SUSSEX

Mist on the Downs. The lower slopes are given over to arable farming; the higher hills the preserve of sheep grazing. The South Downs stretch for more than seventy miles, comprising some 260 square miles, much of it within the South Downs National Park, formed on 1 April 2011, with a well-managed network of 2,000 miles of trails for walkers. The Downs are bounded on their northern side, where they abut the Weald, by a steep escarpment, and form one of the most important chalk landscapes in England.
DAVID MOYES PHOTOGRAPHY

a history of Sussex

Professor Philip Payton

For Angela, Christopher, David,
Graham, Karen, Lesley, Neil

and in remembrance of the two Michaels

A History of Sussex

First published in 2017 by
Carnegie Publishing Ltd
Chatsworth Road,
Lancaster LA1 4SL
www.carnegiepublishing.com

British Library Cataloguing-in-Publication data
A catalogue record for this book is available from the British Library

ISBN 978–1–85936-232-7

Designed, typeset and originated by Carnegie Publishing
Printed and bound by Multiprint Ltd

Contents

Preface ix

1 Ancient landscapes, ancient peoples 1
- The Long Man of Wilmington 1
- Iguanadon 5
- Piltdown Man 8
- Boxgrove Man and Neolithic Sussex 10
- From Bronze Age to Iron Age 13
- The Roman invasion 16
- The Saxon Shore 19

2 The South Saxons 21
- The *Bretwalda* 24
- Conversion to Christianity 25
- Christian folklore and Saxon churches 29
- Settlement and governance 36
- The kingdom of Cnut 38
- From Edward the Confessor to King Harold 40

3 The Normans 42
- William the Conqueror 42
- Tostig and Hardrada 43
- The invasion of the Normans 45
- The Battle of Hastings 46
- The death of King Harold 49
- Bayeux Tapestry, Battle Abbey and the *rapes* of Sussex 51
- Domesday Sussex and religious revival 57
- Conflict renewed 60

4 Medieval Sussex 63
- A licence to crenellate 63
- 'An old soldier's dream home' 66
- The Black Death 68
- The Peasants' Revolt 69
- From Simon de Montfort to the Wars of the Roses 71
- The Rise of the Weald 74

5 Early modern Sussex: wealth and war in the Tudor and Stuart era 77
Andrew Boorde 77
'The great rebuilding' 81
Sussex iron 85
The Dissolution of the Monasteries 90
The Reformation and its aftermath 93
Civil War 95
'This war without an enemy' 98
Interregnum and Restoration 100

6 Hanoverians and early Victorians: high society and social crime 102
The pursuit of leisure 102
Militia Mutinies 106
Smuggling 111
Radicals 118
Captain Swing 120
Poor Law Amendment Act and Chartism 122
A changing countryside 126

7 Sussex in the Railway Age 129
'... highly desirable that there should be a railway to Brighton' 129
'Crash, crack, / Brighton and back, / All the way for a shilling' 135
The Clayton Tunnel disaster 137
Brighton locomotive works 141
'London, Brighton and South Coast religion' 145
Beyond Brighton – country lines and Colonel Stephens 150
Brighton Belle 155

8 Literary Sussex 159
Johnson, Dickens, Thackeray 159
Virginia Woolf and Sussex 163
Vita and death 164
Eric Gill and Arts & Craft 168
To Ditchling and beyond 170
The Catholic world of Hilaire Belloc 174
'The great hills of the South Country' 178
'Yea, Sussex by the sea!' 180
Kipling at Bateman's 183
From *Winnie-the-Pooh* to *Mapp and Lucia* 186

9 War and an uncertain peace, 1914–1939 190
'Sussex by the Sea' 190
'The most tremendous cataclysm that has ever happened' 192
An armed camp 194
Military hospitals and convalescence 196
The home front 199
'My boy Jack' 200
Undertones of War 203
'A land fit for heroes'? 207
The road to war … again 216

10 Sussex at war again 221
The trauma of war 221
From the 'phoney war' to Dunkirk 222
HMS *King Alfred* 228
The Home Guard 230
The Battle of Britain 232
Canadians and the Dieppe Raid 237
The Blitz 238
The Women's Land Army 241
D-Day and Victory in Europe 244

11 Into the new millennium 247
Rations and bonfires 247
'And we're going up to win the cup/For Sussex by the sea' 250
From Crawley to the 'Haywards Heath-Burgess Hill axis' 253
All things Brighton beautiful 257
Holidays and 'Hoppers' 264
'Does Sussex still exist?' 271

Notes and references 279

Index 287

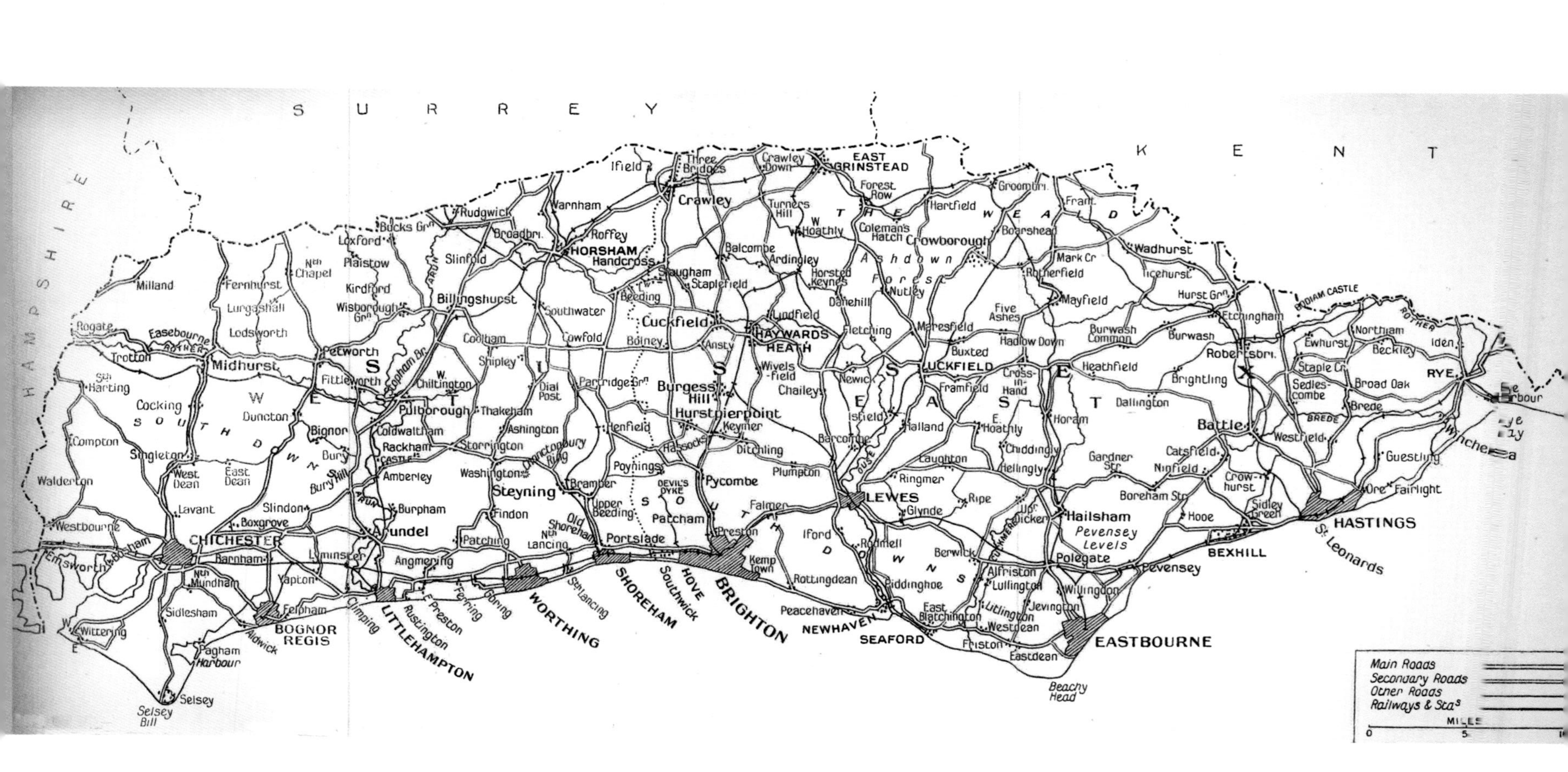
SURREY
KENT
HAMPSHIRE
WEST SUSSEX
EAST SUSSEX
SOUTH DOWNS
WEALD
Ashdown Forest
Main Roads
Secondary Roads
Other Roads
Railways & Stas
MILES
0
5
Milland
Rogate
Trotton
Sth Harting
Compton
Walderton
Westbourne
Emsworth
Bosham
W. Wittering
Selsey Bill
Selsey
Pagham Harbour
Sidlesham
Nth Mundham
CHICHESTER
Lavant
West Dean
Singleton
Cocking
East Dean
Easebourne
Midhurst
Fernhurst
Lurgashall
Lodsworth
Nth Chapel
Loxford
Plaistow
Kirdford
Wisborough Grn
Bucks Grn
Rudgwick
Petworth
Fittleworth
Duncton
Bignor
Bury
Bury Hill
Slindon
Boxgrove
Barnham
Yapton
Felpham
BOGNOR REGIS
Aldwick
Climping
LITTLEHAMPTON
Rustington
E. Preston
Ferring
Goring
WORTHING
Sth Lancing
SHOREHAM
Southwick
HOVE
BRIGHTON
NEWHAVEN
SEAFORD
Lyminster
Arundel
Amberley
Burpham
Angmering
Patching
Findon
Nth Lancing
Old Shoreham
Portslade
Rackham
Coldwaltham
Pulborough
W. Chiltington
Storrington
Ashington
Thakeham
Washington
Steyning
Bramber
Upper Beeding
Chanctonbury Ring
Shipley
Coolham
Billingshurst
Slinfold
Broadbri.
HORSHAM
Warnham
Roffey
Handcross
Southwater
Cowfold
Dial Post
Partridge Grn
Henfield
Poynings
DEVIL'S DYKE
Patcham
Pycombe
Hassocks
Keymer
Ditchling
Hurstpierpoint
Burgess Hill
Bolney
Cuckfield
Beeding
Slaugham
Staplefield
Ifield
Three Bridges
Crawley
Crawley Down
EAST GRINSTEAD
Turners Hill
W. Hoathly
Balcombe
Ardingley
Horsted Keynes
Lindfield
HAYWARDS HEATH
Ansty
Wivelsfield
Chailey
Plumpton
Falmer
Preston
Kemp Town
Rottingdean
Peacehaven
Iford
Rodmell
Piddinghoe
LEWES
Barcombe
Isfield
Newick
Fletching
Danehill
Nutley
Coleman's Hatch
Forest Row
Hartfield
Crowborough
Groombri.
Boarshead
Frant
Mark Cr
Rotherfield
Wadhurst
Ticehurst
Mayfield
Five Ashes
Maresfield
Buxted
UCKFIELD
Framfield
Halland
Laughton
Ringmer
Glynde
Ripe
Berwick
Alfriston
Lullington
Litlington
Westdean
East Blatchington
Friston
Eastdean
Beachy Head
EASTBOURNE
Jevington
Willingdon
Polegate
Pevensey
Pevensey Levels
Hailsham
Upr Dicker
Hellingly
Chiddingly
E. Hoathly
Cross-in-Hand
Hadlow Down
Heathfield
Horam
Dallington
Gardner Str.
Boreham Str.
Ninfield
Catsfield
Hooe
BEXHILL
Sidley Green
Crow-hurst
Battle
Westfield
Brightling
Burwash Common
Burwash
Hurst Grn
Etchingham
Robertsbri.
Sedlescombe
Staple Cr
Ewhurst
Northiam
Beckley
Broad Oak
Brede
BREDE
BODIAM CASTLE
ROTHER
Iden
RYE
Winchelsea
Guestling
Fairlight
Ore
HASTINGS
St. Leonards
ARUN
OUSE
CUCKMERE

Preface

ALTHOUGH I have lived none of my adult life in Sussex, formative parts of my childhood were spent there, and I remain a frequent visitor, not least as an ardent Bluebell Railway enthusiast and as an admirer of Sussex landscape and architecture – especially Bodiam Castle, which I have loved since my schoolboy days. In a sense, part of this book is 'autobiographical', not only re-visiting in words and picture the places that have special meaning for me, but also telling (sometimes overtly, sometimes not) the entwined stories of the Payton and Williams families – my Sussex and Cornish sides – against the background of the county's history. In recounting the travails of Sussex in the Second World War, for example, I have been especially fortunate to draw on the diaries of my late maternal grandmother, 'Dottie May' Williams, and also the wartime memories of my late mother and father, Hazel and Tom Payton.

Although it is obvious to even the most uninformed observer that Sussex is a maritime county, and that its close proximity to Continental Europe has ensured that it has been perpetually in 'the front line', I have been struck afresh just how much Sussex history is 'invasion' and fear of invasion. It is a theme, in its myriad forms, that is detectable from earliest times to the present day, from those early hunter-gatherers who wandered across what was then the land bridge to those twenty-first-century migrants who, to the discomfort of some Brexiteers at least, arrive from the European Union via the Channel Tunnel in search of work. Such 'invasions' have often been enriching – one thinks, for example, of Huguenot and Fleming refugees in the early modern period. But there have also been invasions on the grand scale, violent and traumatic, bringing death and destruction and sometimes wholesale upheavals in governance, religion and culture. Romans, Saxons, Vikings, and Normans are obvious examples, with their profound impacts on Sussex life, but in more modern times constant fear of French and then German invasion was, until comparatively recently, a constant pre-occupation.

If 'front line' status and exposure to 'invasion' – some benign, some not – is an enduring theme of Sussex history, then so too is 'violence'. Civil conflict, again detectable from earliest times, has been a regular feature of Sussex life, and the Civil War itself had a particular and vivid Sussex dimension. Most astonishing of all, perhaps, is the violence endemic in the Sussex countryside in the eighteenth and nineteenth centuries – encompassing smuggling, mutinies, riots, and protests – an aspect of the county's past that has almost disappeared from popular memory. Comprehensively 're-invented' by literary figures, the railway, tourists (of which George IV was an early but important example), and a host of other agencies, especially since the Second World War, Sussex today may seem remote from the rural upheavals of two hundred years ago. But, as observers are often keen to acknowledge, although Sussex has generally embraced and benefited from change, it is has retained its distinctive identity to a remarkable degree. For some, Sussex is still the kingdom of the 'South Saxons', its Saxon inheritance traceable in place-names, early architecture and other features of Sussex life – some tangible, some not – where they detect a primordial Saxon influence. For others, Sussex is quite simply the epitome of England and Englishness, its apparent distinctiveness actually exhibiting all that is quintessentially English.

Be that as it may, in this book I have attempted to chart continuity as well as change, to demonstrate the dynamic quality of identity, and also to entwine the narrative story of the Sussex past with thematic insights. Inevitably, I have been greatly influenced by those writers who have gone before, and all students of Sussex history must acknowledge their debt to J.R. Armstrong's splendid *A History of Sussex*, first published in 1961, and Kim Leslie's and Brian Short's edited *An Historical Atlas of Sussex*, published in 1999. More recent volumes include Denys Skinner's portrait *Sussex: People and History* (2002) and Peter Brandon's wide-ranging survey *Sussex* (2006). But I am most especially indebted to John Lowerson's *A Short History of Sussex*, published in 1980. I had the immense good fortune to meet the late John Lowerson at a conference at the University of Exeter in the early 1990s, where we struck up an acquaintance, comparing notes on aspects of Sussex and Cornish history. Later, John was gracious enough to contribute an article on 'Celtic Tourism' to my series *Cornish Studies*, but it is as a scholar of Sussex that I remember him best. I also value the friendship I shared with the late John Rule, the distinguished social historian, who among many other things introduced me to the work of Roger Wells and Cal Winslow, who between them in a series of magnificent articles examined in depth popular protest and social crime in eighteenth- and nineteenth-century Sussex.

I am also, of course, indebted to the many other writers on whose works I have been privileged to draw, as detailed in the references. At the University of Exeter, I have benefited especially from the advice and assistance of my colleague, Nicola Whyte, leading specialist on early modern landscape and identity, who introduced me to the debate concerning late-medieval castle building in England, particularly that surrounding my beloved Bodiam. Former schoolmates – to whom this book is dedicated – have kept alive memories of our early Sussex days, rekindled in periodic reunions; some of them, indeed, within the county. Likewise, I have been helped in various ways by other friends and relations in Sussex, and here, especially, I should like to thank my cousin Paul Williams for the enthusiasm with which he readily agreed to material concerning the wartime experiences of his late father, my Uncle Cyril, being included in the book.

Alistair Hodge at Carnegie Publishing deserves particular acknowledgment and thanks. It was he who first approached me to write this book, to turn my enthusiasm for Sussex into a history of the county from earliest times to the present day, and he has been extremely supportive, commenting on early drafts of chapters and sourcing a number of the illustrations which grace the volume. Likewise, I am enormously indebted to Anna Goddard at Carnegie, who has embraced the book with such great enthusiasm, saving me from numerous errors, and who with great skill and commitment has turned my rather raw manuscript into this volume. Without Anna, this book would never have seen the light of day. I should also like to thank the rest of the Carnegie team who have worked on the book – especially Ben King-Cox for his splendid assistance with the illustrations and Lucy Frontani for her superb typesetting.

And finally, of course, I owe so much to my wife Deidre – Dee – who has loyally accompanied me on our periodic pilgrimages to the Bluebell Railway and to Bodiam Castle, and who has completed this book's formidable index – a task I could never have undertaken myself. Thank you, Dee.

Philip Payton
Flinders University,
Adelaide, Australia

The Long Man of Wilmington, also known variously as the Wilmington Giant, the Green Man, or plain Wilmington Man, was long considered to be of Iron Age or even Neolithic provenance, a timeless figure in the Downland landscape at Windover Hill. However, investigations in 2003 by archaeologist Professor Martin Bell of the University of Reading, together with Aubrey Manning's Open University programme *Landscape Mysteries*, dated the Long Man of Wilmington to the early modern period of Tudor and Stuart England. Many of the Long Man's adherents were distressed by this conclusion, and said so. But Professor Ronald Hutton of the University of Bristol, leading historian of early modern Britain and folklore specialist, was more philosophical. As he put it, 'we can at least celebrate the fact that we have our first, apparently unequivocally, early modern hill figure, and historians now have to reckon with it.'

ALISON AVERY, WWW.BEAUTIFULENGLANDPHOTOS.UK

ONE

Ancient landscapes, ancient peoples

The Long Man of Wilmington

AT WINDOVER HILL, high on the Sussex Downs some five or so miles north-west of Eastbourne, stands the Long Man of Wilmington. Scored deep into the chalk of the steep north-facing slope, the Long Man is all of 235 feet tall. He exhibits none of the war-like virility of his Dorset downland cousin, the Cerne Abbas giant, but he remains an imposing figure. Best observed from the lane at Wilmington village, he was cut with an expertise that shows him perfectly in proportion when viewed from below. Arms outstretched, he holds two upright parallel staves, each as high as the top of his head. Who is he?

T.C. Lethbridge, onetime keeper of Anglo-Saxon antiquities at the Archaeological Museum in Cambridge, thought the Long Man a Sun worship totem. Perhaps he was opening wide the doors of heaven, thought Lethbridge, or maybe his twin staves were once topped with Sun discs, in imitation of ancient Scandinavian rock carvings. Indeed, some believed the Long Man to be a representation of Thor himself, the Viking god, or Woden, or perhaps the eponymous Anglo-Saxon hero, Beowulf, subject of the famous tenth-century Old English poem. When, in 1964, a belt-buckle depicting a helmeted warrior carrying two spears – one in each hand – was uncovered in a seventh-century Anglo-Saxon burial site at Finglesham in neighbouring Kent, archaeologists thought they had found more than a clue to the provenance of the Long Man of Wilmington. But others continued to insist upon his far greater antiquity, Iron Age or even earlier, an enduring memorial of a pagan, prehistoric past long before the coming of the Romans, let alone the Angles and the Saxons. Perhaps even, as legend averred, he had been a giant killed in battle on Windover Hill, his outline scored for posterity where he had fallen.[1]

When, controversially, new twenty-first-century scientific evidence suggested that the Long Man was, after all, no older than the sixteenth or seventeenth century, present-day pagans were appalled. In defiance,

Morris Men danced at the Long Man's feet each May Day morn, and in June 2010 fertility ritualists endowed him with a massive phallus, picked out in white playing-field marker to match his chalk-cut outline. The appendage washed away in no time, succumbing to summer showers. But, in claiming common cause with the Cerne Abbas giant, Long Man's devotees had insisted upon their version of the chalk figure's past. In the face of modernity, they had asserted a timeless Sussex, rooted in pagan prehistory. Moreover, in championing the Long Man's longevity, they had struck a wider Sussex chord – the Long Man of Wilmington as icon of a classic, defining Sussex landscape: the Down country. He is, as his keeper, the Sussex Archaeological Society, has put it so aptly, the 'mysterious guardian of the South Downs'.[2]

Hilaire Belloc, author of the topographical guide *The County of Sussex*, published in 1906, wrote passionately of his adopted county, and also saw the Downs as the epitome of all that was quintessentially Sussex. 'Sussex is Sussex,' he wrote, 'on account of the South Downs. Their peculiar landscape, their soil, their uniformity, give the county all its meaning.'[3] Yet the Downs, archetypal as they are, are really but one element of a distinct Sussex landscape, as Rudyard Kipling (Belloc's near contemporary) knew. Living first at Rottingdean, a stone's throw from the sea, and later at Bateman's, his country house at inland Burwash,

Chanctonbury Ring, inland from Worthing, is an ancient hill-fort crowning Chanctonbury Hill. A familiar landmark for miles around, the site is best known for its magnificent beech trees, planted in 1760 by Charles Goring. Although the copse was much thinned in the great storm of October 1987, it still retains its almost mystical presence in the Downland landscape.

Fulking escarpment, East Sussex, illustrates the steep, almost cliff-like, northern slopes of the Downs, where they meet the Weald. Owned and managed by the National Trust, Fulking escarpment is popular with hikers and ramblers.
DAVID MOYES PHOTOGRAPHY

Kipling the poet and novelist had encountered Sussex in all its moods, and appreciated its diversity:

> I'm just in love with all these three,
> The Weald and the Marsh and the Down countrie;
> Nor I don't know which I love the most,
> The Weald or the Marsh or the white chalk coast.[4]

As Kipling had described it, the essential Sussex was partly maritime – a varied coastal plain with shingle beaches, rising to high chalk cliffs at Beachy Head and descending to the wetlands of the Pevensey Levels and Romney Marsh – with the adjacent South Downs and the Weald beyond. Between Brighton and Eastbourne, the Downs intruded upon the coast, accounting for that majestic cliffscape, and further east around Bexhill, Hastings and Rye, the Weald stretched down to the sea. But for the most part, the Sussex landscape exhibits – as it has done since the end of the last Ice Age *c.*8000 BC at least – what Desmond Seward has called its 'geological symmetry' of coastal plain, chalk Downs, and wooded Weald.[5]

Even today, despite modern developments of all kinds and the intrusions of the built environment and extensive transport and other

Ouse Valley sunset – a quintessentially Sussex scene, viewed from Beddingham Hill, and ranging from Kingston Ridge on the left through Lewes to Mount Caburn on the right. The River Ouse rises near Lower Beeding and meanders through east Sussex, flowing into the English Channel at Newhaven.
DAVID MOYES PHOTOGRAPHY

infrastructures, this pattern is still readily discernible. Looking north from Ditchling Beacon, for example, 813 feet above sea level on the steep escarpment slope of the South Downs, or from Chanctonbury Ring, all of 783 feet high, the Weald stretches out almost as far as the eye can see. The prospect appears overwhelmingly rural, the countless towns and villages and teeming populations somehow camouflaged by the forest, woodland, hedgerows and small pasture farms that unfold below. There is bracken-covered common land, such as that at Chailey and Ditchling, and pine and birch. But it is oak that is commonplace, everywhere abundant, emblematic still of the Sussex Weald. The Downs themselves, although their slopes today are partly under the plough, remain largely as Belloc and Kipling saw them in those areas where sheep still safely graze, keeping bracken at bay and accounting for the characteristic, smooth close-cropped grassland hills. The coastal plain, meanwhile, remains the most heavily populated part of Sussex, with large towns such as

Chichester, Bognor Regis, Littlehampton and Worthing, and with some of the county's best farming country.

Geologically, Sussex is young compared to many parts of Britain, the earliest rocks being those laid down in the Jurassic period, the rest in the subsequent Cretaceous. It was the latter, with its marine incursions, that accounted for the Downland chalk, formed from the compacted remains of countless millions of tiny marine organisms. Likewise flint, common as a building material in parts of Sussex, was formed from the numberless skeletons of marine sponges laid down in similar fashion. The heavy Wealden clay, so characteristic of inland Sussex, was also the product of the Cretaceous period, the result of deposits from a large freshwater lake, or perhaps from a series of rivers traversing a large plateau.

Iguanadon

As all schoolchildren know, the Cretaceous period was also the high noon of the age of dinosaurs, when giant lizards roamed the earth – including what is now Sussex. In the early Cretaceous, some 125 million years ago, as the continents moved and reshaped, so new animals and plants emerged. Among the former were *iguanodontids*, as scientists now describe them, huge herbivores that could grow as long as 30 feet and stand 10 feet high, weighing all of 30 tons. Roaming in herds, they grazed among the ferns and conifers of the prehistoric landscape. When they died, their skeletal remains were fossilised in stone, and for the most part lay undisturbed across the vastness of geological time. Although occasionally stumbled on by those digging or quarrying, who no doubt marvelled at the massive bones of these fearsome monsters, it was not until the early nineteenth century that dinosaur remains began to attract serious scientific attention. Inevitably, palaeontology, as it was soon known, appealed especially to the gentlemen antiquarians of the day. Among them was Dr Gideon Mantell, a surgeon, born in 1790 in Lewes, the county town of Sussex. Mantell developed a youthful enthusiasm for the locality's geology and archaeology, his article on 'Geology and the Environs of Lewes' appearing in the *Sussex Advertiser* as early as 1813, and kept a journal in which he recorded his excavatory escapades.[6] In an entry in July 1818, for example, he described the opening of eight tumuli near Mount Caburn, outside Lewes. 'In one of them,' he recorded, 'was deposited a skeleton of a warrior.' On either side was a large urn, he explained, one containing burnt human bones, the other holding 'calcined bones also, and a necklace of beads of various forms and materials'. Some were jet, some were of amber, and others appeared to be 'green porcelain'.[7]

This artist's impression, based on current estimations of the Iguanodons' appearance, shows a herd of these fierce-looking but herbivorous dinosaurs grazing in a Cretaceous landscape.

Mantell had also begun collecting fossils, notably from a quarry at Whiteman Green, near Cuckfield. Legend has it that one day, while he was visiting a patient in the country, Mantell's wife Mary (whom he had married in 1816) went for a stroll along a nearby lane and picked up a strange tooth that had caught her eye. She showed it to her husband, leading shortly to the discovery of further 'iguana teeth' – as he described them – among waste rubble. Eventually more teeth were found, and Mantell uncovered the full twenty-five foot long fossil of the giant dinosaur to whom these had belonged: 'Iguanodon', as he dubbed the monster. In 1825, a year after his wife's all-important find, Mantell

In 1852, following the removal of Crystal Palace to its new home at Sydenham Hill in south London, Benjamin Waterhouse Hawkins was commissioned to create a number of life-like models of dinosaurs for a new Dinosaur Court. Although critics today complain that his representation of Iguanodon is wholly inaccurate, Hawkins' work was inspirational and attracted admiring crowds who marvelled at his impressive representations of life millions of years before.
IAN WRIGHT/WIKIMEDIA COMMONS/ CC BY-SA 2.0

read a paper to the Royal Society entitled 'Notice on the Iguanodon, a Newly Discovered Fossil reptile, from the Sandstone of Tilgate Forest, in Sussex'. He was propelled immediately into the forefront of the new science of palaeontology, and among other things was elected Fellow of the Royal Society. He published widely, and in 1852 was further honoured when a (highly inaccurate, as we now know) brick-built model of his Iguanodon was given pride of place at Crystal Palace's new home in south London. Alas, Gideon Mantell's personal life was by now dogged with ill fortune. Mary, his wife, had left him in 1839, and in 1841 he suffered an appalling accident (he fell from a carriage) which damaged his spine and left him in constant pain. He died in 1852, from an overdose of opium.

The 1852 Iguanodon model still exists in south London, with the dinosaur's thumb spike mounted incorrectly – rhinoceros-like – on its nose, its body constructed as a lumbering quadruped quite unlike that imagined by scientists today. But it remains an enduring memorial to the pioneering work of the unfortunate Dr Mantell, and is for us an important reminder of the significance of Sussex in early palaeontology, as well as an insight into the county's almost impossibly far-distant past. An intriguing postscript is that, as recently as 1979, an Iguanodon bone was noticed in the Natural History Museum in London in a hitherto unregarded collection. It had been found near Cuckfield, Gideon Mantell's stamping ground, in 1809 – some thirteen years before his wife Mary had made her discovery in that country lane. No doubt there were other such early finds, in Sussex and perhaps elsewhere in southern England, but the Mantells' reputation as discoverers of Iguanodon remains undiminished – Gideon and Mary are united in posthumous fame, just as they were estranged in life.[8]

The story of the Mantells and their Iguanodon continues to capture the public imagination, in Sussex and far beyond. Yet their renown pales significantly alongside Sussex's other great claim to 'prehistoric' fame – or infamy – the extraordinary hoax surrounding the discovery of 'Piltdown Man'. Having made for itself an important niche in the emerging science of palaeontology, it was perhaps understandable that Sussex should wish to consolidate its position in the forefront of the study of fossils. At any rate, in the latter nineteenth century, as Charles Darwin's *On the Origin of Species* and theory of evolution gained scientific and popular attention, so the hunt was on – in Sussex, as elsewhere – for a 'missing link', the discovery of which would reveal the evolutionary connection between apes and modern men and women, and clinch Darwin's arguments, providing incontrovertible evidence of their veracity. At last, in 1912, the scientific journal *Nature* was able to reveal that the remains of a human skull and jaw, thought to date from the early Pleistocene period, some 500,000 years ago, had been discovered in a Sussex gravel pit by one Charles Dawson. It was the news the world had been waiting for – the elusive 'missing link' had been found.

Piltdown Man

Charles Dawson, already Fellow of both the Geological Society and the Society of Antiquaries, acquired an instant reputation and prominence, comparable to that of Gideon Mantell almost a century before. Writing in 1944, as she compiled her book *Sussex* for the prestigious Robert Hale 'County Book Series', Esther Meynell penned a deferential account of Dawson's dramatic discovery. A keen supporter of the Sussex Archaeological Society, she was thrilled that the find had been made in her home county (she lived at Ditchling, near Lewes, at the foot of the Downs). 'People who have never set foot in Sussex, people in other continents,' she exclaimed, 'have heard of Piltdown because of that bit of skull.' Piltdown village, she added for the benefit of those not fortunate enough to know Sussex, was 'a retired little place … near Fletching and about seven miles north of Lewes'.[9]

In Meynell's account of the discovery, Dawson was taking a walk in the country near Piltdown when he encountered some labourers digging for gravel, 'and the eye of a geologist being always attracted by any fracture of the earth's surface, he stopped to look'. He asked the men to be on the look-out for fossils, and was later handed a fragment of 'remarkably thick' skull-bone. Horrified to learn that only recently the skull had been whole, and had been wantonly smashed by the ignorant workers who had thought it a coconut, Dawson immediately launched a systematic search of the whole area. Assisted by his friend Sir Arthur Smith-Woodward, by 1912 a keeper at the British Museum, Dawson eventually uncovered other pieces of skull – enough, as Esther Meynell observed, 'to enable a conjectural model to be made of the bony structure of the head of this

Eoanthropus, Dawn Man, as Sir Arthur Smith-Woodward christened him'. She was proud that this model of the head of Piltdown Man – 'or woman, as some authorities consider' – could be viewed in the museum of the Sussex Archaeological Society at Barbican House, adjacent to Lewes Castle. And it was gratifying that the extraordinary story of the discovery 'always comes to my mind when I walk past the charming old house within the Barbican Gateway at Lewes where Charles Dawson was living at the time of the discovery of the Piltdown skull'.[10]

Esther Meynell died in 1955. Alas, two years earlier, in 1953, her fond imaginings of Charles Dawson and his Piltdown Man had been shattered by the announcement that the whole episode had been a hoax. It was a fraud that would not have survived for five minutes under the scrutiny of twenty-first-century forensic science. But it was not until after the Second World War that sufficient advances had been made for doubts to be cast on Dawson's claims. Even as Meynell's book appeared in 1947, so scientific opinion was increasingly puzzled by the fact that Piltdown Man seemed entirely outside the evolutionary ascent of mankind revealed by recent fossil discoveries in Africa, China, Israel and Java. In 1949 the British Museum conducted a fluorine test (the amount of fluorine in fossils increases with time), which showed that the skull could not possibly be half-a-million years old, as Dawson had claimed. Ironically, it was Esther Meynell who had unwittingly put her finger on the crux of the forgery. As she had admired the model in the museum in Lewes, she had admitted to herself 'that it is not a very attractive countenance'. But this was hardly surprising, she thought, for in appearance 'it is the mixture of a skull of a man and a monkey ... the teeth are not quite human, but the eye-sockets and forehead have the look of humanity.'[11] How right she was, if only she had known it. It was found subsequently that the skull was indeed that of a modern man, the lower jawbone that of a Sarawak orang-utan, the latter fitted with artificially abraded teeth from a chimpanzee, the whole ensemble stained to give it uniformity and the patina of age.

The news broke in the press in 1953, and thereafter the search for the culprit has continued more or less unabated. The chief suspect, inevitably, is Charles Dawson himself. Even in his own time he was notorious for 'unreliability' among his fellow Sussex archaeologists and geologists, and was thought to be pushy and self-seeking. By the time of his Piltdown 'discovery' in 1912, he was already an honorary collector for the British Museum, and coincidentally (or not) was also a steward of Barkham Manor, in whose grounds the finds were made. Yet there is no firm evidence that he planted the remains. Sir Arthur Smith-Woodward may have been an unfortunate victim of the deception, but perhaps he was party to the hoax, and a further possible accomplice was a French priest resident in Sussex at the time, one Pierre de Chardin. De Chardin participated in later digs, locating another tooth and unearthing assorted animal bones, and in 1915 he, Smith-Woodward and Dawson claimed to have found further skull fragments – Piltdown II – at another site, some two miles from the original gravel pit. Although Dawson died a year later, in 1916, this further discovery bolstered the credibility of the original find, confirming – for the time being – its honoured place as 'missing link' in the pantheon of human evolution. Intriguingly, in 1996, there was a new twist to the story when a trunk inscribed with the initials MACH – probably Martin A.C. Hinton, one-time keeper of zoology – was found in the British Museum. When opened, it contained bones stained in exactly the same manner as the original Piltdown fossils. Hinton had suffered a bumpy relationship with his boss, Sir Arthur Smith-Woodward, and so perhaps, it has been suggested, it was *he* who planted the Piltdown remains in a deliberate plot to discredit his master.[12]

Boxgrove Man and Neolithic Sussex

Alongside this long-running 'whodunnit', the revelations of 1953 had the disappointing effect of demolishing the by now long cherished belief, held by Esther Meynell and many others, that early human beings had lived in Sussex all of 500,000 years before. It was a lingering disappointment that lasted until 1993–94, when significant discoveries were made in another gravel pit, this time at Boxgrove, about three miles from Chichester on the edge of the Goodwood-Slindon 'raised beach', situated today a hundred feet above sea level. Initially, flint tools, together with animal bones from long-extinct species such as rhinoceros and giant deer, were uncovered, evidence (it was thought) that the site was a prehistoric butchers' yard, where early hunters had stripped carcasses of their flesh and crushed bones to obtain marrow. A year later there was an even more startling find, when a tibia (shin bone) was found at the same site.

'Boxgrove Man', as he was dubbed, turned out to be the oldest proto-human yet discovered in the British Isles, said to date from 500,000 years ago. At a stroke, Sussex was restored to its important position in European – and, indeed, global – prehistory, the ignominy of the Piltdown fraud at last overshadowed by a modern, scientifically verified discovery of international significance. Boxgrove Man – the hunter-butcher, if that is what he was – proved to be a particularly fine specimen, his shin bone suggesting a twenty-year-old man at least six feet tall, weighing more than twelve stone. Intriguingly, his tibia showed signs of teeth marks made by wolves – had he fallen victim to these animals, one wonders, the cause of his untimely death, or had his remains been scavenged from a shallow grave? Either way, his discovery was followed in 1995 by the uncovering of a human tooth several hundred years older than his tibia, further confirmation of the importance of the site for the nomadic hunters who roamed southern England during the warmer spells (or interglacials) of the last Ice Age, a time when a land bridge still connected Britain with continental Europe.[13]

Even when rising seas caused by the melting ice sheet resulted in physical separation, the nearby Continent continued to have an important impact on Sussex prehistory, accounting among other things for the wealth of archaeological discoveries and artefacts. During the Mesolithic period, from about ten thousand years ago, groups of hunter-gatherers moved about the coastal areas and river valleys, collecting berries, fishing, and ensnaring game. They fashioned harpoons and fishhooks from bone, and worked flints into finely crafted arrowheads. Knives, spearheads and other implements have also survived from this period. One site at Selmeston, near Firle, a gravel pit, contained some 6,500 worked flints, evidence of large-scale activity over an extended time span, a veritable prehistoric industry. Similar sites have been discovered at Westhampnett, near Chichester, and at several spots near Midhurst.

Later, about 3,500 BC, new settlers arrived from what is now northern France, bringing with them cereals and herds of domesticated animals. No longer hunter-gatherers, these Neolithic people – as they are called – appear to have settled mainly on the downland areas, spreading from Sussex across to Windmill Hill in Wiltshire, which has lent its name to their culture. These Neolithic farmers knew how to weave and to make pottery, and in Sussex their 'Windmill Hill' way of life is still readily observable in the landscape – in causewayed camps, flint mines, and long barrows. Of several known causewayed camps across southern England, eight are in Sussex – the best known being Whitehawk, near Brighton; the Trundle at Singleton, north of Chichester; at Barkhale above Bognor; and on Coombe Hill at Eastbourne. Situated on prominent hilltops, they are designated 'causewayed' on account of their construction – circular or oval ramparts and ditches punctuated by what appear to be undefended gaps or 'causeways'. Perhaps, as Derek Simpson once suggested, these unexcavated areas may simply indicate that different groups of workmen were responsible for different parts of the camp, leaving un-dug ground between their sectors.[14] Alternatively, perhaps, the causeways are a deliberate feature, facilitating the movement of people and animals through the fortifications. Either way, the camps seem to be not so much military defensive structures as seasonal gathering places where the various tribes of the locality could meet to trade cattle or artefacts. Such gatherings might also have political, social and religious significance, affirming the power relationships between different territorial groups in the region and providing a focus for collective religious observance.

Several of these Sussex camps have been excavated – notably Trundle and Whitehawk – the latter by far the largest of the group. Covering almost twelve acres, Whitehawk appears to have served several purposes.

Big enough to provide protection for herds of livestock from predatory wild animals, it was also a site of feast and ritual. Thrown together in untidy rubbish heaps with broken pottery, animal bones and other detritus, were traces of human remains. Perhaps, as John Lowerson has argued, cannibalism was part of camp life, a social activity that bound groups together, or a form of religious worship where dead children were consumed as sacrifice.[15] Yet alongside the hastily discarded remnants of the eaten, there were careful – even reverential – interments of other humans, such as the young woman whose excavated skeleton showed that after death her body had been decorated with chalk pendants and fossilised sea-urchins. Likewise, the careful burial at Whitehawk of animal parts – and occasionally whole animals – indicated equally sensitive treatment of the once living, perhaps in religious celebration of Creation.

Neolithic agriculture was based on the grazing of cattle and sheep, and the cultivation of wheat and barley. Both these activities required the clearing of woodland and bracken, which in turn rested on the manufacture of high-quality flint axes. Just as their Mesolithic predecessors had relied upon Sussex gravel pits, so the Neolithic farmers exploited local deposits of flint – but now through underground mining. Superior flint deposits lay sometimes as much as fifty feet below the surface, although generally it was the more accessible seams a dozen or so feet below ground – such as that at Blackpatch, near Patching – which were exploited consistently. Seven such sites have been identified in Sussex, some worked for as much as 500 years, and their filled-in shafts and waste dumps can still be discerned in the downland landscape. At Cissbury, near Findon, there is evidence of no fewer than 200 shafts. Galleries radiating from the bottom of each shaft allowed miners to follow the flint seams, sometimes interconnecting with other galleries to create a complex underground maze. At Church Hill, near Findon, remains of a wooden shaft ladder have been discovered, and at other sites antler picks and shovels fashioned from the shoulder blades of animals such as oxen and pigs have been found. At Harrow Hill, Angmering, there are traces of soot on the gallery roofs, deposits from the primitive lamps which helped the Neolithic miners find their way and undertake their work, poignant survivals that speak to us across the millennia of their toil and courage. Again, the impression is of an organised and widespread industry, although it is doubtful whether occupational specialisation had emerged at this early period. It seems unlikely that there were full-time miners. Rather, farmers or groups of farmers probably visited the mines on occasion to hack out flints themselves, when they needed to make new implements.

The discoveries at Whitehawk indicated the significance of ritual in 'Windmill Hill' culture. Neolithic long barrows, a dozen or so of which have been found in Sussex, were also evidence of ritual, of the elaborate interment of society's notables – tribal chieftains, perhaps, or religious leaders – and may have been used to bury dynastic dead over several centuries, not unlike family vaults much later. In West Sussex, near North Marden, Bevis' Thumb barrow is an impressive 150 feet in length and twenty feet wide; at Wilmington in East Sussex the extensive Hunter's Burgh barrow is all of 180 feet long and some seventy feet wide. Like the causewayed camps, these barrows may have served as symbols of territorial power, visible reminders in the landscape of the wealth and authority of regional rulers.

From Bronze Age to Iron Age

Today, archaeologists largely play down the old idea of waves of Continental invaders, who successively slaughtered or drove off the existing populations to establish their own hegemony. Instead, they offer a more careful and nuanced picture, in which the 'invaders' were often relatively few in number but possessed certain advantages – usually technological – that enabled them to dominate the localities in which they settled. Existing peoples were assimilated rather than killed or banished, and alongside the cultural and economic dominance of the new elite there could also be compromise and accommodation. In this way, it has been argued, the older hunter-gatherer communities were introduced to – and adopted – new agricultural methods, leading to what some have deemed 'hybrid' cultures, such as that seen in the 'Secondary Neolithic' pottery sherds discovered in the causewayed camp at Combe Hill, Jevington. Similarly the Beaker 'invasion', about 2,000 BC, was probably as much to do with the arrival of new techniques as new people, not least the distinctive beaker-like drinking cups after which the latter were named. Beaker culture spread across Sussex, reflected, for example, in new funerary practices in which the dead – along with their beakers – were buried individually in round or 'bell' barrows. These Beaker folk could also work metal, a significant technological breakthrough, first copper and later iron, and among the artefacts retrieved from a bell barrow near Hove was a bronze dagger.

The Beaker culture marked the transition from the Neolithic to the Bronze Age, from an economy that relied on stone implements to one which crafted metal. Several large bronze hoards have been uncovered in Sussex – mainly axes and spearheads – at places as disparate as Bognor, Black Rock (Brighton) and Wilmington – and one remarkable find was made in the Wealden sandstone country between Horsham and Crawley. Important evidence that early folk inhabited the 'impenetrable' Weald as well as the downland and coastal plain, this Bronze-Age burial mound also showed the longevity of such sites. Almost 200 feet in diameter, the mound appears to have remained a sacred place until at least Roman times – evidenced by the large number of Roman coins found within the site.

Growing wealth and trading contacts with the Continent were reflected in the exotic items often placed in graves – the bell barrow at Hove, for example, also included a finely made cup fashioned from red amber, the raw material for which had probably been imported from the Baltic. As such trading routes grew, so new peoples and new cultures continued to arrive. Among these were Celtic-speaking settlers, armed with weapons forged from iron, who first emerged in Sussex around 600 BC, bringing with them their so-called Hallstatt culture, named after Hallstatt in Austria where it had originated. To these first Iron Age settlers was added a second group, so-called La Tene Celts, who introduced a new continental culture to Sussex around 250 BC. Initially strong in West Sussex, they constructed a number of their characteristic hill-forts – massive constructions with great ramparts and steep ditches – at Goodwood, Cissbury and elsewhere. Later, their influence spread across the county, and as it did so the profusion of smaller hill-forts diminished, leaving a line of major forts – the Trundle (where the builders intruded on the old causewayed camp), Devil's Dyke, Mount Caburn – that dominated their hinterlands. Caburn has retained its Celtic name – perhaps Caer Bryn, as Candida Lycett Green has mused, literally 'fort hill', or maybe Cam Bron (as in Camborne in Cornwall), 'crooked hill', as its distinctive profile suggests.[16] Unlike the earlier causewayed camps, these later Iron Age forts were occupied permanently. At Caburn there were more than 140 grain storage pits, evidence perhaps of sizeable agricultural surpluses, or maybe a sign of more turbulent

Seven Sisters – a reflective portrait of the breath-taking cliff-scape between Seaford and Eastbourne, where the South Downs meet the sea in a series of the dry valleys characteristic of the chalk Downland. With all the appearance of an impregnable rampart, this is part of the coastline as it would have appeared to successive waves of invaders and settlers.
DAVID MOYES PHOTOGRAPHY

Mount Caburn, about a mile from Lewes and some 480 feet above sea level, is crowned with a Celtic Iron Age hill-fort. Today, Mount Caburn lies within the Lewes Downs Site of Special Scientific Interest.
DAVID MOYES PHOTOGRAPHY

times, with the need to hoard provisions against the possibility of siege or attack. The hill-forts were also places of potential retreat for local farming communities, should they be threatened by hostile outsiders.

By now Roman expansion in Gaul (modern-day France) had displaced tribal groups, who sought refuge across the Channel, bringing further Celtic-speaking newcomers to Sussex. Around 100 BC the first of the Germano-Celtic Belgae people arrived in south-eastern Britain. They brought coinage and left behind evidence of both literacy and cash exchange, marking a new cultural and economic sophistication as Sussex emerged from prehistory into the historical record. The introduction of new, heavy-wheeled ploughs allowed further advances in agriculture, which enabled cultivation of the difficult clay soils of the Weald. Wheel-turned pottery was another indication of Belgic technical advance. Metalworking was commonplace, and Sussex iron-ore deposits were increasingly important to the regional economy. Textiles and leather were also significant, and salt-workings were commenced in the coastal area around Selsey. By virtue of these several innovations, the Belgae established their overlordship in large areas of the county, creating something like a local military and political confederation. This was perpetuated after the arrival of Commius *c.*52 BC, a Belgic leader who had rebelled against Roman rule in Gaul, fleeing to southern Britain with his people, the Atrebates. These new settlers spread as far east as the Ouse – where Mount Caburn may have become an important border fortress – and into the Weald, also moving westwards into what would become their heartland in Hampshire and Wiltshire.

The Roman invasion

Commius had been an important ally of Julius Caesar, the Roman conqueror of Gaul, and in backing the wrong side in the revolt and escaping across the Channel, he had unwittingly provoked growing Roman interest in the fortunes of Britain. Caesar had already launched punitive raids against the Gaul's south-eastern British allies in 55–54 BC, and little by little Britain was being drawn into Rome's orbit. Belgic culture was in any case increasingly 'Romanised', at least among the elite, as evidenced by the adoption of Latinised personal names and the use of Latin on coins. Commius was succeeded by his son Tinocommius, and, after a series of internecine power struggles, another son, Verica, became leader of the Atrebates in Sussex and environs, ruling a people that became known as the Regni, whose capital seems to have been near Selsey. Verica styled himself *rex*, 'king', a title which appeared on coins and which may have indicated Roman approval as well as influence. At any rate, he was keen to remain on friendly terms with his powerful Roman neighbours, now firmly ensconced just across the Channel.

However, Verica was already under pressure from tribal groups farther north, the Trinovantes and the Catuvellani, who were less inclined to bend to Rome's will. The Atrebates ceded territory to these two expansionist groups, and Rome pondered the possibility of further military intervention in Britain to shore up its allies and secure its interests. When Verica fled to Rome in AD 42, seeking help from the emperor Claudius, the die was cast. The Roman invasion of Britain in the spring of AD 43 involved some 40,000 troops, the majority of whom landed in eastern Kent. At first unopposed, the Romans met stiff opposition as they ventured inland, fighting their way to the Thames. A secondary invasion force, meanwhile, had sailed along the south coast, landing somewhere near Selsey with the aim of joining Verica's supporters. Its exact landfall is unknown, and probably long since lost to coastal erosion, but the Roman general Vespasian established his base at nearby Fishbourne, from which he launched his successful campaign against the tribes of Hampshire and Dorset. This time, unlike Julius Caesar's earlier raids, the Romans were here to stay, with the south coast from Kent to Dorset soon under Rome's sway. It is not clear what happened to Verica. He may have died, been killed, or perhaps never returned from exile. Either way, the Romans installed Cogidubnus as puppet king of the Regni, conferring upon him the flattering title of *rex et legatus Augusti in Britannia* – 'king and legate of the Emperor in Britain' – a reward for his continuing loyalty and co-operation.[17] Like all successful empire builders, the Romans were good at divide and rule, as Tacitus himself observed in his biography of Agricola when he noted that the elevation of Cogidubnus was 'an example of the long-established Roman custom of employing even kings to make others slaves'.[18]

With Cogidubnus now safely installed as client ruler, south-west Sussex was well placed to act as conduit for Roman power and influence. Chichester – Regnum, or Noviomagus Regensium, to give it its full title – was founded as *civitas*, or regional capital, a centre for administration, taxation and political control. It was a 'new market' (*noviomagus*), suggesting a shift from the assumed earlier capital near Selsey, and developed rapidly as one of the principal towns of Roman Britain. A temple dedicated to the gods Neptune and Minerva, a forum, an amphitheatre, public baths, and streets built on a grid system, all reflected the Roman way of doing things – and indicated a high level of prosperity. A main road, Stane Street, was built to connect Chichester with London – Londinium – and another ran north-westwards towards Silchester. Other Roman roads ran west from Brighton via Chichester to Southampton, from Anderida (Pevensey) to London by way of Lewes, and into the iron country of the upper Weald. The iron industry had been further developed by the Romans, evidenced by considerable furnace slag deposits at Maresfield and Beauport Park, near Battle. Recognising the strategic importance of iron, the Roman navy based in Britain managed several iron pits and associated bloomeries (furnaces) directly, tiles from the bathhouse at Beauport Park being stamped with the tell-tale CLBR, designating the Classis Britannica or Roman fleet.

Economic wealth was mirrored in the elaborate villas which sprang up after the Roman conquest, especially those at Fishbourne and Bignor. Fishbourne, no doubt constructed as Cogidubnus' palace, was unparalleled in its magnificence anywhere in Britain. A central courtyard some 250 feet across, with fountains and formal gardens, was surrounded by four wings of the great house, which contained decorations of the highest order, including mosaics, paintings and stucco, each betraying detailed Roman cultural influence and a lavish lifestyle modelled on that of the Roman elite. Bignor villa, on Stane Street south-west of Pulborough, also exuded luxuriance and the trappings of opulent living, with under-floor heating and a complex system of baths. Again, four wings were built around a courtyard, and, together with well-executed paintings on stucco, there was a remarkable series of very fine mosaics. Today, both sites have been excavated (although part of the Fishbourne complex remains hidden beneath the modern A27 road), preserved and interpreted, providing visitors with a rare window on to aristocratic life in Roman Sussex.[19]

However, beneath the so-called *Pax Romana*, this veneer of progress and stability, there was an underlying sense of insecurity. After little

The museum buildings at Bignor Roman villa, situated about nine miles north-east of Chichester. The villa dates from the period AD c.200 to c.300, when a simple farmhouse was first constructed and then later vastly expanded to create the large villa whose remains we see today. The villa was discovered in 1811 by George Tupper, a local farmer, leading to excavations by Samuel Lysons, but there was no further work until 1929 when some of the mosaics were restored. In 1935 S.E. Winbolt, the Sussex archaeologist, undertook further work, followed by limited excavations by Professor S.S. Frere between 1956 and 1962, after which the museum was constructed.
USER: POLIPHILO/WIKIMEDIA COMMONS/ CC0 1.0 UNIVERSAL

Among the several important mosaics at Bignor villa is the depiction of Medusa, in Greco-Roman mythology one of the hideous Gorgon sisters, who had venomous serpents for hair and whose countenance was so terrible that anyone who looked upon her would be immediately turned to stone. Medusa was eventually killed by the hero Perseus, who was able to approach and decapitate her by looking at her reflection in his polished shield, instead of gazing upon her directly, and thereafter he used her severed head as a weapon against his enemies.
WWW.BRITAINEXPRESS.COM

more than a century since the Roman occupation, internal unrest and external threats began to re-emerge. In response, around AD 200 Chichester was fortified with new walls, a time when the northern frontier of Roman Britain was under pressure and in danger of complete collapse. Towards the end of the third century, Chichester's defences were further strengthened, and the old hill-forts at Cissbury and Mount Caburn were re-fortified. The Classis Britannicus patrolled the coastline against marauders from the sea, and a mighty new fort was built at Anderida (Pevensey), the Roman naval base. For a time, these measures

A detail of the extensive mosaic 'Venus and the Gladiators' at Bignor villa, depicting a contest between two well-armed gladiatorial opponents, a *Secutor* (on the left) equipped with helmet, breast-plate, leg-guards, sword and shield, and a *Retiarius* (centre) who carries a net, trident and short sword. On the right is the *Redarius*, or umpire, who adjudicates the match from close quarters, holding his *Rudus* or wand of office.
WWW.BRITAINEXPRESS.COM

appeared successful. But by now Rome itself was under pressure from the barbarian hordes that were threatening it from all sides. When the legions finally departed Britain around 410, withdrawing to defend the Empire's heartland, local leaders were left to their own devices.

The Saxon Shore

The fort at Anderida (Pevensey) had been conceived as part of a series of defences along the coasts of both southern Britain and northern Gaul, known as 'the Saxon Shore'. Their nomenclature gives us more than a clue to the identity to the Germanic marauders who had given such trouble: these 'forts of the Saxon Shore' had provided a co-ordinated defence under the direction of a military Count of the Saxon Shore.[20] But after the departure of the legions, this network broke down. In Sussex, there appears to have been some attempt to construct strong points against invasion – at Chichester in the west, Hassocks in mid-Sussex at the northern foot of the Downs, and at Pevensey in the east. But by now Saxon newcomers were already settling in the Sussex countryside. Ironically, some may have come as Roman mercenaries, employed to man the Saxon Shore defences. Others were raiders who had decided to stay. The burning of Fishbourne palace late in the third century may have been a deliberate act by such intruders; either way, the site was abandoned thereafter, with no attempt at rebuilding.

The *Anglo-Saxon Chronicle*, part history and part propaganda, observed the process of invasion with satisfaction. Its entry for AD 477 (actually *c.*457) reported: 'This year Ella [or Aella] came to Britain, with his three sons, Cymen and Wlenking, and Cissa, in three ships; landing at a place that is called Cymenshore. There they slew many of the Welsh; and some in flight they drove into the wood that is called Andred Sley.'[21] 'Cymenshore' is thought to be Selsey, 'Andred' is surely Anderida (Pevensey), and the 'Welsh', of course, are actually the Celtic-speaking native Britons. Thus, in vivid detail, the *Chronicle* described the manner in which Ella and his three bloodthirsty sons had confronted the defenders in their strongholds. And, like others, they were there to stay. Over the next dozen years or so, Ella established his overlordship in Sussex at the point of a sword. The old capital Noviomagus Regensium was renamed Cissa's Castra, or Cissa's fort (the Saxon form of modern Chichester), evidence of the collapse of the *civitas* and the triumph of the newcomers. Likewise, Cissbury – now captured from its British defenders – had become Cissa's camp. By 490 (*c.*470) the *Anglo-Saxon Chronicle* could note with the sense of a job well done: 'This year Ella and Cissa besieged the city of Andred, and slew all that were therein, nor was one Briton left there afterwards.'[22] The kingdom of the South Saxons was in the making.

Pevensey Castle is possibly the most interesting, historically, of all Sussex fortresses. Its origins predate the medieval era by several centuries, having been constructed initially by the Romans in the fourth century as part of their 'Saxon Shore' defences. Remarkably, the majority of this early work, with its towers and walls, still stands, although augmented by later fortification. In 1066 William of Normandy built a wooden castle within Pevensey's protective walls, and this was superseded in the 1070s by a stone-built Norman castle. Subsequently, there were further additions to this Roman and Norman work, and Pevensey Castle remained in more or less continual occupation until the sixteenth century. During the Second World War, the castle was re-occupied, first by the Home Guard and later by the Canadians and Americans. Originally situated on a peninsula projecting into a tidal lagoon, subsequent shifts in the coastline have left Pevensey Castle stranded almost a mile from the sea.

TWO

The South Saxons

The fierce Saxons, of ever execrable memory, [were] admitted into the Island [of Britain], like so many wolves into a sheep's fold, to defend them from the Northern Nations. A thing more destructive and pernicious than was ever done to this Kingdom. O the mist and grossness of this sense and apprehension! O the dullness and blockishness of these souls![1]

'The fierce Saxons, of ever execrable memory …'

THOSE CONQUERING SAXONS – Ella and his three sons, Cymen, Wlenking and Cissa – who had arrived in Sussex in AD 457 (see pp.19–20) were part of a wider Germanic intrusion in post-Roman Britain, lamented here by the British monk Gildas in his book *De Excidio et Conquestu Britanniae* (*On the Ruin and Conquest of Britain*). Gildas, who died *c.*572, had witnessed first-hand the Saxon invasions and settlement, and had viewed with horror and disbelief the destruction of Romano-British civilisation – including Christianity – that was wrought by the pagan Saxons. In his version of events, the Saxons had first been enticed to Britain as mercenaries by local leaders after the departure of the legions, their task being to help stem attacks from the marauding Picts and Scots, those 'northern nations'. But, once invited, the Saxons had arrived in ever-increasing numbers, outstaying their welcome and precipitating the calamity that so distressed Gildas.

His story has a ring of truth: we know that Germanic troops may already have been employed by the Romans to man the Saxon Shore forts, and that some Saxon raiders had by then decided to settle permanently – and his account is echoed in that of another early commentator, the Welshman Nennius. Although not written until *c.*830, Nennius' *Historia Brittonum* (*History of Britain*) is the first to name the individual responsible for this Saxon influx, pointing the finger of blame at Vortigern, erstwhile overlord of southern Britain. According to Nennius, it was Vortigern who had enlisted the Saxon mercenaries, under the command of their tribal leaders Hengist and Horsa, to join the fight against his 'northern' enemies. But having opened the floodgates to these newcomers, Vortigern was now powerless to prevent the treacherous Saxons establishing a fledgling kingdom of their own, probably in Kent. Thereafter, the Saxon invasion continued apace; further settlers from northern Germany arrived in south-east England, and others sailed up the Thames and the rivers of the Wash and the Humber to create new kingdoms all along the eastern coast. The *Anglo-Saxon Chronicle* gloried in the scale and pace of the conquest, smiling at the betrayal of Vortigern, and advancing 'the worthlessness of the Britons' and 'the excellence of the land' as full justification for this invasion and appropriation. As the *Chronicle* explained:

> Hengist and Horsa, invited by Vortigern, King of the Britons, came to Britain … at first to help the Britons, but later they fought against them. They then sent to Angeln [in Germany], ordered [them] to send more aid and to be told of the worthlessness of the Britons and the excellence of the land. They sent them more aid. These men came from the three nations of Germany: from the Old Saxons, from the Angles, from the Jutes.[2]

Today, the old story – that the invading Saxons (and Angles and Jutes) slaughtered the indigenous Britons or drove them off to the wilds of Wales and Cornwall – has been modified. Now we are encouraged to imagine relatively small numbers of invaders who, through military prowess and by taking advantage of political turmoil, were able to impose their will on the existing populace. Sometimes the Britons were evicted, perhaps, or even enslaved, and at other times there was intermarriage and assimilation into the dynamic culture of the newcomers. Sometimes the contact between peoples may have been hostile; at others, friendly or even welcoming. Maybe the Saxons benefited materially from their contacts with the Britons, acquiring a variety of new goods and wares produced in the towns, and perhaps they even provided a measure of local security – protecting Romano-British settlements from other groups of marauding barbarians. As Lloyd and Jennifer Laing once observed, on the Continent the Saxons had demonstrated 'time and again that they wanted not to massacre and annihilate, but to eat of the fruits of civilisation: we have no reason to suppose it was otherwise in Britain.'[3] However, even allowing for their propaganda agenda, the hand-wringing accounts of Gildas and Nennius tell a different tale, speaking eloquently of catastrophe and ruin on the grand scale, while the unrestrained triumphalism of the *Anglo-Saxon Chronicle* reveals all too readily the victors' contempt for the vanquished.

The experience may well have varied across England: in some areas the indigenous population was perhaps left relatively undisturbed; in others the Britons were more readily displaced or killed. But one senses that it is in the south-eastern corner of England that the old story of slaughter and banishment, if it still has any credibility, comes nearest to the truth.[4] Celtic place-names in Sussex are virtually non-existent – unless one counts the element *combe*, a valley, one of the few Celtic words incorporated into Old English – but everywhere apparent are the tell-tale Saxon names: *hurst*, a wood; *ley*, a clearing; *den* or *dene*, a wooded valley; and *ing*, a patronymic suffix meaning 'people of'.[5] The paucity of Celtic names suggests considerable displacement, or at least comprehensive cultural subordination, while the Saxon place-names are themselves a clue to how the Saxon colonisation of Sussex progressed. 'Saxon place-names are thick-scattered all over the map,' wrote the distinguished early twentieth-century teacher and archaeologist, S.E. Winbolt.[6] Indeed they are. But *ing* is the earliest Saxon element, found on the coastal plain and in southerly areas along the river valleys, indicating areas of initial settlement and subsequent consolidation in the sixth and seventh centuries. Also relatively early is the familiar suffix *ham*, at first meaning an isolated pasture but later describing a hamlet or small settlement. Later, when the forests of the Weald were at last penetrated, *hurst*, *ley* and *den* became commonplace, as did the ending *field* in more eastern parts of the Weald and *fold* in the west.

As we know, among those Saxons who followed in the wake of Hengist and Horsa were Ella and his three sons – and just as Hengist and Horsa were said to have founded the embryonic kingdom of Kent, so Ella's people forged neighbouring Sussex. In its territorial extent, Ella's Sussex mirrored, more or less, both the old British kingdom of the Regni and the later Roman *civitas* (based on Chichester), stretching from Selsey to Pevensey or thereabouts and establishing boundaries that would prove remarkably durable over time – more so than for almost any other English county. Yet despite this continuity, Ella and his successors transformed Sussex, laying the foundations for one of the most distinctive periods of its history – one that would last for all of six centuries, until the Norman Conquest. As Esther Meynell put it, Sussex was 'no longer the Kingdom of the Regni, or a Roman province, but the country of the South Saxons'.[7] It was an identity that would endure, and the notion of Sussex as quintessentially Saxon has come down to our own time. In the eighteenth century, for example, Horace Walpole, the novelist and antiquarian, could muse that 'the whole county has a Saxon air'.[8] Two hundred years later, S.E. Winbolt could still insist that: 'Vestiges of the Saxons … are probably more richly represented in Sussex than in any other English county.'[9]

The *Bretwalda*

It is not clear whether Ella used the term 'South Saxons' to describe his kingdom (the first documentary evidence of the name does not appear until 687). But he was aware of the importance of his newly won territory as a power base from which he could attempt to project his authority. He absorbed the neighbouring pocket of *Haestingas* or 'Haestas's folk' (who gave their name to modern Hastings), expanding and strengthening his eastern frontier, and for a time he was recognised as *Bretwalda* – or overlord – of all Britain. Although 'England' as a unified political entity did not emerge until the tenth century, there were clearly much earlier aspirations towards English unity, together with early designs on Cornwall, Wales and Scotland. In his eighth-century *History of the English Church and People*, the Venerable Bede – the Northumbrian monk and historian, writing in his monastery at Jarrow – listed the *Bretwalda*. First had been Ella, king of Sussex, who was succeeded by Ceawlin of Wessex, who in turn was succeeded by Ethelbert of Kent, then Raedwald of East Anglia, and finally Edwin, Osiu and Oswald of Northumbria. *Bretwalda* was a title of distinction, of honour and prestige, a measure of a leader's standing among his peers, but it carried little if any political power. Bede suggested that Ella's sway was felt in all the provinces south of the Humber. But it is unlikely that his rule extended far beyond the bounds of Sussex. Besides, the *Bretwalda*-ship could sometimes be contested – although they did not appear in Bede's list, the great Mercian kings Ethelbald and Offa adopted the title 'king of Britain' and certainly considered themselves *Bretwaldas*. That Ella had been proclaimed *Bretwalda* was an indication of the esteem in which he was held. But on his death the title passed to neighbouring (and more powerful) Wessex, the land of the West Saxons, and the brief national prominence of the South Saxons was already on the wane.[10]

Moreover, the aspirations towards English unity had bred jealousy and rivalry between the several kingdoms, as they jostled for position and engaged in an extended struggle for dominance. Ultimately, it became a battle for supremacy between the big three – Mercia, Northumbria, and Wessex – in which the latter eventually triumphed. The Wessex heartland was Dorset, Wiltshire and Hampshire. But as its power grew, so the kingdom expanded west and east. Before his accession as king, Caedwalla of the West Saxons had already attempted to carve out a principality for himself in Sussex, and after gaining the Wessex throne in 685 devoted three years to 'warfare, loot and arson' in Sussex, Kent, Surrey, and the Isle of Wight. His son Ine, who came to power in 688, continued the subjugation of Sussex, and thereafter it appears to have survived as a sub-kingdom under West Saxon suzerainty. By the time Egbert of Wessex (another self-styled *Bretwalda*) defeated the Mercians in 825, Sussex – like Essex and Kent – had become entirely dependent upon the West Saxons, token 'kingships' that were handed out from time to time by Egbert and his son Aethelwulf on a grace and favour basis.

Conversion to Christianity

The struggle for political mastery was mirrored in a contest between religious faiths. The Roman Empire had formally converted to Christianity in the fourth century, following the Emperor Constantine's decree in AD 314 that Christians be allowed to practise their religion unmolested. However, there is no evidence that this had much impact in Sussex, and in the years before the Saxon intrusion the Romano-British populations no doubt continued to worship their pantheon of Roman gods – such as Neptune and Minerva, commemorated in the temple at Chichester – and other, lesser deities inherited from the pagan Celts. When Ella arrived with his Saxon invaders, he brought another kind of paganism, with its celebration of the cults of 'heroes' and much feasting and story telling, its distinctive funerary practices, and its own array of gods. Chief among these was Woden, the creator. There were also Tiw, the god of war, and Frig – the goddess of love and mother of humanity – and Thunor (or Thor), the god of thunder. Near Alfriston are the remains of an extensive pagan Saxon cemetery, containing more than one hundred and fifty graves – all inhumed burials, male and female – and a wide variety of material objects. Alongside iron swords, spears and shield bosses, were discovered conical glass drinking horns, large quantities of beads, pottery, gilded bronze fibulae, pins and brooches, silver finger rings, and a bronze bowl. Another Saxon cemetery, at Highdown, revealed both inhumations and cremations (the ashes placed in urns), together with iron knives and spearheads and four glass drinking horns – one of which, with its frieze of hare and hounds on the body and an inscription in Greek on the neck, may be of Mediterranean origin.

Such funerary practice – the burial with the dead of all the things that had been useful or given pleasure in life, and which might come in handy in the hereafter – was symptomatic of pagan Saxon religious belief. In Sussex, such beliefs and practices survived longer than anywhere else in England. Sussex was not officially converted to Christianity until 681 (and no doubt thereafter the traditional worship of rivers, woods and hills lingered on regardless, not least in the remote Weald), almost a century after Pope Gregory had sent St Augustine on his celebrated mission to save the pagan Saxons. Augustine had arrived in Kent in 597. Here King Ethelbert, soon to become the first Christian *Bretwalda*, had an already Christian wife (a Frankish princess), who in turn had close links with Continental Christianity. Keen to take advantage of this promising situation, Augustine arrived with the full pomp and authority of Rome – decked out in his vestments, preceded by a silver processional cross, and with an illustrated Gospel, fragments of which still survive in Cambridge. A reluctant Ethelbert allowed himself to be baptised, and gave permission for Augustine and his missionaries to operate in his kingdom, establishing themselves at Canterbury. Meanwhile, Raewald, the pagan king of East Anglia, had been earmarked as the next *Bretwalda*, and so, having successfully preached the Word in Kent, Augustine now turned his attention northwards – without ever having penetrated neighbouring Sussex. Thereafter, the Weald would continue to act as a barrier to the spread of Christianity from the north and east, and when the new faith finally did arrive in Sussex, it would be by sea.

By the year 625, Augustine's followers had reached as far north as Northumbria. Here they were to find themselves in competition with a rival missionary effort, that of the Celtic Church. Today, scholars are wary of the terms 'Celtic Church' and 'Celtic Christianity', sceptical of any suggestion of a cohesive ecclesiastical organisation and a coherent liturgy and theology. Yet, however inchoate, there was undoubtedly an evangelical impulse in the Celtic lands, which saw Celtic 'saints' – holy men and women – crisscrossing the seas between Brittany, Cornwall, Wales, Ireland, the Isle of Man, and Scotland, taking the Christian faith to distant corners of these islands. In this way, Celtic monks from the island of Iona in western Scotland had founded a mission on Lindisfarne, off the coast of Northumbria. Its leader, Aidan, set about the conversion of the Northumbrians but soon found himself up against Augustinian teaching and the competing claims of Rome. To resolve the conflict, in 664 the famous Synod of Whitby was held (in present-day Yorkshire) to decide whether the 'Celtic' or 'Roman' form of Christianity should prevail in Northumbria – and, by implication, in the Isles of Britain. The saintly Cuthbert, abbot of Lindisfarne, argued the Celtic case, but he was out-manoeuvred by the wily Wilfrid, bishop of Ripon. Ostensibly, the debate was about such arcane matters as determining the date of Easter or the style of tonsure to be worn by monks. But in reality it was a political contest as significant as that of the struggle between the several English kingdoms – and Rome won.

Meanwhile, Sussex had had its first taste of Christianity when in the 660s a Scottish (or Irish) monk, Dicul – another of those Celtic missionaries – had established a modest monastery, with no more than half a dozen brethren, at Bosham. As the Venerable Bede noted, somewhat patronisingly, 'none of the natives cared either to follow their course of life, or to hear their preaching', and Dicul's mission proved less than successful.[11] But serendipity intervened, and in 666 none other than bishop Wilfrid – the victor of Whitby – turned up unexpectedly, when his ship was driven ashore on the Sussex coast in a violent storm. His welcome was no more friendly than that Dicul had received a few years before. Indeed, Wilfrid claimed to have been confronted by an angry crowd of pagans, bent on killing him and his followers, and it was only with the safe return of the tide – expedited, we are told, by God's timely intervention – that he was able to escape. Wilfrid's outrageous treatment at the hands of the pagan South Saxons confirmed all the worst fears of the Christian kingdoms in England, which tended to look down on their wayward Sussex cousins. Bede himself wrote of the unparalleled ignorance of the Sussex pagans – they were so primitive that they did not even know how to fish, he said, and during times of dearth they leapt lemming-like from the great chalk cliffs.

Yet, despite his harrowing experiences, Wilfrid was back in Sussex in 681. This time his political intrigues had led to his expulsion from Northumbria, and perhaps the rest of England, by the angry King Ecgfrith – and it was no doubt a measure of Wilfrid's desperation that he sought exile in hostile Sussex. Now, however, he was altogether more successful, and he spent five years ministering to the South Saxons before he was allowed to return to Northumbria. Among other things, it is said that Wilfrid taught the locals to fish using nets, winning their gratitude and persuading their King, Ethelwalh (perhaps already nominally Christian), to embrace the faith unequivocally. Thus baptised, Ethelwalh set an example that his subjects were required to follow – evidence, perhaps, of the nature of kingly authority in Saxon England. At any rate, the whole of England was now officially Christian. Theodore of Tarsus (Archbishop of Canterbury, 668–90) divided the country into fifteen dioceses. Among these was the new bishopric of Selsey, where Wilfrid established a monastery, endowed with land – some eighty-seven *hides* all told (roughly 120 acres each) – to generate income to support his monks. Alas, nothing remains of Wilfrid's monastery – nor of the great Minster that was built later on the site – for much of the Selsey 'island' or Manhood peninsula was subsequently inundated by the sea.

The Venerable Bede, writing not long after, noted how the fortunes of the South Saxons had changed for the better since Wilfrid's arrival. The long drought that had precipitated sacrificial suicide – the leaping from the cliffs – had been broken at a stroke. As Wilfrid baptised the first of his converts, so Bede reported, the rain began to fall, changing the face of the land and bringing an abundant harvest in its wake. Wilfrid also ordered the freeing of some 250 slaves – male and female – on his monastic estate, these no doubt descendents of the defeated Britons. St Wilfrid, as he became, was lauded for his efforts, not only by Bede but also in the biography penned by one of his followers, the monk Eddius Stephanus – or Eddi, for short. According to Eddi, who conveniently neglected to mention his master's political indiscretions, Wilfrid was simply 'affable to all, penetrating in mind, strong in body, expert at all good works, never with a sour face', to be celebrated for all time as the man who had brought Christianity to Sussex.[12]

Eddi himself is still remembered for his own role in the conversion of the South Saxons. Rudyard Kipling, in one of his several poems about the county, 'Eddi's Service (AD 687)', sketched an amusing account of the difficulties encountered by missionaries in persuading recent converts to conform to the practices of their new religion:

Eddi, priest of St Wilfrid
  In his chapel at Manhood End,
Ordered a midnight service
  For such as cared to attend.

But the Saxons were keeping Christmas,
  And the night was stormy as well.
Nobody came to the service,
  Though Eddi rang the bell.

'Wicked weather for walking',
  Said Eddi of Manhood End.
'But I must go on with the service
  For such as care to attend'.[13]

In time, of course, part of the success of Christianity – in Sussex, as elsewhere – was its ability to accommodate elements of pagan belief within the Christian faith, and to endow them with Christian meaning. Thus the mid-winter feasting which had traditionally marked the pagan Saxon calendar was neatly re-invented as part of the celebration of Christmas, in which believers might both feast *and* attend midnight mass. Yet the progress of Christianity in Sussex was not always straightforward. When Caedwalla, king of Wessex, descended on the South Saxons bent on conquest, he brought turmoil and uncertainty, not least when (it is said) he slew King Ethelwalh in battle. Nominally a Christian, Caedwalla was also a warrior in the old Saxon tradition, and thought nothing of wreaking death and destruction on his co-religionists. However, in the midst of this mayhem, he suddenly had second thoughts. Tradition insists that he was converted anew by St Wilfrid, who for his pains was gifted the little town of Paganham (a telling play on words!) as his personal possession. At any rate, Caedwalla abandoned his warlike ways, gave up his kingdom, and set off to Rome on a pilgrimage of penitence. Perhaps he had been injured in battle, and recognised that his days were numbered. Arriving in Rome, he was baptised once more, being given the holy name 'Peter' by the Pope. There he died, in his white baptismal robes, on 20 April 689. Intriguingly, his son Ine, who had continued the subjugation of Sussex, followed his example, and after his long career as king of Wessex, he too retired to Rome to die in peace.

Christian folklore and Saxon churches

No doubt superstition remained commonplace among the converted South Saxons, such as belief in *puca* – the mischievous woodland sprite – whose persistence in the supposedly Christian landscape is evident in the modern place-name 'Pook's Hill', near Burwash. Rudyard Kipling, always a keen observer of Sussex lore, penned his children's stories 'Puck of Pook's Hill' in 1906, in which Puck – *puca* – is the last of the people of the hills, the 'oldest thing in England', who mysteriously charms the fictional children Una and Dan with his tales of England's past.[14] But to such superstition was progressively added a patina of Christian folklore (Kipling's Pook even has a story to tell about St Wilfrid), such as the well-known life of St Cuthman. His mother, so the legend goes, had lost the use of her legs, and dutiful St Cuthman took her everywhere in a wheelbarrow, even when he was out on the Downs tending his sheep. His ability to perform miracles was apparent to all who knew

The Church of St Andrew and St Cuthman stands on the site of the original church, reputedly founded by St Cuthman as an act of atonement for his hasty punishment of cheeky farm labourers. Given to the Abbey of Fécamp in the eleventh century, the church was lavishly rebuilt, with Caen stone imported from Normandy. Elements of Norman work survive in the church today. The contemplative figure gazing upon the church is a sculpture of none other than St Cuthman himself.
ALISON AVERY, WWW.BEAUTIFULENGLANDPHOTOS.UK

him – when he needed to leave his sheep unattended, for example, he simply drew a circle around them with his crook, preventing them from straying and protecting them from predators. Yet one day, when the ropes on the barrow conveying his mother broke, some haymakers working in an adjoining field were foolish enough to laugh at his misfortune. St Cuthman promptly called down a great deluge, which ruined the haymakers' efforts – and ever since, according to legend, it has always rained in that very field during haymaking.[15]

A story of retribution, the haymakers' punishment had taught the cheeky farm labourers a lesson in manners. But it had also given hasty St Cuthman pause for thought. Even as the haymakers had smirked, so he had fashioned a withy out of some elder twigs from a nearby bush to replace the snapped ropes. Subsequently, when the withy finally wore out, he was compelled by his conscience – or Divine intervention – to build a church at the place where now he had had to stop. In this way, he founded the church at Steyning, constructing it at the confluence of two small rivers under the shadow of the Downs, where he discovered some elder bushes among an overgrown tangle of brambles and thicket, enabling him to make a new withy. Tradition insists that St Cuthman was eventually buried there, along with King Ethelwulf (father of Alfred the Great), although the latter's body was afterwards removed to Winchester. A measure, perhaps, of the significance of St Cuthman in Sussex lore, the much-prized church at Steyning was later given to the Norman abbey at Fécamp by Edward the Confessor, the penultimate Saxon king of England, an important diplomatic gesture which marked the growing relationship with Normandy in the years before the Conquest.

Almost as well known as St Cuthman's tale is the story of St Dunstan,

St Dunstan's church at Mayfield was founded by St Dunstan himself, *c.*960, when he was Archbishop of Canterbury. Originally a wooden structure, it was replaced by a stone building in the twelfth century. The church was all but destroyed by fire in 1389, and was eventually rebuilt between 1410 and 1420.
JOHN FRIEND

the tenth-century Saxon monk who rose through a number of important ecclesiastical appointments – among them Abbot of Glastonbury, Bishop of Worcester, and Bishop of London – to become Archbishop of Canterbury. Despite this hectic trajectory, legend insists, St Dunstan found time to practise his skill as a metalworker, not least in the tiny forge he had built alongside the church at Mayfield in Sussex. Here he would craft gold chalices and iron horseshoes, and on one such occasion while busy working he was interrupted by an unexpected visitor, a beguiling young woman. However, St Dunstan was not taken in by this cunning disguise, and recognised at once that the attractive maiden was none other than the Devil himself. He grabbed the red-hot tongs from his forge and tweaked the Devil's nose as hard as he was able. Howling in rage and pain, the Devil immediately assumed his usual horrific visage, and sped to Tunbridge Wells to cool his sizzling nose in the springs. Dunstan was canonised after his death, and for the next two centuries remained among the most popular saints in Sussex and the rest of England. So ingrained in Sussex folklore was the story of St Dunstan and the Devil, that when the travel writer Louis Jennings visited Mayfield in the 1870s, conducting research for his volume *Field Paths and Green Lanes in Surrey and Sussex*, he was shown what were purported to be the very tongs with which St Dunstan had repelled the Devil's advances. Jennings called at Mayfield Convent, where one of the sisters allowed him to view the famous tongs. As he recounted:

> 'These are the tongs with which St Dunstan worked his miracle,' said the worthy sister.
>
> 'I have read of the legend in my book,' said I, meaning no offence.
>
> 'It is not a legend,' replied the sister in a tone of slight reproof.
>
> 'No, no,' said I, 'I did not mean to throw any doubt upon the story.'[16]

The popularity and persistence of such Devil stories reflects the perpetual struggle between Good and Evil, as it has been imagined over the centuries, and perhaps too a lingering Christian fear of a malevolent residual paganism lurking in the countryside.

The legend of Devil's Dyke is another good example of the *genre*. Here, to explain the natural defile in the Downs north-west of Brighton, it was suggested that under the cover of darkness the Devil had begun to dig a massive dyke across the hills, to allow the ocean to rush through and inundate the Weald beyond, with its many churches which so infuriated him. However, he had not reckoned with the old woman who lived nearby: she, expecting her son home from sea at any moment, had lit a lamp in her cottage window to guide the sailor-boy in the inky blackness. The Devil, mistaking the light cast from the lamp as the first sign of dawn, panicked, stopped digging and fled – and thereafter the cleft that he had started was known as Devil's Dyke.[17]

Inundation, from which the old woman had saved the Weald, was a constant fear all around maritime Britain in early times, and not without reason. The drowned landscape of the Isles of Scilly had no doubt prompted stories of Lyonnesse – the legendary lost land off the coast of Cornwall – and in Sussex a similar, if perhaps less well known, drowning accounted for tales of a sunken land off Selsey, the 'Isle of Seals'. Bede had written that Wilfrid's monastery at Selsey was surrounded on all sides by the sea, except on the western edge where there was an entrance 'of about a stone's throw', presumably a causeway rather like those of Lindisfarne or St Michael's Mount. However, Wilfrid's monastery – and the subsequent Minster – was more low-lying than these other holy

Devil's Dyke, a steep valley in the Downland chalk created by river erosion, has long attracted explanatory legends. One suggests that, as the Devil dug his dyke, intent on flooding the Weald, he stubbed his toe on a large rock. In pain and anger, he added to his injury by kicking the rock towards the sea, then promptly abandoned his task to nurse his wounds. Meanwhile, the rock had landed at the spot that is today Hove Park, where it may still be seen and wondered at. A further story insists that the Devil had taken the form of a giant goat, with the intention of trampling the Wealden churches into oblivion. However, scenting a whiff of the sea, he feared that his coat would become damp (such was his vanity), so he turned and fled, leaving only his hoof-print – Devil's Dyke.
ALISON AVERY, WWW.BEAUTIFULENGLANDPHOTOS.UK

Holy Trinity Church at Bosham, situated about two miles west of Chichester, is steeped in Sussex history. The church features in the stories of King Cnut and King Harold, and is represented in the Bayeux Tapestry as well as rating a mention in Bede's *The Ecclesiastical History of the English Nation.* A pleasing legend insists that when Viking raiders stole the tenor bell from Bosham church, the other bells were rung in defiance – as the Viking longship sailed away, the tenor miraculously joined in the ring of bells, destroying the ship and its occupants.
BILL BROOKS, WWW.BILLBROOKSIMAGES.COM

islands, and, as we know, was lost when shortly after the sea radically redefined that part of the Sussex coast. William Camden, writing later in his *Britannia* in 1586, could note that even then the 'ancient little city where the bishops had their seat' was 'hidden quite with water at every tide, but at low water evident and plain to be seen'.[18] This is no longer the case today, although, in the immediate post-Second World War years at least, a stretch of local water was still generally known as 'The Park'. Likewise, tales persisted of occasional relics brought to the surface by fishermen, while, as in many other inundation stories, it was said that at certain times cathedral bells could be heard tolling from their watery resting place beneath the waves.

Although the monastery and Minster have disappeared, the church at nearby Bosham remains as testament to the area's importance in Saxon times. Parts of the church's fabric are pre-Conquest, revealing the enduring quality of Saxon architecture, and beneath the chancel arch are earlier arch bases still *in situ*, said variously to be remains of a Roman basilica or from Dicul's pioneering monastery. In Victorian times, early Sussex churches tended to get a bad press, and were thought plain and uninteresting. Even W.S. Mitchell, writing the notes on Sussex for John Betjeman's otherwise sympathetic *Guide to English Parish Churches*, published in 1958, considered them 'not among the most magnificent'.[19] More recently, however, Simon Jenkins has pointed out that the relative poverty of early Sussex ensured both the simplicity and survival of these modest structures, which in more prosperous areas would have been comprehensively rebuilt in medieval times. In this way, precious examples survive to give us at least some physical insight into the world of the Christian South Saxons. Nikolaus Pevsner considered the chancel arch at Bosham 'one of the best Saxon arches in England',[20] and the extraordinary tower at Sompting church has been described by Simon Jenkins as 'England's supreme Saxon steeple', the only example anywhere in Britain of a gabled pyramidal style known as a 'Rhenish helm'.[21] Utterly unique, Sompting nonetheless seems incomparably Saxon in ambience and character. Intriguingly, there are also traces of Roman brickwork in its tower walls, presumably tiles recovered from abandoned Roman buildings.

The church at Worth, meanwhile, in the north of Sussex is, according to Jenkins, 'in the front rank of Saxon structures' with as much as 95 per cent of the structure dating to before the eleventh century – especially noteworthy are the three impressive Saxon crossing arches which dominate the interior.[22] As an admiring Pevsner put it, Worth is 'one of the most powerful of Anglo-Saxon churches, large in scale and bold in conception'.[23] However, Worth is atypical, a giant among the typically much smaller Sussex churches of the era, especially the tiny

The Church of the Blessed Virgin at Sompting, situated between Lancing and Worthing in West Sussex, is justly famous for its 'Rhenish helm' tower, unique in England. The tower dates from *c.*1050, and the church boasts other distinctive Saxon survivals, notably the characteristic window and bell openings. In 1154 the church was acquired by the Knights Templar, who added the transepts, and following their suppression it was given to the Hospitallers – the Knights of St John – in 1324.

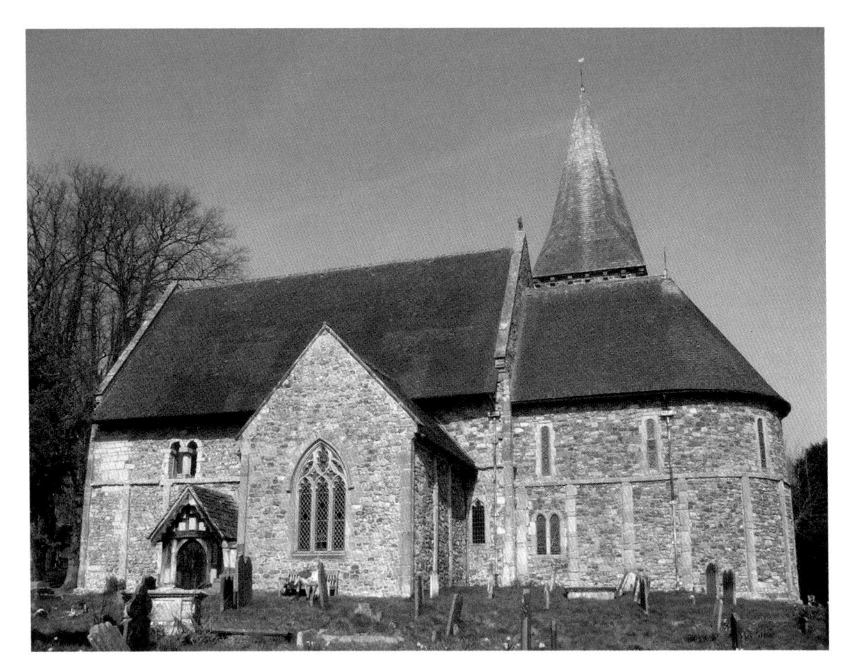

St Nicholas' church at Worth, near Crawley, sports much Saxon work, dating to the tenth century. Compared to most medieval church buildings in Sussex, Worth is of massive construction, especially its prominent and strongly built eastern apse. USER: HASSOCKS5489/ WIKIMEDIA COMMONS/CCO 1.0

Downland chapels such as Didling (where only a Saxon font remains in a mainly thirteenth-century building), or Selham – on the sandstone ridge which follows the northern flank of the Downs – and Up Marden, 500 feet above sea level, which appears to be a partial rebuilding of a Saxon original. Near Up Marden church is a Saxon cemetery, thought to date from the late fifth to early eighth centuries: the later interments are clearly Christian, suggesting that the church was built on the site of an earlier pagan place of worship, further evidence of the accommodation of the old and the new. The same seems to have occurred at Hamsey, Piddinghoe, Southease, Tarring Neville, and Berwick, where the churches are built on or alongside earlier burial mounds.[24]

Interestingly, the simple Saxon architectural style survived the Conquest in Sussex, and in the late eleventh century and after there were many examples of what Ian Nairn has called 'Saxon-Norman overlap', where traditional features were complemented by new innovations, especially during new builds and the refurbishment of existing structures.[25] The towers at Jevington, Sullington and Singleton just pre-date the Conquest, and so too perhaps do the wall paintings in Clayton church, thought now to date from *c.*1050–1100. Said to be unique in England for their extent and degree of preservation, the Clayton wall paintings exhibit stylistic influences reminiscent of early eleventh-century Saxon manuscripts. The figures are long and lean, with tiny heads, and they appear to bend forwards as if swaying. Of the lower tier of instructional religious stories, only fragments survive, but the upper tier is remarkably intact. We see

Christ delivering the keys of Heaven to St Peter, there are angels blowing trumpets, and we witness the fall of the Antichrist. There is a depiction of the Heavenly Jerusalem, groups of the blessed and the damned and the Day of Judgement, a Horseman of the Apocalypse, the Instruments of the Passion, and other graphic illustrations designed to grip the South Saxon imagination.

Settlement and governance

There may have been as many as 150 churches spread across the Sussex landscape on the eve of the Norman Conquest (although the Domesday Book records rather fewer), their distribution reflecting the scattering of the population. The majority were in the west and the south, mirroring population density, but by now settlement had penetrated almost the whole county. Initially, the Saxons had not been an urban people, and although Chichester survived it was but a shadow of its former self, overtaken now by neighbouring Selsey. The fertile coastal plain spawned large estates, presided over by powerful *thegns* or chieftains. Early settlers had also moved inland along the river valleys and on to the productive soils along the northern scarp slope of the Downs. The Downs themselves, with their poorer soils, were less closely settled. The Weald was tackled, as John Lowerson has explained, in almost military fashion, with a series of well-organised 'campaigns' designed to clear large areas of the forest. Land thus opened up was often used by the arable coastal estates as 'swine pastures', where extensive herds were allowed to roam, their herders responsible for the pattern of hamlets that we observe today. Farmers followed where the swine had led, burning or chopping down the forest to create small fields, and leaving as hedge boundaries the wide *shaws* of woodland characteristic of the Weald. In contrast to the wheat and barley and rye of the coastal plain (whose surpluses were collected in co-operative granaries called *berwicks*), these Wealden farmers grazed sheep and cattle, and no doubt hunted game in the extensive forest that remained.[26]

The villages which sprung up across Sussex in the wake of rural settlement were generally built of wood, and rarely of stone. A typical dwelling was the so-called *grubenhaus* – or 'dug house' – where the building, rectangular or oblong in shape, was sunk a few feet into the ground, and fitted with a gabled roof resting on rafters and supported by posts. An early, fifth-century *grubenhaus* was uncovered at Bishopstone, near Seaford, in 1968. A much later building, dating from the ninth century, had been excavated at Erringham, near Shoreham, a few years before, in 1964. Remarkably, although separated by four centuries, these two huts were very similar in construction, evidence that this simple method of building had endured throughout the whole period.[27]

Most villages were self-sufficient, weaving their own cloth, for example, or keeping bees for making mead, and although there is evidence of co-operative behaviour, social distinction and variation in wealth became features of South Saxon life. Chieftains or *thegns* lived in more impressive wooden halls. These chieftains deferred to the bishop and *ealdermen* of the shire, but ranged beneath them were the *cearls* (or churls), mostly freemen and landholders, and below these were the *geburs*, nominally free cottagers who nonetheless owed extensive services to their *thegns*. And then there were the slaves, such as those liberated by St Wilfrid, among them the defeated Britons and their descendents. The *thegns* also exercised legal jurisdictions in districts which, after the Conquest, would be known as *rapes*. These, in turn, were divided into *hundreds*, groups of parishes that would organise the *fyrd* or local militia. Hundred courts also dispensed local justice.

This emerging social and governmental system, alongside the spread of Christianity, no doubt encouraged a sense of community and security. However, all this was challenged in the ninth century when a new wave of marauding pagans began to ravage the shores of Britain. These were the Danes and Norwegians, the 'Vikings' or pirates as the Saxons called them, who began raiding along the Kent coast in 852. Politically, these Viking incursions and their subsequent settlement led to both the concentration and consolidation of Saxon power in the kingdom of Wessex *and* the division of England into two, the north-eastern part becoming the Danelaw where the invaders held sway. Alfred became king of Wessex in 871 and, after a series of defeats at the hands of the Danes, began to organise a stout military and naval resistance. As part of this defence, Alfred built a series of forts or *burghs* along the south-eastern coast of England from Porchester to Dover. Five of these *burghs* were in Sussex – at Chichester, Burpham (near Arundel), Lewes, Hastings, and possibly Pevensey. Of these, Lewes and Hastings, as well as Chichester, were by now towns of some importance. Lewes, in particular, had emerged as a regional focus in its own right, a counter to the weight of population and political authority vested in Selsey and environs, a foretaste of the day when Lewes would share power with Chichester as the respective county towns of East and West Sussex. By Edward the Confessor's reign, Lewes may have been the legal centre of the shire, as well as having its own mint and cattle market, and had already begun to spawn suburbs alongside the navigable river Ouse.

The wisdom of creating these defensive *burghs* was demonstrated in 895 when a large force of raiders was repulsed at Chichester. The *Anglo-Saxon Chronicle* recorded breathlessly that the 'Danish Army went up plundering in Sussex nigh Chichester; but the townsmen put them to flight, and slew many hundreds of them, and took some of their ships.'[28] Of course, it was not the townsmen themselves who performed these noble deeds but rather the professional troops stationed in the *burgh*. It may be a measure of the effectiveness of this defensive system that the Sussex coast was spared major incursions until 994 when, during the reign of Ethelred 'the Unready', the Viking menace returned suddenly. Swegan the Dane and Olaf the Norwegian, having been defeated at London, turned 'the fury of the Norsemen' on Sussex. According to the *Anglo-Saxon Chronicle*, they 'advanced and brought the greatest evil that any army could, burning, plundering and manslaughter … in Sussex and Hampshire'.[29] In 998 the Vikings established their winter quarters on the Isle of Wight, which would become their base for raiding along the south coast of England. In 1000, for instance, as the *Chronicle* reported: 'everywhere in Sussex they plundered and burnt as is their custom.'[30]

The kingdom of Cnut

In 1016, when Ethelred died, the Wessex Witan – the supreme Saxon governing council – decided that enough was enough, and in a 'if you can't beat 'em, join 'em' strategy, passed over Ethelred's son Edmund 'Ironside' and instead offered the throne to Cnut, king of the Danelaw. That the Danelaw had turned to Christianity made the deal possible. At last there was peace, and all England was unified under Cnut's rule. From 1016 until his death in 1035, Cnut was king of England and – for most of the time – king of Denmark and Norway too, as well as lord of Sweden. In many ways, despite creating the united England that Saxon kings had long yearned (and fought) for, this was a self-inflicted defeat. But peace was the prize, and in Sussex there was a brief flowering of Saxon culture, for the period after 1016 was the time of church building and wall painting, of Sompting and Worth, of Jevington, Sullington and Clayton. However, Cnut was ruthless in his peacemaking. Having achieved his objective, the throne of England, he dispensed with the Saxon hostages he and his father had collected over the years – mutilating them before execution – and killing or driving off into exile Ethelred's remaining sons. Other leading Saxons were murdered at Cnut's command, and to make sure that he had everything sown up he married Ethelred's widow, Emma of Normandy. However, although nominally a Christian, Cnut had not yet lost the Viking taste for polygamy, and so he did not divorce his existing 'temporary wife', Elgifu of Northampton, but dispatched her to Denmark where they ruled together as king and queen.

Yet Cnut tried to rule fairly in his newly united kingdom, and stressed his status as successor of Alfred the Great and inheritor of the Wessex dynasty and tradition. He also cultivated his image as a pious man, deeply devoted to the Church. In 1027 he went on a pilgrimage to Rome, consciously following in the footsteps of Caedwalla and Ine and Alfred who had done the same. When his followers suggested that he could achieve anything, even turn back the tide, Cnut in his humility – or so the story goes – demonstrated that this was not so and that there were limits to kingly power. In some versions of the tale, it was at Bosham in Sussex that Cnut unsuccessfully commanded the waves to retreat. If so it was a telling choice of location, for the inundation that was so to alter the coastline thereabouts may already have begun, groins perhaps having been built only recently to retard the ingress of the sea. It may also help to explain the enduring legend that one of Cnut's daughters, having died unexpectedly in childhood, was buried in Bosham church. In 1865 the Revd Henry Mitchell decided to test the story, as he explained in the following year's edition of *Sussex Archaeological Collections*. The floor of the church was taken up at the spot traditionally thought to mark the grave of the child princess. As Mitchell reported: 'The iron bar at once struck upon a stone, and on removing the mould which covered it a stone coffin was presented to our delighted gaze.' Moreover, when the lid was raised, 'the remains of a child were distinctly visible. ... From the size of the body the child must have been, as handed down by tradition, about eight years of age at the time of her decease.' Mitchell also considered that the stone coffin 'corresponds in rudeness of style with coffins of Canute's [*sic*] period', and so the legend was proved beyond doubt as historical fact – to his satisfaction at least.[31]

Cnut also died relatively young, aged about forty, in 1035. By then, despite the early firmness of his rule, he had devolved day-to-day authority to trusted but increasingly rival earls (Saxon as well as Danes), with the Earl Godwin governing in Wessex, including Sussex – where he was especially popular. Cnut also had two queens, one of whom was Norman, creating the potential for dynastic muddle. This atmosphere of political uncertainty ensured that, after his death, Cnut's kingdom would be plunged into factional fighting and jostling for position. Cnut had produced one son by Emma of Normandy, Harthancnut, who had already been given the kingdom of Denmark and was now fully preoccupied in fighting in Norway. Emma and Earl Godwin pressed his case, nonetheless, but were out-manoeuvred by Elgifu of Northampton and Earl Leofric (the governor of Mercia) who arranged with Elgifu the 'temporary wife' that Cnut's 'illegitimate' son Harold should become regent, and then king. Meanwhile, Alfred, eldest surviving son of Ethelred and Emma had returned from exile in Normandy to press *his* claim, only to be murdered in a plot hatched by Godwin. Then Harold, the new king, died in 1040 and so the throne of England passed to Harthacnut, by now the consensus candidate. In the meantime, Harthacnut had made his peace with Magnus of Norway, the two agreeing that each would succeed to the other's throne if either should die without an heir. Magnus and his successor, Harald Hardrada, insisted that this pact also applied to England. But Harthacnut dismissed this interpretation, and instead in 1041 invited Edward – Ethelred's last surviving son – to join him at court. Edward duly returned from his own exile in Normandy and, having been named as successor, suddenly found himself king of England when Harthacnut died in June 1042, aged just twenty-three. Edward was great-great-great-grandson of Alfred of Wessex, and his mother Emma had been queen to both Ethelred and Cnut. His succession thus won approval across the kingdom – and he became the first Saxon king of all England proper, although in culture and sympathy his long exile had made him Norman in outlook.

From Edward the Confessor to King Harold

Edward the Confessor, as the new king became known, married Godwin's daughter, Edith. But the couple remained childless, and Edward, who in the early years of his reign has deferred to Godwin's advice and direction, was now increasingly hostile to the man who had plotted the murder of his brother Alfred. Accordingly, in 1051 Edward acted against him. Godwin was exiled, Edith was ejected from court, and a Norman was appointed Archbishop of Canterbury. Most important of all, the kingdom of England was promised to Edward the Confessor's cousin, William of Normandy. However, it was immediately apparent that Edward had gone too far, and for the sake of equanimity in his kingdom he allowed the return of Godwin and Edith in the following year. Godwin died in 1053 but his son Harold stepped into his shoes, winning the confidence of Edward the Confessor to such an extent that the promise to William of Normandy was quietly forgotten, with Harold earmarked for the succession instead.

As we shall see, this bewildering turn of events in the first two decades since Cnut's death had enormous consequences for the kingdom of England, not least for Sussex, the stage upon which would be acted out some of the most momentous events of the next few years. Edward the Confessor, with his pro-Norman sympathies, had already donated St Cuthman's church at Steyning to the Benedictine abbey of Fécamp, together with other land in that vicinity and at Hastings, Rye, and Winchelsea. To his Norman chaplain, Osborne, he gave the church and harbour at Bosham. The latter gift was resented locally, not least as Godwin and his son Harold had used Bosham – along with Pevensey – as a naval base from which operated the ships protecting the coastline from pirate raids. When Godwin returned from exile in 1052, he had received a hero's welcome in maritime Sussex.[32]

Ironically, it was from Bosham that Harold sailed in 1064 on a journey that ended with his being wrecked on the coast of Normandy, and falling into the hands of the local count, Guy of Ponthieu, who dutifully passed him on to William. The purpose of Harold's journey remains unclear. One suggestion is that Edward the Confessor had sent him on a diplomatic mission to William – if so, plucked from the wreckage of his foundering ship, Harold was now on a decidedly unequal footing with his host. He was treated as an honoured guest but, it is said, was forced on oath to support William's claim to the English throne. Less than two years later, in January 1066, Edward the Confessor died – plunging England into crisis. As Harald Hardrada in Norway and William in Normandy both pondered their respective claims to the succession, the English *thegns* chose Harold as king – the one man, they considered, who could keep the country united and see off the threats of Norway and Normandy. It seemed an obvious and sensible decision, and yet within the year William and his conquering Norman army would be landing on the shores of Sussex.

THREE

The Normans

William the Conqueror

THE BATTLE OF HASTINGS IN 1066 is among the most famous events of English history. It led to the Norman Conquest – not only to William of Normandy's coronation as king of England but to an array of political, cultural, social, economic and ecclesiastical innovations which changed the face of the country rapidly and for ever. Nowhere were these felt more immediately or more comprehensively than in Sussex, which emerged not only as front line for the Norman invasion but as lasting conduit between England and Normandy, the principal channel of communication and exchange between the two territories. Norman French became the language of polite society as well as the state, and Normans and their allies (notably Bretons) were appointed to key positions of authority and power in England. Social and economic distinction became more organised and more rigid, as feudalism on the Norman model was imposed on English society. To some later observers this was 'the Norman yoke', the moment when traditional English liberties were fatally undermined by Continental intrusion. But for others the Conquest heralded the welcome emergence of England into the mainstream of European life and ushered in a new period of prominence and greatness. Either way, Sussex was to play a major role in what lay ahead.

William the Conqueror – as he became after his victory at Hastings in 1066 – was born in 1027 or 1028, the illegitimate son of Robert I, sixth Duke of Normandy, and Herleva, teenage daughter of a humble tanner in the town of Falaise. Although he was thus 'William the Bastard' to his numerous detractors, who whispered against him and thought him unfit to rule, William's ambiguous status did not prevent his succession to the dukedom. Despite the growing influence of the Church, eleventh-century Normandy in many ways continued to betray its Viking origins. No less than nominally Christian Cnut, with his two wives (see pp.38–9), the Norman dukes were slow to adjust to ideas of monogamy. They were notorious as the feared *Duces Northmannorum* – dukes of the Norsemen – and were descendents of Rollo the Viking, who had been granted land in northern France by the Frankish king, Charles the Simple, in 911. As part of this deal, in which he was able to settle his Viking army within the diocese of Rouen, Rollo acknowledged the overlordship of the Frankish king and agreed to convert from paganism to Christianity. But old habits died hard. As late as 996 the Duke of Normandy was denounced by a neighbouring French nobleman as a 'pirate thief', and a mere quarter of a century before William's birth his grandfather had welcomed to the Norman capital in Rouen a marauding Viking army which had only recently laid waste to much of adjoining northern France. Yet we also know that by 1025 Viking speech had disappeared from Rouen, replaced by a dialect of French, although the Scandinavian language lingered for a time in Bayeux and other places across the dukedom. In other ways, too, the Normans had become increasingly 'French' and 'Continental' rather than 'Viking' and 'Scandinavian' in culture, outlook and politics. Indeed, as David C. Douglas has pointed out, one of the principal outcomes of the Norman Conquest was to be the realignment of medieval England away from Scandinavia and towards the near Continent.[1] Again, this was a reorientation which was to have profound consequences for Sussex.

William himself, having inherited the dukedom of Normandy at the age of eight, suffered a chaotic minority in which all his guardians were murdered, and was threatened by almost constant rebellion as he tried desperately to assert his authority. Enjoying for a time the support of the French king, Henry I, William became intimately embroiled in the territorial conflicts of the various rival principalities, such as Brittany, Anjou and Flanders, which characterised mid-eleventh-century France. As well as steeping him in French (as opposed to Viking) politics, this intimacy gave William his taste for territorial ambition and aggrandisement, with England the ultimate prize. Promised, as he thought, the English throne – first by Edward the Confessor, and then under oath by Harold, son of Godwin – William had also married Matilda (daughter of the count of Flanders), a descendent of Alfred the Great. His English credentials thus marshalled, William was dismayed when in January 1066 the crown was handed to Harold. Garnering support from his Norman barons – enticing them with the prospects of rich territorial pickings in conquered England – William also won the backing of the Pope, persuading him of the legitimacy of his claim to the English throne and insisting that he would ensure the compliance of the 'backward' English church with new papal reforms.[2]

Tostig and Hardrada

Meanwhile, in England, King Harold – as he now was – had ejected his unreliable brother Tostig from the earldom of Northumbria. Tostig sought exile in Flanders, and in neighbouring Normandy William saw his chance. Tostig was invited to base his troops in Normandy, and encouraged to acquire ships for an attack on southern England. In early May 1066, Tostig sailed from Normandy with a motley army of perhaps 1,200 men – English, Flemish, Norman – in more than thirty vessels. When the earl of Godwin had returned from exile in 1052, the people of Sussex had turned out in force to cheer him home. But Tostig received no such welcome. Landing first on the Isle of Wight, he then conducted a series of exploratory raids along the Sussex coast. None came to join his cause, so he turned instead to plunder and burning, eventually occupying the strategic port of Sandwich in Kent. In response, Harold gathered his fleet and mobilised the *fyrd* – the English militia – but by the time he reached the south coast, Tostig had already disappeared.

Perhaps an expedition to test the English defences, or maybe just an opportunity to preoccupy and embarrass Harold, Tostig's adventure was clearly to William's advantage. Even as Tostig had harried the Sussex coast, William had begun to assemble his own invasion fleet in Normandy. This was altogether a more ambitious affair, at least 700 ships (some estimates suggest as many as 2,000 vessels) and more than 11,000 men, supplied with horses, weapons, and all the necessary paraphernalia of warfare – including wooden forts in kit form, the forerunners of the Normans' famous motte-and-bailey castles. Expecting an amphibious landing to occur in the wake of Tostig's incursions, Harold held a large reserve army – the *fyrd*, together with *housecarls*, the elite professional soldiery – in Sussex, with concentrations of troops in key strategic areas such as Hastings and Pevensey, and Bosham. The latter, close to the Isle of Wight where the English navy was mustered, was probably Harold's military headquarters, where he could be kept informed of activities along the Sussex coast as well as communicating with London. Fearing William's arrival at any moment, Harold maintained this state of readiness until early September – a considerable feat of supply and logistics – when at last his stores began to run low, and men started to slip away to reap the harvest before the onset of autumnal rain and gales.

Yet there was still no sign of William, and on 8 September, the Nativity of St Mary, the order was given for the fleet to disperse and the army to stand down. As the *Anglo-Saxon Chronicle* confirmed: 'When the festival of the Nativity of St Mary came, the men's provisions had run out, and no one could keep them there any longer: they were therefore given permission to return home.'[3] However, even as the order was made, news appeared to reach Harold that Harald Hardrada, king of Norway – aided by the treacherous Tostig – was heading towards the north of England to press *his* claim to the English throne. In the nick of time, Harold rallied his troops in preparation for what would be their epic march northwards. Convinced now that William, after all, was not about to invade, he set about dealing with the imminent threat of Harald Hardrada. Gathering reinforcements as he went, Harold caught up with the Norwegian army at Stamford Bridge, some eight miles from York, on 25 September. Achieving complete surprise, he roundly defeated the Norwegians, killing both Harald Hardrada and Tostig.

The invasion of the Normans

For the moment Harold's grip on his kingdom was safe. But just two days later, on the evening of 27 September, William at last set sail for Sussex, landing unopposed at Pevensey on the following morning. It is said that William, leaping from his ship as it landed, slipped and fell as his feet touched English soil – a potentially disastrous omen in an age when such tokens were taken seriously. But as he scrambled up, he grabbed handfuls of mud or sand, and the knights accompanying him exclaimed that he had seized the land of England. This was a sign, they insisted, that victory would be theirs and that William would soon be king.[4]

The Normans were well acquainted with Sussex – many held land there and enjoyed close trading links – and knew that the coastal plain around Pevensey and Hastings was well suited for amphibious operations. Some of William's ships may have entered Pevensey harbour, and others no doubt ran ashore on the shingle beach to the east. Only two vessels were lost. One of these had strayed as far as Romney, where the local inhabitants slaughtered the entire crew and passengers, including the expedition's official soothsayer – no great loss, according to William, since he had failed to foresee his own demise. Otherwise the landing was successful, although William soon recognised that Pevensey itself was not ideal. The surrounding salt marshes and myriad channels made movement difficult and hampered defence. Instead, he decided to move on to Hastings, which made a fine base port and was more easily defended. Robert Wace, the twelfth-century chronicler, described the first few days of the invasion in his *Roman du Rou*, a history of the dukes of Normandy:

> Then the carpenters landed. They had great axes in their hands, and planes and adzes hung at their sides. … They had brought with them from Normandy the elements of three wooden forts, ready for putting together, and they now took enough material for one out of the ships. … Before evening set in, they had completed a good fort on English soil, and there they placed their stores. Everyone then ate and drank well, right glad that they were ashore.[5]

This initial fort was probably erected within the walls of the old Roman fortress at Pevensey, providing additional security for equipment and men. Wace considered that the subsequent shift to Hastings was made by land, although it seems more likely that the short journey was by sea, avoiding the salt marshes and channels, rather than a circuitous inland route. In Wace's version of events:

> The next day they marched along the coast to Hastings. Near that place William fortified a camp, setting up the other two wooden strongholds. The foragers, and those on the lookout for booty, seized all the clothing and provisions they could find in case their shipborne supplies should fail them. And the English could be seen fleeing before them, driving off cattle and quitting their homes. Many took shelter in burying places, and even there were in great alarm.[6]

There is certainly evidence of the reduction of local villages, perhaps to bolster supplies – as Wace suggested – or possibly to demonstrate to the English the ruthlessness and determination of the invaders, and the futility and folly of resistance. Perhaps, too, knowing of Harold's popularity in Sussex, William hoped that he might provoke him into an early and ill-conceived counter-attack. If this was William's plan, it succeeded. In a second forced march, Harold arrived back in London from Stamford Bridge on 6 October, having completed the 190-mile journey in only eight days. There he allowed himself just five more days to recuperate and reinforce his army. Some of his seasoned troops – notably the archers – had still not arrived from Stamford Bridge, and yet Harold was anxious to press on. Hoping to achieve the same degree of surprise which had heralded his great victory against Harald Hardrada, he moved swiftly through the Weald, expecting to catch William unawares. But three days later, arriving near Hastings, it was Harold who was surprised, finding William prepared and waiting. Harold mustered his army near the tiny hamlet of Senlac, and then took up position on Caldbec Hill, the well-known landmark of 'the hoar apple-tree' at the meeting point of the Sussex hundreds of Baldstow, Ninfield and Hailesaltede.[7] William, whose scouts had seen the English coming, arrayed his army – Normans in the middle, Bretons on the left flank, and French and Flemish allies on the right – on the twin peaks to the south, the Telham and Black Horse hills. In between, the ground over which the two armies would clash was rough pasture and marsh.

The Battle of Hastings

In composition the two armies were different. Harold's force, perhaps 8,500 strong, comprised some 2,500 professional warriors – the trusted *housecarls* and the so-called Danish *lithsmen* – the remainder select *fyrd*: 'select' in the sense that they were better trained and better armed than the mass of the *fyrd* militia. The select *fyrd* came from Sussex and the adjoining counties of Kent, Surrey and Hampshire, as well as further afield in Wessex – Berkshire, Somerset and Dorset – and more distant shires such as Gloucester, Northampton, Lincoln and Nottingham. There were even Yorkshiremen, who had fought at Stamford Bridge. To the modern observer, this sounds like a scratch force – but it was one of the most formidable armies in Europe. Although the English *thegns* rode horses, they usually fought on foot (typically with axes). To attackers Harold's army presented a tight, well-armed and extremely intimidating but relatively immobile defensive wall of shields. William committed about 8,000 of his men to the fight, some 2,400 armoured knights on horseback, together with 1,000 archers, and the remainder foot soldiers.

Dawn broke at about 5.30 a.m. on the morning of 14 October 1066. Harold raised his standard, the celebrated Wessex dragon, while William marshalled his army under the papal banner and the two leopards of Normandy. There was the usual exchange of messages, including ritual challenges to single combat, which were often the prelude to medieval battles, and around 9 a.m. the trumpets sounded – signalling the commencement of battle. 'God help us!' roared the Normans. 'Out, Out!' cried the English in response.[8] Today, the details of the battle are contested. Even the exact location is open to dispute, revisionists insisting that most of the action occurred on Caldbec Hill rather than the traditional spot marked by Battle Abbey, and historians continue to argue whether King Harold was killed by an arrow in the eye (the traditional explanation), or was instead cut down and dismembered by a Norman 'hit squad'.[9] But whatever the precise facts, it is clear that this was a close-fought contest between two evenly matched armies very different in make-up and style yet each bringing its particular strengths (and weaknesses) to the battlefield. Apologists for the English suggest that, had Harold's army not been weakened and disorganised by the forced march to Stamford Bridge and back, it might have carried the day. Others point to the greater discipline and versatility of the Norman forces, and to the superiority of their archers. Either way, the battle lasted a gruelling eight hours, until the sun went down and the English fled the field.

The action had begun with a rain of arrows from the Norman short-bows. Advancing to within one hundred yards of the English line, the archers stuck their quivers in the ground, and began to shoot uphill at the enemy positions. Most of the opening volleys were taken harmlessly on the *housecarl's* shields, with those arrows that had been shot high sailing safely over the heads of the English army. The majority of English archers had still not arrived from Stamford Bridge, so the reply was feeble. An enemy's arrows were critical to maintaining an adequate flow of ammunition, and the Norman archers soon fell silent for fear of exhausting their reserves, so few English arrows having come their way. Next the heavy infantry advanced uphill against the English, to be met by a terrifying hail of missiles and, as it closed with the *housecarls*, the debilitating effects of the English two-handed axe. These axes smashed the Norman shields and cut easily through chain-mail armour, inflicting heavy casualties on the attackers. The Bretons, advancing on the left flank where the hill was less steep, were the first to engage the English and, unsupported on their right, suffered appallingly. They fell back in confusion, taking with them the Norman cavalrymen who had been waiting to exploit any breakthroughs in the English line. Seeing their opportunity, the English on Harold's right – among them perhaps relatively ill-disciplined *fyrd* – rushed after the retreating Bretons. In response, the Normans occupying the middle position and the French and Flemings on their right flank also fell back, and for a moment the battle was held in the balance. Panic spread through the Norman army, which was in danger of being driven from the field. Taking drastic action to retrieve the situation, William galloped into the midst of the fighting. But soon the rumour swept through the Norman ranks that he too had been killed. Again he tried to seize the initiative, pushing back his helmet to reveal his face and shouting that he was still alive. Decisive and courageous in the face of the enemy, William succeeded in steadying his army, and the immediate crisis was over.

Manoeuvring his cavalry, William managed to cut off the English who had pursued the fleeing Bretons, hacking them down in the open and pursuing the survivors to a hillock, where they held out for a time before they too were slaughtered. Among those who fell were the king's brothers, Gyrth and Leofwine, and it may be that it was this sudden and stunning loss that paralysed Harold into inaction. At any rate, he failed to exploit the tactical advantage offered by the Breton collapse, and had allowed William to save the day for the Normans. Apologists for Harold suggest that the flight of the Bretons was just the first of several feigned Norman retreats, designed to tempt the English to break out from their own line, and then to cut them off, isolate them and destroy them. But this seems unlikely, and after these exhausting initial contacts the two opposing armies settled into an interlude or stalemate, reforming their lines, gathering up spent weapons, and eating and drinking whatever was available. During this time, William pondered his next move. Thus far his tactics had been largely unsuccessful and, perhaps in desperation, he decided upon a full frontal attack on the English line by his cavalry – hoping that they would succeed where the archers and heavy infantry had failed. As the Norman knights thundered towards their enemy, they encountered another furious storm of missiles – clubs, stones, spears, throwing axes, and anything else the English had to hand – and the force of their assault had been checked by the time they reached the formidable ranks of *housecarls*. Again the English deployed their two-handed axes to devastating effect, and once more the Normans fell back in disarray (or feigned retreat?). As before, they were pursued by English troops who, breaking ranks, charged down the hill after the retreating horsemen. This time William was ready, and he sent a waiting troop of cavalry after the English, outflanking and annihilating them. Weakened now, and unable to hold the entire ridge, the English army began to draw in, clustering around the king's standard on the summit.

The death of King Harold

By now the Norman archers had been re-supplied with fresh arrows from the baggage train, and William began to use them in conjunction with both his infantry and cavalry in co-ordinated attacks. In contrast to their action earlier that day, the archers were now able to approach the English far more closely, screened by cavalry in front, and over whose heads they rained a shower of arrows onto the *housecarls*. This time the arrows found their mark, and the hitherto disciplined wall of *housecarls* began to waver. This was the decisive moment, and among those who fell under the onslaught of Norman arrows was King Harold, struck in the eye. This, at least, is the fate suggested in the 'Bayeux Tapestry', the self-congratulatory pictorial record made by the Normans after the event, which shows a warrior clutching an arrow in his eye, above which reads the caption: 'Here King Harold was killed.' It was also a story common in England in the next generation, quite independent of the Bayeux representation, and of course has come down to our time as common knowledge. However, critics have objected that the Bayeux commentary may be referring to the *next* illustration in the Tapestry, where a Norman knight is shown trampling an English warrior beneath his horse, smiting him with his sword as he falls. Yet perhaps, as Michael Wood has argued, *both* warriors depicted here may represent Harold, the Tapestry simply moving the story along from Harold's initial wounding in the eye to the subsequent *coup de grâce* administered by the Norman knight. If so, then this makes sense of other contemporary accounts, which suggest that, as the English defence began to crumble, a party of Norman knights managed to fight its way through to King Harold. William of Poitiers, in his *Deeds of King William*, names these knights: Guy of Ponthieu, Walter Giffard, Hugh de Monfort, and Eustace of Boulogne. Guy of Amiens, in his *Song on the Battle of Hastings*, tells a slightly different story, substituting duke William himself instead of de Monfort. Either way, Harold came to a grisly end. Already wounded in the eye, Harold was found kneeling by his standard. One knight stabbed him in the chest, another severed his head, a third disembowelled him, and a fourth hacked off his leg at the thigh – or, according to one reading of the evidence, sliced off his genitals.[10] This was the supposed spot where, less than a decade later, the high altar was placed in the great abbey built to commemorate and thank God for William's victory.

'Here King Harold was killed'. The death of Harold is perhaps the most famous scene from the Bayeux Tapestry. The arrow-in-the-eye has been the traditional explanation for Harold's death, 'common knowledge' from the immediate aftermath of the Battle of Hastings in 1066 down to our own time. Modern interpretations are more nuanced, however, suggesting that, following his initial wound in the eye, Harold was ridden down by a Norman knight on horseback who slashed him with his sword, both episodes being represented here in the Tapestry.
USER: MYRABELLA/WIKIMEDIA COMMONS/CCO 1.0

As the sun set, at about 5 p.m., groups of determined *housecarls* continued to offer resistance. But as word of Harold's demise spread, increasing numbers fled the field. The *fyrd*, according to William of Poitiers, escaped 'some on horseback, some on foot, some taking to the roads, most by bye-paths'.[11] The remaining *housecarls* retreated into the Weald, maybe planning to fight another day. Yet even as they disappeared into the forest, there was a heroic eleventh-hour stand – perhaps by *fyrd* reinforcements who had just arrived on the scene – at a place later remembered by the Normans as *malfosse*, the evil ditch.[12] Here, in a ravine thick with brambles, a detachment of Norman cavalry swept down on the English, only to tumble into the steep ditch were they were swiftly slaughtered. At that moment, Eustace of Boulogne, fresh from the mutilation of King Harold, arrived with fifty horsemen. Seeing what had befallen the others, he made to turn back, only to be confronted by William, who urged him on into the fray. Eustace was promptly struck down by an axe (though not mortally wounded), leaving William himself to direct the rout of this last pocket of English resistance. By now darkness was upon the battlefield, and pursuit of the few survivors impossible.

To commemorate his victory, William built a cairn of stones – or *mountjoy* – on the summit of Caldbec Hill, on the site of the 'hoar apple-tree', at a place known even now as Mountjoy.[13] The day after the battle, 15 October, was given over to the burial of the fallen. William of Poitiers noted that English families were allowed to take away their dead, although this appears to have applied only to local Sussex soldiers whose kith and kin lived nearby. The other English corpses were left to rot where they lay, another kind of memorial to the Norman victory. William ordered that Harold's remains be interred on the beach, but it is not clear whether this was actually carried out – if it was, the remains were later exhumed and taken to Waltham Abbey, where they rest today. On 16 October, William returned to Hastings, where for five nights his badly bruised army licked its wounds, rested and reorganised. On 21 October he reviewed his forces at Northiam, on the Kentish border, before they set out for Dover and to occupy London. However, it is apparent that he also sent detachments out into Sussex to secure the subjugation of the county, the first part of England to fall fully under Norman sway. The Domesday Book, the great survey of landed property and ownership carried out across England after the Conquest was complete, is a clue to the Norman progress across Sussex. In the entries for Sussex there is a noticeable drop in recorded property values in land presumably laid waste by the Normans as they traversed the county. The Normans appear to have taken the strategically important town of Lewes shortly after the battle, and then to have moved speedily westwards – by way of Plumpton, Keymer, Hurstpierpoint, Steyning and Arundel – to join up with reinforcements landed near Selsey to capture equally important Chichester.[14]

Bayeux Tapestry, Battle Abbey and the *rapes* of Sussex

William was anointed and crowned king of England in Westminster Abbey on Christmas Day 1066. Although there still remained some resistance to Norman rule – particularly in a great rebellion in the North in 1069–70 – the Conquest was already a fact of English life. To record this achievement, William's half-brother Bishop Odo of Bayeux, commissioned the famous Tapestry, a continuous embroidered frieze some 230 feet long by about two feet high, which tells the story of the Conquest from Edward the Confessor on his deathbed to William's triumph at the Battle of Hastings. Early in the Tapestry, Harold is depicted in the hunting lodge on his estate at Bosham (there is a remarkably accurate representation of the church), where he is feasting on the eve of his ill-fated voyage to Normandy in 1064. There, as we know (p.40), he fell into the custody of Guy of Ponthieu – one of the knights who later put him to the sword on the battlefield at Hastings – and he is shown promising under oath the English crown to William. Elaborate preparations for the invasion of the Sussex coast, including shipbuilding, are depicted in detail, as is the voyage itself and the landing at Pevensey. The erection of a wooden fort at Hastings is also shown, including men shovelling earth to build up the 'motte' or mound upon which the fort was built. The Tapestry also records the torching of Sussex villages after the landing – a woman and her child are seen outside their burning home

A key episode in the story of the Norman Conquest as it unfolds in the Bayeux Tapestry is the oath sworn by Harold son of Godwin (later King Harold) to support the claim of William, duke of Normandy, to the English throne. Given under duress, following Harold's shipwreck on the Norman coast, the oath was later discounted as Harold became king of England, triggering the sequence of events that led to the Norman invasion and William's seizure of the English Crown.
USER: MYRABELLA/WIKIMEDIA COMMONS/CC0 1.0

Often referred to as the 'crypt' at Battle Abbey, this is the thirteenth-century vaulted undercroft of the monks' dormitory, probably also used as a novices' common room. Founded by William the Conqueror *c.*1071, the Benedictine Abbey at Battle was dedicated to the Trinity and the Virgin, together with St Martin of Tours for good measure. Intended as a memorial to the dead of the Battle of Hastings, and as an atonement for the bloodshed, the abbey was founded and largely endowed by William, who insisted that the high altar be placed at the spot where Harold fell. Until its suppression in 1538, the abbey was a dominant ecclesiastical, economic and political influence in Sussex and far beyond.

– and provides graphic illustrations of the battle itself, including (as noted above) the death of King Harold.

A further commemoration of the Conquest was the founding of Battle Abbey in Sussex. William had promised that, should he prevail against Harold, he would build a religious house on the site of his victory, and he was as good as his word. Work commenced around 1075, and by 1094 the abbey was complete. William ensured that it became one of the most richly endowed religious houses in England. It owned great estates scattered across the country, and was declared free from all episcopal and royal jurisdictions, effectively a law unto itself where its bishop was also one of the most powerful barons in the land. Indeed, his word *was* law within the so-called *legua*, his personal territorial fiefdom which extended over a radius of one-and-a-half miles from the abbey gates; the abbot's economic influence in Sussex and beyond was immense.[15]

In addition to the *legua* of Battle Abbey, Sussex was divided by the Normans into five *rapes*, new administrative subdivisions and landholdings based on the old Saxon *burghs*. As William had promised, these *rapes* were awarded to his most loyal supporters, lending Sussex an early, prominent and enduring place in the political and economic settlement that followed the Conquest. Elsewhere in England, earlier forms of local government had remained unchanged; Sussex was the exception. Robert of Eu (William's cousin) was given the *rape* of Hastings, Robert of Mortain (William's other half-brother) received Pevensey, William de Warenne got Lewes, William of Braose acquired Bramber, and William of Montgomery had the important prize of Arundel – which included Chichester.[16] Each *rape* encompassed a defended river valley, where the newly installed Norman barons built castles designed to protect their territory but also as visible symbols in the landscape of their power and authority. Initially timber constructions, such as those depicted in the Bayeux Tapestry and described by Robert Wace, they were soon

Bramber Castle was founded *c.*1070 by William de Braose. It was among the earliest Norman castles built in England, and most of the surviving masonry dates from this period. Perched on a high knoll overlooking the River Adur, the castle was designed as the defensive as well as administrative centre of the new-found *rape* of Bramber, one of the six (originally five) administrative sub-divisions in Sussex established by the Normans. The de Braose family held Bramber Castle continuously until 1450, when it passed to the Mowbray family.
MARGARET ANNE CLARKE/WIKIMEDIA COMMONS/ CC BY-SA 3.0

Knepp Castle, near West Grinstead, began life as a Norman motte-and-bailey castle in the twelfth century, constructed by William de Braose, and was rebuilt in stone in 1214 by King John, who reputedly used it as a hunting lodge.
USER: ANTIQUARY/ WIKIMEDIA COMMONS/ CC BY-SA 4.0

developed on the motte-and-bailey principle as impressive stone-built structures.

The *rape* of Bramber was something of an afterthought, not created *c.*1073 to guard the Adur estuary, but its flint-walled fortress – situated at what was then the port of Bramber, near Steyning – was one of the earliest Norman castles built in England. A substantial natural mound was surmounted by a smaller motte and large stone-built tower-keep. At first the bailey was surrounded with a wooden palisade but this too was replaced with a stone curtain wall early in the twelfth century. Today,

Arundel Castle represents almost a thousand years of Sussex history, and although much of what is immediately apparent is of relatively recent construction, especially the 'restoration' work of Henry 15th Duke of Norfolk (1847–1917), there are still significant survivals from the Norman and later medieval periods. The castle has been the seat of the dukes of Norfolk and their ancestors for over 850 years. Considered the premier duke and earl in the realm, the duke holds the traditional position of Earl Marshal, responsible for the organisation of important state occasions, such as the opening of Parliament. The current duke is Edward Fitzalan Howard, 19th Duke of Norfolk.
ALISON AVERY, WWW.BEAUTIFULENGLANDPHOTOS.UK

only fragments of the castle remain: it was comprehensively 'slighted' by Cromwell's Roundheads during the Civil War, and may have suffered subsidence as early as the fifteenth century. Nonetheless, the towering remnant of the keep – some 76 feet high – is an indication of the scale and former magnificence of this building. The de Braose family, which built Bramber, was also responsible for nearby Knepp Castle, on the Worthing road close to West Grinstead, constructed in the late eleventh or early twelfth century, where a fragment of masonry some thirty feet tall is all that survives of a large sandstone tower.[17]

Further west, at Arundel, Roger of Montgomery laid the foundations for what has become one of England's most romantic castles, early Norman and medieval elements later incorporated into eighteenth-century reconstruction and nineteenth-century Victorian Gothic work to produce the extraordinary edifice we see today. Nickolaus Pevsner objected to the modern accretions, considering them 'silly' and unconvincing, and concluded that there 'is no getting away from the fact that Arundel Castle is a great disappointment'.[18] Yet for many the castle embodies a thousand years of Sussex history, and is still an arresting sight on its elevated spur overlooking the river Arun, just as the Normans had intended it to be.[19] Montgomery's principal legacy at Arundel is the motte, all of a hundred feet tall, originally capped with a wooden fort which was replaced by a shell keep less than a century later, together with the inner gatehouse and adjacent stretch of curtain wall. There is also Norman work hidden away beneath the showy Victorian exterior, no longer visible to visitors to the castle, including a large undercroft or vaulted lower room beneath the main floor, silent and unseen testament to Norman ambition and self-confidence.

Equally impressive in its way is Lewes Castle, further evidence of the enduring Norman presence in the Sussex landscape. Situated on its distinctive twin mottes above the town, and looking out across the flood plain of the river Ouse, it dominated the locality in Norman times, a formidable symbol of William de Warenne's grip on the district. Parts of the original bailey wall and Norman gatehouse still exist today (the famous barbican – perhaps the finest in England – is a later, early fourteenth-century addition) to give us something of the flavour of de Warenne's imposing stronghold. Further east, at Pevensey, the existing Roman fortifications were added to by Robert of Mortain, who erected a massive keep, with a great tower added about 1100. Further east still, at Hastings, site of one of William's original prefabricated forts, a stone castle was constructed *c.*1070 by Robert of Eu on a promontory jutting out into the sea, designed to protect what was then an important

The keep of Lewes Castle stands on the highest ground in Lewes, county town of East Sussex, dominating the locality and overlooking the floodplain of the river Ouse. Commenced as early as 1067 by William de Warenne, first Earl of Surrey and son-in-law of William the Conqueror, the castle was subsequently extended during the later medieval period, the most notable accretion being the fourteenth-century barbican. Today the adjoining Barbican House is home to the Museum of Sussex Archaeology.

Hastings Castle was initially built of wood, to the Norman motte-and-bailey template, but was reconstructed *c.*1070 in stone. The castle was held by the Count of Eu (of which the first was Robert) for much of the Norman period but suffered a chequered history. Following the loss of Normandy during King John's reign, the castle was slighted to prevent its capture by the marauding French. Although rebuilt by Henry III in 1220, erosion of the nearby cliff in the fourteenth century caused part of Hastings Castle to fall into the sea, leaving it in the ruinous condition we see today.
ALISON AVERY, WWW.BEAUTIFULENGLANDPHOTOS.UK

port. Today the port has disappeared, while much of the castle and its promontory have tumbled into the sea (erosion at the site was recorded as early as the fourteenth century). Yet the ruins that have survived are again a very visible reminder of the overwhelming presence of Norman power in post-Conquest Sussex.

Domesday Sussex and religious revival

Across England, Saxon *thegns* were systematically dispossessed as landowners, to be replaced by incoming Normans. The old earldoms were likewise allowed to lapse. The house of Godwin (Harold's line) was now eclipsed, its erstwhile influence in Sussex replaced by the new authority of William of Montgomery, who was appointed Earl of Sussex in 1070. The Domesday Book, completed in 1087, was designed to provide a survey of landholdings in England, as comprehensive as possible, partly for taxation purposes and also to provide an economic portrait of the newly conquered kingdom. It listed fifteen landowners in Sussex. Principal among them was King William himself, who acquired two estates previously held by Harold – Bosham in the west, and Rotherfield in East Sussex. The Domesday returns indicated that most settlements continued to be in the coastal areas and along the Downs, with the Wealden districts still relatively uninhabited by permanent settlers. Only one iron works, near East Grinstead, is mentioned in the survey, and for the rest the economy remained a mix of pasturing, farming and fishing. Bristelmestune (Brighton) was one centre of the fishing industry – it tenants paid their annual rent to the lord of the manor in the form of 4,000 herrings – and no fewer than 280 saltpans, mainly along the estuaries where sea-water was trapped and evaporated, provided the salt so necessary for the preservation of fish and the salting-down of slaughtered meat for the winter.[20]

The Domesday entry for Hooe, near Battle, is typical of the manner in which the survey recorded the newly acquired Norman lands in Sussex:

> The Count of Eu holds in demesne a manor which is called Hou. Earl Godwin held it, and in the time of King Edward, as now, it was assessed for 12 hides. There is land for 44 ploughs. On the demesne are 2 ploughs and 44 villeins while 12 bordars have 28 ploughs. There is a chapel and 1 mill yielding 7 shillings and 71 acres of meadow, and 30 saltpans yielding 33 shillings. Wood land yielding 10 swine from the pannage [fallen acorns and beech mast]. From the pasturage 7 swine.[21]

Mention of 'villeins' and 'bordars' indicates the hierarchy of Norman feudalism. The villeins held strips in the common fields of their villages, and in return owed a variety of payments and services to their lords of the manor. Below the villeins were the bordars, who held smaller holdings but paid similar dues. Beneath them were the lowly cottars, who held little or nothing and survived by working the land of those above them in the social order; and lower still were the serfs who toiled directly for the lords of the manor. Rich and poor together, Norman counts and English serfs, the total population of Sussex at the time of the Domesday survey was probably somewhere between sixty and seventy thousand souls, bound together in the system of feudal dues which characterised the Norman regime.

Norman power in Sussex was also exercised in matters ecclesiastical. Aethelric II, the English bishop of Selsey, was pushed aside after the Conquest. The centre of the diocese was moved to Chichester in 1070, with a Norman enthroned as the new bishop. Construction of a new cathedral at Chichester commenced around 1075 but progress was slow, with a complete rebuilding ordered in 1091 by Bishop Ralph de Luffa. A fire in 1114 further impeded progress, and it was not until 1184 that a more modest version of the original plan was at last completed and consecrated – only to be damaged again by fire in 1187. Stylistically, Luffa's design owed much to Romanesque influence from Normandy, especially the Abbaye aux Hommes at Caen, built in 1066–86, which is regarded as the prototype for Chichester.[22] Elsewhere in Sussex, similar influence is apparent. At Steyning, for example, a new church was constructed by the monks of Fécamp, with distinctively Norman nave arcades, clerestories and arcade capitals – the latter with densely carved abstract patterns which make them, as Simon Jenkins observes, 'the best of their time in Sussex'.[23]

Climping church, on the outskirts of Littlehampton, sports a fine Norman 'zig-zag' pattern on the doorway beneath its squat Norman tower, tribute to the French craftsmen who worked the Caen stone brought over from Normandy. USER: CHARLESDRAKEW/ WIKIMEDIA COMMONS/CCO 1.0

Similarly, many other Sussex churches were rebuilt or started afresh after the Conquest. At first, there was an overlap between traditional Saxon and new Norman styles, as there had been before 1066 when Norman ideas and preferences had already made themselves felt in Sussex. But gradually the latter predominated, and by the Late Norman period (from about 1170) there was a great spate of church building across Sussex. St Mary's, at New Shoreham, was begun as early as 1130, part of the infrastructure to support the new harbour then being built to replace its silting-up neighbour, Old Shoreham. Still a large church today, it was perhaps twice the size when first constructed in the early twelfth century. Tradition insists that it was commissioned by Philip of Braose, who intended it as a monastery to give thanks for his safe return from the First Crusade in 1103. If so, this original aspiration was soon lost sight of, St Mary's becoming an ordinary parish church, albeit built on the grand scale. Interestingly, this preoccupation with New Shoreham did not mean the neglect of the earlier church, St Nicholas, at Old Shoreham, where new Norman work led to a remarkable sequence of carvings on capitals and corbels – a cat, an elf, a monster, shells and rosettes, and other figures. Elsewhere in Sussex, there is equally fine Norman work, such as the intricate dogtooth and zigzag carving in the doorway at Climping, executed by French masons on Caen stone imported from Normandy.[24]

Alongside this architectural influence, the Normans brought their religious enthusiasms to Sussex. The Pope had lent his support to William on condition that he address the lacklustre state of the English Church. In Continental Europe, much of the energy of religious revival had emanated from the great Benedictine Abbey at Cluny, in France, which had been founded in 910. Cluny emerged swiftly as the leader of western monasticism, and its influence spread quickly from France to the neighbouring countries of western Europe – but not across the

Channel to 'backward' England. By the early eleventh century, Cluny had hundreds of daughter houses across the Continent but it was not until after the Conquest that Cluniac influence reached English shores. Founded by William de Warenne in 1076, the Priory of St Pancras at Lewes was the first Cluniac establishment in England – another example of the post-Conquest intimacy of Sussex and Normandy, and of the early and pervasive Norman impact in the county. Belonging to the network of Cluniac monasteries, Lewes sent representatives to the triennial convocations called by the Abbot of Cluny, and was determinedly Continental in outlook. But this did not mean that local conditions were ignored. Far from it: the priory led the way in educational work and the provision of hospitals, and under its influence the arts prospered.[25] In the small Norman church at Hardham, for example, twelfth-century Cluniac artists from Lewes executed a sequence of biblical and other religious scenes that encompassed the entire interior of the building. The story of Adam and Eve rubbed shoulders with the Flight into Egypt and an intriguing depiction of St George fighting the Infidels – the latter a favourite English medieval theme and, given the context, maybe another Sussex remembrance of the First Crusade.[26] Indeed, the Crusading orders of the Knights Templar and the Knights Hospitaller, both founded in the aftermath of the First Crusade, were for a time important in Sussex, the former in 1115 acquiring the church and manor of Shipley, together with Sompting in 1154 and other significant possessions.

Conflict renewed

The impact of the First Crusade on religious observance and popular memory in Sussex is a reminder that the Conquest, though bringing strong government, did not usher in a lasting peace. Indeed, King William's untimely death in September 1087 precipitated a new period of political instability. Although by now about sixty years old, a good age for early medieval times, William remained in excellent health and as robust as ever. However, relations with his French neighbours had deteriorated to the extent that the French were now raiding into Normandy from their base at Mantes, situated strategically about midway between Paris and the Norman capital at Rouen. Characteristically, William, returning to Normandy from England, decided to teach the French a lesson and marched against Mantes, setting it ablaze. But as William admired his handiwork, his horse stumbled, throwing him against the iron pommel of his saddle, inflicting a wound from which he would not recover. He died on 9 September, and was buried in the Abbaye aux Hommes at Caen, leaving three sons to argue over his inheritance.[27]

William Rufus, as he was known (on account of his florid complexion), lost no time in rushing to England, where he claimed the throne and was crowned William II at Westminster Abbey by Archbishop Lanfranc, his late father's most trusted advisor and confidant. Robert, the Conqueror's eldest son, inherited Normandy as he had expected but was dismayed by his younger brother's seizure of the English crown. There was a stand off between the two, and once again Sussex seemed ripe for invasion. Rufus swiftly won the support of William de Warenne, the powerful Earl of Sussex, but Robert of Mortain – the late king's half-brother – declared in favour of Robert and held Pevensey Castle against Rufus. Robert of Montgomery bided his time at Arundel, waiting to see which way the wind would blow.[28] Eventually, Rufus and William de Warenne starved Pevensey into submission, averting the immediate crisis in Sussex, while in Normandy a disgruntled duke Robert resigned himself to the *de facto* partition of the combined territory that he had hoped to inherit in its entirety. Indeed, when an increasingly impecunious Robert left to participate in the First Crusade, he had little choice but to mortgage a large part of his dukedom to Rufus, who now had clear designs upon it. Before his departure, Robert had made a pact with Rufus in which each was the other's heir – Rufus no doubt hoping that his brother would not return from the Crusades. But Rufus's plan to absorb Normandy never materialised, for on 2 August 1100 he was struck by an arrow and killed while out hunting in the New Forest – a mysterious death that has never been satisfactorily explained. Present in the hunting party was Rufus's younger brother, Henry, who at once galloped to Winchester to secure the royal treasure and then made immediately for London, where he was crowned king of England on 5 August. Robert, away at the Crusades, was powerless to intervene, although on his safe return he plotted invasion and was not without sympathisers in England.[29]

Eventually, the deadly rivalry between Henry I (as he had become) and duke Robert was settled on the battlefield of Tinchebrai in Normandy in 1106. Robert was defeated, his dukedom confiscated, and he was imprisoned for life. Henry, king of England, was now also duke of Normandy, bringing the two territories together once more. In doing so he perpetuated the close links between Sussex and Normandy. But, in seizing Normandy by force, he had placed himself dramatically in the centre of French affairs, and in the subsequent wars – over several centuries – between England and France, Sussex found itself more or less continually in the front line. In 1216, for example, the French invaded England in support of the barons against King John (of *Magna Carta* fame). William de Casingham led the defence of Sussex, hiding in the Weald with a thousand men and harassing the French until they were finally driven out the following year.

The Hundred Years War, which broke out in 1338, meant that Sussex was almost perpetually militarised, with the coming and going of armies, navies and supplies destined for the Continent, and in 1360 a French fleet sacked Winchelsea, the first of a new series of raids along the Sussex coast. In 1377, when they occupied the Isle of Wight as an operating base, the French again attacked Winchelsea, only to find it stoutly defended by the abbot of Battle Abbey. The raiders moved on to Hastings – which they found abandoned and already fired by its fleeing inhabitants. Suitably enraged, the French promptly razed Rye to the ground. Rottingdean was also attacked, the raiders making inland up the river Ouse towards Lewes before being halted by the prior of St Pancras and his armed retainers. During the chaotic reign of Edward II (1307–27), the French were not the only problem with which the confederation of Cinque Ports – principally Rye and Winchelsea – was confronted. For a time, there was almost open warfare between the 'Gallants' of Fowey in Cornwall and the Cinque Ports, with the latter accused of molesting Cornish ships as they passed up-Channel.[30] The Gallants responded by attacking Rye and Winchelsea, alongside the French. In the longer term, this continual raiding – the French were again burning Rye and Winchelsea in 1448 – did permanent damage to the commercial potential of maritime Sussex, although the prestige of Hastings, Winchelsea, Rye and the other Cinque Ports was enhanced through their provision of ships to the king to support expeditions against France. Such was the nature of the county's front-line status, confirmed by the Conquest of 1066 and in the often traumatic experience of subsequent decades and centuries.

Amberley Castle was the result of Bishop Rede's license to 'crenellate' in 1377, permission to rebuild and fortify his existing manor house. Designed to impress his peers rather than to deter an enemy, Bishop Rede's imposing creation has continued to attract the attention of admirers down the ages. Today it does so as a luxury hotel, for which role it was converted (although retaining a great many original features) in 1989.
ALISON AVERY, WWW.BEAUTIFULENGLANDPHOTOS.UK

FOUR

Medieval Sussex

A licence to crenellate

IN 1377, at the height of the French raids along the Sussex coast, Bishop Rede of Chichester was granted a licence to 'crenellate' – to rebuild and fortify his manor house at Amberley, near Pulborough, nine miles inland on the navigable river Arun. Perhaps it was feared that the French might penetrate this far, striking out into the interior in the hope of threatening London. Or maybe the invasion scare offered a timely opportunity for the good bishop to engage in a little self-aggrandisement, to construct a pile that befitted his social and ecclesiastical status as well as responding to the French threat. The impressive castle that emerged at Amberley, with its formidably high curtain walls, may indeed have given any invader pause for thought. Yet its defensive capacity was limited. The gatehouse lacked machicolations (stone galleries projecting from the parapet which allowed defenders to drop or pour offensive items on attackers below) or gunports, and the walls were without any flanking towers – the only projection being a massive protruding block for the garderobes or privies. Moreover, the entire castle was overlooked by the nearby church tower, fatally compromising its security.[1] How Amberley might have fared under sustained assault is difficult to say. What is clear is that Bishop Rede had built for himself a substantial, modern dwelling, one designed to impress – would-be assailants, possibly, but most certainly his social peers.

The same might be said of Bodiam. Situated at the eastern extremity of the county, Bodiam Castle occupied a triangular tongue of land close to the Kent Ditch – the border between Sussex and Kent – with the river Rother to the south, a dozen or so miles from the coast. Long recognised for its strategic importance, the locality had boasted a river port in Roman times, built to serve the Sussex iron industry. The Rother remained navigable in the medieval period, and, with its quays and bustling commerce, was considered an integral part of the port of Winchelsea. By 1372, however, almost halfway through the Hundred Years War, the English had lost control of the Channel, the French now raiding with impunity, sacking both Rye and Winchelsea. In October 1385, with the French still in ascendancy, Richard II issued Sir Edward

Dalyngrigge with a licence 'to strengthen and crenellate his manor house at Bodyham near the sea in the County of Sussex ... and to construct and make thereof a castle in defence of the adjacent countryside and for resistance against our enemies'.[2]

The Dalyngrigges were a long-established Sussex family, from Dalling Ridge near East Grinstead, and Sir Edward himself had fought during the Hundred Years War. In 1367 he had gone to France with Lionel, Duke of Clarence, second son of Edward III, and had served alongside his friend and patron, Richard Fitz-Alan, the Earl of Arundel. But he made his money as part of Sir Robert Knollys' private army, one of the many 'free companies' of mercenaries which operated on behalf of the king, although always with more than an eye to their own interests and opportunities. Knollys, for example, was reputed in 1358 to have amassed 100,000 gold crowns from his plundering of Picardy, and in the Loire valley – where his name struck terror into the hearts of the local peasantry – the charred gables of towns he had destroyed were known as 'Knollys' mitres'.[3] Sir Edward Dalyngrigge fought under Knollys' banner in his bloody campaigns in Picardy, Normandy and Brittany, all the while amassing the fortune that was later to finance the construction of Bodiam Castle – where he was careful to have Knollys' coat of arms carved in relief on the postern gate, a suitable recognition of his indebtedness to his erstwhile commander and patron.

Retiring at length to his native Sussex, Sir Edward welcomed the opportunity to crenellate, building his castle anew in 1386–88 in Sussex sandstone, rather than modifying his existing manor house nearby. For this new dwelling, Sir Edward selected a site close to the Rother. This, according to Catherine Morton in her brief history of Bodiam, was a logical choice. It was, she wrote, 'the obvious place for a fortress to stem the devastating raids which the south coast of England was then suffering from the French'.[4] Nikolaus Pevsner agreed. 'No wonder,' he exclaimed, explaining why the licence to crenellate had been issued, 'as the French had burnt Rye in 1377 and Winchelsea in 1380.'[5] It was an opinion shared by the noted castle historian M.W. Thompson, who in 1987 listed Bodiam among those castles built 'for a specific purpose: on the south coast, after the French raids'.[6] However, even as this conventional wisdom was being repeated, doubts were now expressed about the true purpose of Bodiam. Charles Kightly, another specialist, agreed that the castle 'was, indeed, well equipped to repulse the King's enemies'. But, he added, 'Bodiam's aggressive exterior ... belies something of its character, for its builder [Sir Edward Dalyngrigge] was a courtier as well as a soldier, and his castle was a sumptuous residence as well as a fortress'.[7] Tom McNeill went further, writing in his authoritative *English Heritage Book of Castles* in 1992 that the wide windows open to the exterior at Bodiam 'jeopardized the military strength of the whole castle'. As he concluded

Bodiam Castle, Sussex, 'is not large', admitted Catherine Morton in her 1981 pamphlet on the subject, 'yet both the grandeur and symmetry of its well-preserved outer walls and towers, mirrored in their moat, and its perfect setting, enhanced by Lord Curzon's careful landscaping, add to its charm as a "castle in miniature"'. A decade later, and David Thackray, Head of Archaeology at the National Trust, could add that the 'impressive and beautiful symmetry of Bodiam Castle, with its massive towers and broad moat, appears the very epitome of the medieval castle ... a romantic reminder of England's past'.

Despite its forbidding exterior and seemingly formidable moat, Bodiam Castle was not all that it seemed. An 'old soldier's dream home', it was more a flight of fancy designed to impress important visitors rather than a serious attempt to construct an impregnable fortress. It did, however, serve to stamp the authority of its owner, Sir Edward Dalyngrigge, on the local populace in the aftermath of the Black Death and the Peasants' Revolt.

An imposing image of the castle, showing the main gatehouse as viewed across the causeway. The excellent state of preservation that we see at Bodiam today is largely a result of the work carried out lovingly by Lord Curzon after the First World War. Recognising its historic as well as aesthetic significance, Curzon purchased Bodiam in 1916, and in 1919 he began the restoration of parts of the castle, assisted by the architect William Weir. Vegetation was removed from stonework, and excavations uncovered a well in the base of the south-west tower. The moat was drained to remove mud and silt. In 1925 Bodiam Castle was bequeathed to the National Trust, and today it attracts over 170,000 visitors each year.

wryly, 'Dalyngrigge was as much interested in displaying his position, both in society and within his castle, as in strict military concerns'.[8]

Indeed he was. Sir Edward Dalyngrigge had married well. His wife was Elizabeth, heiress of the Wardedieu or Wardeux family fortune, through whom he had acquired the Bodiam estate in the first place. Sir Edward was also conscious of his position as a leading member of the Sussex gentry. Between 1379 and 1388 he was knight of the shire for Sussex in parliament, and in 1380 he was appointed to the commission examining the expenses and income of the royal household. In the same year he was asked to survey Winchelsea and to make recommendations for its improved defence. Likewise, in 1384 he investigated and commented on the fortifications at Rye. In the previous year he had received royal approval for the holding of a weekly market at Bodiam, and for an annual fair – on 25–26 May, the vigil and feast of St Augustine. Sir Edward's prominent status in Sussex was a matter of considerable personal pride, and in 1384 it brought him into conflict with John of Gaunt, Duke of Lancaster, whose recent acquisition of property in the county had caused resentment among the local gentry. Giving voice to that disquiet, Sir Edward sought to interfere in the Sussex affairs of John of Gaunt, only to be faced with a successful lawsuit demanding his restraint. Momentarily wrong-footed by the powerful Duke of Lancaster, who sued for trespass and illegal hunting, Sir Edward soon regained his composure, his patron the Earl of Arundel representing his side of the story to the king, and only a year later he received his coveted licence to crenellate. His position at the head of Sussex society was thus assured, while John of Gaunt learned to live with his assertive and headstrong neighbour.

'An old soldier's dream home'

As the above suggests, Bodiam has become an important case study for those castle historians re-evaluating the role of English fortresses in the later medieval period. Today, Bodiam is seen less as a bastion against the French raiding up the river Rother, and more as 'an old soldier's dream home', built by the aging Sir Edward to impress his peers and neighbours, and to reflect his status as war veteran and pillar of Sussex society.[9] During his time in France, Sir Edward may well have observed castles built in a style similar to that he would later adopt at Bodiam, some examples dating back to the early thirteenth century, more than a hundred and fifty years before. If so, he would not be the first Englishman to have been impressed by French design. Edward I's mighty castle at Harlech, in Wales, was built in like fashion *c.*1285, reflecting all that was best in current practice. But that was almost exactly a century before Sir Edward's licence to crenellate at Bodiam, by which time such design was already archaic. Moreover, Bodiam was on a considerably smaller scale than Harlech, a 'castle-in-miniature' as Catherine Morton called it, built to create an impression of military prowess rather than to engage in actual conflict.[10] The moat, for example, was crafted to make Bodiam look bigger than it really was, its purpose to deceive the eye rather than to defeat an enemy.

It seems that Sir Edward's design at Bodiam was actually an elaborate exercise in nostalgia, deliberately harking back to the halcyon days of Edward I's castle-building programme of a century before. Unlike Harlech, where the castle had the clear military objective of subduing the Welsh, the defences at Bodiam had little practical value. They were, as Matthew Johnson has described them, 'sham defences', such as 'flanking towers that do not really flank, drawbridges and portcullis grooves that do not really work'.[11] Robert Liddiard, writing in similar vein, has added that at Bodiam the 'gunports and murder holes [for pouring boiling or corrosive liquids] are impractical and could never be militarily effective, the battlements are too small, the moat is shallow and easily drained, access around the parapets is difficult, and the whole site is overlooked by higher ground'.[12] In fact, as O.H. Creighton has argued, the castle was not sited for defensive reasons at all but was placed in a 'carefully contrived monumental landscape' for maximum aesthetic effect.[13] Landscaping features even included a viewing platform, from which admiring guests could look down upon the fine building Sir Edward had created for his retirement.

In 1387 an English naval victory significantly diminished French capability, and the threat to the Sussex coast became less immediate. The Hundred Years War began to lose its momentum, and in 1390 Sir Edward Dalyngrigge was plucked from retirement to help negotiate a truce with the king of France. He also conducted negotiations with the earl of Flanders, and with the burgesses of Bruges, Ghent and Ypres, as well as surveying English-held castles in Calais and Picardy. A measure of his success, on his return he was in 1392 appointed Keeper of the Tower and Governor of the City of London. In 1396 a peace treaty was at last concluded in which Richard II was married to the infant daughter of the French king as part of the deal. Later, when Henry IV deposed Richard in 1399 and the young queen was ignominiously sent home, hostilities were resumed – although not on the same scale in the English Channel. Fortunately, Sir Edward Dalyngrigge had never had to put his 'defences' to the test against the French.

Nonetheless, for all their 'sham' ineffectiveness, the defensive features of Bodiam Castle served to impress, as Sir Edward had intended – not only those visitors who marvelled at what he had achieved, but also the ordinary folk of the locality who were expected to defer to his authority and status. Not versed in the finer points of military practicalities, these peasants were very likely intimidated by the 'aggressive exterior' of this imposing new fortress which had risen up so suddenly and impressively in their landscape. This, no doubt, was part of Sir Edward's plan, to stamp his presence unequivocally on a countryside so recently unsettled by the ravages of the Black Death and the turmoil of the Peasants' Revolt. As Robert Liddiard has argued, seen in this light Bodiam Castle was 'an assertion of traditional forms of authority in a period of anxiety on the part of the aristocracy'.[14]

The Black Death

In 1348–49 the Black Death, a virulent form of bubonic plague that swept the whole of Europe, wreaked havoc across Sussex. At Battle Abbey, for example, the abbot and over half of the monks died. Perhaps as much as half of the population of Sussex as a whole perished within a few months, leading to social dislocation and to an acute shortage of agricultural labour. In some parts of the county landowners had to raise wages by up to 75 per cent (albeit temporarily) to secure sufficient workers for their estates. Those labourers who survived the Black Death found themselves much sought after, and able to command far more favourable treatment and conditions than hitherto. In some places this meant renegotiating working arrangements, with enclosure of small fields replacing the strip system of agriculture. At Wiston, near Chanctonbury, for example, a surviving early fourteenth-century custumal – the record of the customs of the local manor – elaborates in great detail the obligations of every tenant which had obtained before the Black Death. Thus 'Henry Calwe holds 1 ferling of land and gives rent yearly at the feast of St Thomas the Apostle 8*d*., and at the feast of the Nativity of St John the Baptist 8*d*., and to Sheriff's Aid 2*d*., and to Parksilver 1*d*. And he shall give at the feast of St Thomas the Apostle 1 cock and 1 hen and at Easter 5 eggs', and so on.[15] However, between 1349 and 1352 more than half of the tenants at Wiston succumbed to bubonic plague, making a nonsense of the intricate relationships and dues defined in the custumal. As elsewhere, rent and wages replaced the feudal system of traditional services and payment in kind.

Meanwhile, marginal land was abandoned as no longer profitable to cultivate, and in the Weald forest clearance came to a halt. Some communities simply disappeared, given up as no longer viable. Coastal and downland settlements suffered most, such as Barpham, near Worthing, which vanished entirely, its makeshift children's graves a poignant memorial to the village's sudden demise. Even in the remote Weald communities were often badly affected. Isfield and Buxted, for example, were abandoned completely. In all, more than 40 settlements across Sussex ceased to exist during this traumatic period, the depopulation caused by the Black Death aggravated by the effects of agricultural change. Hangleton, today subsumed in Hove, is one 'lost' village which has been investigated by modern archaeologists. Already in decline when the Black Death struck (its sheep flocks were then a mere one-third of the strength they had been forty years earlier), the settlement was reduced swiftly by the plague to little more than one or two cottages.

Elsewhere along the coast, inundation added to the deleterious effects of plague, agricultural decline, and French raids. In the twelfth and early thirteenth centuries, marshland around Pevensey had been reclaimed, turning levels into pasture. However, by the late thirteenth century, changing weather patterns were beginning to have a distinctly adverse effect on the coastline. In 1288, for example, Winchelsea was overwhelmed by storms and high tides. As J.R. Armstrong observed, so 'complete has been its obliteration, that it is impossible to say exactly where Old Winchelsea stood'.[16] A large area of Romney Marsh disappeared under the sea at the same time, and the ports of Seaford, Shoreham, Pevensey and Hastings suffered likewise. Between 1315 and 1321 crops failed repeatedly due to exceptionally poor weather, and in 1324–25 thousands of sheep were drowned by further inundations of Romney Marsh. During the Black Death, several communities on the Manhood peninsula were completely overwhelmed by the encroaching sea, as were the remains of Old Selsey. An intriguing postscript is that it was planned to rebuild Winchelsea anew on the grand scale. But the work was never finished. The streets were laid out and walls completed but already the anchorage was found to be too shallow – in time, the proposed harbour turned to pasture, as the coastline altered in response to the changed environment.

The Peasants' Revolt

For those individuals who survived the Black Death, there was at least the prospect of improved conditions. However, landowners stood to lose much in the changes that had occurred – both control of the agricultural workforce and their grip on economic production. Accordingly, throughout England a series of reactionary labour laws, the 'Ordinance of Labourers', was enforced with the aim of undoing as far as possible the advantageous position enjoyed by peasants and yeomanry in the aftermath of the plague. Popular resistance to this 'Ordinance' was redoubled in 1381 when the introduction of a new poll tax (a tax levied per head of population) stirred up general discontent, especially in the south-east of England. This was the third such tax levied since 1377. But this time it had tripled in size and was no longer graded according to rank. The resultant 'Peasants' Revolt', as it was termed, began in Essex and soon spread to neighbouring Kent. The rebels marched on London, where others joined them from Sussex and Surrey. The Sussex Weald appears to have been a particular focus of the rebellion, where the peasantry was less subject to feudal control and where early religious nonconformity found a ready audience among the individualistic and independent-minded populace – included in the rebel ranks in 1381 were Lollards, drawn to the preaching of John Wycliffe, and followers of the radical cleric John Ball, author of the famous couplet:

> When Adam delved and Eve span,
> Who was then the gentleman?[17]

In an orgy of violence and destruction, the rebels pillaged great houses and palaces, set prisoners free from gaols, and killed several unpopular ministers – including the Archbishop of Canterbury (who was also Chancellor) – as well as murdering Flemish immigrants. The Kentish contingent, with its Sussex and Surrey allies, camped on Blackheath, later joining the Essex rebels at Smithfield. Here they were met face-to-face by the courageous boy-king, Richard II, then only fifteen years old. As the two sides parleyed, the rebel leader, Wat Tyler, was cut down and killed by Sir William Walworth, the Lord Mayor of London. Thereafter, Richard II acceded to many of the rebels' demands, including the insistence that feudal bondage be formally abolished, and he granted them all free pardon. However, having regained control of the situation, the king's men promptly executed the remaining rebel leaders, immediately revoking the concessions that had been made. Among those who participated in the savage repression that followed the Peasants' Revolt were Sir Robert Knollys and Sir Edward Dalyngrigge, the latter determined to reaffirm his authority in Sussex.

Before long the poll tax was quietly dropped, and the decline of feudal bondage continued apace in response to the changed economic conditions. However, the authorities had been careful to crush this popular uprising, and to reassert their control in the countryside. It was in this repressive climate that the licence to crenellate at Bodiam had been issued, the new castle visible evidence to the local 'peasantry' – and to the artisans and yeomen who had actually constituted the bulk of the rebel force – that political power continued to rest firmly in the hands of the aristocracy. But the countryside was not entirely subdued. Outlaws retreated into the depths of the Weald, beyond the reach of authority, and the atmosphere of repression that had provoked the revolt of 1381 was still widespread. In 1383, for example, a mob overwhelmed and looted the Earl of Arundel's castle at Lewes.

In 1450 there was a further rising, again initiated in Kent, but soon spreading to neighbouring Sussex. The village of Brede, in later centuries notorious as a centre of rural unrest, emerged as a focus for rebellion in the county. This time it was not only the 'peasantry' that rose up. The leader of the rebellion, Jack Cade, claimed to be a cousin of the Duke of

York, courting favour with the esquires, gentlemen and clergy of Sussex and Kent, men who also considered themselves overtaxed and unjustly treated by the Exchequer. Among those Sussex worthies who expressed keen support for Cade's stand were the mayor of Chichester and the prior of Lewes, although both men were careful to distance themselves from the rebels when events began to get out of hand. The rebels marched on London, as their predecessors had done in 1381, and executed the Lord Treasurer before being forcibly dispersed to their counties of origin. Jack Cade himself was overtaken and cut down at Heathfield in East Sussex by one Alexander Iden, an 'esquire of Kent', an event celebrated in William Shakespeare's *Henry VI Part 2*. Cade did not expire immediately but died in a wagon on the way to London, presumably en route to Tyburn or some other place of execution. On 16 July 1450 his lifeless body was drawn and quartered and dragged through the streets of the capital on a hurdle: one quarter was displayed on Blackheath, the others despatched to Norwich, Gloucester and Salisbury. His head was exhibited on London Bridge. Later, in the 1790s, a commemorative pillar was erected in the hamlet of Cade Street, outside Heathfield: 'Near this spot was slain the notorious rebel Jack Cade.'[18] Vilified down the centuries as a vainglorious failure, only recently has Cade been rehabilitated as 'a Sussex hero' by those seeking to understand the motives and aspirations of 'a host of Sussex gentlemen, yeomen, wealthy clothiers and craftsmen' who, as Peter Brandon describes it, 'flocked to his standard in revolt against the corrupt government of Henry VI'.[19]

From Simon de Montfort to the Wars of the Roses

As Jack Cade's rebellion had hinted, the gentry, while keen to assert its authority in the countryside, was not above challenging royal power when it was in its interests to do so. Earlier, in 1264, Sussex had been the scene of confrontation between the embryonic English parliament and the king, when Simon de Montfort, earl of Leicester, defeated Henry III at the Battle of Lewes. King Henry's penchant for expensive foreign wars had made him unpopular, and de Montfort sought to expand the representational base of parliament by summoning four knights from each shire (county) to sit alongside the greater nobles and higher clergy. The ensuing struggle between royal and baronial power spilled over into armed conflict. Sussex was an important centre of support for Henry III – the lords of Arundel, Lewes, Pevensey and Hastings had all declared for the king – and de Montfort feared that the county might serve as a back door for royalist reinforcements from France. He decided to act. As de Montfort marched south into Sussex to confront these various enemies, Henry moved *his* forces westwards from Tonbridge and Battle, the two armies clashing at Offham Hill, near Lewes, on 14 May 1264.

De Montfort seems to have achieved the element of surprise, driving a sizeable part of Henry's cavalry over the precipice to its destruction at Chalk Cliffs, the panicked king fleeing the battlefield to take refuge in Lewes priory. It was a decisive victory, celebrated at the time in the popular *A Song of Lewes*, which insisted that 'England breathes again, hoping for liberty'.[20] In 1265 de Montfort summoned two knights from each shire and two burgesses from each of certain important towns to sit in his rudimentary parliament. When Edward I became king in 1272, he accepted parliament thus constituted as integral to the governance of England. But he had no intention of actually submitting to parliament, and killed Simon de Montfort at the Battle of Evesham, wiping 'the viper's brood' – the de Montforts – from the landowning class of England.[21]

If Sussex had played a decisive role in the clash between Simon de Montfort and Henry III, then it was less prominent in the Wars of the Roses, which were generally played out farther north. Yet there were conflicting allegiances. Sir Edward Dalyngrigge had died some time before 1395, and was succeeded by his son John. Like his father before him, Sir John Dalyngrigge was prominent in Sussex and national affairs. But he died in 1408, leaving his widow Alice to inherit Bodiam. They had had no children, so when Alice died Sir John's cousin Richard Dalyngrigge acquired the estate. Neither Richard nor his brother William produced offspring, and eventually Bodiam passed to their sister Philippa, whose husband was Sir Thomas Lewknor, representative of another prominent Sussex family. Sir Thomas had decided to support the Lancastrian side in the Wars of the Roses, despite the uncomfortable fact that his two uncles were leading Yorkists. In 1483, therefore, when Richard III acceded to the throne, Sir Thomas Lewknor was attainted for treason, his titles and estates forfeited permanently. He was reputed to have made 'traitorous proclamations' and to have armed his 'rebellious' followers. Accordingly, on 8 November that year King Richard issued a commission authorising the Earl of Surrey 'to levy men in the counties of Kent and Sussex to besiege the castle of Bodyham which the rebels seized'.[22] The castle appears to have offered small resistance – ill-equipped as it was for siege warfare – and a little over a month later Nicholas Rigby, the new constable-designate of Bodiam, was already drawing his salary. He took up his post formally in August 1484, although he was dismissed the following year after Henry Tudor's famous victory over Richard III at the Battle of Bosworth Field. Sir Thomas Lewknor's attainder was likewise reversed, although his son Roger – who was appointed sheriff of Sussex in 1532 – did not acquire full possession of Bodiam until as late as 1542.

It was once considered that the slighting of the internal buildings within the castle at Bodiam was a product of Rigby's short stewardship. But archaeological evidence suggests that the buildings were still inhabited in the seventeenth century, the ruinous state that we see inside today the result of slighting by Cromwellian forces during the Civil War, or perhaps of gradual decay once human occupation had ceased. Fortunately, whatever the explanation for the destruction within, the curtain walls and towers remained intact, surviving the ravages of time and the hand of man until the castle was restored by Lord Curzon – onetime Viceroy of India – in the years after the First World War. Bodiam endures as a magnificent example of late medieval English castle building. Equally impressive, in its way, is Herstmonceux Castle, also in East Sussex. Perhaps even more than Bodiam, Herstmonceux was built with nostalgic grandeur rather than military defence in mind. Luckily, its impressive exterior has survived the turbulent centuries without slight or decay, although the interior was dismantled in 1777 and not restored until after the First World War. In 1440 Sir Roger Fiennes, a veteran of Agincourt, had received his licence to crenellate. He began his new castle at Herstmonceux in 1441, ostensibly to strengthen the defence of Sussex against French incursion, and in particular to guard the Pevensey Levels. But, instead of stone, Sir Roger chose to build in brick, employing Flemish bricklayers to undertake the task and producing the first brick-built building of significant size in England since Roman times. As at Bodiam, Herstmonceux's defensive features are largely ornamental, the use of brick betraying the castle's real purpose, to provide a splendid residence for an old soldier who had fought alongside Henry V and served

Herstmonceux Castle, built unusually of brick in the fifteenth century, is one of several late medieval English castles (such as Amberley and Bodiam) designed to afford impressive homes for local grandees rather than to engage in serious military conflict, their ostensible purpose. The interior of Herstmonceux was dismantled in 1777 and not restored until the twentieth century, with work commenced by Colonel Claude Lowther in 1913. From 1957 until 1988, the castle was the home of the Royal Observatory (which moved to Cambridge), and in 1994 it became the Queen's International Study Centre, a focus for Queen's University in Canada's study abroad programmes.
MICHAEL COPPINS/WIKIMEDIA COMMONS/CC BY-SA 4.0

as Treasurer to the Household of Henry VI. The brick exterior would have provided no protection against late medieval siege engines and early cannon. As Robert Liddiard has observed, Herstmonceux's 'insubstantial walls [are] less than two metres thick, which could not have resisted any kind of sustained bombardment'.[23]

The Rise of the Weald

It might have been ineffective militarily, but Herstmonceux represented a new level of sophistication and achievement in Sussex architecture. Indeed, in the later medieval period there was a remarkable upsurge in building, as the economy and society bounced back after the depredations of plague, agricultural decline, inundation, rebellion and war. Much of this new activity was in the Weald, in contrast to the period before the Black Death where the growth of towns – Chichester, Lewes, Arundel, Midhurst, New Shoreham, Hailsham, Pevensey, Battle, Rye, Winchelsea – had been along the coastal plain and its hinterland. But these were the localities which had suffered most, and they were the slowest to recover. They had exported wool, imported wine, held markets, and – in the coastal towns – built stout ships of Sussex oak, together exuding an air of busy commerce and prosperity. Yet much of this had been undone. North of the Downs, meanwhile, older industries were revitalised and the economy flourished as a result. It may be, as J.R. Armstrong has suggested, that merchants of troubled towns such as Shoreham, Hastings and Winchelsea simply moved their operations inland, responding to the new opportunities they found there.[24] Continental craftsmen, fleeing religious persecution in nearby Europe, also brought their skills to the Sussex Weald, stimulating industries such as timber, iron and clothmaking. No longer a byword for the remote and impenetrable, the Weald had become a focus of economic creativity.

Proximity to London was suddenly a virtue for Wealden towns such as East Grinstead, and in the north-western corner of the county between Kirdford and the Surrey border the glass-making industry received an important boost from a series of prestigious commissions such as stained-glass windows for Winchester cathedral. The long-established iron industry similarly flourished anew, especially in the Worth and Tilgate Forest areas near Crawley, and wealthy ironmasters began to build themselves comfortable Wealden dwellings – a trend which grew apace in the subsequent Tudor and Stuart periods, of which a later but classic example would be Bateman's, near Burwash, built of Sussex sandstone *c.*1634, eventually to become the home of Rudyard Kipling. Another measure of this new-found Wealden prosperity was the establishment of new grammar schools at Cuckfield and Billingshurst.

A further measure was the continuous improvement of farmsteads in the Weald, a trend first noticeable before the Black Death but much accelerated thereafter. Here the plentiful supply of timber for building purposes enabled the construction of larger and more durable farmhouses than those encountered elsewhere in Sussex, complementing the more compact and more efficiently managed farms that had resulted from forest clearance. Increasingly, these timber-framed farmhouses featured 'jettying', a late-medieval technique – possibly imported from Scandinavia but made fashionable by London practice – that allowed great flexibility in design. 'Jetted' upper storeys extended over lower ones, saving space in built-up areas such as towns and villages and affording pedestrians some protection against the elements. These were hardly considerations in more rural locations but nonetheless 'jettying' caught on in Wealden Sussex.

The earliest jetted building in the county dates from the fourteenth century. By the beginning of the fifteenth, a distinctive local variant had already emerged, the so-called 'Wealden house' design – 'one of the most attractive forms of timber building that has ever been conceived',

(*Left*) The Old Market House (now an annex of the Spread Eagle Hotel) at Midhurst is a fine example of Sussex 'jettying', where timber-framed buildings featured 'jetted' upper storeys that extended over lower ones.
ALISON AVERY, WWW.BEAUTIFULENGLANDPHOTOS.UK

(*Right*) Robin Cottage in Mermaid Street, Rye, is a picturesque example of Sussex vernacular architecture.
ALISON AVERY, WWW.BEAUTIFULENGLANDPHOTOS.UK

according to Armstrong – which soon became characteristic of the Sussex Weald, spreading out into the adjoining Downland and neighbouring Hampshire.[25] Its most important feature was the combination of jetted upper floor with open hall, a solution that required heavy timberwork and considerable skill in its execution. It was a style that found favour with the increasingly prosperous yeomen, merchants and craftsmen, in towns and villages as well as farmsteads. The market hall at Midhurst, dating from the early sixteenth century, is an excellent though much altered survival from later in the period, and preserved late fifteenth-century cottages at Tarring exhibit a 'modified Wealden' design with the gable end fronting the street. At Bignor, the 'Old Shop', built *c.*1485, is another important survival. Here the timber framing is in-filled with brick, set alternatively herringbone-style and horizontal. At the front of the house, the two outer portions are jetted, supported on massive oak joists. The central portion, by contrast, does not overhang but continues upwards direct from the ground floor, adding grace and individuality to this version of Wealden design.[26]

Wealden churches were likewise improved in the later medieval period. Holy Trinity at Cuckfield, for example – described appreciatively by Simon Jenkins as 'pure Sussex, all flint, red tiles and white wooden fences' – has elements dating back to the thirteenth and fourteenth centuries, but its dominating feature is its impressive late fifteenth-century wagon roof.[27] Similarly, at West Grinstead the church of St George is redolent of 'nowhere else but the Weald', according to Nikolaus Pevsner. Some aspects date back to the Normans but were added to in successive centuries, culminating in excellent fifteenth-century work, including a 'delightful wooden porch', as Pevsner called it, 'about the best in Sussex'.[28] Here again was evidence of high craftsmanship as characteristic of the late medieval Weald, and of increasing economic prosperity after the dislocation of the Black Death and other misfortunes suffered in fourteenth-century Sussex. Most noticeable of all, of course, was the decided shift in economic life from the declining coastal towns to the interior of the county, a trend that would continue into the Tudor and Stuart periods, with important social consequences.

Holy Trinity Church at Cuckfield was altered and improved in the later medieval period, benefiting from the increased wealth in the Weald in this period.
USER: HASSOCKS5489/ WIKIMEDIA COMMONS/CCO 1.0

FIVE

Early modern Sussex: wealth and war in the Tudor and Stuart era

Andrew Boorde

IN THE LATE MEDIEVAL AND TUDOR PERIODS, the Weald rose suddenly to prominence. In his intriguing and inimitable way, Andrew Boorde, born in 1490 at Borde Hill, near Cuckfield, seemed somehow to epitomise this flowering of Wealden society and economy. He rose from obscurity to become one of the celebrated literary figures of his day, living a life of extraordinary richness and diversity which captured attention far beyond his native Sussex. But until 1511 he was merely a feudal bondman, existing simply under the direction and control of his manorial lord, George Neville. In that year, however, an enlightened Neville emancipated 'Andrew Boorde, son of John Boorde ... belonging to his manor or lordship of Ditchling [in which Borde Hill was located] in the County of Sussex'. Thus, it was written, 'the said Andrew [was] made free from all bondage, villeinage, and servile condition; so that neither he, the said lord, nor his heirs ... should for the time to come have any right in or upon the said Andrew, nor his goods and chattels'.[1] A free man at last, twenty-one-year-old Andrew Boorde went on to study at Winchester and at Oxford – under whose patronage, it is not clear – although he did not take his degree. He then decided to become a Carthusian monk, and was appointed briefly suffragan bishop of Chichester. But he found his order's discipline too exacting, complaining to his prior that 'I am nott able to byde the rugosite off your relygon'.[2] He went back to Oxford, this time to study physic, and in consequence becoming a doctor of medicine.

Subsequently, Boorde travelled extensively in Europe, reporting on the reputation and standing of England in Continental courts, and warning that 'Few frendys hath Ingland in theys part of Europe'.[3] He likewise journeyed throughout Britain, advising Thomas Cromwell – chief minister under Henry VIII – to 'Trust you no Skott', explaining the 'devellyshe dysposicion of a Scottysh man, not to love nor favor an Englishe man'.[4] His wanderings also took him as far as Cornwall, where he recorded words and phrases from the Cornish language, and noted

Andrew Boorde was reputedly born at Borde Hill, near Haywards Heath, *c.*1490. The Tudor house we see at Borde Hill today was constructed in 1598 by Stephen Borde, and is renowned for its magnificent gardens, which are open to the public. The estate was acquired by Colonel Robert Stephenson Clarke in 1893, and the gardens – which include numerous rare shrubs collected by Victorian enthusiasts – have been carefully nurtured by four generations of the Stephenson Clarke family.
HELEN HADEN

that 'In Cornwall is two speches; the one is naughty Englyshe, and the other Cornyshe speche'.[5] Staunch Englishman that he was, Andrew Boorde's suspicion of the Scots extended to his contempt for Cornish beer. 'Iche cham Cornysche man,' he wrote in his spoof verse, 'al[e] che can brew; / It will make one to kacke, also to spew; / It is dyke and smoky, and it is dyn; / It is lyke wash, as pygges had wresled dyn.'[6] But Sussex beer, presumably, was a different matter, for he was of the firm opinion that 'water is not wholesome, sole by itself, for Englysshe men', advocating instead the regular imbibing of ale.[7] Being a doctor, his prescriptions were taken seriously. Indeed, for a time he was physician to Henry VIII (his reputation built in part on his having observed the intricacies of surgery during a sojourn in Rome). He acquired property at Pevensey, and he regularly sold his medicines at fairs and markets in that locality.

Pevensey still remembers its Boorde connections; or at least it did until relatively recent times. In 1904 E.V. Lucas, in his *Highways and Byways of Sussex*, visited the town and was told that Andrew Boorde was notorious as 'a thorn in the side of municipal dignity'. Here we glimpse

Boorde's impish sense of humour – in his irreverent dictum 'I am still but a man, although Mayor of Pevensey', and in the tall story, attributed to him, that a Pevensey jury once convicted an individual of manslaughter on account of his stealing a pair of breeches. Lucas was shown the house in Pevensey reputed to have belonged to Boorde, and where, it was said, he had entertained the boy-king Edward VI with his jests. 'The oak room in which Andrew welcomed the youthful king is shown at a cost of threepence per head,' wrote Lucas, 'and you may buy pictorial postcards and German wooden toys in the wit's parlour.'[8]

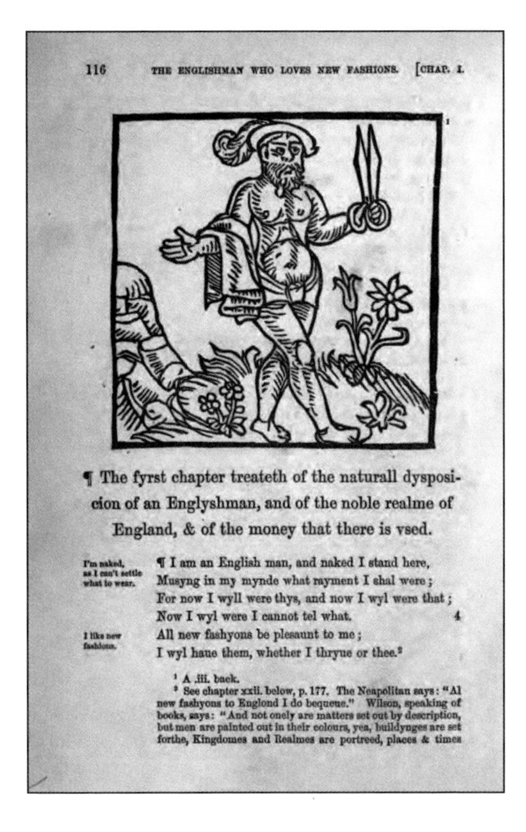

116 THE ENGLISHMAN WHO LOVES NEW FASHIONS. [CHAP. I.

¶ The fyrst chapter treateth of the naturall dysposicion of an Englyshman, and of the noble realme of England, & of the money that there is vsed.

I'm naked, as I can't settle what to wear.

¶ I am an English man, and naked I stand here,
Musyng in my mynde what rayment I shal were;
For now I wyll were thys, and now I wyl were that;
Now I wyl were I cannot tel what. 4

I like new fashions.

All new fashyons be plesaunt to me;
I wyl haue them, whether I thryue or thee.[2]

[1] A .iii. back.
[2] See chapter xxii. below, p. 177. The Neapolitan says: "Al new fashyons to Englond I do bequeue." Wilson, speaking of books, says: "And not onely are matters set out by description, but men are painted out in their colours, yea, buildynges are set forthe, Kingdomes and Realmes are portreed, places & times

(*Left*) The 1870 edition by F.J. Furnivall of Andrew Boorde's *The Fyrste Boke of the Introduction of Knowledge* reproduces Boorde's sketch of the naked Englishman, complete with shears and cloth, along with Boorde's accompanying explanation that 'The first chapter treateth of the natural dysposition of an Englyshman'. In the Introduction to his edition, Furnivall explored Boorde's character and preoccupations, noting with rare insight his great interest in architecture and the planning of buildings. As Furnivall observed, 'he'd have enjoyed ordering where the moat was to be, the stables, and all the belongings, and lecturing the owner as to how to manage his house and servants, wife and child, pocket and body'.
AUTHOR'S COLLECTION

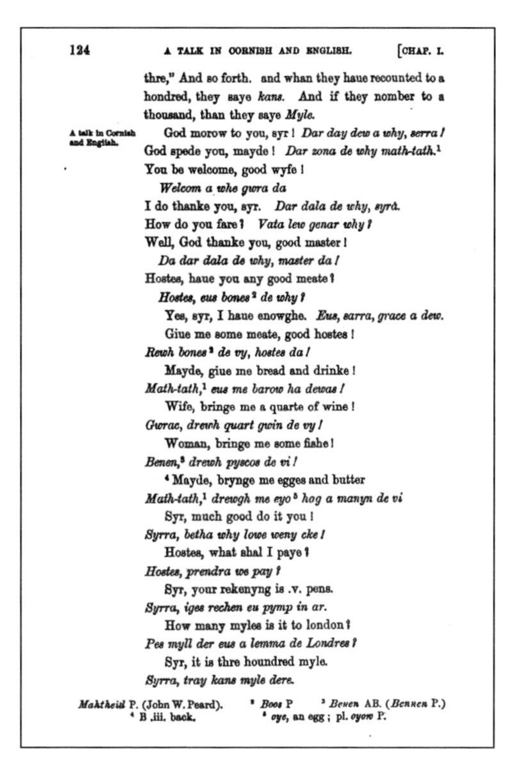

124 A TALK IN CORNISH AND ENGLISH. [CHAP. I.

thre," And so forth. and whan they haue recounted to a hondred, they saye *kans*. And if they nomber to a thousand, than they saye *Myle*.

A talk in Cornish and English.

God morow to you, syr! *Dar day dew a why, serra!*
God spede you, mayde! *Dar zona de why math-tath.*[1]
You be welcome, good wyfe!
Welcom a whe gwra da
I do thanke you, syr. *Dar dala de why, syrà.*
How do you fare? *Vata lew genar why?*
Well, God thanke you, good master!
Da dar dala de why, master da!
Hostes, haue you any good meate?
Hostes, eus bones[2] *de why?*
Yes, syr, I haue enowghe. *Eus, sarra, grace a dew.*
Giue me some meate, good hostes!
Rewh bones[2] *de vy, hostes da!*
Mayde, giue me bread and drinke!
Math-tath,[1] *eus me barow ha dewas!*
Wife, bringe me a quarte of wine!
Gwrac, drewh quart gwin de vy!
Woman, bringe me some fishe!
Benen,[3] *drewh pyscos de vi!*
[4] Mayde, brynge me egges and butter
Math-tath,[1] *drewgh me eyo*[5] *hog a manyn de vi*
Syr, much good do it you!
Syrra, betha why lowe weny cke!
Hostes, what shal I paye?
Hostes, prendra we pay?
Syr, your rekenyng is .v. pens.
Syrra, iges rechen eu pymp in ar.
How many myles is it to london?
Pes myll der eus a lemma de Londres?
Syr, it is thre houndred myle.
Syrra, tray kans myle dere.

Maktheid P. (John W. Peard). [2] *Boos* P [3] *Benen* AB. (*Bennen* P.)
[4] B .iii. back. [5] *oye*, an egg; pl. *oyow* P.

To demonstrate his acquaintance with the several languages of the British Isles, Andrew Boorde in his *Boke of Knowledge* included a guide to Cornish phrases. His choice of utterances reflects the gender relationships of the day:

'Mayde, give me bread and drinke!
Math-that, eus me barow has dewas!

Wife, bringe me a quarte of wine!
Gwrac, drewh quart gwin de vy!

Woman, bringe me some fishe!
Benen, drewh pyscos de vi!

AUTHOR'S COLLECTION

CHAP. VII.] *INTRODUCTION.* ANDREW BOORDE. 143

¶ The .vii. Chapytre sheweth howe the auctor of thys boke, how he had dwelt in Scotland and other Ilandes, did go thorow and rounde about Christendom, and oute of Christendome; declarynge the properties of al the regions, countreys, and prouynces, the whiche he did trauel thorow.

[2] OF noble England, of Ireland and of Wales,
And also of Scotland, I haue tolde som tales;

[1] On this woodcut the late Mr Dyce remarks in his *Skelton's Works*, i, "the portrait on the title-page of *Dyuers Balettys and Dyties solacyous* (evidently from the press of Pynson; see Appendix II. to this Memoir) is given as a portrait of 'Doctor Boorde' in the *Boke of Knowledge* (see reprint, sig. I)." The pinnacle over the Doctor's head is complete in A, broken in B as in our cut. The cut that Wyer used for Boorde is on the title-page of Barnes's *Treatyse* on Beards below, p. 305. [2] sign. E .i.

Boorde's seventh Chapter, illustrated with an elegant portrait of 'Doctor Boorde' himself, detailed his travels beyond England, both within Christendom and beyond.
AUTHOR'S COLLECTION

Boorde also wrote widely, his books eagerly sought after in his time. There were the sensible medical books, *Dyetary of Health* and *Brevyary of Health*, dealing with medicine and hygiene. But his most amusing volume is his *The Fyrste Boke of the Introduction of Knowledge*, written before 1542, which, as well as admitting his own foibles and shortcomings, gives a geographical account of Britain (such as his notes on Cornish speech and ale) in which he records something of his native Sussex – including the old story that no nightingale would ever sing in the Forest of St Leonards. But it was Englishness that Andrew Boorde especially wished to celebrate, and the frontispiece of his *Boke of Knowledge* (as it is known routinely) pictured a naked Englishman with a pair of shears in one hand and a piece of cloth over the other arm, explaining:

> I am an English man and naked I stand here,
> Musing in my mund what raiment I shall were;
> For now I wyll were this, and now I wyl were that;
> Now I wyl were I cannot tel what.[9]

Boorde is sometimes celebrated as the original 'Merry Andrew', the author of several jest books, including the *Merry Tales of the Mad Men of Gotham*, his advocates insisting that the village so-named was the one near Pevensey, rather than in Nottinghamshire as is usually assumed. Be that as it may, we can safely presume that it was Boorde's contemporary reputation as a merry fellow which saved him from a fate no worse than a short imprisonment in the Tower when he protested against the Dissolution of the Monasteries. Remembering his Carthusian allegiances, he also continued to fast and to wear hair shirts, maintaining a simple piety seemingly at odds with his worldly ways – not least when, in 1549, the year of Catholic unrest across the kingdom, he was convicted of keeping in his house three loose women of ill repute. He was committed to the Fleet Prison, where he made his will on 9 April 1549 and died shortly after.

‘The great rebuilding’

Among Andrew Boorde’s prejudices and aphorisms, was his opinion that: ‘I had rather not to buylde a mansion or a house than to buylde one without a good prospect in it, to it, and from it.’ As he explained: ‘For if the eye be not satysfyed the mynde cannot be contented, the heart cannot be pleased.’[10] It was a judgement shared by many Sussex gentlemen, who during the early modern period – the Tudors and the Stuarts – built a series of fine houses across the county. The century 1540 to 1640 has been dubbed the era of ‘the great rebuilding’, when the gentry throughout England – made newly rich as a result (as we shall see) of religious and socio-economic change – expressed its increasing wealth through the erection of conspicuously impressive dwellings. Nowhere was this more apparent than in Sussex, where the landscape north of the Downs was littered with houses rebuilt, enlarged or constructed anew by individuals anxious to demonstrate their new-found wealth or status. Between 1540 and 1640, Sussex participated vigorously in the ‘great rebuilding’, and, after the interruption of the Civil War years, began building again in the second half of the seventeenth century, by now adopting increasingly geometric and classical designs.

Evidence of the great rebuilding is still plentiful in the Sussex landscape. Rowfant House, for example, was built in the late sixteenth century (the

Danny Park, near Hassocks, at the foot of the South Downs, was built in distinctive red brick in 1593–95 by George Goring. It remained in the Goring family for four generations, until sold to Peter Courthorpe in 1650. Today the house exists as up-market serviced apartments for retired people.
USER: CUPCAKEKID/WIKIMEDIA COMMONS/CCO 1.0

fireplace in the entrance hall is dated 1597) for the successful ironmaster Robert Whitfield, its fabric incorporating survivals from an earlier timber-framed residence. Slaugham Place (today a ruin) was likewise erected for Sir Walter Covert, also made rich by the iron industry, as was Wiston Park (delightfully situated under the Downs near Chanctonbury), built *c.*1575 by the self-aggrandising Sir Thomas Shirley shortly after he had received his knighthood. Following the trend established at Herstmonceux in the 1440s, brick became an increasingly important Sussex building material during this expansionist period. Danny Park, near Hassocks, Legh Manor and Cuckfield Park, both near Cuckfield, and Bolebrooke, near Hartfield, were four late Tudor houses constructed entirely of brick. Danny Park, tucked under Wolsonbury Hill, was built *c.*1582–93; Legh Manor dates from *c.*1550, Cuckfield Park from 1579; and at Bolebrooke there are today substantial remains of the original sixteenth-century mansion – including a fine brick-built gatehouse. Even where new houses were made of stone, brick was often used for special features, not least the characteristic Elizabethan 'twisted' chimneys observable on many Sussex dwellings. To this inventory of 'the great rebuilding' in Sussex might be added numerous other notable examples – Wakehurst Place, near Ardingly, perhaps, where elements date back to the 1590s, or New Place and Ecclesden Manor, both at Angmering; the former exhibiting fragments of the house built by Sir Thomas Palmer in the sixteenth century, the latter (despite its Tudor ambience) built as late as 1634.

The construction of Parham House, situated near the village of Cootham, between Storrington and Pulborough, was commenced in 1577, during the reign of Elizabeth I, the foundation stone being laid by two-year old Thomas Palmer, symbolic of the dynastic power of the Palmer family in early-modern Sussex. Today, the house and gardens are open to the public.
CHRIS BROCKBANK

Mention should also be made of Uppark, near Midhurst, erected towards the end of this period, in about 1690, after the hiatus of the Civil War, built for Lord Grey of Werke, later earl of Tankerville. Writing in 1978, Nigel Nicolson, younger son of the celebrated Vita Sackville-West and her husband Harold Nicolson, thought Lord Grey 'a mean man, a seducer, a political turncoat and a trickster', such was Grey's reputation in the late seventeenth century. But, as Nicolson conceded, 'he did build Uppark, and for that much can be forgiven him'.[11] Indeed, when Celia Fiennes, on her famous sidesaddle journeys across England, passed that way in 1694, she was much impressed. 'I went to Chichester,' she wrote, 'through a very fine Parke of the Lord Tankervailes [*sic*], stately woods and shady tall trees for at least 2 mile: in the middle stands his house which is new built, square, 9 windows in the front and seven in the sides, brickwork with freestone coynes and windows.' She added: 'It's in the midst of fine gardens, gravell and green walks with bowling green.'[12] Unfortunately, Uppark was largely destroyed by fire in August 1989, although it has been faithfully restored to its late twentieth-century condition by its current owner, the National Trust.

However, pride of place in this great Tudor and Stuart building extravaganza must go to three splendid Sussex houses which, together, span the entire period and typify the phenomenon: Parham, Cowdray and Petworth. Parham, near Storrington, begun in 1557 by Sir Thomas Palmer, was constructed with the usual Elizabethan 'E' pattern facade, comprising central entrance and two wings, while the interior work was largely of the late sixteenth and early seventeenth century, completed on 'the cusp of the Elizabethan and Jacobean eras' as Simon Jenkins has observed.[13] 'It is a house of magic,' concludes Jenkins; it is a perfect 'Tudor house in a Tudor landscape', agrees Nikolaus Pevsner, the whole estate, with its many large trees and extensive bracken, an impressive memorial to the wealth and power of the Palmer family in early modern Sussex.[14]

Yet even more breathtaking was Cowdray, near Midhurst, today a romantic ruin but in its time the very 'epitome of Tudor architecture' (as Pevsner opined), which took all of sixty years to build.[15] Its earliest traces date to 1492, built by Sir David Owen (son of the Welsh patriot, Owain Glyn Dwr), who died in 1535. By then the property had been acquired by Sir William FitzWilliam – soon to be elevated as earl of Southampton by an admiring Henry VIII – who added the gatehouse, porch, and hexagonal tower at the north-west corner. On Southampton's death in 1542, Cowdray passed to Sir Anthony Browne, his half-brother and another favourite of Henry VIII, one of those well-placed individuals who gained enormously from the Dissolution of the Monasteries. He had been given Battle Abbey in 1538, rebuilding it as a private residence, as well as acquiring Easebourne Priory and Bayham Abbey – both in Sussex – and

The ruins of Cowdray House, along with its fine granary, are situated just east of Midhurst. Although almost destroyed by a catastrophic fire in 1793, Cowdray still betrays its pedigree as one of the grandest of England's Tudor houses, palatial in style and imposing in design. During the twentieth century the ruins were carefully conserved, and since 2007 the house has been open to the public.
ALISON AVERY, WWW.BEAUTIFULENGLANDPHOTOS.UK

Waverley Abbey and St Mary Overy Nunnery, the former in Surrey the other in London. Sir Anthony, as Pevsner remarked, was 'a dissolution profiteer indeed', his wealth and prestige built firmly on the back of social and religious upheaval.[16] He also added significantly to the fabric of Cowdray. His son, Viscount Montague, inherited the estate, where in 1591 he entertained Elizabeth I, further evidence of the family's status, although Montague's principled adherence to the Catholic faith meant that his power and influence went into decline, gradually but inexorably. Cowdray itself, alas, was gutted by fire in 1793. But the handsome façade and walls remain as evidence of the building's former glory.

Petworth House, by contrast, is very much extant, today one of the brightest jewels in the National Trust's English crown. In the late sixteenth century the Percy family, earls of Northumberland, greatly enlarged the existing manor house (some of it dating back as far as the thirteenth century), thus adding yet another fine example to the already impressive list of 'great rebuilding' properties in Tudor Sussex. However, almost a century later, in 1682, Charles, the 6th Duke of Somerset, acquired the house through his judicious marriage to a Percy heiress. He then began a great rebuilding of his own, lasting from 1688 to 1696, which transformed the house in what is supposed to have been a 'French' style, producing an enormously long façade, its forty-two tall windows encompassing and defining the two main floors. Petworth's setting was equally grand and spacious, including artificial landscapes and an especially created lake (the latter further enlarged by Capability Brown in the 1750s), together with an extensive deerpark. Charles, the 6th Duke, was known to his contemporaries as 'the Proud Duke', and he spared no expense in fashioning a residence that befitted his exalted status, in the process becoming a leading patron of some of the most prominent artists and craftsmen of his time.[17] Samuel Fulkes, for example, who worked on St Paul's Cathedral, is supposed to have undertaken much of the carving on the façade, while inside the house the murals adorning the grand staircase were by Louis Laguerre, who also painted the great mural at Blenheim Palace depicting Marlborough's victories. In acting as patron of the arts, Charles behaved in the same manner as many other aspiring gentlemen. Yet his lavish extravagances were on the grand scale, evidence of his great power and wealth. Indeed, by the closing decades of the seventeenth century, landholding in Sussex had become concentrated in fewer and fewer hands, a result of carefully calculated marriages and the aggressive amalgamation of estates, producing a tight-knit dominant class – of which the 'Proud Duke' was an exemplar – who would lead Sussex county life for the next two centuries at least.

Sussex iron

How did all this happen? First of all, the Wealden iron industry had continued its rapid expansion for much of this period, generating wealth and employment as well as responding to mushrooming demand for ironware of all kinds, from domestic items such as pots and ironwork for house building to cannon and firearms. Until 1496, when the first blast furnace arrived from the Low Countries, iron had been produced by the slow and inefficient 'bloomery' method, dependent on the layering of charcoal and ore in a primitive furnace, with a draught provided by bellows. By then, however, a new technique had been developed in the Ardennes Forest of northern France, based on the construction of a permanent smelting structure with a substantial furnace chamber and wide chimney. A number of large bellows projected into this chamber, each of which was compressed in turn to force a continuous blast of air into the furnace. This compression was driven by a wheel, perpetually in motion through the harnessing of waterpower, or sometimes horses or oxen. The result was a greatly increased and more consistent draught, with much higher temperatures, allowing the far more efficient production of iron. The furnace was continually top-filled with ore, and at the bottom of the chamber the molten iron was drained into moulds. In this way, the process could be kept going indefinitely by the furnace operators, producing a steady stream of iron to meet the growing demand. Indeed, it has been estimated that a blast furnace of this type could equal the output of perhaps as many as thirty of the earlier bloomeries.

The installation of blast furnaces across the Weald was accompanied by a wave of Flemish migrant iron workers eager to transfer their skills to this rapidly developing Sussex industry, as well as to escape religious persecution at home. The very first blast furnace and attendant hammer forge were erected at the end of the fifteenth century at Newbridge, in Ashdown Forest, to be followed swiftly by scores more across the county. The strategic importance of Sussex iron was quickly appreciated: Continental supplies were unreliable and vulnerable to interference by an enemy, while changing technologies at home demanded increased quantities of iron. The first successful casting of an iron cannon, at Buxted in 1534, was a significant advance. Hitherto, early banded cannon – such as those produced at Eridge – had consisted of wrought-iron strips bound together with iron hoops. These were almost as big a danger to their operators as to the enemy, and the advent of the safer, more efficient and more accurate cast-iron cannon was a huge step forward. Wealden entrepreneurs of all types clamoured to join the iron industry, bringing much needed capital – the £80 required to erect a furnace at Worth in 1547 was easily raised from a group of such men. At Buxted, where the first iron cannon was cast, the furnace was owned by the local vicar, Revd William Levett. He rented it out to one Ralphe Hogge, who in turn employed Peter Baude, a Flemish migrant, actually to run it.[18] It was an arrangement typical across the Weald, where local landowners and other worthies formed what were effectively small collaborative syndicates with skilled craftsmen, the necessary casual labour being recruited from the district. It was a formula that would serve for a hundred years and more, and its abundant fruits helped fund the 'great rebuilding' of Sussex houses as well as stimulating the local economy more generally. By 1574 there were reckoned to be 110 ironworks scattered across the county. In the 1580s William Camden could write that Sussex

> is full of iron mines, all over it; for the casting of which there are furnaces up and down the country, and abundance of wood is yearly spent; many streams are drawn into one channel, and a great deal of meadow ground is turned into ponds and pools for the driving of the mills by the flashes, which, beating with hammers upon the iron, fill the neighbourhood round about it, night and day with continual noise.[19]

Even today, Ashdown Forest maintains an air of mystery, even impenetrability, although in reality it is one of the largest free public access spaces in the south-east of England, and in the height of the early modern period was a centre of the Sussex iron industry. Two-thirds of the Forest's 6,500 acres comprise heathland, and are at the centre of the High Weald Area of Outstanding Natural Beauty. Originally a deer-hunting forest in Norman times, Ashdown Forest has experienced a rapid growth in deer numbers in recent decades. Together with fallow deer and the native roe deer, are the recently introduced muntjac and sika deer. They pose a considerable hazard to motorists in the locality, especially at dawn and dusk, and unfortunately there are some 250 deer casualties each year.
DAVID MOYES PHOTOGRAPHY

As Camden intimated, extensive iron-ore deposits and plentiful timber for the furnaces also facilitated the rapid advance of the industry. But, like all natural resources, both were finite. Large tracts of Ashdown Forest and other areas were soon denuded of their trees, causing much alarm. A royal commission in 1573 drew attention to the deleterious effect of the iron industry upon the Sussex landscape, and in the following year there was an attempt to control this damaging impact, the Privy Council requiring all manufacturers of cannon first to obtain a licence to cast. This concern was not merely environmental (although in 1581 an Act of Parliament forbade the erection of new iron works within twenty-two miles of London) but reflected the fear that too much good timber, needed for shipbuilding, was disappearing without replacement. Consequently, it was decreed that timber might not be cut for the iron industry within twelve miles of the Sussex coast, and in 1585 a ban was announced on the construction of new iron furnaces in the east of the county. Sussex ironmasters reacted by shifting their attention to Fernhurst and the upper Arun valley. Here they found themselves in stiff competition for timber with the similarly expanding glass industry. New techniques and migrant Huguenot craftsmen from France had, as in the iron industry, boosted glass production in Sussex. In 1567, for example, one Jean Carree had opened a large glass furnace at Farnefold Wood, near Wisborough Green. Yet it soon became clear that there was insufficient timber in the district to support both the glass and iron industries. By the early seventeenth century, competition for this increasingly scarce resource had reached serious proportions – so much so that in 1615 an Act prohibited the use henceforth of timber for glassmaking. In the deadly struggle for control of local fuel, the Sussex ironmasters had won.

In 1607 the traveller and cartographer, John Norden, worried in his *Surveyor's Dialogue* that those who had known the Weald of Sussex, Surrey and Kent, that 'grand nursery of oak and beech', would 'find an alteration within less than thirty years as may well strike fear lest few years more as pestilent as the former will leave as few good trees standing in those wealds'. Moreover, he added, such 'a heat issueth out of the many Forges and Furnaces for the making of iron, and out of the glass kilns as hath devoured many famous woods within the wealds'.[20] Yet the Sussex iron industry continued to flourish for several decades yet. It was not until the Civil War, in the 1640s, that the first hints of a fall from grace became apparent. To increasing shortages of timber and renewed attempts at regulation (including enforced contributions to repair roads ravaged by the industry), were added the effects of the Civil War itself. Many furnaces were owned by Royalists loyal to Charles I, and were subsequently destroyed or closed down by Cromwell's Roundhead forces. Additionally, coke was found to be a viable alternative to charcoal, and so the iron industry gradually relocated to the coal-rich Midlands. By 1717 there were only twenty furnaces left in Sussex, and the last of these fell silent in 1810. Yet this decline was gradual; so much so that when Daniel Defoe passed through the Weald in about 1720 he could note that 'the deep, dirty, but rich part of these two counties [Sussex and Kent]' was dependent on 'the great foundaries [*sic*] or ironworks' which 'in this county [Sussex] … are carry'd on at such a prodiguous [*sic*] expense of wood'.[21] For Defoe, the Wealden iron industry remained vibrant and impressive. The country was

> exceedingly grown with timber, has abundance of waste and wild grounds, and forests, and woods, with many large iron-works at which they cast great quantities of iron cauldrons, chimney backs, furnaces, retorts, boiling pots, and all such necessary things of iron; besides iron cannon, bomb-shells, stink-pots, hand-grenadoes [*sic*], and cannon balls, &c. in an infinite quantity.[22]

However, the decline of Sussex iron-making was inexorable. Despite Daniel Defoe's enthusiastic estimation of the industry, there were probably no more than thirty ironworks still operating in the whole of Sussex, Surrey and Kent at the time of his visit to the area. Thereafter, one by one these were abandoned until, early in the next century, they were but a memory. At some places, the waterways and ponds and waterwheels were put to new uses. At Beech, near Battle, for example, a flour mill was constructed on the site of an old furnace. Likewise, at Maresfield and at Brede gunpowder mills made use of existing water provision. At Eridge, a hammer pond was pressed into service as an ornamental lake at the (now demolished) Eridge Castle, while other disused ponds were simply reclaimed by the Wealden woodland, to sometimes eerie effect. In churchyards at Hartfield, Rotherfield, Uckfield and Wadhurst, iron grave slabs survived as memorials to the versatility of the industry and the multiplicity of uses to which the metal was put. Place-names such as Huggetts Furnace, near Crowborough, Furnacefield Wood, south of Ticehurst, Hammerwood, near East Grinstead, and Hammer Wood at Chithurst, together with the Iron River between Uckfield and Lewes, were also enduring testament to the erstwhile ubiquity of this once great industry which in its heyday had driven economic expansion and social change across Sussex.

To the impact of Sussex iron on the Tudor and Stuart economy should be added development and expansion in other sectors. There was a general improvement in farming skills throughout the early modern period, and a marked increase in demand for agricultural produce pushed up prices and land values. Inflation was sometimes rampant, as in the first half of the seventeenth century when a holding of thirty acres within the manor of Plumpton increased in value by almost 300 per cent. Individual landowners made astonishing profits as a result of such rises, fuelling the social aggrandisement noted above and the tendency to concentrate estates in fewer and fewer hands. On the Downs sheep farming continued to be important, and in the hard-pressed coastal areas a growth in corn production helped regenerate the economy, encouraging a new export trade which (as Defoe was to note) enriched the merchants of Chichester. Cattle breeding also increased significantly during this period, the red Sussex cow becoming commonplace across the county. Almost two dozen market towns scattered across Sussex provided important centres for trading and exchange, and acted as foci for their surrounding rural localities. Arundel, Battle, Chichester, Cuckfield, Ditchling, East Grinstead, Lewes, Midhurst, Petworth, Steyning, and other urban communities offered an extensive range of goods and services. Leatherworkers, tailors, cobblers, builders and other skilled tradesmen ensured a comprehensive self-sufficiency in each locality. As before, Lewes and Chichester remained the largest towns, with populations of about 2,000 apiece during this period. Lewes especially, strategically placed on the navigable river Ouse and adjacent to Weald, Downs and coastal plain, flourished. By comparison, Chichester languished – at least until the upsurge in local corn production.[23]

The Dissolution of the Monasteries

Alongside the iron industry, the principal impetus to economic and social change was the Dissolution of the Monasteries. By the late medieval period, many considered that the Church had become increasingly lax and complacent, as well as distanced from the ideas and ambitions of the more progressive elements of the socio-economic elite in England, influenced as it was by the mores and norms of Continental Renaissance thinking. Viewed from this perspective, the Church was ripe for reform, and heading the list of doubtful institutions ready for radical change were the religious houses – said to own one-sixth of all the land in England. Henry VIII, looking to replenish his coffers after expensive military campaigns against France and Scotland, was keen to identify new sources of income, and Cardinal Wolsey was likewise anxious to secure sufficient funding to found a new Oxford College (Christchurch, as it eventually became). Accordingly, the property of the smaller monasteries and convents across the country was appropriated forthwith. The first to go in Sussex was Bayham. Although rich in land, by 1525 the Abbey was badly in debt and notorious for corruption and inept administration. Declared to be beyond redemption, the house was dissolved and its lands seized. Local people, not yet used to the principle of dissolution, resisted the closure and sought to reinstate the abbot. But their protest was short-lived – the rising was put down, its leaders imprisoned.

Thereafter, the business of dissolution became inextricably entwined in Henry VIII's 'Great Matter' – his attempt to divorce Catherine of Aragon and his subsequent marriage to Anne Boleyn – and the break with Rome. The Act in Restraint of Appeals in 1533 formally severed the jurisdictional links between England and Rome, and the Act of Supremacy in 1534 confirmed Henry VIII as both head of state and head of the Church of England. At the same time, Thomas Cromwell – who had replaced Cardinal Wolsey as Henry's principal advisor – began the dissolution of all religious houses whose income was less than £2,000 a year. This soon escalated into a full-scale assault on all monasteries and convents, carried out with such diligence and severity that by 1540 no religious order survived anywhere in England. The famous Priory at Lewes was formally surrendered in November 1537, followed by Robertsbridge and then Battle some sixth months later. Lewes was subsequently acquired by none other than Thomas Cromwell, who took great delight in the systematic demolition of the priory buildings, before he too fell from favour and was executed for 'treason' in 1540. The dispossessed prior, ironically, was treated relatively lightly, and was found various ecclesiastical positions around the country, working for the newly constituted Church of England, as were the friars and nuns who had also toiled at Lewes. Likewise, the abbot of Battle was able to retire on a comfortable pension. But the real beneficiaries were those, such as Sir Anthony Browne, Pevsner's 'dissolution profiteer' *par excellence*, inheritor of Bayham, Battle and a string of other properties, who acquired the land, ornaments and other riches of the surrendered religious houses. They became wealthy, and their social and political status was enhanced accordingly. The fortunes of the ordinary people altered hardly at all, although they were glad enough to partake of the building materials made available by the demolition of Lewes Priory – and, indeed, at Robertsbridge, where the locals eagerly participated in the destruction of the abbey. Elsewhere, buildings survived – at Rye they became storehouses, and Michelham was converted into a moated manor house.

Boxgrove Priory, in the village of Boxgrove, was built at the time of the Norman Conquest by one Robert de Haye as a Benedictine foundation. Considered wealthy (in 1535 its assets were worth more than £180), it was ripe for 'dissolution' by Thomas Cromwell, and was acquired by Sir Thomas West, Baron de la Warr. The fourteenth-century lodging house fell into disrepair but the priory itself survived as the Anglican parish church of St Mary and St Blaise.
BILL BROOKS, WWW.BILLBROOKSIMAGES.COM

Anne of Cleves' House in Southover High Street, Lewes, is today a museum managed by the Sussex Archaeological Society. A typical Wealden hall building, it was constructed in the fifteenth century and became part of Queen Anne's settlement on the annulment of her marriage to Henry VIII in 1541. She appears never to have visited it, although she also acquired a second property – also sometimes known as Anne of Cleves' House (or, less confusingly, as Wing House) – at nearby Ditchling.
USER: CHARLESDRAKEW/WIKIMEDIA COMMONS/CC0 1.0

The small priory at Boxgrove was happily reinvented as a parish church of the new Church of England. As an aside, we might also note that one of the knock-on effects of the Henry VIII's 'Great Matter' was his later and very brief marriage in 1540 to Anne of Cleves – the 'Flanders Mare', as Henry unkindly dubbed her – who acquired 'Anne of Cleves' House' (as it is known today) in Lewes as part of the deal when their union was annulled.

On the whole, despite the objectors at Bayham and the vocal opposition of individuals such as Andrew Boorde, the population of Sussex appears to have accepted the Dissolution of the Monasteries with little more than a murmur. However, this did not mean that all aspects of the Reformation – the break with Rome and the creation of the Church of England – passed without resistance. In the years before his death in 1547, Henry VIII had reopened hostilities with France (the castle at Camber, built in 1511, was extended and modernised to meet the French threat during the 1540s, although this did not stop the enemy burning Brighton in 1544). As before, Henry dug deep into his coffers and was forced to debase his currency, which precipitated a new round of steep inflation. This, in turn, prompted a degree of labour unrest not seen since the days of Jack Cade. Although violence was endemic in English society in the sixteenth century, with riotous assembly, forcible entry, murder and manslaughter frequent offences, something more serious was brewing now. In 1549 the sickly boy-king, Edward VI, replaced the old Latin liturgy with a new English-language *Book of Common Prayer*. This new order of service was first used on 6 June that year, to mark the feast of Pentecost, and represented a significant shift towards Protestant practice in the Church of England. There was discontent across the realm among the common people (in Cornwall there was open rebellion), as resistance to these liturgical innovations combined with existing economic and other grievances.

There were riots in Sussex in 1549. At Angmering, the tenants of Ecclesden Manor were at loggerheads with their lord, John Palmer. In a complaint that anticipated what would in subsequent centuries be commonplace resistance to the process of enclosure across England, the tenants alleged that Palmer, with the assistance of armed servants, had ejected them from their farms. They accused him of wanting their land for his own purposes, something which Palmer strenuously denied.[24] On 29 June the earl of Arundel wrote to government officials to warn of the danger of rural unrest in Sussex and Surrey. He judged that 'these parts remain as may be in a quavering quiet', and recommended decisive action to meet the complaints of the common people.[25] Meanwhile, at Witley Park in Surrey a riot had broken out in response to the enclosure of common land by a local landowner, and there was further disquiet in Sussex, not least at Arundel itself, where protestors railed against changes in Church ritual. The earl was hard pressed to manage the situation across both counties during the summer of 1549 but succeeded in preventing a widespread breakdown in law and order. Eventually, in what was perhaps one of the very last exercises of feudal authority in England, he took the initiative himself, summoning to Arundel Castle all those with grievances. There he dined them in the Great Hall, listened to their complaints, and passed judgement. Those gentlemen he decided had acted unjustly in enclosing common land were required to return it to the commoners, which they did willingly in due deference to his authority. But he also arrested and dispensed summary justice to those he considered ringleaders and agitators. Thereafter, the people, acknowledging the earl of Arundel as 'their ancient and chiefest lord of that country', dispersed quietly, content that at least some of their complaints had been addressed.[26] Ironically, the earl was himself a Catholic, and no doubt sympathised with those who criticised the new Protestant Prayer Book. But he also recognised his feudal obligation to the Crown and was determined to exercise his responsibilities, as he saw them. Although he had little need to deploy military force, he possessed the means to assert his authority in Sussex: according to the muster rolls of 1539, he had at his disposal 123 armed servants as well as ready access to twice that number more if need be, together with the dozen or more men at arms that each other leading Sussex gentlemen would be required to supply in a moment of crisis.

The Reformation and its aftermath

As the earl of Arundel's Catholicism evidenced, not all the elite – in Sussex, or in the country as a whole – had embraced the new Church of England, and many remained deeply suspicious of Protestantism. Henry VIII's motive in breaking with Rome had been to solve his 'Great Matter' but also to ensure greater national control over the Church and its resources. However, this English 'Reformation' – as its many supporters interpreted it – was seen by some enthusiasts as a timely opportunity for Protestants to introduce their ideas and practices into the new Church. Edward VI, indeed, proved highly receptive to Protestant thought, not least through the influence of those ministers who managed his affairs. As well as introducing the new English-language Prayer Book, he approved the stripping of images and the removal of rood screens from parish churches across the country. In London and the south-east of England, despite the enduring Catholicism of gentry such as the earl of Arundel or Viscount Montague, this increasingly militant Protestantism found growing support – especially among the merchants and artisans. Important here was the impetus lent by Protestant Flemings and French Huguenots, those bricklayers, ironfounders, glass makers, weavers and brewers who had fled religious persecution in Continental Europe, bringing their advanced ideas with them. These skilled craftsmen and their families found a ready home in Sussex, especially in busy urban centres such as Lewes, where they became influential members of the community.

Thus Protestantism was already well entrenched in Sussex when Edward VI died in 1553. Having no offspring, the crown passed to his half-sister Mary – daughter of Henry VIII and Catherine of Aragon – who had remained firmly committed to the Catholic faith. Moreover, her new husband was Philip of Spain, feared and loathed across the realm as the embodiment of Continental Catholicism. 'Bloody' Mary, as she is known to popular history, planned a comprehensive return to Rome. In this she was thwarted by an obstructive Parliament which dragged its feet on all the main issues: it would not allow her to renounce her supremacy over the Church of England; nor would it allow her husband to be crowned king of England. Likewise, Parliament resisted the re-enactment of the heresy laws in November 1554 until especial dispensation for the purchasers of former religious property was incorporated. Similarly, Parliament rejected Mary's attempt to appropriate the lands of Protestant exiles seeking refuge abroad from the new heresy laws. Nonetheless, the re-emergence of heresy as a serious religious crime had drastic effects. Spurred on by the enthusiastic bishop of London, Edmund Bonner, Mary inaugurated a programme of persecution and punishment across the country, aimed at advanced Protestants. In Sussex, between 1555 and 1558 no fewer than twenty-seven men and women were convicted of heresy and burned alive, a considerable proportion of the 300 or so people who were executed in England as a whole. Among the first of these Sussex 'martyrs', as they were later proclaimed, was a Flemish brewer, Derryk Carver, who was burned in Lewes in July 1555. Brighton, Chichester, East Grinstead, Mayfield and Steyning supplied their own victims, but the most notorious execution was that of July 1555, when ten Protestants – five men and five women – were burned in the market place in Lewes.[27] Perhaps as a result, Lewes remained a stronghold of Protestant Dissent in subsequent centuries, home, for instance, to the Sussex 'Bonfire Societies' who to this day celebrate Bonfire Night at the Martyr's Memorial in Lewes with the insistent cry of 'No Popery'.

'Bloody' Queen Mary died in 1558, to be succeeded by Elizabeth I – daughter of Henry VIII and Anne Boleyn. Elizabeth viewed her relationship with the Church of England much as her father had done, and the break with Rome was renewed – this time for ever. Clergy were now required to take an oath of allegiance to Elizabeth's Church of England, and the forty or so in Sussex who refused to do so were deprived of their livings. In an upsurge of Protestant enthusiasm, a mob at Hailsham desecrated the parish church, smashing its 'papist' images and prefiguring an era of growing suspicion between the county's Protestant Dissenters – or 'Puritans', as they were increasingly known – and the remaining Catholic or 'recusant' families. It was an atmosphere aggravated by Richard Curteys, newly appointed bishop of Chichester in 1570, whose Puritan zeal irritated many of the more moderate Sussex gentry but won the support of advanced Protestants, not least in Lewes. Curteys was unwise enough to pick a legal fight with Thomas Lewkenor of Selsey, a leading merchant in the Chichester area, and at length the central government felt that it could no longer ignore the antagonisms he had engendered. Accordingly, he was removed from office. Nonetheless, as the threat from Catholic Spain became acute, so anti-Catholic sentiment grew apace. Viscount Montague, son of Sir Thomas Browne, and inheritor of Cowdray and Battle, owed his wealth and position to the Dissolution of the Monasteries. Ironically, he remained a committed Catholic and, although his loyalty to the Crown was not in question, he suffered for his beliefs as his authority in the county dwindled. Other Sussex gentry suffered more acutely, such as Richard Shelley of Warninghurst who was imprisoned in 1580 for recusancy. His kinsman, Edward Shelley, was executed at Tyburn in 1588 for concealing a Catholic priest, a harsh penalty that nevertheless did not deter Sir Thomas Leedes of Steyning, and others like him, from keeping a secret priest's hole in his house. Meanwhile, fines for non-attendance at church were increased drastically and enforced with greater vigour, part of a sustained campaign to force conformity to the Church of England. Two Catholic priests who were exposed were executed on Broyle Heath, near Chichester. But when the Spanish Armada arrived off the English coast in 1588, Sussex provided a united front – Catholic as well as Protestant – as the county raised some 4,000 men for the defence of the realm.[28]

Civil War

However, by time of Elizabeth's death in 1603, and the accession of James I & VI (of Scotland), the first of the Stuart line, this solidarity had already begun to break down. By the 1620s a new wave of religious and social conflict was apparent, no longer Protestant versus Catholic but rather a struggle for the soul of the Church of England between the Puritans and their 'Arminian' or 'High' opponents. The latter, dismissed as 'papists' by their Puritan critics, had the support of Charles I (who had succeeded his father James in 1625), and their hand was strengthened when he appointed the High Church William Laud as Archbishop of Canterbury in 1633. Bishops with Arminian sympathies had been appointed to Chichester in the 1620s and 1630s, where they managed to upset the Sussex gentry just as Curteys had done before them. But, perhaps more importantly, they also clashed openly with the Puritan districts of the county, notably

Lewes and Rye, creating new enmities and division. As historians such as David Underdown and Mark Stoyle have shown, the patterns of loyalty and local allegiance which emerged in the English Civil War – and the wider 'War of the Three Kingdoms' across the British Isles in the 1640s – depended not only on the major issues of the day but on deep divisions at county or regional level.[29] And in Sussex, as elsewhere, it was not just the opinions of the gentry and aristocracy that counted. Ordinary men and women, especially among the artisans and merchants, had views that mattered and which could influence events. In the deteriorating climate between king and parliament which led eventually to the outbreak of civil war in 1642, such opinions in Sussex helped to determine the patchwork of allegiances to one side or the other – or to none – that were to emerge.

In 1642, for example, as the king's supporters were denounced as quasi-papists, so there was an outburst of Puritan enthusiasm throughout East Sussex, which did much to promote the parliamentarian cause. Elsewhere in the county Puritan adherents also proved likely to plump for Parliament, although, as in many other areas, there was no clear division of allegiance. Of the thirteen urban boroughs returning Members of Parliament, five were divided in their allegiance, three had both Members who supported the King, and five had both Members supporting Parliament. This seems a fair representation of Sussex opinion – a clear inclination towards the Parliamentarian/Puritan camp but with considerable indecision and a strong minority remaining loyal to the king. Inevitably, families were often divided – brother against brother, cousin versus cousin – and old friendships were at last broken. A poignant insight into the personal agonising which often underpinned difficult and sometimes reluctant decisions, is provided in the touching letter written by Sir William Campion of Danny Park to his dear friend, Colonel Herbert Morley of Glynde. As Sir William explained, he was no papist, and he believed in the rights of Parliament. A sense of duty, however, compelled him to side with the royalists. He desperately wanted his old friend to understand his position, for Colonel Morley had emerged as a leading advocate of the parliamentarian cause in Sussex. 'I did not rashly or unadvisedly put myself upon this service,' confessed Sir William, 'think not that I fight for Popery, God knows my heart, I abhor it.' Indeed, he insisted, 'God Prosper me no further than my desires and endeavours tend to the preservation of the Protestant religion settled in Queen Elizabeth's days, the just prerogative of the King, and just privilege of Parliament.' Sir William's support for 'the Protestant religion settled in Queen Elizabeth's days' was tacit admission to his hostility to Puritanism. But in declaring for the cause of the king, he wanted to extend the hand of continuing friendship to his reluctant enemy: 'I heartily thank you for your desire of the preservation of mee and mine, and if ever it lie in my power to do any courtesy to you, it shall not be wanting in your faithful friend and servant.'[30]

Chichester Cathedral, with its blend of Norman (Romanesque) and Gothic features, was in the estimation of Nikolaus Pevsner 'the most typical English cathedral'. Its free-standing fifteenth-century bell-tower (or campanile) makes it unique in England, however, while its double aisles arrangement is also unusual. Luckily, it survived the depredations and despoliation of the Civil War. Like all cathedrals, Chichester contains many items of exceptional interest and national importance, from medieval sculptures to the grave of the composer Gustav Holst and a pennant presented by Sir Francis Chichester after his successful circumnavigation of the globe in his yacht *Gypsy Moth IV* in 1966–67.
BILL BROOKS, WWW.BILLBROOKSIMAGES.COM

Although Sussex was spared the mighty clashes of the royalist and parliamentarian field armies – the Cavaliers and Roundheads – that occurred elsewhere, the county did play a significant role in the Civil War. The Wealden iron foundries were important to both sides for the production of arms and ammunition, and those in royalist hands attracted the attention of parliamentarian adherents, who tried to seize, decommission or sometimes destroy the furnaces – perhaps to the permanent detriment of the industry's fortunes. Likewise, the Sussex coast was close to Continental Europe, and, although Hastings was the only coastal town to declare unreservedly for the king, Parliament feared that the county might become a conduit for the illicit import of arms, bullion and other material designed to bolster the royalist cause. For this reason alone, Parliament considered it vital that its writ should run in Sussex. But the royalists made the first move. In November 1642, less than two months after hostilities in England had commenced,

Sir Edward Ford led elements of the hastily impressed local 'trained bands' – the part-time militia – in an attack on Lewes. However, they were intercepted and scattered by an opposing parliamentarian force at Haywards Heath. Ford retreated to Chichester, to join a group of royalist gentry determined to seize control of the town from its Puritan aldermen. Hitherto, an uneasy peace had existed between opposing sides in Chichester, even to the extent of their drilling daily in different parts of the town. But now the royalist initiative drew a robust response from Parliament. A force some 6,000 strong, under the command of General Sir William Waller, advanced on Chichester. After an eight-day siege, the royalist garrison surrendered. Entering the town, the triumphant parliamentary soldiers ransacked the houses of the royalist gentry and laid waste to the 'papist' cathedral. The dean, Bruno Reeves, could do no more than record the violent behaviour of the Puritan soldiery and the thieving tendencies of their masters. 'The Commanders having in person executed the *covetous part* of Sacrilege, they leave the *destructive* and *spoiling* part to be finished by the common soldiers.' As he complained, they 'broke down the organs and dashing the pipes with their pole-axes, scoffingly said "hark how the organs go"'.[31]

'This war without an enemy'

Meanwhile, a detachment of Waller's force had been sent to Arundel Castle, a formidable stronghold and yet lightly garrisoned – so much so that it surrendered with hardly a fight. For the moment, Parliament held sway in Sussex. However, in December 1643 a powerful royalist force under General Sir Ralph Hopton entered the west of the county from Petersfield, in Hampshire, capturing the lightly defended houses at Stansted and Cowdray before confronting Arundel Castle. Again, Arundel's defence collapsed without much of a fight, this time a royalist garrison replacing the captured parliamentarians. In an echo of the heartache experienced by the old friends, Sir William Campion and Colonel Herbert Morley, who found themselves on opposing sides in the Civil War, so Ralph Hopton and William Waller – the principal protagonists in the clashes in Sussex – had been close for many years. In June 1643 Waller had written to Hopton – much as Campion had written to Morley the year before – to confess that the 'experience I have had of your worth, and the happiness I have enjoyed in your friendship are wounding considerations when I look upon this present distance between us'. As he explained: 'My affections to you are so unchangeable, that hostility itself cannot violate my friendship in your person, but I must be true to the cause wherein I serve.' He emphasised 'with what a perfect hatred I detest this war without an enemy', and, although resigned to the fact that both men 'must act those parts that are assigned to us in this tragedy', implored: 'Let us do it in a way of honour, and without personal animosities, whatever the issue be.'[32]

Nonetheless, Hopton's recapture of Arundel Castle could not be allowed to stand, and Waller was soon again on the scene, crossing into Sussex on 17 December with an army perhaps 10,000 strong. Cowdray was swiftly retaken but this time Arundel proved a much harder nut to crack. Although Waller conducted the siege with his customary good manners – he wined and dined the royalist ladies, offering them safe passage away from the fight – he was ruthless in his prevention of supplies reaching the besieged garrison and in his effective use of artillery to bombard and reduce the castle. When water ran out, the thousand or so royalist defenders had little alternative but to surrender. They did so on the morning of 6 January 1644. 'I never saw so many weak and feeble creatures together in my life,' wrote one contemporary observer, 'for almost all the common soldiers were half starved, and many of them hardly able to set one foot before another.'[33] Indeed, for some it seemed more like liberation than defeat, and half of the royalist garrison promptly opted to join Waller's forces instead. Meanwhile, Waller had already met and defeated Hopton's main force at Alton, across the border in Hampshire, and a further victory at nearby Alresford opened the way for the parliamentary capture of Winchester. Hopton wrote despairingly to his old friend and adversary Waller – 'God give a sudden stop to this issue of English blood' – but the fighting continued.[34] They met on the battlefield as friendly enemies for the last time at Newbury in October 1644. A dispirited Hopton complained that he was 'so perfectly tired with the drudgery of it', and, having failed to pierce Waller's stout defence of Surrey and Sussex, went into voluntary exile – first in the Channel Islands, and then in Holland, where he died in 1652.[35] Ironically, after the Restoration Waller also fled to Holland, subsequently returning home to a dismal life of imprisonment and seclusion. The Civil War had worn out and ultimately ruined the two old friends.

The recapture of Arundel Castle and the defeat of Hopton secured Sussex for Parliament for the rest of the Civil War. However, the county was by no means quiet, for Sussex emerged as an important centre of the large popular movement – the Clubmen – which supported neither side and instead protested against the widespread destruction of agricultural produce and property, and the cost in lives, money and other resources. The Clubmen were especially prominent in the southern, south-western and Welsh border counties. In Sussex, local neutralism and resistance to the war had been apparent for some time, not least in the Weald, being expressed, for example, in the severe beating meted out by a mob to a parliamentary recruiting sergeant at West Hoathly fair in 1643. Colonel Herbert Morley, the parliamentarian leader, feared that the Civil War would 'raise a storm in Sussex, which county is full of neuters and malignants; and I have ever observed neuters to turn malignant upon such occasions.'[36] He was right. By early 1645 the Clubmen had emerged as organised groups, composed mainly of yeomen, tenant farmers and labourers but sometimes also appealing to the minor gentry and even elements of the clergy. They saw themselves as defenders of ancient local traditions in the face of unwelcome and disruptive external intrusion. In Sussex, the Clubmen appealed to Magna Carta as the source of just and true government, and regretted that it had been subverted by unscrupulous men from both sides of the conflict. As they saw it, 'some particular persons crept into authority who have delegated their power to men of sordid condition whose wills have been laws ... by which they have overthrown all our English liberties'.[37] Such rhetoric was calculated to inflame the passions of the ordinary people, and by the autumn of September 1645 parliamentarian forces were having to deal with Clubmen risings across Sussex. On 18 September, for example, a crowd of more than a thousand protesters gathered round the medieval chapel of St Roche, which then crowned the Trundle at Singleton in West Sussex. There were similar protest meetings at Duncton Down, near Petworth, and Bury Hill, near Amberley, each dispersed by parliamentary troops. Trouble flared again in 1648, when protests at Horsham and Pulborough against food taxes and low agricultural wages revealed a continuing propensity for rural unrest and resentment.

Interregnum and Restoration

The final victory of Parliament, and the execution of Charles I, on 30 January 1649, was followed in 1651 by Prince Charles's abortive return to England from exile. Although crowned King Charles II of Scotland, his fortunes south of the border were less happy – he was defeated by Oliver Cromwell's forces at the Battle of Worcester and forced to flee to France from the Sussex port of Shoreham. Ten Sussex gentry, including Colonel Herbert Morley, had served among those sitting in judgement of Charles I, although all of them abstained from signing the execution warrant. Thereafter, former royalists in Sussex were fined heavily for having been on the wrong side, or, as in the case of John Ashburnham, had their estates confiscated altogether. Generally, however, Sussex was relatively quiet during Cromwell's Commonwealth and Protectorate, notwithstanding Dutch raids along the coast during the 1650s, although religious adherence continued as a political issue. An experiment in the creation of a strict Puritan 'Common Wealth' at Rye, led by its clergy, was short-lived, the populace soon tiring of its unbending public morality. However, Sussex remained a centre of religious dissent, and during the 1650s Quakerism gained in popularity. In 1655 George Fox, founder of the Society of Friends, visited the county, recording in his journal that near Horsham he conducted 'a great meeting and many were convinced'. Two years later he was back: 'I travelled into Sussex visiting Friends, among whom I had great meetings; and many times I met with opposition from Baptists and other jangling professors, but the Lord's power went over them.'[38] Fox's comments indicate the antagonism that often existed between competing dissenting sects, along with the potential for violent public confrontations over theological matters. The threat of renewed disorder alarmed the local gentry, who were still recovering from the travails of the Civil War, and measures were taken to suppress the Quakers – Thomas Haycock of Horsham, for example, went to gaol for his beliefs in 1656.

When the Cromwellian Protectorate eventually collapsed, and in 1660 Charles II was invited to return as king, there were Puritan clergymen in Sussex who could not accept this Restoration. Perhaps as many as one third left or were ejected from their Church of England livings, to become Dissenters or Nonconformists of various persuasions. Despite continuing persecution (between 1665 and 1690 almost 200 Friends were incarcerated in Horsham gaol), the Quakers continued to attract adherents; by the end of the seventeenth century there were a dozen meeting houses across the county. One of their number, William Penn, who held meetings at his house in Warminghurst, later became a founder of the colony of Pennsylvania in America. In 1669 a rudimentary survey was made of dissenting 'conventicles' (or meeting places) in Sussex. It identified forty-nine such 'conventicles' (probably a conservative figure, as the survey appears incomplete), among them eleven Anabaptist, six Quaker, four Presbyterian (their meeting place at South Malling said to be 500 strong), three Independents, and twenty-four others. East Sussex especially remained a home of religious Dissent.

The Restoration in 1660 undid much that had been enacted during the Interregnum. John Ashburnham, for example, who had been dispossessed and forced into exile, was welcomed home by Charles II and rewarded for his loyalty with gifts of land. Other royalists, together with those who had been prudent enough to alter their allegiance during the Interregnum, were rewarded likewise. Such patronage, and the wealth that it engendered, precipitated a renewal of the 'great rebuilding' – houses such as Uppark and Petworth date from this time – and further encouraged the concentration of property and power in the hands of the relatively few great landowners who came to dominate Sussex life. The 'Glorious Revolution' of 1688 – when James II was displaced in favour of William of Orange and his wife Mary (elder daughter of James II) – passed peaceably enough in Sussex, as did the Act of Union between England and Scotland in 1707. In 1714 Queen Anne, the last of the Stuart line to sit on the British throne, died, ushering in what was to become known as the Hanoverian period after the new king, George I, son of the Elector of Hanover.

SIX

Hanoverians and early Victorians: high society and social crime

The pursuit of leisure

When Douglas Hay and his fellow historians wrote their ground-breaking book *Albion's Fatal Tree*, first published in 1975, they observed that Hanoverian England was often presented as a world of 'landscaped parks and polite culture', a tranquil picture of 'quiet elegance'. Yet behind this peaceful façade, they argued, was an altogether more unstable society, marked by violence, gangs and organised crime (such as smuggling and poaching), and kept in check only by the severity of the penal code.[1] If this was true for England as a whole, then it was doubly so for Sussex. The county was dominated by a small social group of aristocracy and gentry which continued to build or rebuild its fine country houses, as it had done in previous centuries, and to design or redesign in impressive Italianate classical style the splendid gardens that surrounded these noble seats. But at the same time, from the accession of George I until at least the middle of the nineteenth century, rural Sussex beyond the great estates was characterised by almost continual unrest and lawlessness.

Petworth underwent a second rebuilding in the 1780s, under the direction of the third earl of Egremont, maintaining its position as the most grand of the Sussex seats. At Glynde Place, the existing Tudor house was ingeniously upgraded by the insertion of Italianate features – Tuscan columns in the great hall, and a completely redesigned entrance – while at Stanmer a new 'Palladian'-style house was built in the 1720s. Here the unsightly village belonging to the estate was relocated farther away, so as not to spoil the view. Goodwood House, near Chichester, the seat of the dukes of Richmond, built originally in the seventeenth century, was substantially extended in 1800–06 by James Wyatt, with assistance from John Nash. Sheffield Park was likewise the work of James Wyatt, erected before 1779 for the earl of Sheffield, an early essay in the Gothic Revival style at the very moment when Wyatt's interests were shifting from the classical to the gothic. And so it went on. Expressions of power and wealth, as well as artistic and architectural taste, the great houses and parks of Sussex were also centres of stylish and leisured living. They exercised their authority in the landscape – Petworth and similar seats continued their traditional role in the receipts of petitioners and the consideration of grievances – but increasingly they were devoted to pleasure.

The pursuit of health was another major obsession of the leisured classes, in Sussex as elsewhere in England, and many made their way to Tunbridge Wells, across the Kentish border. Here they could sample or bathe in the spa water but also, as John Lowerson has explained, take advantage of the opportunities for 'social and sexual intercourse, flirtation, gaming and marriage-broking' which were available at such rich gatherings, all *de rigueur* for those wishing to advance their social positions in this ambitiously leisured world.[2] By the 1750s, the focus had begun to shift from such inland destinations to the coastal areas, as seawater was identified as having special healing and reviving qualities. A key advocate of seawater treatment was Dr Richard Russell, from Lewes, who in 1750 published his *A Dissertation concerning the use of Sea-Water in the Diseases of the Glands*. Seawater cured everything from toothache to abdominal trouble, or so he claimed, and 1754 he set up practice in Brighthelmstone – or Brighton as it would shortly be known – devising strict regimens to restore to full health the ailing and the anxious. He died in 1759, but by then Brighton's reputation as a watering hole was already well established. Indeed, it was to receive a major boost when, in the 1780s, George, Prince of Wales, began staying with his uncle, the rakish duke of Cumberland, at Grove House near the Steine. 'Prinny', as the young George was called by his admiring friends, came to Brighton to escape the constraints of his father's court. But he had also been advised by his physicians that seawater might cure the unpleasant swelling of the glands in his neck that he so often experienced.

Prince of Wales, Prince Regent and George IV, 'Prinny' (as he was known by his pals), did much to establish the Brighton we know today, not only conceiving the Royal Pavilion and Dome but confirming the town (as it was then) as a desirable watering-hole within easy reach of the metropolis and with all the benefits of a leisured seaside existence.
NEW YORK PUBLIC LIBRARY

Inevitably, fashion followed suit: the number of visitors annually to Brighton increased from a modest 400 in 1760 to some 11,000 by 1821, while the town's permanent population grew from around 2,000 to almost 25,000 over the same period. Meanwhile, in 1786, George installed the beautiful Mrs Fitzherbert (a Roman Catholic, whom he had married secretly and illegally) in a house in Brighton, intent now on focusing his life in the town. In the following year he commissioned

Brighton (or Royal) Pavilion, the brain-child and plaything of the Prince Regent (later George IV), was commenced in 1787, enlarged in 1801–2, and further extended in 1815 by John Nash, who was responsible for its exotic 'Oriental' domes and minarets – a style known in architectural circles as 'Indo-Sarasenic Revival'. Later, Queen Victoria, who disliked Brighton and needed the money to redevelop Osborne House on the Isle of Wight, sold the Pavilion to the town in 1850 for £35,000. Ten years later, the adjacent stables, known as the Dome, were converted into a concert hall and assembly rooms. During the early years of the Great War, the Pavilion served as a hospital for wounded Indian soldiers. Thereafter, the Pavilion developed apace as a tourist attraction – today its draws more than 400,000 visitors a year, and is also a popular venue for weddings.

Henry Holland to design the early version of the 'Pavilion', initially a modest neo-classical structure based around a central domed rotunda. In 1801–02 the Pavilion was enlarged to cater for George's expanding social life, and between 1803 and 1808 a grand stable building (the 'Dome', as it became) was erected alongside. Built in the 'Indian style', this impressive building could accommodate some sixty horses, and in its size, grandeur and opulence overshadowed the Pavilion itself. The solution was to rebuild the Pavilion, a project that was initiated in 1815 under the direction of John Nash. The work was not completed until 1823, by which time alterations to the original building had been complemented by the erection of the Great Kitchen, a Music Room and a Banqueting Room. The external appearance of the greatly expanded Pavilion was now decidedly 'Indian', and internally the design reflected the current enthusiasm for all things Oriental.

As Jessica Rutherford has pointed out, the development of the Pavilion, from its modest neo-classical beginnings to John Nash's magnificent Oriental palace, reflected George's own progress: from Prince of Wales, to Prince Regent (1811–20), and then to King George IV (1820–30).[3] In each of these incarnations, George was determined to enjoy life to the full. He was, in the words of historian Simon Schama, 'a fat, often drunk lecher', and the Pavilion was his 'funhouse'.[4] George was also a keen horseman (hence his impressive stable), and would often drive across to Uppark to visit his close friend, Sir Harry Fetherstonhaugh, who had succeeded to the estate in 1774, where he would 'enjoy Sir Harry's excellent table and string of race-horses'.[5] Sir Harry, like George, was also an admirer of fine women. One of the ladies entertained at Uppark was the lovely Emma Hart, universally acknowledged as a great beauty, who later became the famous Lady Hamilton. She was a mere sixteen years old when she first met Sir Harry, who speedily recruited her as his mistress, installing her at Uppark for a year before dismissing her just as summarily. The other great woman in Sir Harry's life was his wife,

The opulence of the more fashionable parts of early nineteenth-century Brighton is still seen in some of its imposing architecture today. Originally known as Kemp Town, after its founder Thomas Read Kemp, this area of eastern Brighton is now more usually known as Kemptown. As initially conceived, Kemp Town was a series of fine Regency precincts. Work commenced in 1823 on Arundel Terrace, Chichester Terrace, Lewes Crescent and Sussex Square (the latter shown here) and was completed in 1855.
USER: HASSOCKS5489/WIKIMEDIA COMMONS/CC0 1.0

Mary Ann, whom he first met in 1825 when he was over seventy. One day, so the story goes, as he strolled along the west terrace of his house, he was captivated by the singing emanating from the dairy. Investigating further, he found that the possessor of the perfect voice was a dairymaid, one Mary Ann Bullock. He proposed marriage shortly after. 'But do not answer me immediately,' he said: 'If you will have me, cut a slice out of the leg of mutton that is coming up for my dinner today.'[6] When the mutton duly arrived at Sir Harry's table, the slice was indeed cut, and his youthful dairymaid became Lady Fetherstonhaugh. It was a pretty tale, and one that would have appealed to George IV, yet somehow it also epitomised the narrow self-seeking, self-centred life of upper-class Sussex in what was otherwise a period of great instability and upheaval.

Elsewhere in Sussex, coastal towns struggled to emulate Brighton's success at becoming fashionable resorts – a trend alighted upon by Jane Austen in her satirical portrayal of fictional 'Sanditon', where she lampooned an aspiring 'village [that] contained little more than cottages, but the spirit of the day had been caught'.[7] One such village was Bognor, briefly renamed Hothampton after the London speculator, Sir Richard Hotman, who in the 1780s invested and lost a fortune there, to little visible or enduring effect. Hastings fared better, attracting growing numbers of visitors, but the only real success outside Brighton in this period was the new town of St Leonards-on-Sea. Offering a yet more exclusive destination than Brighton (there was none of the slums that had begun to blight George's *beau monde*), St Leonards attracted those looking for an unsullied life-style of uninterrupted leisure.

Militia Mutinies

That Britain was at war with Revolutionary and then Napoleonic France for much of the period from 1789 until 1815, may have impinged little on this pleasure-seeking minority. But there were those among the Sussex gentry who saw as it as their traditional duty to serve in the Militia. They were led from the 1780s until early in the following century by the Duke of Richmond, at Goodwood, with the able assistance of Lord Pelham and other officers drawn from leading county families. There was little visible popular support in Sussex for the French Revolution when it erupted in 1789. Indeed, yet again in the front line, Sussex rallied to prevent a French invasion. Some 15,000 local men had been called up into the Militia by 1805 (and many others claimed exemption), and a measure of the supposed vulnerability of the county was the construction in 1804 of the Royal Military Canal from Rye to Shorncliffe in Kent and the forty-seven defensive Martello Towers built at 600-yard intervals along the Pevensey Levels and at points eastwards. The canal was intended as a moat, cutting off the marshland near Rye, rather than as a military

Goodwood House, near Westhampnett, was built *c.*1600 and acquired by Charles Lennox, 1st Duke of Richmond, in 1697. It has remained ever since as the seat of the Richmond family, a leading Sussex dynasty. In modern times the estate has diversified its interests, including a golf course, motorsport events (the 'Goodwood Circuit'), and horse racing and cycling.
IAN STANNARD

transport system, while cannon mounted on the towers were designed to provide enfilading crossfire to impede the progress of any invading army.

Although many sought to avoid military service altogether, the Militia was seen as an attractive alternative to the regular army. The latter fought set-piece battles of terrifying proportions and appalling casualties, while postings to the disease-ridden Caribbean were seen as virtual death-warrants. The Militia, by contrast, was expressly excluded from overseas service, offering the much safer prospect of duty at home, and promising a more or less full stomach to those whose diet was often indifferent and infrequent. Not surprisingly, the Militia was deployed mainly along the southern and eastern coasts of England, where a French invasion might be expected. Troops mobilised from elsewhere in the kingdom supplemented locally raised militiamen, and their concentration in maritime counties such as Sussex caused acute accommodation problems. In 1795, for example, the mayor of Hastings explained that he had been unable to find sufficient billets, leading to 'great complaint among the troops', private houses being 'crowded with soldiers' and 'every Alehouse housing

Martello Towers were constructed as coastal defence fortifications throughout the British Isles and across the Empire, but they are especially redolent of the eastern fringe of Sussex, where they were erected between 1804 and 1808 in response to the threat of French invasion. A number survive to this day, striking and sometimes forlorn monuments along the coastline, and one, the Wish Tower near Eastbourne, is now open to the public. This example is at Seaford.
ALISON AVERY, WWW.BEAUTIFULENGLANDPHOTOS.UK

above twenty men billeted upon it'.[8] Indeed, when the Surrey Militia arrived in Rye and Winchelsea in 1793, the innkeepers went on strike, refusing to provide rooms for the troops, and when barracks were hastily constructed they became breeding grounds for disease, such as the outbreak of typhoid fever at Battle in 1809. To these difficulties were added the drunkenness, brawling and wenching that routinely attended the arrival of the Militia, causing anxiety among the local populace.

However, during 1795 the Militia found itself making common cause with the locals. The harvest of 1794 had been poor, leading to price rises, and in the unusually harsh winter of 1794–95 there was real hardship. The wholesale price of a quarter of wheat at Chichester had risen from 52 shillings in December 1794 to 64 shillings by the following April. The Poor Law protected the impoverished from the worst consequences of want, but the militiamen were more exposed. Their rations of bread and meat were reduced as prices rose; as the duke of Richmond observed, while the country folk were relieved by their parishes, the Militia received no such support. And as discontent grew in the countryside, the Militia was inclined to throw in its lot with the common people, resisting orders to quell disturbances and instead turning to lawlessness itself. Near Eastbourne in March 1795, for example, privates of the Cheshire Militia caught poaching threatened the local landowner with violence, 'advising him ... to prepare his coffin, as he would soon have occasion for it'.[9] In the following month, soldiers from the Herefordshire Militia demonstrated in support of 'fair prices' at Arundel, while others joined a crowd several thousand strong in Chichester calling for price reduction. Two militiamen and a civilian were arrested but promptly released when the mob became violent. As one observer wrote, 'such riot could not be quelled otherwise than by assurances given to the Rioters of their being, on the Morrow, supplied with Meat and Bread at a reduced price'.[10] The redoubtable duke of Richmond took action, instructing the officers of the Herefordshire Militia to remove their troops from their billets and to organise a field day out of town, where the miscreant soldiers would be made 'sensible of the impropriety of their Conduct'.[11]

Even where the militiamen were routinely separated from townsfolk, as in the barracks at Blatchington, near Seaford, there was still scope for trouble. The men of the Oxfordshire Militia found that the hurriedly constructed barracks were incomplete – there were no beds, and the roof leaked. Fever was rife, and rations meagre and poor. Their commanding officer, to his credit, saw that his men were not happy, and on investigation found their meat 'very thin and indifferent and one piece not sweet'.[12] In disgust, he returned the foul meat to the supplier in Seaford. But the butcher protested that this was the best meat that could be obtained for the modest 4½*d.* per pound allocated by the Militia. The colonel arranged for better quality meat to be supplied at 5*d.* per pound by another Seaford butcher, but explained to his men that the extra expense would be deducted from their pay. Not all were happy with this arrangement, and some 150 to 200 malcontents set off to teach the

By the Edwardian era, when this photograph was taken, Seaford had acquired a more genteel reputation as a welcoming seaside town, its fortunes having been revived by the coming of the railway. Previously, it had been a centre for 'wrecking' – the looting of ships that had foundered along the local coast – its inhabitants thus acquiring the unflattering nicknames 'cormorant' and 'shag'. Likewise, Seaford was a focus for the Militia Mutinies of the late eighteenth century, as well as being notorious for smuggling.

butchers of Seaford a lesson. They were halted by their officers, but overnight plotted to march on Seaford the next morning. By 7.30 a.m. no fewer than 400 militiamen, with bayonets fixed, entered the town, where they were met by a local justice of the peace, Thomas Harben, who undertook to buy them ten loads of wheat if they would refrain from violence. The militiamen agreed but nonetheless sought out the butchers, forcing them to sell their meat for 4*d.* per pound and to reduce the prices of cheese, butter and other provisions. Flushed with their success, the troops adjourned to the local inns, again demanding price reductions. But their intervention was not over yet, as they had heard that a consignment of flour was about to be despatched by sea from Newhaven harbour.

Insisting that locally produced flour should be preserved for local consumption, the militiamen requisitioned horses and carts from farmers roundabout and marched on Newhaven. They arrived at the flour-mill, hoping to find the owner so that he 'should be stuck … full of bayonets', but luckily for him he was absent.[13] However, his assistants were forced to load the carts with flour, while some of the soldiers boarded the sloop *Lucy* in the adjoining creek, discovering that she was full of flour, which they promptly landed. The Militia was now in full control of Newhaven, and word was sent via the county town of Lewes to the War Office for military assistance. The Royal Horse Artillery was swiftly despatched and there was a stand-off with the Oxfordshire Militia, the latter drawn up with bayonets fixed, as representatives of the two sides parleyed. Eventually, the Militia agreed to return to barracks, but a small hardcore of mutineers refused, intent on guarding their newly won flour overnight. That evening they joined local civilians in carousing and looting, which continued until early the following morning, Saturday 18 April, when the Artillery returned, reinforced now by the Lancashire Fencibles from Brighton. A pitched battle erupted in the streets of Newhaven and the surrounding countryside, with several militiamen seriously wounded. Some 200 militiamen were arrested and marched back to Blatchington barracks, while nineteen ringleaders were sent to Lewes gaol.

There were rumours abroad that the militiamen had been encouraged by radicals and democrats among the people, and it was decided that such subversion – in the military and among civilians – would not be tolerated. While the assiduous duke of Richmond was successful in persuading the government to address the worst of the militiamen's grievances, increasing the rations of bread and meat, he was also clear that the mutineers should be made an example of. Some were tried by courts martial, with three men sentenced to be shot, and six to receive between 500 and 1,500 lashes. One of those earmarked for execution was later pardoned on condition that he served as a soldier in New South Wales, while the number of lashes for those to be flogged was reduced. Others were tried at the county assizes, with two militiamen, Sykes and Sanson, sentenced to death, and a third later condemned at the Summer assizes. The executions were scheduled for 13 June 1795, at Brighton camp and at Horsham gaol. Popular sympathy clearly lay with the militiamen, and at Brighton local people managed to smuggle food and drink to the condemned men. The government had decreed that the executions and floggings should be a public spectacle, with all troops in the vicinity – regular as well as Militia – ordered to take part. On the appointed day, the troops paraded, infantry lining both sides of the arena, and artillery drawn up at their rear, cannon pointing at the men under sentence. After the floggings were completed, it was time for the executions. According to one eye-witness account:

> The men capitally convicted were then marched up between the two lines of the army accompanied by a clergyman, and escorted by pickets, from the different regiments of horse and foot; at the upper end of the line, after a short time spent with the clergyman, they were shot by a party of the Oxfordshire Militia who had been very active in the ... riots, but had been pardoned ... the awful ceremony was concluded, by the marching of all the regiments round the bodies ... laid upon the ground.[14]

The Brighton ceremony completed, it was Horsham's turn. Sansom's wife had travelled down from Oxfordshire to be with her husband in his final moments, and there were emotional scenes as the two embraced for the last time. Unfortunately, the two professional hangmen hired to undertake the grisly work did a 'bungling job' in despatching poor Sansom, according to the local press. Local gentlemen, moved by the horrific spectacle, it was reported, organised a subscription to cover Mrs Sansom's expenses and 'to comfort her under her distress'.[15]

Smuggling

Behind the veneer of sumptuous good living, epitomised by George, Prince of Wales, and his new Pavilion, the Militia mutinies of 1795 had revealed an altogether different Sussex. Rural deprivation and hunger had brought crowds onto the streets, demanding price reductions, and the Militia joined the protests, prompting alarming scenes of near anarchy, culminating in the violence of Seaford and Newhaven. The government, and its military representative in Sussex, the duke of Richmond, had been swift and ruthless in their reaction, and an air of repression and vengeance now hung over the county. Yet, in one sense, nothing here was new. As Cal Winslow has observed, in eighteenth-century Sussex 'crimes of protest, riots and forms of collective or popular action' were commonplace.[16] Poaching, sheep-stealing and other thefts were rife, and for many ordinary people these were 'social crimes' against an unjust establishment – 'crimes' in that they were technically against the law of the land but 'social' in that they were generally approved of by those (not least the perpetrators) who saw them as an expression of natural law or a legitimate means of addressing grievances and asserting freedoms. Most notable of these 'social crimes' in Sussex was smuggling.

For Rudyard Kipling, writing at the turn of the twentieth century, there was a certain romance in Sussex smuggling, although even he caught the sense of widespread complicity, and with it an underlying hint of malice:

> If you wake at midnight, and hear a horse's feet,
> Don't go drawing back the blind, or looking in the street.
> Them that asks no questions isn't told a lie –
> Watch the wall, my darling, while the Gentlemen go by!
>
> Five and twenty ponies
> Trotting through the dark –
> Brandy for the Parson,
> 'Baccy for the Clerk;
> Laces for a lady, letters for a spy,
> And watch the wall, my darling, while the Gentlemen go by!
>
> If you meet King George's men, dressed in blue and red,
> You be careful what you say, and mindful what is said.
> If they call you 'pretty maid', and chuck you 'neath the chin,
> Don't you tell where no one is, nor yet where no one's been![17]

In fact, there was nothing at all romantic about this brutal and bloodthirsty business, Kipling's 'Gentlemen' being ruthless and violent gang bosses and their willing acolytes. War with France in the early eighteenth century had disrupted trading relations with France, but the peace of 1712 encouraged new cross-Channel contacts, including smuggling. In 1715, for example, a ship landed a quantity of brandy at Cooden Beach, then sailing into Cuckmere Haven, near Seaford, to load an illicit cargo of wool, where it was intercepted. Two years later, in another incident, a preventive officer by the name of Reeves was killed by smugglers outside Eastbourne, the authorities pointing their accusing finger at the notorious Mayfield gang. Equally infamous was the gang at Groombridge (situated near the gracious spa town of Tunbridge Wells) on the route from the coast to London, where smuggled items were disposed of. During the 1730s the Groombridge gang was led by John Bowra and Robert Moreton, who received smuggled goods on the beaches near Pevensey and arranged for their transference to the metropolis. Sometimes working with the

The Cuckmere meanders its way down to Cuckmere Haven, near Seaford, once the haunt of smugglers and wreckers. DAVID MOYES PHOTOGRAPHY

Hawkhurst gang, across the border in Kent, or the so-called 'Hooe Company' at Hooe, near Pevensey, Bowra and Moreton were reckoned to have sold 3,000 pounds of tea per week during the winter of 1735–36. In the following March they had a narrow escape when confronted by preventive men. Two smugglers were killed in an exchange of fire, and some of the contraband was lost. Yet, such was the web of clandestine

The Real Cause of the present HIGH-PRICE of PROVISIONS.
or, a View on the Sea Coast of England, with French Agents smuggling away Supplies for France.

A contemporary cartoon depicting smugglers on the Sussex coast negotiating with French agents who have crossed the Channel. Intriguingly, the sketch is entitled 'The Real Cause of the present High-Price of Provisions', suggesting that smuggling was a two-way process, in this case flour and livestock being smuggled from England to France.

activity, and the sheer range of opportunity that presented itself, that the Groombridge gang and its associates were hardly inconvenienced. Bowra himself was arrested for smuggling tea in 1737, although it is not clear what happened to him thereafter, but Moreton continued to head the Groombridge gang until he was apprehended over a decade later in the purges of 1749.[18]

At Hastings there was another local gang, the Hastings 'Outlaws' or 'Transports', who built and crewed their own smuggling vessels, bringing contraband across the Channel and then arranging for its removal to London. Farther west, Seaford had enjoyed a reputation as a smuggling centre since the late seventeenth century, and by the 1720s the Mayfield gang was active in the area. A decade later and the Rottingdean smugglers were in the ascendancy, on occasion clashing violently with preventive officers at Seaford and Newhaven, and all along the coast towards Shoreham and beyond smuggling was by now a routine way of life. At Chichester, it was reported, one ship-owner in the 1720s had taken his vessel to and from France once a week for all of five years, and every night a wagon train brimming with contraband had made its way inland from Selsey Bill. One local farmer was reputed to have made over £10,000 in half a dozen years for his part in the operation.[19]

By 1740 the situation was clearly out of hand. Charles Fleet, author of *Glimpses of Our Sussex Ancestors*, published in Lewis in 1878, maintained that between 1740 and 1750 there was 'a guerrilla war between the smugglers of Sussex and Kent and the officers of the government'. It was a war, he said, of 'organized resistance to the government, in which towns were besieged, battles fought, Customs Houses burnt down, and the greatest atrocities committed'.[20] Wool, he said, had always been smuggled out of Sussex, but now these traditional smugglers (or 'owlers') had been joined by those engaged in the illicit import of tea and other contraband, and it was these desperate gangs that were responsible for the new levels of lawlessness and violence. Daniel Defoe, an eyewitness, had seen soldiers on the Sussex coast 'on horseback, riding always about as if they were huntsmen berating up their game', and Horace Walpole had encountered rival armed camps of smugglers and preventive men on a night journey from Tunbridge Wells to Battle: 'as we were neutral powers,' he wrote, 'we passed safely through both armies.'[21]

Even more graphic was the testimony of one 'Gentleman of Chichester' who in 1749 described the conditions that had only recently obtained in the county. 'The smugglers had reigned a long time uncontrolled,' he said, 'the Officers of the Customs were too few to encounter them; they rode in troops to fetch their goods, and carried them off in triumph in daylight.' Indeed, he added, so audacious had the smugglers grown, 'that they were not afraid of the regular troops that were sent into the country to keep them in awe'. Moreover, if 'any of them happened to be taken, and the proof ever so clear against him, no magistrate in the country durst commit him to gaol', for if he did so 'he was sure to have his house or barns set on fire, or some other mischief done to him, if he was happy to escape with his life'.[22] Yet, despite these accounts, the best evidence, as Cal Winslow has noted, lies in the records of the trials of scores of smugglers at East Grinstead, Lewes and the Old Bailey, the result of several especially gruesome murders and the subsequent efforts by the authorities – led by the duke of Richmond (father of the Militia leader above) – to stamp out smuggling once and for all. As Winslow added, in pursuit of this aim the authorities 'unleashed nothing less than a reign of terror on the smuggling communities of the south coast'.

In 1740 a Customs officer, Thomas Carswell, was shot dead during a confrontation with smugglers. A large quantity of tea had been landed on the shore between Hastings and Bulverhythe, and was transported by thirteen or fourteen horses to a barn near Hurst Green. However, their movement had been detected by soldiers and preventive men, who discovered the tea and made off with it towards Hastings. Obtaining firearms from Hawkhurst, the smugglers began their pursuit, having first, in the words of one participant, 'stript themselves to their shirts and drank brandy, wishing damnation might take him that returned before they had retaken the tea'.[23] As they caught up with the troops, Carswell gave the order for the dragoons to fire on the smugglers, and in the exchange that followed he was mortally wounded. Several horses were also hit, and in the mayhem the smugglers recovered the tea and escaped unscathed. A reward was offered for the apprehension of Carswell's killers, but there was no conviction until ten years later, when the duke of Richmond intervened. Likewise, when three dragoons were murdered by smugglers near Arundel in early 1743, there were no arrests; nor was there when another soldier was badly wounded a year later. In November 1744 a preventive officer at Bexhill had his house invaded by 'a large gang of smugglers, at least sixty in number … armed with blunderbusses, carbines, and other offensive weapons … [who] destroyed his household goods and furniture and insulted his wife and family in a violent manner'.[24] The next morning three large cutters disgorged their illicit cargo at Pevensey Bay, which was then taken inland by some 500 or 600 horses. Such was the scale of smuggling operations, and the lengths taken to intimidate the local population and incapacitate the preventive service. In August 1747 the *Gentleman's Magazine* reported that about '24 smugglers well-armed and laden with prohibited goods rode through Rye, Sussex, and stopping at the Red Lion to refresh, fired several times to intimidate the inhabitants'. Ominously, the report added that the smugglers, 'observing one, James Marshall, a young man too curious of their behaviour, carried him off, and he has not been heard of since'.[25]

In response to such outrages, the government introduced a range of draconian anti-smuggling laws, while also reducing the duty on imported tea in the hope of making smuggling less attractive. But the event which, as Winslow remarked, 'finally fixed the attention of the entire nation on Sussex', was the murder in February 1748 of William Galley, a revenue officer, and Daniel Chater, an informer.[26] Following an audacious operation by Sussex smugglers on the Hampshire–Dorset border, William Galley was accompanying Daniel Chater to Stanstead, near Chichester, where the latter was to be examined by Major Battine, the Surveyor of Customs for Sussex. However, while *en route* Galley and Chater were intercepted by smugglers who took them both prisoner and decided that the only way to secure their silence was by killing them. Both men were tied to horses, and Galley was forced to ride with his head under the horse's belly, 'wounded, bruised and hurt', with one of the smugglers 'all the time squeezing his private parts'. Eventually, he was taken down from the horse. The smugglers 'cut off his nose and privities' and, breaking as many of his bones as they could, buried his expiring body in a shallow grave near Rake, in Sussex.[27] Chater was dealt with in similar fashion, and was thrown down a well at Harting, where he died. When the bodies of both men were recovered in the autumn of 1748, the duke of Richmond decided it was time to act, initiating a campaign against the smugglers that was to last until his death almost three years later.

Richmond organised a special commission which was empowered to try suspects directly, and diligently collected evidence throughout Sussex and beyond. Initially, seven smugglers were indicted at Chichester. They appeared before the Special Commission on 16 January 1749 in a trial that lasted three days, resulting in guilty verdicts. The men were sentenced to be hanged in chains, one of them, petrified at the prospect, dying in prison before the executions could be carried out. On Thursday 19 January the remaining six were marched by a party of soldiers to a place of execution, known as the Broyle, just outside Chichester. One of them, John Hammond, hitherto known as a hard man, broke down before the gallows, pleading for his life for the sake of his 'poor wife and children'.[28] Shortly after, his dead body, together with that of his comrade, John Cobby, was taken to Selsey Bill where it was hung up, visible for miles, to act as a gruesome warning for all thereabouts. Another body was hung in chains at Rake, and one at Rook's Hill near Chichester. There were further trials. In March 1749 another group of smugglers was indicted at East Grinstead, including Henry Sheerman, accused of murdering William Galley, and all were sentenced to death, with the exception of one, Richard Savage, who received seven years' transportation. A trial at Rochester, in Kent, resulted in further executions, as did indictments at the Old Bailey. At the summer assizes in Lewes in 1749, eight more smugglers were found guilty of murder and other offences, and at East

Grinstead in the following year there was yet another conviction. Before his own death in 1750, the duke of Richmond reflected with great satisfaction upon his good work. Thirty-five smugglers had gone to the gallows; a further ten convicted men had died in gaol.

The establishment heaved a collective sigh of relief – its authority had been restored in the countryside and along the coast, or so it was imagined, while the government would no longer be defrauded on the same scale as hitherto. However, there were many who had resented the extreme tactics employed in dealing with the smugglers, including what appeared to be random arrests, perfunctory trials, and widespread intimidation of local communities. Moreover, there were those whose sympathies were with the smugglers, in their open opposition to government authority and in their insistence upon 'fair trade' in the face of government attempts to impose duties on imported goods. The campaign against smuggling had broken the power of the big Sussex gangs, but it had not stamped out the practice altogether. Sometimes smugglers turned to piracy, as in 1758 when Hastings men boarded a Danish ship and relieved it of part of its cargo, or in 1768 when another Hastings gang known as Ruxley's Crew apprehended a Dutch vessel off Beachy Head, killing the captain. The perpetrators were swiftly captured (and several executed), and two hundred Irish dragoons were billeted on the town, to its great terror. On another occasion in 1790, preventive men were held captive when they tired to interfere with the landing of contraband on the strand under Beachy Head. Increased military activity along the coast during the Revolutionary and Napoleonic wars inhibited the activity of the smugglers – several vessels were intercepted in 1805 and 1806 – and the peace of 1815 brought new difficulties. As Hastings and the new town of St Leonards tried to emulate fashionable Brighton, there was the curious prospect of smugglers and visitors living in close proximity: indeed, at Eastbourne, the son of the proprietress of the town's new bathing machines was shortly convicted for smuggling.[29]

Nonetheless, smuggling continued into the 1820s and beyond. Men from Hooe and Herstmonceux routinely landed contraband along Pevensey Bay (one of their boats, the *Ann* of Pevensey, was confiscated in 1826), and in January 1828 there was a major confrontation at Bulverhythe. In the early hours of 3 January, upwards of twenty smugglers, armed with 'bats', ran an illicit cargo ashore. A party of preventive men attempted to intervene but was outnumbered. Reinforcements arrived but were likewise beaten off by the smugglers, leaving one of the preventive men dead. Subsequently, ten men were sentenced to death but were later transported. Again, popular sympathy was often with the smugglers. When, in 1833, George Pett, commander of a preventive boat operating near Eastbourne, was killed in a clash with smugglers, none came forward to claim the £1,000 offered as a reward for information leading to the arrest of his murderers.[30] In the following year, 1834, it was claimed that rural Sussex, despite everything that had been done in the previous half century and more, remained irretrievably beyond the law: 'Labourers have acquired the habit of acting in large gangs by night and of systematic resistance to authority. High living is become essential to them, and they cannot reconcile themselves to the moderate pay of lawful industry.'[31]

Radicals

The worthy parliamentarians who took this dim view of the undeserving poor and their illegitimate desire for 'high living', conveniently ignored the fact that agricultural Sussex had been in decline since the eighteenth century. The iron industry had all but disappeared by the 1750s, to be replaced in only one or two places by the gunpowder mills that survived until the 1870s. Sussex had not participated in the mass switch to arable farming that characterised (and made wealthy) East Anglia and the Midlands, although hop-growing in the eastern Weald – where oasthouses became a defining feature of the local landscape – had increased markedly by the turn of the nineteenth century. Stock and sheep-breeding also advanced. John Ellman of Glynde, born in 1753, had developed a technique of selective breeding which produced the hardy but productive Southdown sheep, ensuring that the Sussex downland would continue to be given over to grazing, rather than, as elsewhere, being put under the plough. By 1801 there were no fewer than 350,000 sheep in Sussex. But observers of Sussex agriculture generally condemned it for its backwardness and inefficiency. When, in 1815, the French wars came to an end, there was a slump in demand for agricultural produce, and the hardship was made worse by a series of disastrous harvests. John Ellman himself, observing the plight of the Sussex countryfolk, especially the blacksmiths, wheelwrights and other tradesmen who depended for their livelihoods upon a buoyant agricultural economy, worried that 'nothing can be done to save many from absolute ruin'.[32]

Paradoxically, the years of agricultural decline had witnessed an increase in population in Sussex (only partly explained by the rise of Brighton), reaching 160,000 by 1801 and an astonishing 260,000 by 1831. This expansion put intolerable pressure on the existing system of parochial poor relief, which dated back to the early seventeenth century and was dependent upon occasional rates levied on landowners. But, in Sussex as elsewhere, the system had begun to creak badly by the 1790s, and in 1801 the county had the highest poor law rates anywhere in England, with some 37,000 in regular receipt of relief. Agricultural wages were low (around £28 per year in the late 1790s), hardly enough to keep a growing family above the breadline. Supplements from the poor rates were handed out to married men with children, who in return were made available to be hired out for road working and similar projects. The system kept the wolf from the door, perhaps, but it made for a sullen and dependent agricultural working class, while the land-owning ratepayers were frustrated by the ever-increasing demands on their pockets. Sometimes these resentments boiled over into violent confrontation, as at Bexhill in 1821 when local labourers, refused supplements by the Battle magistrates, went on the rampage to express their disappointment. Skilled tradesmen, thrown out of employment by economic conditions, considered it degrading to be put to work on roads alongside common labourers. At Midhurst in 1818, for example, a party of brickmakers, sawyers, joiners, papermakers, fishermen, and a 'hog-butcher', were given just such a task, much to their annoyance. Some decided that emigration to the colonies was the only solution, those game enough to take the plunge often assisted by eager landowners happy to see the back of them.

Although few in Sussex had openly claimed common cause with the French Revolution, radicalism had by now taken root in Sussex, giving a new political dimension to the underlying hostility to authority. One early adherent was Thomas Paine, later famous as author of *The Rights of Man* (published in 1791) and supporter of American independence, who had arrived in Lewes in 1768 and spent six years in the town. Ironically, Paine had found government employment as an excise officer, an occupation unlikely to recommend him to fellow radicals, or to those townspeople complicit in smuggling activities. As Samuel Edwards, Paine's biographer, has observed: 'Lewes had made life thoroughly uncomfortable for his predecessors, and it seemed likely that Paine would not last long or, if he persisted, would be incapacitated by an accident in the night.' Indeed, at first 'Paine was unpopular with his fellow citizens', yet he soon 'became acclimated to the life of Lewes'. There is, according to Edwards, no proof that Paine accepted bribes, 'although the excise service was badly crippled by corruption at the time'. He did, however, become involved in the tobacco trade on the side, and it 'may be that he did not take his official duties too seriously'. He also spent increasing amounts of time in the White Hart inn, where he joined a tradesmen's debating society called the Evening Club whose members 'sometimes interrupted their drinking to discuss politics and philosophy'. It was there that Paine 'acquired a reputation as a man who refused to accept defeat in a debate', becoming a frequent recipient of the Headstrong Book, presented to the most obdurate speaker at each gathering. His reputation as advocate recommended him to his fellow Sussex excise officers, who persuaded him to compose and distribute to both Houses of Parliament a pamphlet entitled *The Case of the Officers of Excise*, which was designed to illustrate the disabilities under which they laboured and to call for improvements to their lot. Paine's reward was dismissal from his employment, and shortly he left for America.[33]

It is difficult to decide the extent to which Tom Paine (as he was known) influenced radical opinion in Sussex – when he became a hate figure in the 1790s, the inchoate mob, encouraged by the establishment, happily burned him in effigy. However, there is evidence of radical continuity from the 1790s through to the 1830s and beyond – in Lewes, but also in Chichester, Horsham, Brighton and smaller rural communities across the county. Issues of agricultural decline were exacerbated and compounded by agitation surrounding the Reform Bill of 1832, the 'Captain Swing' outrages of 1830, and the Poor Law Amendment Act of 1834, together with attempts at rural trade unionism, discontent surrounding the payments of tithes, and the growth of Chartism. A product of Sussex rural radicalism, Richard Cobden, a farmer's son, was born near Midhurst, and became an ardent free-trader and leader of the Anti-Corn Law League, securing the Corn Law's eventual repeal in 1846. William Cobbett, a visiting radical, addressed crowded meetings during his famous 'rural rides' across Sussex during 1825, and although he later wrote that, 'I have not seen wretchedness in Sussex; nothing to be at all compared to that which I have seen in other parts', he was nonetheless eyed as a dangerous subversive by landowners in the county.[34] He was imagined, for example, to have incited labourers at Battle to arson and riot, and was supposed by his rhetoric to have 'much excited the feelings of the paupers'.[35]

Before 1832, elections to parliament – where Sussex had twenty-four MPs in the House of Commons – were dominated by the aristocracy, who nominated their own representatives. There were rarely contested elections (these were too expensive), and the minor port of Seaford and the decaying town of Bramber were honoured with their own seats in parliament, such was the rot inherent in the system. There was a brief demand for reform in 1779 and in early 1780, when a county meeting in Lewes went so far as to call for universal male suffrage and annual parliaments. The movement came to little but radical agitation continued. At Rye, for instance, the return of an unpopular Tory MP in 1830 sparked violent protests, while the extended national debate which preceded the Reform Act had the effect of politicising the lower classes. The Act itself abolished some of the worst excesses of the previous regime – including the disenfranchisement of the boroughs of Bramber, Midhurst and Seaford – but universal suffrage remained a distant dream.

Captain Swing

By now, however, popular discontent had already turned to violence. In the autumn of 1830 came the first of the 'Captain Swing' protests which would shortly sweep across much of southern England. Underemployed, pauperised and often dependent on parish relief, the rural populace vented its rage on the agricultural infrastructure, destroying threshing machines and setting fire to hayricks, as well as threatening landowners and poor-law overseers. The first outrage was at Canterbury in Kent on 28 August, and by October machine-breaking and arson had spread across the border into the Sussex Weald. A barn was set on fire at Hartfield overnight on 17 October, and on 3 November there was a blaze in the George Inn at Battle, where the local overseer of the parish poor was domiciled. To demands for higher wages were added calls for reductions in rents and tithes (presumably to allow farmers to pay those increased wages) and, following further arson attacks at Battle and Icklesham, a large meeting of labourers was held at the village of Brede. As well as reaffirming their demand for higher remuneration, to which the farmers apparently agreed, the labourers determined to seize Thomas Abel, the overseer, and cart him to the parish boundary, where he was unceremoniously dumped on the other side. Three hundred men, led by smugglers, it was said, with ribbons in their hats, accompanied Abel on his undignified journey. The spectacle was evidently adjudged a huge success, for the expulsion or threatened expulsion of overseers was repeated in following days at Burwash, Ticehurst, Fairlight, Warbleton and Brightling, Mayfield, Heathfield, Ninfield, and Battle.[36]

At Robertsbridge on 8 November 1830 there was arson and rioting, followed by mass meetings across some twenty-four East Sussex parishes: Bodiam, Frant, Hurstfield, Newenden, Northiam, Salehurst, Herstmonceux, Ringmer, Buxted, Crowborough, Withyam, and elsewhere, with Ashdown Forest fast emerging as a centre of the insurrection. Increasingly, the labourers were joined by artisans – a butcher and a baker at Wakehurst, for example, a wheelwright and a carpenter in Rotherfield – including the townsfolk of radical Lewes who demonstrated on 15 November. On the same day, 'large mobs' (as it was reported) assembled in Mayfield and Rotherfield parishes for the purpose of attacking an experimental farm in the vicinity owned by one Mr Howis, and they succeeded in destroying his threshing machines. By now the 'Captain Swing' protests were moving into more western parts of Sussex. On 13 November threatening letters were received by farmers and overseers in the neighbourhood of Horsham, and there were outbreaks of violence at Petworth workhouse. Shortly after there were blazes at Angmering, Ashington and Watersfield, while at Pulborough the locals announced that 'we know what they have done in Kent' and promised to do the same. They meant what they said. It was soon reported from Chichester that bands of labourers had destroyed all the threshing machines at Arundel, Bersted, Bognor and Yapton, and had forced wage rises from 10*s.* to 14*s.* a week. At Chichester itself, up to 1,000 men gathered to parley with local magistrates and farmers, and there were similar meetings at Pagham and Goodwood. Horsham, with its reputation as a centre for radicalism, played host to yet another mass assembly of rural workers. Beyond Chichester, threshing machines were destroyed at Bosham, Emsworth, Fishbourne, Funtington, and Westbourne, as they were farther north at Chithurst and Rogate. From there, 'Captain Swing' passed swiftly into Hampshire, although this was by no means the end of the Sussex disturbances. In all, there were 103 separate incidents in Sussex, two-thirds of them in the eastern half of the county.[37]

Inevitably, once the authorities had gathered their wits, repression followed. At the Assizes in Lewes, fifty-two men and women were tried for their parts in the disturbances. One was executed, seven transported to Australia, sixteen gaoled, and eighteen acquitted. In the western areas of Sussex, the duke of Richmond implemented what became known as the 'Sussex Plan', which was soon copied in other counties that had experienced 'Swing' disturbances. Richmond recruited a special constabulary, drawn from shopkeepers, yeomen and 'respectable' labourers, and marshalled them into sections under local commanders, forming mobile units which could be deployed swiftly to occupy villages at the first sign of trouble. It proved highly successful in deterring further disturbances, or for nipping them in the bud. The government, meanwhile, considering that the old poor law had failed irretrievably, passed the Poor Law Amendment Act of 1834. Parishes were to be grouped into unions, and there was to be an end to outdoor relief, all work now to be done within the workhouse itself. The implementation of the Act in 1834–36 represented a major upheaval for the poor, especially in Sussex and other southern counties where rural poverty remained a significant problem.

Poor Law Amendment Act and Chartism

There was considerable resistance to the new measures, especially in the east of Sussex. In May 1835 the newly appointed relieving officer for the new Chailey Union, a man named Webb, was accosted by thirty labourers at Ringmer, who demanded relief in cash rather than food vouchers. He readily complied, but this did not prevent him being carted, 'Swing' fashion, across the parish boundary, a humiliation also visited upon the Battle relieving officer when he visited Brede. There were similar demonstrations at Ewhurst, Mountfield, Sedlescombe and Willingdon, as the spectre of 'Captain Swing' began again to stalk the land. There were arson outbreaks at Seaford, and at Eastbourne disturbances led to the temporary postponement of the separation of families in the workhouse. At Maresfield, several men committed to the workhouse turned up, consumed their dinners, and then promptly left again. At Ardingly workhouse, one inmate, Henry Stapeley, regularly absented himself to visit his pregnant wife at Arlington workhouse, despite the frequent strictures of the local magistrates and a spell in Lewes gaol. At other places, there was resistance to transfer to workhouses beyond the parish. At Steyning, where troops were called in to restore order, the poor objected that they had never been to Henfield, where now they were to be removed. One response was for the despairing labourers to try to form rural trade unions, such as the 'Agricultural Labourers' Conjunction Friendly Society' which appeared in East Sussex in 1835 and was especially active around Battle, Eastbourne and Rye. But the movement disintegrated when farmers threatened to lock out members, and rural malcontents resorted to more individualist forms of protest: on the Downs, for instance, crowbars were forced through the heads of sheep; at Arundel cattle were driven into fields of growing corn; and at Buxted horses' tongues were cut out. Cows were maimed, ducks poisoned, chickens decapitated.[38]

Opposition to the Poor Law Amendment Act was also articulated in more considered ways. Charles Brooker, for example, a shopkeeper and dissenting lay preacher at Alfriston, objected to the separation of husband and wife in the workhouse, insisting that it was 'unscriptural and un-christian'.[39] A committee was formed at Cowfold to oppose the Act, monitoring its implementation and gathering evidence, and Chichester, Horsham, Lewes and Rye repeatedly petitioned against the Act during 1835–37, keeping it alive as a political issue and acting as a continuing stimulus to radicalism in the county. This helped to explain the influence of Chartism in Sussex, not only in Brighton, where in 1838 the radical *Brighton Patriot* newspaper attached itself to the Chartist cause – universal male suffrage, no property qualification for the vote, all votes to count equally, annual parliaments, paid MPs, the secret ballot – but in towns such as Lewes and in the countryside. But Brighton remained the focal point of Sussex Chartism, not least because in Parliament it continued to be a three-way marginal, the Whigs, Tories and Radicals having held the seat in turn during the 1830s. It was an unpredictability that the Chartists exploited, maintaining high visibility in the town's affairs. Their confidence boosted by this apparent success, they decided to contest the seat themselves. The Brighton Chartists selected Charles Brooker, the Alfriston Congregationalist, as their candidate, but in the 1841 general election he received a mere nineteen votes. Some Chartists were accused of wrecking his chances by voting for the Radical candidate instead, but when Brooker stood again in 1842 his support declined to a derisory sixteen votes. To such tactical reversals was added the tendency of landowners in Sussex to treat rural Chartists as potential 'Swing' incendiarists and saboteurs, and to deal with them accordingly. Such victimisation retarded Chartist activity beyond the towns, driving it underground or thwarting it altogether. To this was added the national calamity of April 1848 (the 'Year of Revolution' which had toppled

Today Burwash seems the epitome of the typical Sussex village, all tea-rooms and hanging terracotta tiles. Made famous by Rudyard Kipling's residency at nearby Batemans, Burwash was before that notorious as a centre of lawlessness and 'social crime', an exemplar of the rural unrest that characterised Sussex for much of the eighteenth and nineteenth centuries.
WWW.CASUALWALKERS2.WORDPRESS.COM

governments across Continental Europe) when the Chartists were seen to have blinked first in their mass confrontation with the government in London, and when their ostensibly impressive petition demanding reform was found to contain pages of signatures in the same handwriting, including numerous 'Mr Punches' and 'Queen Victorias'. The failure of the London rally was not the end of Chartism, but much of its credibility had been dented, in Sussex as elsewhere.[40]

Yet, despite the fading of organised political radicalism, resistance of a sort remained in the Sussex countryside. As Roger Wells' splendid micro-history of the parish of Burwash in the period 1790 to 1850 reveals, the parish was a microcosm of all that we have seen above, illustrating the manifold links over time between popular protest and social crime. In the 1820s and subsequently, Burwash was implicated in smuggling, and readily resorted to all manner of independent behaviour. The poor law overseer had his barn burned down, and when the local church vestry decided not to make its traditional contribution to celebrate Guy Fawkes night, the local bonfire boys raided the parish wood store and carried off ample supplies of faggots. Likewise, when it was decided not to ring the church bells on Christmas Day in 1820, locals insisted upon their customary celebrations. In November 1830, Burwash was the third Sussex parish to rise in the 'Captain Swing' protest, and it opposed the Poor Law Amendment Act of 1834, in 1838 forming a local Chartist branch. As the *Brighton Patriot* put it in April 1839, 'democratic principles continue to be held in this populous village'.[41] Local labourers attended an anti-Corn Law rally in 1843, and wood-stealing and poaching remained socially acceptable 'crimes' that did not receive the censure of ordinary people. When Tom Vidler was arrested in 1840 for the theft of twenty hop-poles, he explained incredulously that he had just 'picked up the wood for fuel'.[42] Local inns – the Bell, the Bear and, most especially, the Wheel – were centres for illegal activities of all kinds, from receiving stolen goods and gambling to planning raids to steal poultry or sheep. They were also the scenes of hard drinking and brawling. The 1839 Rural Constabulary Act led to the provision of local constables, and in East Sussex Burwash became a favourite target for their activities. Such policing was effective, and from about 1850 there was a noticeable decline in criminal activity in Burwash parish. However, by the 1850s agriculture had become more prosperous, while the excess in the supply of farm labour over demand had been much reduced. These upturns in local economic conditions account in part for the improvement evident in Burwash society. Nonetheless, the local rector, who had been in the parish since 1824, could still complain in 1859 that he wished for 'less drunkenness, fewer illegitimate children, more religion', admitting that he was disappointed to 'see so little good from his labours' and that he 'could not say that his was a model parish'.[43]

Windmills were a familiar part of the Sussex landscape, well suited to the breezy uplands of the Downs. This rather dilapidated wooden structure, near Winchelsea, was sketched during the nineteenth century.

Machine Reaping in Sussex, 1887. Despite the Captain Swing protests and other rural disturbances in the 1830s, when agricultural machinery was destroyed by angry mobs, by the late nineteenth century mechanisation had become an everyday feature of the Sussex countryside. In this photograph, taken by Colonel Joseph Gale (*c*.1835–1906) in 1887, a farm worker ties bundles of wheat newly reaped by his colleague operating the harvester, which is drawn by two horses. A couple of children, to the right of the photograph, sit playing. Joseph Gale specialised in photographs of rural life and figures in landscapes. He was one of the first members of the Linked Ring Brotherhood, which aimed to promote photography as a high form of artistic expression.

A changing countryside

As economic conditions improved the decline in popular protest evident at Burwash was replicated elsewhere across Sussex and southern England. To some extent it remained ritualised in the excesses of the bonfire boys. At Lewes in 1846, for example, they tried to burn down the house of an unpopular justice of the peace, Sir Henry Blackman, piling three tar barrels against the building and setting them ablaze. When Sir Harry came out into the street to protest, he was promptly knocked unconscious by the mob. In the following year the authorities were prepared for a repeat performance, and were taking no chances. The Riot Act was read from the steps of County Hall, and one hundred

Metropolitan policemen, armed with cutlasses and especially brought in from London, helped local forces to dispel the crowd in what was described as a pitched battle.[44] But thereafter the savagery of such events dissipated, although the Sussex bonfire societies were to remain long after as exuberant expressions of popular enthusiasm. As such, they were eyed with suspicion and discomfort by the county establishment.

Attired in oilskin smocks and tarred straw hats, these fisher-folk are engaged in making nets beneath the East Cliff at Old Town, Hastings, in 1864. This traditional scene was captured by Francis Frith (1822–1898), famous for many historic illustrations of people and places across Britain, and was part of a series of sixteen photographs of Hastings, St Leonards, Rye and Winchelsea which Frith published in 1864 in his book *The Gossiping Photographer of Hastings.*

There were further agricultural depressions, especially in the 1870s, but the gradual diversification of the Sussex rural economy helped the county to weather the worst effects. In particular, the railways, which had been extending their tentacles across Sussex in recent decades, played a major role, creating new employment opportunities and opening up agricultural hinterlands. Market gardens and orchards sprang up, their produce able to be sped to Covent Garden by train, and new activities – from chicken-fattening around Heathfield to jam-manufacture at Battle – were established across the county. When the Royal Commission on Agriculture reported in 1895, it was full of praise for the new industries that had been established. The rural poor were still there. But now they were generally better fed and more gainfully employed, and no longer the dire threat that the establishment had so recently feared. The railways, for their part, had brought 'civilisation' to the Sussex countryside, the county's rustic inhabitants increasingly imagined as harmless and amusing countryfolk, rather than the dangerous savages of the recent past. Commonplace now was the charming image of the worthy ploughman or shepherd – 'what used to be called in Sussex a "round frock farmer"' – toiling contentedly in the fields all day and 'sitting in those solid pews on Sunday, red-faced and slightly somnolent after his week-day labours … accompanied by his wife and numerous offspring'. Here was a placid rural timelessness that could not fail to impress the visitor: 'He sat in the same seat that his father occupied before him, and maybe his grandfather before that.' As Esther Meynell mused: 'So close to our own time could have been found some Sussex country-people to link hands with Chaucer.'[45]

SEVEN

Sussex in the Railway Age

'... highly desirable that there should be a railway to Brighton'

By 1820, when the Prince Regent had ascended the throne as George IV, Brighton's future as a desirable destination seemed assured. Following his illustrious example, as we have seen, others with means and status clamoured to acquire properties in Brighthelmstone – or Brighton, as it was now more conveniently known – or at least insisted on the ability to visit the Sussex coast from the metropolis as frequently, swiftly and comfortably as possible. Turnpike roads and the network of stage-coach routes had now reached their apogee, enabling the constant coming and going between London and Brighton. In 1823 William Cobbett could note that: 'Brighton is so situated that a coach, which leaves not very early in the morning, reaches London by noon: and starting back in two hours and a half reaches Brighton not very late at night.' As he observed, the speed and regularity of the service had allowed the growth of what would later be called 'commuting'. He explained: 'Great parcels of stock-jobbers stay at Brighton with the women and children. They skip backward and forward on the coaches and actually carry on stockjobbing in Change Alley though they reside in Brighton.'[1] In this way, as Cobbett suggested, financiers resident in Brighton could be sped to the heart of the Square Mile, transact their business in the City, and be home again in time for dinner. Likewise, Brighton lay directly on the route from London to Paris, and those travellers arriving by stage-coach could transfer immediately to packet steamer alongside the Brighton Chain Pier, constructed for the purpose in 1823, for the relatively short journey to the Continent.

However, demand grew for a yet more efficient service, and by the mid-1830s steam coaches began to replace horse-drawn stage-coaches on the Brighton Road. The steam coaches proved more flexible but not entirely reliable, and still could not cope with the rapidly increasing numbers who wished to travel between London and Brighton. Accordingly, thoughts turned to the possibility of connecting the two by rail. As early as 1823 there had been talk of a tramway to link Waterloo Bridge in London with

A London to Brighton stage coach, probably that operated by the Brighton Comet Stagecoach Company, in full cry in 1822. Although efficient and well-patronised (as this illustration shows), the stage coaches had limited capacity, leading to the early public enthusiasm for a railway link between the metropolis and the Sussex coast.

Brighton and Shoreham, part of a scheme to bring coal down from the Midlands by land transport, rather than incurring the prohibitive tax on coals arriving by sea. For the moment, the idea was shelved but it was not forgotten. By 1835, indeed, there were no fewer than six competing schemes in place for a London to Brighton railway. One, advocated by the famous railway engineer, Robert Stephenson, postulated a somewhat circuitous route from Waterloo, which would skirt the Weald in the Horsham area and traverse the South Downs by means of the Adur gap. Another, by Nicholas Cundy, proposed a similar route, and there were others put forward by Alexander Gibb (who in 1828 had made his name in the construction of the Fort Clarence and West Hartlepool Railway) and the well-known Irish-born railway builder Charles Vignoles. A fifth plan, conceived by Henry Palmer – who also designed the first monorail and invented corrugated iron – envisaged a line running south via Oxted and Lewes, a route that would later be adopted by the South Eastern Railway. But it was the sixth alternative, the 'direct line' proposed by John Rennie – who with his elder brother George had been chief engineer of the Liverpool and Manchester Railway in 1825 – that finally won the day. Rennie's route was by far the shortest – only 47½ miles from the existing railhead south of London to Brighton – but it involved heavy (and expensive) engineering works, including a large viaduct across the Ouse valley near Balcombe and five miles of tunnelling, notably that under the Downs at Clayton.[2]

In the event, the selection of John Rennie's 'direct line' as the preferred choice was made only after a prolonged and acrimonious legal and parliamentary battle. His and Robert Stephenson's projects were put before Parliament in 1835, but both were rejected, failing to achieve the required Act of Parliament. They also aroused a good deal of heated public debate. The political economist and utilitarian John Stuart Mill, for example, agreed that it was 'highly desirable that there should be a railway to Brighton'. But, he added, in 'the choice of a line it is disgraceful that

The Royal Chain Pier at Brighton, depicted here in 1824, had been opened in the previous year, and was welcomed by many as providing a maritime link with northern France, and thus Paris. Stage coach passengers from London, it was envisaged, could transfer direct to a packet ship moored alongside the pier for the journey across the Channel. Advocates of the railway entertained similar ambitions. However, the weather was not conducive to regular cross-Channel sailings from the Pier, which was exposed to the full force of the sea, and when the railway reached the sheltered harbour at Newhaven in 1847, the Chain Pier was largely abandoned by the packet ships. It survived until 1896, when it was destroyed in a storm.

ROYAL CHAIN PIER, BRIGHTON.
(Taken from Phillips's, Confectioner, Steine.)

COPYRIGHT.
THE PIER "ON ITS LAST LEGS."—1896.
(From a photograph taken by Mr. THOMAS DONOVAN, of Brighton).

On its last legs in 1896, the Royal Chain Pier at Brighton was completely destroyed in the so-called Great Storm on 4 December that year. Designed by Samuel Brown (1776–1852), a Royal Navy Captain, the pier was essentially a suspension bridge, 350 yards long and thirteen feet wide. During its heyday, the Chain Pier was visited by up to 4,000 people per day, who paid 2d each for the privilege. In addition to the cross-Channel packets that moored alongside, the Pier's amusements included a camera obscura, various sideshows, and brass band concerts. However, when the cross-Channel service switched to Newhaven in 1847, the Pier's popularity declined, its demise hastened by the opening of rival attractions such as the West Pier (1866) and the Aquarium (1871), not to mention the continued battering of the angry winter storms.

not one thought should be bestowed upon the character of the natural scenery which is threatened with destruction'. No Member of Parliament, he objected, had raised a single question about the impact of the proposed railways on the countryside, despite the obvious deleterious potential of the several schemes, 'particularly Stephenson's'.[3] Nonetheless, despite such protests, Rennie's and Stephenson's proposals were again considered by Parliament in 1836, together with those of Gibb and Cundy, in the process provoking a new round of ill-feeling and dispute. This time Cundy accused Stephenson of stealing his ideas, and Rennie criticised Stephenson's plans for allegedly preferring Shoreham to Brighton and coal to passengers. Despite (or perhaps because of) the controversy, the House of Commons decided quickly upon Stephenson's scheme, only for the Bill to be promptly defeated in the Lords. A third attempt at a solution was made in 1837, with a Royal Engineers officer, Captain R. Alderson, appointed as consultant to report on the relative merits of the several proposals. In June 1837 Alderson recommended John Rennie's plan, and the requisite legislation was pushed through Parliament, receiving royal assent on 15 July.

The Ouse Valley Viaduct near Balcombe, opened in July 1841, showed how man-made features could enhance the landscape. Designed by David Mocatta in collaboration with John Rastrick, the Ouse Valley Viaduct is 1,475 feet long, is ninety-six feet high, and has thirty-seven arches. Some eleven million bricks were used in its construction.

Altogether, some £200,000 had been expended in legal fees in the battle to decide the route, and partisan feelings had run high in Brighton as people backed the different schemes. There was general relief, however, that the issue had now been resolved, together with a renewed sense of urgency which drove the project forward. John Rastrick was appointed engineer, and on 12 July 1838, after nearly a year's surveying work, the first sod was cut. The main line ran direct to Brighton, as planned, with a branch from Keymer Junction to Lewes and Newhaven, the latter soon replacing Brighton as the port for Continental sailings (the Chain Pier itself blew down in a severe storm in 1896, and was not rebuilt). There was also an extension to Shoreham, as envisaged back in 1823, and indeed this short stretch was given priority – allowing building materials for the project to be landed at the harbour by sea – and was opened on 12 May 1840.

An insight into the scale and impact of the large army of 'navvies' – railway labourers – employed in the project is lent by the 1841 census. The population of Balcombe, for example, a quiet village deep in the Weald, had swollen to 1,542 – a figure which now included 550 labourers and their families. At Keymer, the normal population of 916 had been expanded by a further 450 souls, the latter 'navvies' and their women and children. At Hassocks a row of houses was built especially, it was

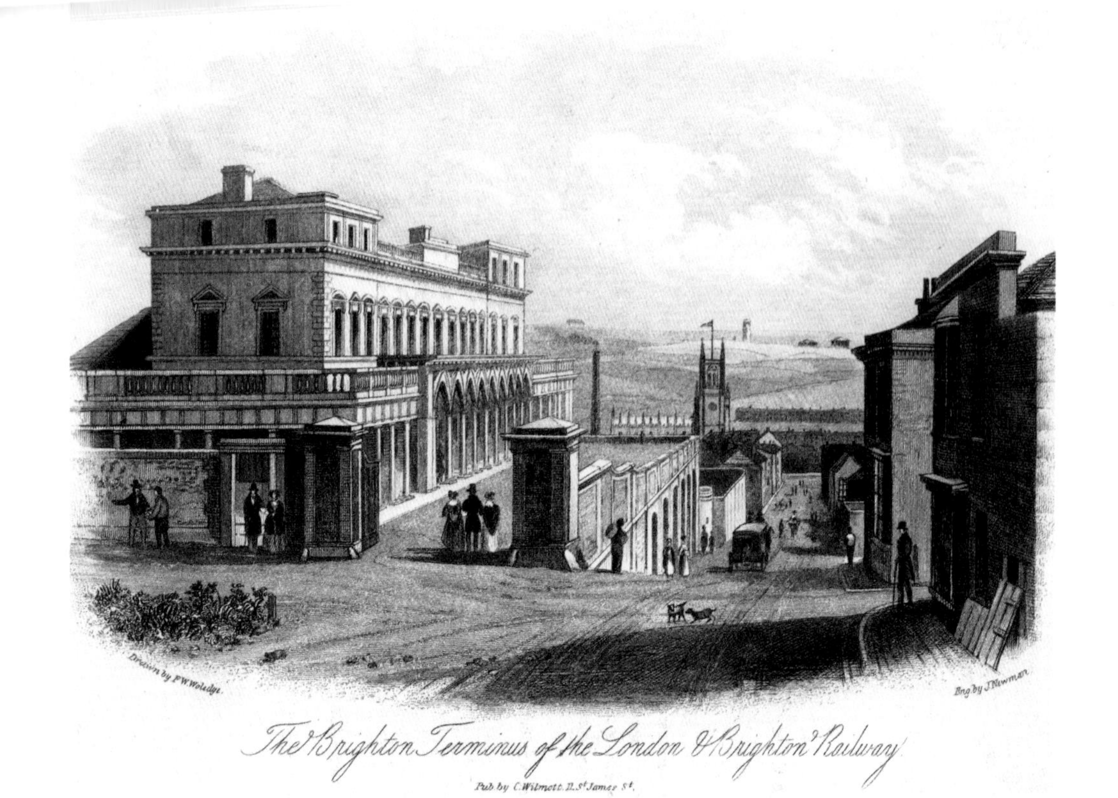

The Brighton terminus of the London & Brighton Railway (precursor of the London, Brighton & South Coast Railway) *c.*1845. Designed by David Mocatta (1806–82), the terminal building was built between October 1840 and September 1841, perched high on the western side of the valley in which the London–Brighton road was located.

said, to accommodate the temporary migrants. By March 1841 the Balcombe 'navvies' had completed construction of the stupendous Ouse Valley viaduct at Balcombe – designed by David Mocatta, who was also responsible for the fine palazzo terminus at Brighton – and nearby Balcombe Tunnel. On 12 July that year services began between London Bridge and Haywards Heath, south of Balcombe, with four trains a day and connecting stage-coaches to Brighton. The final stretch was opened with great ceremony two months later, on 21 September 1841. As the *Brighton Herald* reported breathlessly, from 'Clayton the county poured forth its inhabitants. Hurst[pierpoint] and Ditchling sent out their populations, in holiday array, to meet the train at Hassocks station; and Patcham, Withdean and Preston, all lent their quota to make up one general sum of joy.'[4]

'Crash, crack, / Brighton and back, / All the way for a shilling'

For Brighton, the railway had not come a moment too soon. Although, as Jack Simmons observed in his estimation of Brighton's railway history, the town enjoyed several distinct advantages – its highly fashionable character, 'daring and stylish, a little like what the Victorians came to see in Paris', its proximity to London, and its reputation as 'a health resort, a popular watering place' – in 1841 it was experiencing an economic downturn.[5] Brighton's population had increased rapidly from 7,000 to 47,000 between 1801 and 1841, and the demands on its infrastructure were beginning to tell. The cost of living there was now reckoned to be roughly one-third higher than it was in London, and property speculation had led to a glut of building projects, with houses unoccupied and others always up for sale. More seriously still, the growth in population had not been matched by improvements in sanitary arrangements, and until 1839 Brighton's sewers discharged directly onto the beach, threatening to damage the town's 'health resort' and 'watering hole' reputation. Moreover, Queen Victoria, who acceded to the throne in 1837, did not share her uncle's enthusiasm for the place, and said so. The town's aristocratic allure was beginning to fade, and most frustrating of all was the town's patently inadequate transport system. In the nick of time, however, as Simmons argued: 'The railway transformed Brighton.'[6]

Excursion from London to Brighton. Published in the early 1900s by the London, Brighton & South Coast Railway, this poster advertises the cheap 5/- Third Class fare available 'Every Monday'. In the years before the Great War, railway excursions to Brighton and other south coast destinations grew ever greater in popularity, reaching their apogee in the warm but fateful summer of 1914. A watchful Guard keeps a keen eye on proceedings, ensuring the safety of passengers and train.

In the first place, Brighton became even more accessible for those planning to commute to London. An ordinary stage- or steam-coach could transport no more than fourteen passengers. A single train, by contrast, could accommodate at least ten times that number. Moreover, express services were soon introduced, speeding businessmen to their offices in London and returning them at a reasonable hour. It was now possible to catch a train from Brighton at 8.45, have up to seven hours in London, and be back home again by 6.30 in the early evening. The relatively few 'stockjobbers' noted by Cobbett in 1823, who made the trip by stage-coach and enjoyed but a few hours in London, were now supplanted by an army of commuters who travelled to and from London on a daily basis. As one observer noted as early as 1848: 'Merchants who formerly made Dulwich or Dalston the boundaries of their suburban residences now have got their mansions on the south coast, and still get in less time, by a less expensive conveyance, to their counting-houses in the City.'[7] In 1845 first-class season tickets to London were introduced: £12 monthly, £25 quarterly, and £50 annually. Not surprisingly, the population of Brighton more than doubled between 1841 and 1871, rising to 99,000. Brighton's aristocratic patrons may have faded, but they had given ground to a solid phalanx of affluent, middle-class residents.

The working classes too found Brighton to their taste. In 1845 a Sundays-only second-class excursion fare from London to Brighton was a few shillings, opening up the prospect of affordable day-trips to the seaside. Such excursions proved hugely popular. On Easter Monday 1844 the very first had set out for Brighton. Composed of no fewer than forty-four carriages (most, no doubt, open wagons), it had left London Bridge station hauled by four locomotives. At New Cross six more carriages were added, together with another engine, and yet another six carriages and a further locomotive were attached at Croyden. Eventually, after a journey of four-and-a-half hours, the train arrived at the seaside at 1.30 p.m. Two years later, in June 1846, the *Illustrated London News* noted another Bank Holiday special of similar length, carrying some 4,000 passengers eager to sample the delights of Brighton.[8] By 1866 the West Pier had been completed, a mecca for those bound for the seaside. The minor poet Henry Cholmondeley-Pennell caught something of the excitement and anticipation of those early excursionists. As he put it: 'Crash, crack, / Brighton and back, / All the way for a shilling':

> Oh! Brighton's the place
> For a beautiful face,
> And a figure that daintily made is:
> And as far as I know
> There's no other can show
> At the right time of year – say November or so –
> Such a lot of bewitching young ladies.[9]

But Cholmondeley-Pennell also struck a cautionary note, worrying about the safety implications of such long 'Racketing, reeling, and rocking' trains, which went 'Whack thwack, thump bump' over 'permanent way [that] is shocking!'. There was something inherently dangerous in travelling in all those loose-coupled carriages, he thought, and he did not trust the railway Directors to improve standards:

> Jump, jolt,
> Engines that bolt,

Brighton and back for a shilling –
Jolt jump – but we've children and wives,
Thump bump – who value our lives,
And you won't catch one here again who survives
The patent process of killing.

With our slap dash, crack crash,
And here and there a glorious smash,
And a hundred killed and wounded! –
It's little we jolly Directors care
For a passenger's limbs if he pays his fare,
So away you go at a florin the pair,
The signal whistle has sounded.[10]

Cholmondeley-Pennell was not alone in his concerns, and early travellers had been especially frightened about going through tunnels – a decidedly unpleasant experience in an open carriage behind a steam locomotive belching black smoke. Clayton Tunnel, 2,259 yards long and up to 270 feet below surface, was at first lit by gas, to 'induce a feeling of confidence and cheerfulness' among the passengers, and to allow engine drivers 'to see the road throughout as well almost as in broad daylight'.[11] Maybe fears were allayed by these measures. But they were not enough to prevent a terrible collision in the middle of Clayton Tunnel on the morning of Sunday 25 August 1861 – an appalling event which may perhaps have prompted Cholmondeley-Pennell's trenchant verses. At any rate, it was at that date the worst catastrophe to have occurred on any British railway.

The Clayton Tunnel disaster

On that fateful morning, three trains were booked to leave Brighton station in quick succession after 8 a.m. The first, an excursion to London from Portsmouth, was due to depart from Brighton at 8.05, to be followed by an excursion train from Brighton to London, and lastly by the regular timetabled express. All three were running late, and the excursion from Portsmouth was not despatched until 8.28. The second excursion followed smartly on its heels at 8.31, with the express departing shortly after at 8.35. Signalling in that period was remarkably primitive, and, with the exception of Clayton Tunnel itself, the line was operated according to the 'time-interval system', which allowed five minutes between train departures. Plainly, the quick succession of three trains from Brighton that morning had already contravened the rulebook and, as we shall see, laid the groundwork for the disaster that ensued. The drivers would have been aware of the extremely short intervals between their three trains.

But in covering the four and a half miles from Lovers Walk Junction, at the north end of Brighton, to Clayton Tunnel their visibility was hampered by curves, cuttings, bridges, the 700-yard Patcham Tunnel, and smoke from the engines as they laboured up the continuous 1 in 264 incline. The gaps between the three trains may well have closed as they approached the southern portal of Clayton Tunnel, but they would not have been in visual contact.[12]

Each end of Clayton Tunnel was protected by a signal, under the supervision of signalmen in their respective cabins at either portal. Setting his signal by means of a hand wheel in his cabin, a signalman could inform a driver of the state of the tunnel ahead – the 'off' position indicated that the tunnel was clear but the 'on' position warned that there was a train already in the tunnel, and that the driver should prepare to stop. In passing a signal in the 'off' position, a train would automatically return it to 'on' (or 'danger') by means of a treadle. If, for some reason, the treadle failed to work, an alarm bell rang in the signal cabin to alert the signalman. That morning, signalman Henry Killick was on duty at Clayton Tunnel south signal cabin. Sunday was the change-over day from day to night duty, and it was Killick's practice to work a continuous shift of twenty-four hours, rather than the maximum eighteen stipulated in the rulebook. This allowed him to take a day off work each week, but the price was extreme fatigue. Perhaps for this reason he did not at first notice that the treadle at the south end of the tunnel had not returned the signal to 'on' (the 'danger' position) as the Portsmouth excursion had passed. Killick appeared not to hear the alarm bell when it rang, and he was in any case preoccupied in telegraphing his opposite number in the northern cabin, signalman Brown, to inform him 'train in tunnel'. Only then did he turn to deal with the treadle failure, and to his horror saw from his cabin window that the second train – the Brighton excursion – had already passed the defective signal and was about to plunge into the tunnel. With seconds to spare he showed his red flag, but he could not be certain that the driver of the Brighton excursion had seen it. He again telegraphed Brown with the message 'train in tunnel', intending to indicate that there was now a second train inside. Shortly after, in his anxiety, Killick telegraphed Brown to ask 'is tunnel clear?' At that very moment, the Portsmouth excursion thundered out of the northern portal of the tunnel. Forgetting or misinterpreting Killick's second 'train in tunnel' message, Brown did not realise that the Brighton excursion had already entered the southern portal, and replied 'tunnel clear'. A relieved Henry Killick brought in his red flag and unfurled the white just as the third train, the regular express, approached his cabin. With a cheery wave, driver Gregory acknowledged the white flag and accelerated his express into the tunnel.

Alas, the driver of the second train – driver Scott of the Brighton excursion – *had* glimpsed the red flag shown by Henry Killick. He

The castellated north portal of Clayton Tunnel is a suitably Gothic memorial to the 6,000 men who toiled for three years beneath 270 feet of chalk to fashion the mile-and-a-half tunnel through the South Downs. Clayton Tunnel was also the site of the horrific train crash in 1861.
HELEN HADEN

brought his train to a halt as quickly as he could but it was already half a mile inside the tunnel before it came to a standstill. Assuming that there was a problem with the Portsmouth excursion ahead, he decided to reverse his train to the southern portal of Clayton Tunnel to inquire why Killick had shown his red flag. Scott had set back to within 250 yards of the portal when his train was struck by driver Gregory's on-coming express. Despite running backwards, Scott's excursion train was propelled fifty yards back into the tunnel, such was the force of the collision. In the darkness of Clayton Tunnel, twenty-one people died. A further 176 were seriously injured, two of whom died subsequently. In the inquiry into the accident, conducted by Captain Tyler, much was made of the rulebook infringements but there was also strong criticism of the rudimentary signalling practices in use. Tyler pointed to best practice elsewhere on the British railway system, and urged the directors of the London, Brighton and South Coast Railway [LBSCR] (as the London and Brighton Railway had become in 1846) to follow suit. Remarkably, the directors dragged their feet, resisting the installation of more sophisticated (and expensive) signalling equipment with the retort that such mechanisms tended to undermine the awareness and attentiveness of locomotive drivers – especially when equipment on which they relied did not work properly, as in the Clayton treadle failure. As they put it, complex signalling arrangements 'by transferring much responsibility from the engine drivers, augment rather than diminish the risk of accident'.[13] Indeed, they concluded:

The bucolic scene painted by James Wilson Carmichael (1800–1868) in 1848 was soon to disappear, as the area round the London Road Viaduct (on the Lewes branch) was developed quickly for housing, it inhabitants including many skilled and semi-skilled craftsmen employed at Brighton Works. Carmichael himself had moved to Brighton in 1840, one of the many artistic types attracted to the town.

> it is open to grave doubt whether the circumstances of the serious collision in question do not, when fairly considered, tend to prove that the increasing practice of multiplying signals, and thus lessening the responsibility of the engine driver who is in charge of the motive power, and whose own life is at stake, has not resulted in reducing rather than increasing the safety of railway locomotion.[14]

Perhaps Cholmondeley-Pennell was right to lampoon the directors of the LBSCR. But in the end they could not afford to resist the continuous technical improvements adopted by other railways; nor could they ignore the pressure of public opinion, which demanded ever higher safety standards. Neither could they escape the demands for compensation.

A piano-tuner named Williamson, injured in the Clayton disaster, had to give up work, citing continuous excruciating pain in his head, back and kidneys. The well-known taxidermist, George Swaysland, was so affected by the collision that he too could no longer work. A nervous wreck, 'he could no longer stuff a bird or go out to shoot a fresh one'.[15] Yet despite the Clayton Tunnel disaster and a spate of other collisions across the British railway system, public enthusiasm for railways did not diminish. In Brighton, the beneficial impact of the railway was plain to see. A new thoroughfare, Queen's Road, was cut from the station to West Street and the town's commercial centre, and spacious new town houses sprang up to accommodate the burgeoning middle class. In August 1869 a branch line, less than two miles long but with an impressive fourteen-arch viaduct over the Lewes Road and a 1,024-yard tunnel, was opened to Kemptown in the prosperous eastern suburbs.

Day-tripping was augmented by the growth of holiday tourism, not yet the preserve of the working classes but important enough to warrant a mushrooming of hotels and boarding houses. The establishment of the LBSCR's locomotive works in 1852 added a further string to Brighton's economic bow, creating employment for hundreds of skilled and semi-skilled craftsmen and stimulating the growth of engineering manufacture in the town. Rows of modest terraced houses sprang up on the hillside to the east of the railway station, housing locomotive works employees and other artisans. Firms such as Allen West, which by the early 1900s had evolved from various early manufacturers, lent Brighton a reputation for engineering excellence – among many other things, Allen West went on to provide electrical equipment for the fleet of Brighton trolleybuses introduced in the 1930s.[16]

Brighton locomotive works

By 1871 Brighton locomotive works was employing some 400 men, a figure that had increased to about 600 in 1881. By the turn of the twentieth century, more than 2,000 men in Brighton were employed directly by the railway, with many other workers and their families dependent on the railway's demand for goods and services, and on the activities of allied industries, from tourism to engineering. Brighton Works itself developed as an important centre of British locomotive construction. John Craven, who had established the works, was succeeded in 1870 by William Stroudley, who went on to design and produce some of the LBSCR's finest locomotives, from the diminutive 'Terrier' tank engines to the stately 'Gladstone' class for express services. His engines were a byword for elegance as well as performance, his famous livery of 'improved engine green' (actually a shade of golden ochre) further enhancing their graceful lines. The man himself, William Stroudley,

William Stroudley's classic *Gladstone*, built at Brighton Works for the London, Brighton and South Coast Railway in 1882. The prototype for the B (later B1) class of locomotives, *Gladstone* survived in service until withdrawal in 1927, when it was purchased from the Southern Railway by the Stephenson Locomotive Society for £140. Included in the price was restoration of the locomotive's original 'improved engine green' livery (in reality a golden ochre), and it is in this condition that *Gladstone* is depicted *c.*1930 by the well-known railway artist Leslie Carr. Today *Gladstone* is part of the national collection at the National Railway Museum, York.

created what observers dubbed 'the Brighton legend', a 'mystique' deriving from his 'personal influence ... [as] artist/engineer extraordinary'.[17] He transformed the LBSCR's hitherto poor locomotive stock, introducing design and component standardisation, and insisted on a high standard of turnout for both engines and their drivers and firemen. Sadly, he died unexpectedly on a visit to France in December 1889, cutting short an outstanding career.

Stroudley was succeeded by R.J. Billinton, who continued his predecessor's policy of standardisation and perpetuated what was now the Brighton 'look' or house style in locomotive design. He, in turn, was replaced by D. Earle Marsh in 1905, who moved the construction of railway carriages from Brighton to newly erected works at Lancing, and was responsible for the much loved 'Atlantic' class of locomotives. But not all his designs were successful, alas, and the 'I1' tank engines, built at Brighton in 1906–07, were known to generations of railwaymen and train-spotters alike as 'Wankers' on account of their poor performance, an unflattering nickname recorded solemnly as late as 1948 in a nomenclature listing in the Ian Allan *ABC of British Locomotives*.[18] The last Locomotive Superintendent of the LBSCR was L.B. Billinton (son of

'First in the Field'. Designed at the Southern Railway's Brighton Works during the Second World War, the first of the ultra-modern 'West Country' class steam locomotives, with their stylish 'air-smoothed' body work, was completed at Brighton in June 1945. Although intended for the North Cornwall and West of England lines, several of these new engines were shedded at Brighton in subsequent years. In 1950 Brighton shed played host to *Westward Ho!*, *Clovelly*, *Lynton*, *Boscastle*, *Crewkerne* and *Wilton*. By 1959 they had been allocated elsewhere on the system, to be replaced at Brighton by *Padstow*, *Bideford*, *Holsworthy*, *Templecombe* and *Lynmouth*. Of these eleven locomotives, nine had been constructed at Brighton (*Holsworthy* and *Lynmouth* were built at Eastleigh Works in Hampshire).

Caught by the camera of railway photographer E.D. Bruton, 32424 *Beachy Head* prepares to leave Brighton on Sunday 5 October 1952, bound for London Victoria with a Railway Correspondence & Travel Society special train commemorating the centenary of Brighton Works. *Beachy Head*, one of D. Earle Marsh's much admired H2 'Atlantics', was built and shedded at Brighton, and was the last of her class, being withdrawn from service in 1958. Today, a brand new H2 locomotive is being constructed on the Bluebell Railway.

R.J.), who took over in 1905 and expanded the works at Brighton to cope with the demands of the larger locomotives then being designed. During the First World War the works contributed to the war effort, manufacturing ammunition. In January 1923 when, in the aftermath of war, the government grouped Britain's railways into four main companies, the LBSCR became part of the Southern Railway – the very last locomotive built at Brighton under LBSCR auspices was a large express tank engine, appropriately named *Remembrance*.

Thereafter, Brighton Works came under the control of the Southern's Chief Mechanical Engineers, first R.E.L. Maunsell and then O.V.S. Bulleid. During the Second World War the works were completely re-equipped to meet the demands of the war effort. Large War Department locomotives were produced at the awe-inspiring rate of one every 4½ days, and other military items from tank parts to anti-aircraft components were manufactured. Meanwhile, despite the strictures of the war years, innovative design work had continued apace, leading to the construction at Brighton of 104 Bulleid 'West Country' and 'Battle of Britain' express engines and the prototype of his revolutionary but unsuccessful 'Leader' locomotive. Bulleid, with his radical disdain for aesthetic conventions,

A trainspotter's mecca! Brighton engine shed in the early twentieth century sports a vast array of London, Brighton & South Coast Railway locomotive designs, each conceived and built at the adjoining Brighton Works. Viewed from the top-deck of a bus travelling up the road perched high above the shed, the spectacle of steam engines below delighted generations of young spotters, until the age of steam was finally at an end in the mid-1960s.

was no sentimentalist. But in the centenary celebrations of the Institution of Mechanical Engineers in 1947, he restored two of Stroudley's 'Terriers' to LBSCR livery, and at Brighton Works staged a pageant of historic locomotives to demonstrate the development of engineering design by his predecessors.[19]

After the war and nationalisation in 1948, Brighton participated fully in the building of the new British Railways 'Standard' fleet of steam locomotives. By the end of the 1950s, however, orders were dwindling. The last new locomotive was turned out in March 1957, and thereafter Brighton concentrated on repair work and overhauls, until this was transferred to other workshops on the railway network in 1958. For a time, parts of the premises and machinery were used for motorcar assembly but this came to a halt in 1964. The once famous works then languished until 1969, when the buildings were demolished and the site cleared, to be replaced by that ubiquitous memorial to post-industrial Britain – a car park.[20]

'London, Brighton and South Coast religion'

The growth of Brighton under the aegis of the railway was matched by that of neighbouring Hove. Initially dismissed by the LBSCR in its 1853 *Measom's Guide* as 'a village … now a mere western continuation of Brighton', and served only by the local 'west coast' line, the town benefited enormously from the Cliftonville spur from the Brighton mainline, which was opened in July 1879 and allowed direct running to and from London.[21] Royal patronage was bestowed on Hove by Edward VII, who visited in 1908, twice during 1909, and again in 1910, prompting an upsurge in middle-class tourism and encouraging popular belief that Hove was 'respectable' and 'refined' when compared to more 'common' Brighton next door. It was a prejudice that endured, expressed, for example, in Jennifer Worth's semi-fictional autobiography where an amusing ditty is attributed to the character Sister Monica Joan:

> It's OK to be tight on
> The seafront at Brighton
> But I say, by Jove
> Watch out if it's Hove.[22]

As John Betjeman put it, 'Hove thought of itself as a sort of Westgate-on-Sea to Brighton's Margate'.[23] When, after the First World War, the Angel of Peace memorial was erected on the seafront at the boundary between the two towns, there could be no longer be any doubt about where Brighton finished and Hove began.

Westwards from Hove, the railway served neighbouring Portslade

'A Sea Voyage on Wheels'. This was how the Brighton & Rottingdean Seashore Electric Railway (or Tramroad) was advertised by its optimistic promoters. As the poster explains, this ungainly tramroad connected with the existing Volks Electic Railway (opened by its designer Magnus Volk in 1883) at the latter's Kemptown terminus. Commissioned on 3 August 1883, the tramroad's sole car, named 'Pioneer', plied between Kemptown and Rottingdean, braving the worst of winter storms (including the Great Storm of 1896, which did serious damage) until taken out of service in 1901. Thereafter, the tramroad was dismantled, as Brighton Corporation strove to improve its foreshore.

The grandly named Brighton & Rottingdean Seashore Electric Tramroad, or 'daddy longlegs' in popular parlance, in 1898. When the tide was in, as in this photograph, water covered the tramroad rails, creating the illusion of being at sea – to the alarm of some passengers.

On the Promenade at the boundary between Brighton and Hove, *c*.1893. For the poorer classes, the rise in tourism and day-tripping from London was an opportunity to make a little money. On the left, 'goat boys' with their carts wait for customers looking forward to a ride 'along the prom'. On the right, a 'flower girl' sports her basket-full of bunches.

and Shoreham before continuing on to Angmering, Littlehampton, Chichester and, eventually, Portsmouth. In 1911 the combined population of the Brighton/Hove/Portslade conurbation was some 180,000 souls, who together enjoyed the facility of no fewer than eight railway stations. By 1914 Shoreham was served by over fifty trains a day, London Road (on the Lewes line) by another fifty, and Kemptown by thirty. There was also the steeply graded branch line to Devil's Dyke, opened in September 1887, which boasted eleven trains a day on the eve of the First World War. Electric trams were introduced in Brighton in 1901, further enhancing the transport infrastructure, and in August 1883 Magnus Volk opened his famous 'Volk's Electric Railway' along the Brighton foreshore from the Aquarium to the Chain Pier, with a later extension to Black Rock. Volk, a former electrical engineer at Brighton Corporation, was also responsible for the curious 'Daddy Long-Legs' electric tramroad which was constructed in 1896 along the seashore from Black Rock to Rottingdean. At high tide the rails were covered by the waves, the tramcar riding high above on long stilts (hence the nickname) and taking its electricity from overhead power lines. Not surprisingly this ungainly, expensive to maintain, and possibly dangerous contraption did not survive long, being dismantled in 1901.

Two years earlier, in 1899, the newly constructed Palace Pier (known today as Brighton Pier) had been opened to the public, its superior facilities and amusements soon surpassing the existing West Pier as

St Bartholomew's church in Ann Street dominates its locality and can be seen from many parts of Brighton. Designed by the Brighton-based architect Edmund Scott, work commenced on the building in February 1872 to a neo-Gothic plan, with the ornate interior heavily influenced by the Arts & Crafts movement. The enormous west gable, shown here, boasts its magnificent rose window, set in bands of patterned bricks. When completed, 'Wagner's folly', as it was dubbed by critics, drew mixed reactions. Anglo-Catholics welcomed it as a very visible and self-confident expression of their form of Anglicanism, while 'low church' Protestants were invariably hostile.
USER: HASSOCKS5489/WIKIMEDIA COMMONS/CC0 1.0

the principal focus for pleasure-seeking day-trippers. This development of the promenade and foreshore attracted impromptu entertainers and street-sellers, together with 'happyjackers' – assorted young 'urchins' from Brighton's poorer neighbourhoods – who gathered on the beach and encouraged the trippers to throw down pennies. Seen as a public nuisance, they were periodically chased away by police. The plight of these Brighton poor caught the attention of Revd Arthur Douglas Wagner – 'Father Wagner' as he was universally known – an ardent Anglo-Catholic who saw it as the Church of England's duty to reach out to the working classes. From his own pocket he funded the building of a series of magnificent new churches, mainly in the poorer parts of Brighton, a High Church mission which observers dubbed the 'London, Brighton and South Coast religion' after the railway they fondly imagined to be the patron of all things good in the town.[24]

St Paul, built in West Street in 1846–48, was the first of these mission churches, built by Revd Wagner senior, vicar of Brighton from 1824 until 1870. His son, 'Father Wagner', was the first incumbent, and it became his stepping-stone to still greater things. The soaring tower of St Paul's was soon a local landmark, as well as an enduring memorial to its architect, R.C. Carpenter, one of the great High Church builders of the period. Inside, early work by the Pre-Raphaelite artist Edward Burne-Jones and windows by Augustus Pugin were among the church's Anglo-Catholic splendours. St Mary Magdelene (now demolished) followed in 1862, along with The Annunciation in Washington Street (1864), The Resurrection (1875; also demolished), St Martin in Lewes Road (1874–75), and the incomparable St Bartholomew in Ann Street. To visit this latter church is 'an unforgettable experience', according to Nikolaus Pevsner, perhaps 'the most moving of all churches' in East Sussex.[25] Erected in 1872–74 in the Gothic style, St Bartholomew was the tallest parish church in England, designed by its architect, Edmund Scott, to tower above the rows of terraced houses to the east of Brighton railway works and station, its great west gable and huge rose window set in brick 'a stunning affirmation of architectural and religious self-confidence', as Simon Jenkins has called it.[26] Yet when it was first built, critics dismissed St Bartholomew as 'Noah's Ark' and 'Wagner's Folly', and local residents complained that its huge bulk created a downdraught that made their chimneys smoke. It is said that Father Wagner promptly purchased all their properties, and reduced the rents as compensation for their inconvenience! He also funded the construction of some 400 workers' dwellings along the Lewes Road, in an effort to enhance local housing stock. Father Wagner lived until 1902, having devoted his life and family fortune to the spiritual enrichment of the poor, and to improving their social condition. Yet his was not the only mission. Not to be outdone, the Wesleyan Methodists, under the determined leadership of the evangelical Revd E. Aldon French,

By the early twentieth-century open top electric tram cars had replaced the earlier generation of horse-drawn trams in Brighton and Hove, a prelude to the later motor buses and trolley buses that became essential features of the urban transport scene, complementing the development of the railway system.
© PAST PIX/SCIENCE & SOCIETY PICTURE LIBRARY

organised their own outreach services in the Alhambra Theatre. As the congregation grew, so French looked for larger premises, eventually deciding to rent The Dome. In September 1907 the Dome Mission was launched officially, attracting upwards of a 1,000 people to its Sunday services, many of them recruited – it was averred by the Methodists – from the local public houses.

Beyond Brighton – country lines and Colonel Stephens

By now the railway was seen as vital to so many aspects of Brighton life. Henry James, the novelist, caught something of this public admiration for the LBSCR, when in 1892 one of his fictional characters observes of another: 'He is always splendid, as your morning bath is splendid, or a sirloin of beef, or the railway service to Brighton.'[27] Elsewhere in Sussex, the story was much the same, as localities benefited from the stimulus to trade, access to goods and services, and increased employment opportunities offered by the railways. Lewes was linked to Brighton by the 'east coast' line, which had branches to Seaford (via Newhaven) and continued direct to Bexhill and Hastings. The town also profited from its connection to the Brighton main line at Keymer Junction, allowing through workings to and from London, and from secondary routes which ran northwards to Oxted (and then on to London), one via Horsted Keynes and East Grinstead (the 'Bluebell' line), the other by way of Crowborough and Groombridge. The latter was also joined (at Eridge) by the 'Cuckoo' line, which ran northwards from Eastbourne via Polegate, while a direct 'Hastings line' was built to connect Hastings and Battle to London. As noted above, there was also a 'west coast' line, running from Brighton to Hove, Shoreham, Littlehampton and points west, to which was added a 'mid-Sussex' railway designed to give direct access to Portsmouth from London via Horsham. This route was developed in piecemeal fashion during the 1850s, and was complemented by others in West Sussex, such as the cross-country line that ran from Shoreham by way of Steyning and West Grinstead to Christ's Hospital, near Horsham, and the railways that ran to Midhurst – one westwards from Pulborough on the 'mid-Sussex', the other northwards from Chichester on the 'west coast'. In this way, the rural hinterland of Sussex was comprehensively connected to the main centres of population, with the additional benefit of swift access to and from the metropolis for many parts of the county.

Alongside the social and economic advantages brought by the railways was the impact on the Sussex landscape. Although cuttings and embankments marched across hitherto undisturbed farmland, accompanied by the loud whistling and puffing of smoky steam trains and the clanking and rattling of wagons and carriages, the environmental impact was by no means as negative as John Stuart Mill had feared. Great engineering feats, such as Mocatta's Ouse valley viaduct, were praised for their aesthetic quality, and sympathetic designs for railway stations, workers' cottages, goods sheds, and other buildings often complemented existing vernacular architecture. This was especially true of the design – variously described as 'Old English', 'Sussex farmhouse' or even 'Queen Anne' – employed by the architect T.H. Myres in the 1880s in the construction of eighteen new station buildings. Together with Hassocks on the Brighton main line, these were erected on the latest routes opened by the LBSCR to interconnect rural Sussex – on the 'Bluebell' and 'Cuckoo' lines, and on the Midhurst–Chichester branch. A contemporary account lavished fulsome praise on both the architect and his work. 'Leaving the cold classical style adopted by the first railway engineers and since generally followed,' it opined, 'Mr Myres chose the warm colouring and varied forms of what has, of late years, been termed the Queen Anne School, and the effect of the bright red brick, wooden beams and casemented windows is very pleasing.'[28]

The reference to the Queen Anne School was a nod in the direction of Richard Norman Shaw, the leading architect who had adopted this fashionable style for domestic dwellings, employing hanging tiles, projecting gables, tall chimneys and other devices to reflect vernacular models, an approach not unlike that of the Arts & Crafts movement, with which there were parallels. Norman Shaw had been active in Sussex, where his attractive additions to the built landscape evidently caught the attention of T.H. Myres. Like Norman Shaw, Myres opted for two-storey 'country cottage' brick buildings, with the upper storey hung in typical Wealden red tiles and projecting slightly over the lower storey. Similarly, terracotta was used to ornament the ridge tiles, and sometimes the external walls were plastered, with flower designs added in relief. Gabled timber porches were also a distinctive element of the design. Today, three of Myres' splendid station buildings are preserved on the Bluebell Railway – at Sheffield Park, Horsted Keynes and Kingscote – while others happily survive in private hands.

Beyond the rural network of branch line and secondary routes – built principally by the LBSCR, with minor incursions by the South Eastern and Chatham Railway and the London and South Western – was a handful of Sussex light railways. These existed under the auspices of the legendary 'Colonel Stephens' – Lieutenant-Colonel Holman Fred Stephens (1868–1931) – who was responsible for the surveying, construction and management of light railways throughout England and Wales, which he directed from his offices in Tonbridge, Kent. Often built and run on a shoestring, Colonel Stephens' light railways had a reputation for eccentricity and more than the occasional mishap. The three Sussex lines in question were the Rother Valley Railway (later renamed the Kent & East Sussex), the Manhood & Selsey, and the Rye & Camber. H.C. Casserley, the distinguished railway historian and photographer, writing in 1975, recalled his initial encounters with the Stephens 'empire'. He explained: 'My first acquaintance with the Colonel Stephens railways was with the Kent & East Sussex, now no less than half a century ago, on 29 August 1925 to be exact.' As he remembered with still fresh wonder, 'I had never seen anything quite like it before, and even today that visit remains one of the most vivid recollections of a lifetime of exploration of the railways of Great Britain and Ireland. Anyway,' he continued, 'it started off an enthusiasm which made excursions to other similar concerns essential, particularly those of the Colonel Stephens group, which proved to be the most fascinating of them all.'[29]

The Kent & East Sussex began life as the Rother Valley Railway in 1897, following the Light Railways Act of 1896 which made such ventures possible. It was the fourth of Colonel Stephens' projects, and ran from Robertsbridge in Sussex (on the Hastings main line), via Bodiam and Northiam, to Tenterden in Kent. It opened for goods and passenger traffic in the spring of 1900. Later, in 1905, when the railway changed its name, it was extended to Headcorn on the Ashford and Dover mainline. Locomotives were bought second (or even third) hand from the big railway companies, and likewise an eclectic collection of rolling stock was acquired. Stephens also experimented with a steam-driven railmotor, and in the 1920s purchased Ford 'Tin Lizzy' petrol railcars. After a chequered history, the Kent & East Sussex became part of the nationalised British Railways in 1948, only for the line to lose its passenger services (except for the occasional hop-pickers' special) in January 1954, when the Tenterden to Headcorn section was abandoned entirely. Final closure came in 1961, although by the early twenty-first century a preservation society formed in the 1960s had succeeded in reopening the railway across the Kent–Sussex border from Tenterden to Bodiam. The affection for the line felt by H.C. Casserley and like-minded enthusiasts was shared by the local populace, for whom the railway had been something of a social and economic lifeline as well as a reassuringly familiar part of the rural scene. As one contemporary verse put it:

> Ever seen a railway train
> wheel deep in the wheat?
> Poppies on the boiler dome:
> wreaths of meadow-sweet
> twined about the driving wheel –
> burnished brass and polished steel:
> puffs of steam like woolly lambs,
> on the line to Bodiam?
> He carries grain and he carries hops.
> Wherever you hail him, there he Stops!
> in fact he's a friendly sort of train.
> He takes out shopping farmers' wives:
> he carries a load of bees in hives:
> and he carries pigs,
> and oats
> and goats
> and several boxes of lollipops
> for the village kids
> at the village shops.
>
> He knows the Marsh and he knows the Weald,
> he knows each wood and he knows each field:
> with his bright green paint
> and his glistening brass:
> the rabbits stop
> to see him pass.
> And Arcadia's just another station

on his twice-daily
peregrination![30]

After his foray to the Kent & East Sussex, H.C. Casserley had sought out the even more obscure Manhood & Selsey at the opposite end of the county. 'I paid my first visit to the "Selsey" on 16 July 1927,' he recalled in 1975, where he was met at Chichester not by the veteran steam engine and assorted ancient coaches he had anticipated but instead 'a very disagreeable Ford railcar' of the type Stephens had already installed on the Kent & East Sussex. Nonetheless, on his arrival at the line's Selsey terminus, he found to his delight a motley collection of old locomotives of varying origins hidden away in the engine-shed. 'Fortunately,' he explained, 'there was a co-operative driver (or possibly fireman) still around, who with a little monetary inducement agreed to get up enough steam to pull all the engines out of the shed for photography.'[31]

The Hundred of Manhood & Selsey Tramway, to give it its original and full title, was opened for business in August 1897, linking Chichester on the Brighton–Portsmouth line with Selsey, via Pagham Harbour. Unusually, for the first twenty-seven years of its existence, the railway operated without statutory authorisation because it ran entirely across private land. Even by Colonel Stephens standards, the line eked out a meagre existence, making little or no money, and attracting minimal investment as a result. The permanent way was very unsatisfactory, with rotten sleepers and poor maintenance. Alas, the results were fatal, for on the morning of 3 September 1923 a train was derailed at Golf Club Halt, resulting in the demise of the fireman (who was scalded to death) and injury to the driver. When subsequently cross-examined in court about the state of the trackwork on that fateful day, an indignant Colonel Stephens retorted that it 'was no worse than when the tramway opened'.[32] Perhaps as a result of the accident, in 1924 the line was formally registered in accordance with current legislation, becoming in the process the West Sussex Light Railway. But the change in status and name did not improve the line's fortunes, and it was closed in January 1935.

The Rye & Camber was the second of Colonel Stephens' railway ventures in England. Unlike his other two Sussex lines, it was built not to standard gauge but to a narrow gauge of 3 ft 0 in. Opened in July 1895, it was extended to Camber Sands in 1908. Running along the Rother valley to the seaside, it was frequented by holidaymakers and golfers (the latter alighting at Golf Links halt). By 1925, however, traffic began to decline, and winter services were abandoned. During the Second World War, the line was requisitioned by the government as part of its defensive anti-invasion precautions along the Sussex coast. In some places, the track bed was concreted over to give army lorries easy access to the beach. After the war, the railway was returned to its owners but, despite plans to reopen the line, the cost of restitution proved too great and the remaining infrastructure was sold for scrap.

Brighton Belle

While Colonel Stephens had tinkered with his far-flung empire, mainstream railway services had developed apace in Sussex. The main lines and country routes now complete, the emphasis shifted to enhancement and improvement. By 1905 a through-train dubbed *The Sunny South Special!* was introduced from Manchester and Liverpool, with portions for Brighton and Eastbourne. It was suspended during the First World War but reintroduced thereafter, finally disappearing from the timetable in 1939 on the outbreak of the Second World War after a life of more than thirty years. Of even greater longevity was the London–Brighton Pullman express service, which survived in one form or another until 1972. The first Pullman dining cars had arrived on the LBSCR in 1875, and in December 1881 a weekday all-Pullman train was inaugurated. This was the forerunner of the *Brighton Limited*, as it became in 1899, which ran non-stop from London to Brighton in an unheard-of one-and-a-quarter hours. In 1908 the train was renamed the *Southern Belle* and was soon a by-word for unparalleled luxury, one contemporary account describing its Pullman carriages as 'exquisitely upholstered, lighted by electricity ... comfortably warmed and ventilated and fitted with all the latest improvements'.[33] There was mahogany panelling inlaid with sandalwood, expensive carpeting, damask silk blinds, and 'settees in green morocco'.[34] The LBSCR promoted the service as 'The Most Luxurious Train in the World', a 'Chain of Vestibuled Luxury'. During the First World War the *Southern Belle* was downgraded, sometimes even running without its famous Pullmans, but by 1919 it was back to its pre-war status. After the grouping of 1923, the new Southern Railway continued the *Southern Belle*, its public relations department under the imaginative and energetic J.B. Elliot recognising the train's enduring popularity and prestige. Indeed, Elliot made much of the train's 'coming of age' in November 1929, celebrating twenty-one years of service with a celebratory 'birthday' run and commemorative publication.

By now, however, the Southern Railway had announced its electrification programme. Third-rail 'Southern Electric' services on the Brighton mainline were introduced as far as Three Bridges in July 1932, and reached Brighton itself in time for inauguration on New Year's Day 1933. Dark-green electric multiple units – with prosaic designations such as 4 LAV, 2 BIL and 6 PAN, and variously nicknamed 'juicers', 'flashboxes' or 'emus' – became familiar objects quite literally overnight on the Brighton line, and later on other routes as electrification was extended to destinations such as Lewes, Eastbourne and Littlehampton.

Southern Electric 2 BIL Unit No. 2116, was commissioned during 1937 for the Southern Railway's electrified route to Bognor Regis, one of the penultimate batch of the same class of electric multiple units, the first of which had been introduced in early 1935 for use on the Eastbourne line. During the 1940s and 1950s the 2 BIL units provided the backbone of semi-fast services on most electrified routes in Sussex, and some survived into the early 1970s on stopping-train services such as those on the Brighton–Littlehampton route.
© NATIONAL RAILWAY MUSEUM/SCIENCE & SOCIETY PICTURE LIBRARY

The last steam-hauled *Southern Belle* ran behind the veteran locomotive *Remembrance*, to be replaced by brand-new all-Pullman electric multiple units (designated 5 BEL) which in June 1934 were renamed the *Brighton Belle*. Resplendent in its Pullman chocolate-and-cream livery, the *Brighton Belle* became a firm favourite with the travelling public, its first-class dining cars graced with girls' names fashionable in the 1930s: Gwen, Mona, Doris, Hazel, Audrey and Vera. Despite bomb damage to one of the units, the *Brighton Belle* survived the Second World War, regaining its popularity in the 1950s and 1960s, not least with the many actors and actresses who lived in Brighton but performed on the London stage. Foremost among these was Laurence Olivier, who welcomed the opportunity to relax in the by now fading 1930s' opulence, and relished the traditional breakfast dish of grilled kippers as he sped towards the bright lights of the capital. The *Brighton Belle* had become a legend in its own lifetime. As one observer noted, capturing the mood of celebratory status: 'More stories could be told of the *Belle* than of any other Pullman train … the scene on-board of adventure and romance and also on occasions of sorrow and even tragedy.'[35] Among the latter, unfortunately, was the sad case of a young woman, a student, who, crossed in love, took her own life on the train on 14 October 1960. She was found dead in the lavatory of one of the Pullman cars when, in the late afternoon, it was shunted to the depot at the ironically named Lovers Walk.

The 'Brighton Belle', sporting head-code 4 (non-stop London–Brighton), is seen at speed in this British Railways (Southern Region) advertisement of 1958. Although now rather elderly (its component 5 BEL units were built in 1932), the 'Belle' is still promoted enthusiastically as an up-market ALL-PULLMAN TRAIN, and the juxtaposition of an Art Deco signal-box hints at the continuing robustness of pre-war infrastructural modernity on the Southern's nationalised network.
© NRM/PICTORIAL COLLECTION/SCIENCE & SOCIETY PICTURE LIBRARY

Bexhill-on-Sea. Ronald Lampitt (1906–88) produced a series of highly romanticised illustrations of life and landscapes in Britain and Ireland before and after the Second World War. He was noted especially for his evocative posters produced for the pre-nationalisation railway companies, including this one for the Southern Railway in 1947 advertising Bexhill-on-Sea. Depicting the Bauhaus-inspired De La Warr Pavilion, the poster hints at an up-market modernity while still portraying a traditional landscape and seascape of golden beaches and rolling countryside.
© NRM/SCIENCE & SOCIETY PICTURE LIBRARY

In its last years, the *Brighton Belle* suffered the ignominy of being repainted in the new British Rail corporate livery of blue-and-grey, a portent of its imminent demise in 1972 as it became life expired. The final day, 30 April, included 'Cheese and Wine' and 'Champagne' specials to say 'Farewell to the *Brighton Belle*'. In its prime, the *Brighton Belle* had held a central place in the Southern Railway's marketing strategy, its speed and comfort enticing a new generation of commuting public.

Although the Southern never did come up with a Sussex equivalent of its famous slogans 'Live in Kent and Be Content' and 'Live in Surrey Free from Worry', it did publish an information booklet *Southern Homes – Sussex*, timed to appear after electrification of the Portsmouth via Horsham line in July 1938, extolling the virtues of living in the countryside.[36] A prominent pre-war poster 'Evenings by the Sea', showing a smartly dressed young woman about to board a Southern Electric unit, encouraged after-work trips to the seaside as well as demonstrating the benefits of commuting.[37] Another, showing an eager young man waiting at Brighton station alongside a signboard announcing 'Six Trains Hourly from London', explained: 'She's late, but of course I'll wait for at least six more trains.'[38] Likewise, there were posters advertising the delights of Hastings – now reinvented by the Southern as the 'Conqueror's Coast' – and other destinations such as Bexhill-on-Sea (aimed at long-stay visitors rather than day trippers), Eastbourne (marketed as select and genteel), and Seaford (with its bracing walks and breathtaking cliffs). A Southern Railway booklet also explained that 'Seaford is most excellent for children; for anaemia, debility, convalescence; for tuberculosis, chronic bronchitis and catarrh'.[39]

Something of the stature and lofty atmosphere of Chichester, Sussex cathedral city and county town of West Sussex, is caught in this British Railways poster of 1955. The artwork was undertaken by Claude Buckle (1905–1973), a prolific poster artist, first for the Great Western Railway and then for the nationalised British Railways. Chichester cathedral, featured in the poster, was begun in 1076, a decade after the Norman Conquest, and dedicated in 1108. By the twentieth century it had become a major tourist attraction.
© NRM/PICTORIAL COLLECTION/SCIENCE & SOCIETY PICTURE LIBRARY

Sussex, it seemed, had something for everyone – and in a sense, it did. The railway, from its beginnings in the mid-nineteenth century to its zenith on the eve of the Second World War, had succeeded in transforming the county. Brighton had appeared the principal beneficiary of the new age, but before long the railway bestowed its gifts upon almost all parts of Sussex. Hove, Worthing, Seaford, Eastbourne, Bognor and other coastal towns participated in the growing holiday trade – in its several forms – and the railway, with its ever more efficient services (especially after electrification of the major routes) made commuting from Sussex an increasingly attractive prospect for many businessmen and women. The social and economic fabric of Sussex was generally improved by the coming of the railway, and the people of Sussex were interconnected and mobile in a way that had never been possible before. Even Colonel Stephens had played his part.

EIGHT

Literary Sussex

Johnson, Dickens, Thackeray

Almost a decade before the Prince of Wales, the future George IV, had first visited Brighton, the town's emerging reputation as a resort and watering hole had attracted the inimitable Samuel Johnson. In the 1770s he was in the habit of accompanying his friends, Henry and Hester Thrale, to the town, staying in their holiday house in West Street. Dr Johnson especially enjoyed the company of Hester, who in return later penned the affectionate and amusing *Anecdotes of the Late Samuel Johnson*, published in 1786. Johnson worked on his *Lives of the Poets* when in Brighton, for which Hester Thrale dutifully checked the proofs. The novelist and poet Charlotte Smith was another early literary figure who made Brighton her home (where she was visited by an admiring William Wordsworth in 1791). Her best-known novel *The Old Manor House*, thought by critics to be 'brisk, ironic, and confident', is an adventure story set partly in America.[1] But she also wrote fondly of her home county (she had also lived in Chichester); her final volume *Beachy Head and Other Poems* was published posthumously in 1807.

Most famously, Charles Dickens was among Brighton's early literary devotees, staying variously at the Old Ship Inn and at addresses in Kings Road and East Street, along with the Bedford Hotel. In the summer of 1837, on completion of the last of his *Pickwick Papers*, he paid his first visit to the town. His wife Catherine, already pregnant with their second child (she and Dickens had married in April 1836), accompanied him. But Dickens was yearning for the company of his new friend, John Foster, literary editor and critic, complaining in a letter to him that 'unless I am joined by some male company ... [I am] unlikely to see anything but the Pavilion, the chain Pier, and the Sea'.[2] Still, he enjoyed the atmosphere of Brighton, finding it little altered from the days of the Prince Regent and appreciating the fine terraces of town houses and hotels. Indeed, so successful was the visit, that he was back in early November 1837. Again, he found Brighton exhilarating, although Catherine in her condition was hesitant about venturing out into the blustery gales. 'It is a beautiful day and we have been taking advantage of it,' Dickens wrote to John Foster on

Samuel Johnson (1709–1787), English poet, critic, essayist and lexicographer, reckoned that 'when a man is tired of London, he is tired of life'. However, although he disliked the wind-swept Sussex Downs, Dr Johnson much enjoyed his sojourns in Brighton, where he stayed with his friends Henry and Hester Thrale, and where he worked on his *Lives of the Poets*. For him, and others like him, urbane Brighton would become a kind of 'London by the sea', a maritime version of the metropolis.

The portrait is instantly recognisable as Charles Dickens, as familiar today as it would have been in his own time. Taken *c.*1865, this is a *carte-de-visite* portrait, designed to be mounted on a card of equivalent size to the normal visiting card of the mid-nineteenth century. As well as definitively introducing their bearers, the *carte-de-visite* cards proffered by celebrities such as Dickens were eagerly snapped up by enthusiastic collectors, a craze not unlike autograph hunting today.

3 November, 'but the wind until today has been so high and the weather so stormy, that Kate has been scarcely able to peep out of the door.'[3] By 1841 Dickens was writing *Barnaby Rudge*, and sought a fortnight's solitude in Brighton to help develop the story. In June 1846 it was *Dombey and Son*, serialised like his other books, that brought him to the town. This time he was recovering from the twin traumas of Catherine's latest and very difficult childbirth and a horrific attack by a horse which had ripped the sleeve from his jacket and hurt his arm. Recuperating as well as writing, Dickens pressed ahead with his new story, borrowing Brighton scenes and characters to add colour to his narrative. The Bedford Hotel, for example, where he was staying, was imagined as the abode of Captain

Cuttle. The 'steep bye-street' where lived the unpleasant Mrs Pipchin, to whom the unfortunate young Paul Dombey is sent after his nurse is summarily dismissed, was likewise inspired by Brighton's precincts. So too was Dr Blimber's 'cramming school', to which Paul is sent, the location thought to be based on Chichester House in Chichester Terrace. Dickens described it thus:

> The doctor's was a mighty fine house, fronting the sea, not a joyful style of house within, but quite contrary. Sad coloured curtains, whose proportions were spare and lean, hid themselves despondently behind the window. The chairs and tables were put away in rows, like figures of a sum; fires were so rarely lighted in the rooms of ceremony, that they felt like wells, and visitors represented the bucket.[4]

But if this seemed a bleak estimation of Brighton, it delighted William Makepeace Thackeray, who had nothing but praise for Dickens' portrait of Dr Blimber's cheerless school, and thought the description of poor Paul's demise 'unsurpassed … stupendous'.[5] Thackeray, indeed, was another confirmed Brighton enthusiast, visiting the town frequently in the 1840s and 1850s (he wrote a series of articles about it in *Punch* in 1845–47) and absorbing its invigorating milieu, an essential ingredient for his novel *Vanity Fair*. He wrote appreciatively:

> But have we any leisure for a description of Brighton? – for Brighton, a clean Naples with genteel lazzaroni – for Brighton, that always looks brisk, gay and gaudy, like a harlequin's jacket – for Brighton, which used to be seven hours distant from London at the time of our story; which is now only a hundred minutes off.[6]

The latter observation was an allusion to the impact of the coming of the railway, with its dramatic shortening of the travel time between London and Brighton, and the (relative) comfort and convenience it brought to the journey. Dickens and Thackeray were both devotees of the railway, and we may assume that their journeys to Brighton were usually made by train, such as Dickens' brief visit in 1869 as part of a hectic readings tour that also took him to London, Manchester and Liverpool. Such an extensive itinerary over a short period would not have been possible without the railway network. Thackeray, for his part, mused in his advancing years on the changes that the railways had wrought. 'We who have lived before railways were made, belong to another world,' he exclaimed. 'In how many hours,' he asked rhetorically, 'could the Prince of Wales drive from Brighton to London, with a light carriage built expressly, and relays of horses longing to gallop the next stage? Do you remember … the coachman of the Age, who took our half-crown so affably? It was only yesterday; but what a gulf between now and then!' As he concluded: 'We who lived before railways, and survive out of the ancient world, are like Father Noah and his family out of the Ark. The children will gather round and say to us patriarchs, "Tell us, grandpapa, about the old world".'[7]

William Makepeace Thackeray (1811–1863) was a great admirer of Brighton and Sussex. He first made his name as a writer in 1842 in a series of articles in *Punch* about English snobbery, seen through the eyes of a humble footman. Thackeray also wrote about Brighton in his *Punch* articles, as well as in his well-known novel *Vanity Fair*. He became editor of the *Cornhill Magazine* in 1860, a few years before his death.

As Thackeray recognised, the early allure which had drawn literary luminaries such as Samuel Johnson to Brighton had been enhanced considerably by the coming of the railway. Horace Smith, who lived at Cavendish Place, entertained the town's growing group of literati in the mid-nineteenth century, ably assisted by his daughters – 'the Misses Smith', as they were known – who welcomed writers such as Thackeray, Thomas Hood, Samuel Rogers, and Harrison Ainsworth, the latter also another close friend of Charles Dickens. By then Smith was contributing to Ainsworth's popular *New Monthly Magazine* (which ran from 1814 to 1884), another feature of his aspiring literary life and further evidence of Brighton's emergence as an important centre of literary activity. Ainsworth, indeed, positively enthused about Brighton. A measure of his own regard for the town and its environs, he set his well-received 1860 novel *Ovingdean Grange* – a tale about the flight of the future Charles II across the Channel to France – in the nearby village of Ovingdean, to which he had often walked over the Downs from Brighton. Other writers flocked to make Brighton their home: Robert Surtees, Thomas Hughes, and Herbert Spencer all ended their days there. A.E. Coppard, born in the town in 1872, the son of a tailor, worked as a bookkeeper for a Brighton engineering firm before becoming a full-time author, supplementing his income through prizes won at athletic contests. His short-stories 'Ninepenny Flute' and 'Pomona's Babe' were both set in Brighton, part of a growing literary trend in which writers as diverse as Arnold Bennett, Henry James and Somerset Maugham contrived to compose stories with Brighton themes. It was a trend that reached its apogee in the 1930s, with Graham Greene's celebrated novel *Brighton Rock*.

Virginia Woolf and Sussex

However, just as Brighton's literary scene had benefited from the coming of the railway, so Sussex as a whole was now opened up to the attentions of writers and artists who were attracted to the delights of the deepest countryside. Seemingly remote – in the Weald or on the Downs or in the Marsh – Sussex was now supremely accessible from the metropolis, allowing literary types to commute with ease between their busy London lives and the quiet privacy of their rural retreats. The Bloomsbury Group, for example, formed in 1905–06 around the nucleus of the gifted Stephen family (including Virginia Woolf, as she became on marriage to Leonard Woolf in 1912), spent interludes in Sussex, first at Asheham, near Lewes, where Virginia and Leonard rented a house from 1912 to 1919, and then at Monk's House at nearby Rodmell which the Woolfs purchased in 1919. Virginia, who had happy childhood memories of St Ives, was at first tempted by the alternative prospect of moving to Cornwall. In the gloomy January of 1919, with its post-war shortages, she had spent much of the time ill in bed at her home in Richmond, near London, and envied her friend Ka Cox who had recently relocated to Cornwall. Virginia thought that 'to be ill at the Lizard seems to me better than to be well here', and that, 'sensible people like you go & live in Cornwall'.[8] In fact, she had heard that there was a cottage up for rent at Gurnard's Head, not far from St Ives, and asked Ka to investigate on her behalf. But it was another of Virginia Woolf's literary associates, Katherine Mansfield, who reported that the cottage at Higher Tregerthen, near Zennor, rented during the war by D.H. Lawrence, was now empty and could be had for £5 a year. Virginia jumped at the opportunity, immediately taking the cottage, but it seems unlikely that she ever visited her new acquisition. Instead, recognising that Cornwall was just too far from London to allow them to pursue their literary lives, the Woolfs redoubled their commitment to Sussex. When the lease at Asheham expired, they promptly purchased Monk's House, which remained their home together until Virginia's death in 1942.

Asheham (or 'Asham', as Virginia would spell it) had been an important retreat for the Woolfs during their early married years, and through the First World War. They had spent the first night of their honeymoon there, and, staying at Asheham over Christmas 1912, they considered settling permanently in Sussex. But thoughts of acquiring a few animals and some poultry, and quietly pursuing the life of country smallholders, were soon dismissed, for the draw of London was just too strong. Thereafter, the plan was always to divide their time between the capital and the countryside. Nonetheless, the Woolfs were frequently at Asheham, where literary friends (such as Lytton Strachey) and relations often came to stay, and in 1916 Virginia persuaded her sister Vanessa Bell to rent a farm at nearby Charleston. For Virginia, Sussex was often a welcome relief from the pressures of London life, although she could not escape the bipolar disorder that would often disturb her mental balance: at times she worked with feverish excitement; at others she was overcome by headaches, insomnia and a debilitating sense of personal irrelevance, as well as an irrational belief that her literary output was worthless and ought to be torn up. At Asheham, early in the New Year of 1913, Leonard became very worried about his wife's health, and together the Woolfs decided, although they yearned to have children, that it would probably be better if they did not. By the end of 1915 it had become clear that Virginia's illness was now, more or less, a permanent fact of life. Asheham was part of its management, with holidays there at Christmas and over Easter, another break during May, and then an extended stay from late July until perhaps October.

This pattern was disturbed by the expiry of the lease at Asheham. No sooner had Virginia decided on impulse to rent the cottage in Cornwall, only then to decide against it, than on a whim she bought a house at Lewes. It was a converted windmill, high on the hill near the castle walls, but the environment was essentially urban, not at all the country setting she really wanted. Admitting her mistake, and buoyed by the suddenly mushrooming sales for her new book *Kew Gardens*, she and Leonard managed to extricate themselves from the purchase of the Round House, and acquired instead Monk's House – a two-storeyed brick and flint cottage, weather-boarded on the side facing the street – at Rodmell. They had seen it advertised during a visit to Lewes, and on viewing the cottage had liked it instantly. There was no hot water or bath or indoor lavatory, but Virginia was spartan by nature and used to 'roughing it'. She was also drawn to the extensive gardens and orchard, and by the wonderful views across open countryside.

Vita and death

At Monk's House, Virginia Woolf penned significant sections of some of her most important work – including *Jacob's Room, Mrs Dalloway, To the Lighthouse, Orlando, The Years*, and *Three Guineas* – and entertained literary guests such as E.M. Forster, the economist John Maynard Keynes, Rose Macauley, Raymond Mortimer, and William Plomer. She also formed an intense sapphic relationship with the aristocrat writer Vita Sackville-West, and from Monk's House would visit her at her at Knole and Long Barn across the border in Kent. Vita's son, Nigel Nicolson, thought 'Virginia the most remarkable human being I have ever known'. He and his brother Benedict were then only children. 'To us,' Nigel explained, 'she was not Virginia who had been mad and could go mad again, nor Virginia Woolf who had uncovered a whole new seam

Monk's House at Rodmell, near Lewes, an eighteenth-century weatherboard building, was the Sussex retreat purchased by Virginia and Leonard Woolf in 1919. It was here, in a wooden shed at the bottom of the garden, that Virginia wrote many of her well-known novels. OLIVER MALLINSON LEWIS/WIKIMEDIA COMMONS/CC BY-SA 2.0

of literary perception.' Instead, she 'was Virginia. Virginia who was fun, Virginia who was easy, who asked us questions about school and holidays ... and who floated in and out of our lives like a godmother.'[9] Vita, for her part, told her husband Harold that 'I simply adore Virginia Woolf', and in her diary confided that Virginia was 'delicious', her 'head swimming with Virginia'.[10] And Virginia reciprocated, writing excitedly in *her* diary in May 1926: 'And Vita comes to lunch tomorrow, which will be a great amusement and pleasure. I am amused at my relations with her. ... I like her presence and her beauty.' Virginia asked herself the ultimate question: 'Am I in love with her? But what is love? Her being "in love" (it must be comma'd thus) with me, excites and flatters and interests.'[11]

It was an affair of the heart that lasted until early 1935. One day in March, during a snowstorm, Virginia and Leonard drove across from Monk's House to visit Vita at Sissinghurst, where she was now installed. By the time they left to return home that evening, Virginia recognised that the passion she and Vita had once felt for one another had now dissipated, and that, as her nephew and biographer Quentin Bell observed: 'that particular excitement had gone out of her life, leaving a blankness, a dullness.'[12] Nonetheless, Virginia Woolf had captured much of that earlier intensity in her book *Orlando*, published in 1928, which Nigel Nicolson has called 'the longest and most charming love-letter in literature'. The novel, which, inevitably, was dedicated to Vita Sackville-West, ranges over several centuries, during which the protagonist, Orlando (modelled, of course, on Vita), switches from one sex to the other and back again. As

Nigel Nicolson put it, Virginia 'plays with her, dresses her in furs, lace and emeralds, flirts with her', and finally places her at Long Barn, with her dogs, waiting for Virginia to arrive.[13] Fortunately, Vita was enchanted by the book, recognising it as a lasting testament to her friendship with Virginia.

The journeys to visit Vita Sackville-West in Kent had been made straightforward by the Woolfs' acquisition of a motorcar. Virginia took driving lessons but, having inadvertently driven through a hedge, decided that the car was best left to Leonard and that she would be the passenger. Together, as Quentin Bell noted, the Woolfs explored the 'whole Sussex countryside, with its castles, seashores and great houses', which the car had suddenly made so accessible, as well as visiting Vanessa at Charleston and John Maynard Keynes and his wife, the ballerina Lydia Lopokova, in their new home at nearby Tilton.[14] Virginia's admiration for the Sussex countryside had not diminished – indeed, quite the reverse. In the last decade of her life, she increasingly turned her back on Bloomsbury and 'the hurried London years', as she called them, and cherished the domestic solitude of Monk's House. 'We get snatches of divine loneliness here,' she told her sister Vanessa. She sought 'the old habitual beauty of England', she explained: 'the silver sheep clustering; & the downs soaring, like birds' wings sweeping up & up. … It feeds me, rests me, satisfies me, as nothing else does. … This has a holiness.' She added, presciently: 'This will go on after I am dead.' She enjoyed the freedom of walking on the cliffs and Downs, and Lyndall Gordon, in her life of Virginia Woolf, recounts an amusing incident when Virginia startled a local landowner at Piddinghoe, the 'lean, aristocratic' Mr Gwynne, when she suddenly appeared on his property unexpectedly, scrambling under a barbed-wire fence in her woolly hat.[15] The Woolfs had also recently purchased a gramophone, which added to the cosy domesticity of life at Monk's House. In the morning Virginia would write, then look at the newspapers and have lunch. In the early afternoon, she might take a walk or do some gardening or bread-making, followed by tea. Then it was back to her books and letters before cooking dinner, after which she might listen to the much-prized gramophone, read or embroider before retiring to bed.

Yet Virginia fretted about what she saw as the threat to the Sussex countryside. The open country between Lewes and the coast was increasingly being filled in with a creeping suburbia, and the post-1918 creation of 'Peacehaven', east of Brighton, and the consequent giving over of the cliffs and downland between Rottingdean and Newhaven to bungalow development, distressed her deeply. Worst of all was the establishment of a cement-making plant in full view of Monk's House, fatally obscuring Virginia's vista out across the South Downs and bringing the noise and pollution of industry deep into the heart of the country. Other things disturbed her. A life-long socialist – both she and

Leonard were Fabians – Virginia had nonetheless become increasingly critical of left-wing writers, especially during her later years in Sussex. In a lecture to the Workers' Educational Association in Brighton in May 1940, for example, she criticised the poetry of left-wing intellectuals. The talk was published subsequently as *The Leaning Tower*, in which Virginia Woolf argued that middle-class writers were incapable of escaping the strictures of the English class system, and that, despite their ideological convictions, their whole outlook was the product of their class position. They were in fact entirely ignorant of the working classes, their culture and their social aspirations. As she put it, the 'rising novelist is never pestered to come to gin and winkles with the plumber and his wife ... or start a correspondence with the old lady who sells matches and bootlaces'.[16] Leonard, after the completion of his second and final novel *The Wise Virgins* in 1914, had devoted himself increasingly to political writings and activity. In this, Virginia supported him. She was a member of the Rodmell Labour Party, for example, of which she was secretary for a time. But she was exasperated by its meetings, where attendees found it difficult to focus on the looming international problems of the day and preferred to engage in village gossip. Yet she colluded in the process, seemingly encouraging such chatter. When, in October 1935, she and Leonard had attended the annual Labour Party Conference in Brighton, she had been shocked at the way in which the tough, no-nonsense Ernest Bevin had crushed the pacifist party leader, George Lansbury, in a debate about international security. As far as she was concerned, the entire political system – at home and abroad – had been overtaken by madness.

A pacifist herself, Virginia Woolf was dispirited by the outbreak of war, although she and Leonard were under no illusions about the nature of the Nazi regime or what might happen if Britain were invaded (see p.234). When the Woolfs' London address was bombed in September 1940, and Monk's House perforce became their permanent home, Virginia experienced mixed feelings. When the novelist Elizabeth Bowen visited in early 1941, she found Virginia all smiles and laughter. But already Leonard had detected a dangerous change of mood, and in the March they sought medical assistance. But now Virginia was beyond help, or so she thought. Fearing the onset of madness, and not wanting to become a burden on Leonard, she decided to take her own life. She had wondered before what it might be like to drown. In her novel *Mrs Dalloway*, the character Septimus Warren Smith considers drowning, and decides that it is not to be feared.[17] Rather, drowning was an exciting, challenging journey of discovery in search of the dead. Perhaps this became Virginia's view too. Either way, on the morning of Friday 28 March 1941, she wrote three letters – one for her sister Vanessa, the others for Leonard – explaining that she was hearing voices, and was about to descend into a madness from which she would not recover. Picking up her walking stick, she crossed the fields to the river

Ouse. Putting a large, heavy stone in her coat pocket, she left her stick on the bank and went into the water. Leonard later buried Virginia's ashes in the garden at Monk's House, continuing to live there and writing five remarkable volumes of autobiography. Today, Virginia Woolf is acclaimed as one of the greatest novelists of the twentieth century, whose innovative techniques – such as 'stream of consciousness' composition – have become part of mainstream creative writing. By the 1970s, she had also been acclaimed as a feminist icon.

Eric Gill and Arts & Craft

Among Virginia and Leonard Woolf's literary and artistic friends were Eric Gill and his wife Ethel (or Mary, as she became after her conversion to Catholicism), who lived close by at Ditchling. Like the Woolfs, Eric and Ethel were Fabian socialists. They were also enthusiastic adherents of the Arts & Crafts movement, and of William Morris's 'back to the land' socialism, with its origins in the Pre-Raphaelite Brotherhood of painters (of which Morris was a part), and its desire to create 'little communities' in which people 'had few wants; almost no furniture for instance, and no servants, and studied … what they really wanted'.[18] Morris was a polymath, with a breathtaking range of intellectual and practical skills that encompassed fine art painting, glass and ceramic tiling, weaving, textile and wallpaper design, calligraphy, type design and setting, printing and publishing, poetry, writing and lecturing. He encouraged others to pursue such interests, and envisaged his 'little communities' consisting of similarly skilled craftsmen and women, living simple but productive lives. Morris's influence in Sussex was evident as early as 1891–94 when his disciple, the architect Philip Webb, designed and built his masterpiece, Standen, a fine country house near East Grinstead. The building became the prototype for any number of look-alike Arts & Crafts suburban villas across Sussex and the Home Counties, but is, of course, remarkable in its own right – not least for its extensive use of William Morris wallpapers and fabrics and carpets, together with Arts & Crafts furniture and fittings. Webb became a lifelong Sussex enthusiast, delighting especially in the county's ancient churches, although at length he began to fret at the 'development' and urbanisation of the Sussex countryside.

By 1900 Sussex was beginning to attract other Arts & Crafts devotees, with Philip Webb and William Morris encouraging the establishment of several 'colonies' in the county. A guild of handicrafts was set up at South Harting, and similar communities were founded at Amberley and Storrington. Most important, however, was Ditchling, which developed as a significant centre of the Arts & Crafts movement, where like-minded enthusiasts attempted to put Morris's principles into practice. An early arrival was Amy Sawyer, the dramatist and painter, and among those who followed in her footsteps were Eric and Ethel Gill. Eric Gill was born in Brighton in 1882, his father – the Revd Arthur Tidman Gill – an unconventional and impecunious nonconformist clergyman, at first with the Congregationalists and then in Lady Huntingdon's Connexion. The latter, founded in Brighton in 1760 by Selina, Countess of Huntingdon, was a curious blend of Calvinist Methodist theology and Anglican liturgy, and Sussex was its stronghold. Although Gill, who eventually became a Catholic, played down his early nonconformist background, it is clear that this unusual religious childhood greatly influenced his later life. A further influence was the presence of the London, Brighton and South Coast Railway, whose elegant locomotives and impressive infrastructure fascinated him, prompting his life-long interest in design and in drawing – in 1896, at the age of fourteen, he executed a remarkably accurate sketch of the LBSCR engine *Goldsmit*. Eighteen ninety-six was also the year when Gill's father decided to leave Lady Huntingdon's Connexion, and to join the Church of England, necessitating a move to the cathedral town of Chichester. There the young Eric developed his interests in architecture and art, enrolling at the age of fifteen in the local Chichester Technical and Art School. Later he would reject its highly conventional syllabus, but the techniques and discipline it taught were a useful preparation for his future career. Among other things, he developed his abiding interest in 'lettering'.[19]

Eric Gill (1882–1940), sculptor, typeface designer and sometime devotee of the Arts & Crafts movement, was born in Sussex and spent much of his productive life there, based at Ditchling. Although a convert to Roman Catholicism, his beliefs and sexual behaviour became increasingly wayward, yet his artistic reputation has remained intact and indeed has strengthened over time.
RANDOM HOUSE

At Chichester, Eric Gill also discovered women, soon to be another life-long passion, first in his adoration from afar of fellow art student, Winifred Johnson, and then his far more serious love affair with Ethel Moore – his future wife – daughter of the sacristan at the cathedral. Unfortunately, Gill's parents disapproved of Ethel, and, by now disillusioned with Chichester, the Church of England and, of course, the art school, at the age of 18 he headed for London. There he encountered the Fabian Society and the Arts & Crafts movement, befriending the leading calligrapher Edward Johnston and enrolling in classes in the Morris-inspired Central School of Arts and Crafts. It was there that he received one of his first commissions, for a tombstone inscription. Gill kept in close touch with his beloved Ethel but he also went with prostitutes, another feature of London life that he found appealing, although always careful to tell a forgiving Ethel all about his indiscretions. In August 1904 Eric and Ethel were married. By now Gill was receiving regular commissions, and in 1905 he and Ethel moved to Hammersmith, the heart of Fabian–Arts & Craft London, centred on William Morris's former home, Kelmscott. Among those he met in this hothouse of advanced thinking was Hilaire Belloc, the Sussex writer whose ideas he found especially attractive, not least his devotion to Roman Catholicism. But at length Hammersmith began to pall, and he and Ethel toyed with the idea of returning to Chichester. In the end they decided upon Ditchling, a remote location on the edge of the Sussex downland, where there was already in the making one of William Morris' 'little communities' of Arts & Crafts workers.

To Ditchling and beyond

Although Eric Gill emphasised the role of Ditchling as rural retreat, he was to spend many of his weekdays in London or elsewhere, on commissions or meeting clients. As Fiona MacCarthy has observed, his life in Sussex was 'more or less that of the glorified commuter'.[20] In this, of course, he had much in common with other artistic and literary figures who made Sussex their home. In 1907 the Gills moved into Sopers, a house in Ditchling village which would be their base for almost half-a-dozen years. They now had a young family, and joined in village life to the full, alongside Amy Sawyer, the weaver Ethel Mairet, Fred Partridge the jeweller, Bernard Leach the potter, and other Arts & Crafts adherents. Eric Gill stitched an enormous 'Back to the Land' banner for display at Ditchling, designed as a perpetual reminder to himself and his associates of their essential *raison d'être*. The Gill family also got to know Sussex, going on summer expeditions across the Downs to the Jack & Jill windmills above Clayton and on to Devil's Dyke or Fulking, enjoying the new-found freedom of the countryside. At home, they baked their own bread, part of the drive for self-sufficiency, and tended the garden. A new workshop was erected alongside Sopers, where Gill could undertake his 'lettering' and inscriptions. He also turned his hand to writing, producing articles for the radical journal *New Age* on subjects such as art and engineering. He was likewise a passable poet:

> What is it to the Sussex shore
> That Alfred's bones lie hidden there?
> And how shall Egypt's parched sands
> Remember Cleopatra's hair?[21]

However, just as Gill had tired of Hammersmith, so he began to question aspects of the Arts & Crafts ethos. He recognised that craftsmen and women could only really sell their hand-made products to middle-class enthusiasts, while industrial manufacturing (which he loathed) was able to appropriate their ideas and churn out limitless cheap imitations for the mass market. He also saw some of his fellow practitioners as in insufferably smug: those who turned all too easily to cosy self-congratulation, while the people to whom they ought to have been appealing – the urban poor – lay firmly outside their exclusive circle. It was a criticism not unlike Virginia Woolf's later attack on left-wing intellectuals. But Gill was also scathing about the working people who were themselves the product of the industrial system. The system made 'good mechanics, good machine-minders', he acknowledged, yet moulded 'men and women who in every other respect are morons, cretins, for whom crossword puzzles, football games, watered beer, sham half-timbered bungalows and shimmering film stars are the highest form of amusement'.[22] It was a regret shared by Father Vincent McNabb, a Catholic priest close to Hilaire Belloc, who was also disappointed that the 'back to the land' cry had failed to liberate the workers from their industrial chains, and had merely enticed middle-class eccentrics who had the means to opt out of everyday life. Instead, Father McNabb believed that the answer lay in religion, that the 'back to the land' movement would only ever be successful if it was at root a religious one. As he insisted: 'Nothing but religion will solve the land question. And nothing but a religious order seeking not wealth but God will pioneer the movement from town to land.'[23]

In 1909 Gill had turned to sculpture, using his skills in working stone to produce representations of the human form. It opened a new artistic world to him, drawing him into a new London 'set' with new ideas beyond the Arts & Craft strictures. Out of these he had tried to fashion a 'New Religion'. But as he sought to construct a religious foundation for his own 'back to the land' beliefs, so he came to realise that such a religion existed already – Roman Catholicism. Gradually, the Gills drifted towards Rome. On Eric's thirty-first birthday, Saturday 22 February 1913, he and Ethel (now forever to be known as Mary) were received into the Roman Catholic Church in a ceremony at Brighton. That afternoon, Virginia and Leonard Woolf came to stay for the weekend at Ditchling. The following morning, after mass, the Gills and 'the Wolves' (as Eric dubbed them) went for a hike across the Downs.[24] Not long after, Eric and Mary (as she now was) decided to move out of the village itself and onto Ditchling Common, purchasing a house and two acres of land at a place called Hopkins Crank. This would be the start of Gill's project born afresh, now within the guiding principles of Catholicism. Fortuitously, Gill had just been commissioned by the Catholic Archbishop of Westminster, Cardinal Bourne, to carve fourteen five-foot panels for the Stations of the Cross in Westminster Cathedral, for which Gill produced the first drawings in August 1913. It seemed like a symbolic welcome to the

Church. The following year, in June 1914, Gill met the visionary Father Vincent McNabb for the first time. Father Vincent was a Dominican friar, and had little difficulty in persuading Gill that the new community at Hopkins Crank should be run according to the Order of St Dominic. It was an allegiance that Eric Gill retained for the rest of his life. The Arts & Crafts movement had been essentially agnostic, but now Gill's 'back to the land' community on Ditchling Common had the religious foundation for which he had yearned.

For Gill and his colleagues (notably Hilary [Douglas] Pepler, who arrived at Ditchling Common from Hammersmith in 1915), the manifesto for their 'Distributist' theories was Hilaire Belloc's *The Servile State*, which was published just before the Great War. *The Servile State* which Belloc characterised was capitalist, based on modern industrial society. This produced wage-slaves who, to earn a living, had perforce to work for a small minority of rich employers. The evils of this capitalist world, Belloc thought, were self-evident. However, socialism as conventionally imagined was no alternative. Public ownership of industry and increased taxation would merely hit wage-slaves harder and increase their dependency on the capitalist class. The answer, said Belloc, was – by embracing the far-seeing encyclicals of Pope Leo XIII – to spread the restoration of private property. As Belloc saw it, 'every man' [*sic*] should own 'three acres and a cow'. This, as A.N. Wilson has observed, was 'an anti-industrial, anti-capitalist, anti-modern view'.[25] And it chimed exactly with the religious opinions of Eric Gill. It was a Catholic vision of England, reflecting a particular Catholic reading of English history.

Gill designed a chapel that was built in the meadow adjoining Hopkins Crank, and which became the centrepiece of the new workshop complex, consciously juxtaposing 'work and worship'. A huge crucifix was also erected on the Spoil Heap alongside the Haywards Heath to Brighton road, an impressive calvary which caught the attention of travellers in the locality, proclaiming the Ditchling Common community to a wider, sinful world. It inspired Gill's sister Enid, an accomplished poet, to pen these lines:

> There was a cross on Calvary –
> And stark against the sky,
> There hung the Christ of all the world:
> Men saw – and passed it by.
>
> There is a cross on the wide downs:
> High on the hill its stands: –
> And men have carved and placed it there,
> With love-inspired hands.

They left Him dead on Calvary –
But he is living still: –
His cross against an English sky –
Christ – on a Sussex hill.[26]

In 1921 the Guild of SS Joseph and St Dominic was inaugurated formally on Ditchling Common, and in the following year there were no fewer than forty-one Catholic devotees toiling there. By now, however, Eric Gill's religious vision had begun to explore new and wayward dimensions, as he sought to combine piety with the erotic, to reconcile the sacred and the profane, to blend sex and worship. The erect phallus became a symbol of God's virility, and physical love was the expression of divine love. Following his marriage, Gill had continued to have sexual encounters with other women. He experimented with bestiality, practised incest (with his sisters and daughters), and had an acute sense of *droit de seigneur*. Daisy Hawkins, for example, was the illegitimate daughter of Mrs Hawkins – known to the villagers as 'Hawkie' – the Ditchling dressmaker. They were both part of Gill's circle, and Daisy – perhaps with Gill's support – had attended a convent school in Brighton, being

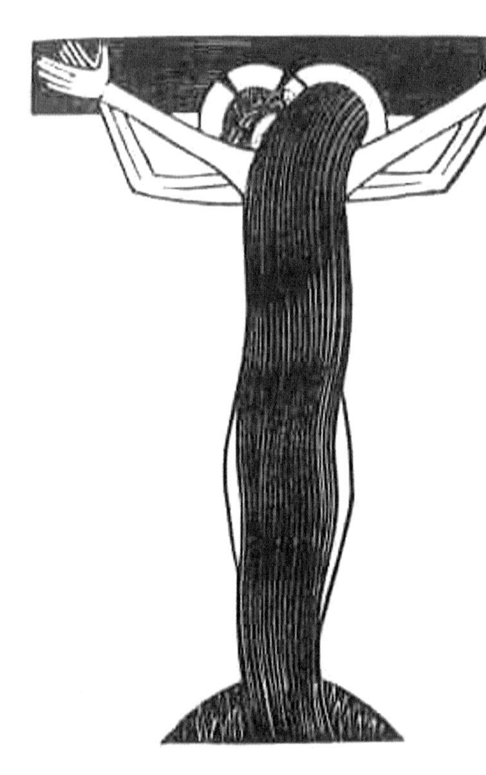

Nuptials of God. This controversial etching by Eric Gill was one of a number that passed into the possession of John Skelton (1923–1999). Gill's nephew (son of Gill's youngest sister, Angela), Skelton was first apprenticed to Eric Gill, just a few months before his death, and later joined the Ditchling community. Subsequently, John Skelton became an assistant at Bridgeman's stonemason's yard in Lewes, and in 1950 set up his own workshop in Burgess Hill. Among several important commissions were a font for Chichester cathedral, a statue of St Augustine for Bexhill-on-Sea, and the sculpture Axiis Mundi for Bishop Otter College in Chichester.
FROM FIONA MACCARTHY, ERIC GILL

received into the Catholic Church when she was twelve. Daisy and Hawkie waited on the Gills at table, adding to the *frisson* of excitement that Eric Gill always felt in Daisy's presence. By the time she was nineteen, Daisy and Gill were engaged in an energetic affair. He drew her constantly, and they made love equally frequently, Gill insisting that sex was an integral part of the creative process.

'All this was far beyond the ken of Father Vincent,' as Fiona MacCarthy has noted with wry understatement.[27] Yet Gill's sexual interests were increasingly reflected in his religious artwork, such as his 1923 wood-engraving *Nuptials of God*, an explicit depiction of the embrace between Christ and His bride (the Church). As well as prompting disquiet in the Ditchling Common community, it also caused dismay in Church circles (which did not know the half of it) where Catholics began to see Gill as unhealthily obsessed with sex. Among Gill's critics was his hitherto close friend, Hilary Pepler, and the two became increasingly estranged, with Gill an ever more isolated figure. In early 1924 a contemplative Gill went to visit the Benedictine community on Caldey Island, off the coast of South Wales, at the suggestion of Donald Attwater, the Catholic writer and author of the *Penguin Dictionary of Saints*. Attwater was interested in Celtic Christianity (his daughter Catherine Rachel John would later write a book on *The Saints of Cornwall*), and his Celtic enthusiasms appear to have rubbed off on Eric Gill, especially when he drew attention to the exciting possibilities of Capel-y-ffin in the Black Mountains. At any rate, feeling that he had overstayed his welcome in Sussex, and that it was time to re-invent his community anew, Gill and his closest relations and friends left for the remote Llanthony valley in south Wales. Here the project was to restore the derelict monastery at Capel-y-ffin which had belonged to the Benedictines before their move to Caldey Island. Eventually, Gill and his followers and their menagerie of animals would move on again, to Pigotts, near High Wycombe in the Chilterns, returning to the English Home Counties and the welcome proximity to London. But the original Guild at Ditchling Common survived until as recently as 1979, and Eric Gill (who died in 1940) – the man who gave the world of printing and design the Gill Sans typeface and executed some of the most outstanding sculptures of his era – has remained linked in popular memory with Sussex and his pioneering community work at Ditchling.

The Catholic world of Hilaire Belloc

Comparable with Eric Gill, perhaps, was Wilfrid Scawen Blunt, the Sussex poet (born at Petworth House) who enjoyed a lengthy career as diplomat, traveller, explorer, and horse-breeder. Like Gill, he was a Catholic and admired the Arts & Craft movement: the Pre-Raphaelite model, Janey Morris – wife of William Morris – was for a time his mistress, and later Morris published an edition of Blunt's poems at his Kelmscott Press. Blunt was also a political radical. A sworn enemy of the British Empire, he supported Egyptian, Irish and Indian nationalist aspirations, in doing so earning something of a reputation as a dangerous revolutionary. He likewise earned a dubious reputation as an amorist. He was married to Lady Anne Noel (granddaughter of Lord Byron) but, like Gill, embarked on a string of extra-marital liaisons. He had a brief affair with Lady Gregory of Coole Park in Ireland, patron of W.B. Yeats, and among his several mistresses was the Irish courtesan Catherine 'Skittle' Walters. When he moved his latest lover, Dorothy Carelton, into the family home, Lady Anne had finally had enough, and she arranged a legal separation in 1906. Blunt had inherited two estates from his brother, Crabbet Park and Newbuilding Place, both in Sussex, and at the former bred Arab horses and rented an estate cottage to Philip Webb, Arts & Crafts architect of Standen. His collected poems were published in 1914, and among them were several extolling the beauties of his native Sussex:

> Say what you will, there is not in the world
> A nobler sight than from this upper Down.
> No rugged landscape here, no beauty hurled
> From its Creator's hand as with a frown:
> But a green plain on which green hills look down
> Trim as a garden plot. No other hue
> Can hence be seen, save here and there the brown
> Of a square fallow, and the horizon's blue.
> Dear checker-work of woods, the Sussex Weald!
> If a name thrills me yet of things on earth
> The name is thine. How often I have fled
> To thy deep hedgerows and embraced each field
> Each lag, each pasture – fields which gave me birth
> And saw my youth, and which must hold me dead.[28]

However, whatever the similarities between Gill and Blunt, the more important connection, of course, was that between Eric Gill and Hilaire Belloc – not a relationship of intimate friendship (they met rarely and moved in different circles) but rather a similarity of vision. For both Gill and Belloc, Catholicism established the guiding principles of everyday life, and it provided the basis of the 'Distributist' political creed to which each adhered. Father Vincent McNabb had acted as conduit between the two men, first as Belloc's confidant and adviser, and then as inspiration for Gill's religious community. But, for the most part, they operated in separate spheres – for a time Belloc was a Liberal MP, until his disillusionment with the parliamentary process – and they pursued their objectives in different directions. Yet Sussex was a constant backdrop for both men, and they drew their inspiration from its soil and landscape. Unlike Gill, Hilaire Belloc was born a Catholic – at La Celle Saint Cloud, a village twelve miles outside Paris, his father a Frenchman, his mother English. And while Gill strayed from Catholic teaching into religious innovations of his own making, Belloc adhered closely to the faith and all that that implied. The circumstances of his birth and upbringing engendered a life-long Europhilia, a passion unusual in England, together with a Catholic imagining of England and English history which placed the country unequivocally at the heart of Europe. Anti-industrial, anti-capitalist and anti-socialist, he looked instead to the land itself for redemption, with his dream of 'three acres and a cow' for Everyman, and in the Sussex countryside he saw distinct possibilities for re-creating this 'Old England' of his imagination.

Hilaire Belloc, photographed in 1908 by Alvin Langdon Coburn. The introspection and melancholy that sometimes affected Belloc (not least when contemplating the future of his beloved Sussex) is apparent in this unsmiling portrait.

Belloc's *The Servile State*, published in 1912, was his defining political and economic analysis, where he set out his critique of existing society and offered a vision of a better future. But 1912 also saw the publication of *The Four Men*, one of a string of travel books that ranged across subjects as diverse as *Paris* and *The Pyrenees*, including the volume that had first made his literary name, *The Path to Rome* – the story of his journey, on foot, from Toul in France, along the Moselle, over the Alps, and finally through Tuscany to his objective, Rome. *The Four Men*, written a decade later, was similar in form to *The Path to Rome*, although the intention this time was to chart a hike through Sussex by four characters – the original 'I' of the journey to Rome, together with a sailor full of salty truths, a gnarled countryman named Grizzlebeard, and a love-struck poet. Each individual, of course, represented a different aspect of Belloc himself. He hoped fervently that the book 'has the sentiment of Sussex running through it', and his biographer A.N. Wilson, comparing the volume to *The Path to Rome*, considered that *The Four Men* 'is different, more poignantly elegiac, more hauntingly religious',[29] an estimation shared by the historian A.L. Rowse who found it 'the most moving' of Belloc's travel writings. As Rowse observed, it was 'a record of those last days when it was possible to walk the length of Sussex, along downs and lanes, through woods and shaws, calling at rustic inns, singing as he went with those shadows, his companions, before the world was polluted by petrol'. As Rowse concluded: 'Those were his days and ways, that was his *floruit.* It is really a strange, autumnal book, touched by melancholy and poetry, the inner Belloc, quiet and questing, which he exposed too rarely.'[30]

In his Preface to *The Four Men*, Belloc addressed himself in intimate proprietorial terms to 'My County', his own 'Dear Sussex', revealing the impulse behind the book, with its sense of deep affection as well as its unsettling portents of passing and decay. 'I have put down in writing what happened to me,' he explained, 'now so many years ago, when I met first one man and then another, and we four bound ourselves together and walked through all your land, Sussex, from end to end. For many years now,' he added, 'I have meant to write it down and have not, nor could I write it down now, or issue this book at all, Sussex, did I not know that you, who must like all created things decay, might with the rest of us be very near your ending.'[31] He mused, sadly:

> For I know very well in my mind that a day will come when the holy place shall perish and all the people of it and never more be what they were. But before that day comes, Sussex, may your earth cover me, and may some loud-voiced priest from Arundel, or Grinstead, or Crawley, or Storrington, but best of all from home, have sung Do Mi Fa Sol above my bones.[32]

The atmosphere of impending loss was prescient, for little more than a year later, in February 1914, Belloc's wife Elodie, to whom he was devoted, died at their home in Sussex, aged only forty-two. For weeks he was inconsolable, and he never really recovered from the loss. Likewise, within the year, Belloc was traumatised further when, for the second time in living memory, his native France was invaded by the advancing hordes of Prussian militarism. Alas, his son Louis, serving in the Royal Flying Corps, was later posted 'missing' in action in Flanders in August 1918.

Belloc's intensely personal, heartfelt, sometimes painful love for Sussex survived these reverses intact. But increasingly it was tinged with fear that the county's days could also be numbered. Here was a note of pessimism which suggested, despite everything he had said and written, that 'three acres and a cow' might after all not be possible. As he put it, writing in 1936: 'Can Sussex endure? No man knows the answer to that question, but in measuring the chances we of the county must admit that they are heavily against our survival.' There were forces, he said, that were 'too powerful to be withstood' and were 'making for the destruction of this county, its traditions, its personality ... they are working at such speed that our own generation may well see the end of the land we knew.'

The motorcar was chief among these assailants, but Belloc also detected 'a spiritual change which destroys our powers of resistance. Men have lost their doctrines, and therefore their manners and morals, and the passing of all the ideas that made our civilisation is due more to this loss of standards than to any material loss.' As he pondered this fading of the Catholic/'Distributist' dream, he added: 'In the midst of so much evil the passing of Sussex would seem a small thing, but to us it is a great one.'[33]

'The great hills of the South Country'

This level of attachment to Sussex – being French-born, decidedly *not* his native heath – is at first difficult to understand. So too is the level of negative introspection which contrasts so startlingly with the bright, energetic comic books that delighted generations of youngsters, *The Bad Child's Book of Beasts* (1896), *More Beasts for Worse Children* (1897) and *Cautionary Tales for Children* (1908). This melancholy, perhaps, is best explained by Belloc's experience of life, of a disillusioned man approaching late middle-age and facing up to the possibility of difficult years ahead (indeed, Belloc was to witness a third German invasion of France, in 1940, and lost a second son, Peter, who died of pneumonia while serving with the Royal Marines in 1941). The extraordinary passion for his adopted county, however, is more complex. A.N. Wilson comes closest to an explanation, perhaps, when he observes that in all the 'wanderings and turmoil' of Belloc's life, Sussex was somewhere where he could feel free and stable: 'Sussex was to be more than the place where he sometimes lived. It was to be an emblem of innocent solidity, of the permanence which forever eluded him.'[34] As Belloc himself put it:

> When I am living in the Midlands,
> That are sodden and unkind,
> I light my lamp in the evening:
> My work is left behind;
> And the great hills of the South Country
> Come back into my mind.
>
> The great hills of the South Country
> They stand along the sea:
> And it's there walking in the high woods
> That I could wish to be,
> And the men that were boys when I was a boy
> Walking along with me.

The 'South Country' is, of course, Sussex, as later stanzas reveal:

I never get between the pines,
But I smell the Sussex air,
Nor I never come to a belt of sand
But my home is there;
And along the sky the line of the Downs
So noble and so bare.

I will gather and carefully make my friends
Of the men of the Sussex Weald,
They watch the stars from silent folds,
They stiffly plough the field.
By them and the God of the South Country
My poor soul shall be healed.

If I ever become a rich man,
Or if ever I grow to be old,
I will build a house with deep thatch
To shelter me from the cold,
And there shall the Sussex songs be sung
And the story of Sussex told.

I will hold my house in the high wood
Within a walk of the sea,
And the men who were boys when I was a boy
Shall sit and drink with me.[35]

Belloc's father had died when Hilaire was only two, and for several years thereafter he lived a strange double life, gravitating between France and Wimpole Street, in London. Belloc disliked Wimpole Street, and his mother, Bessie, having been swindled out of her inheritance by an unscrupulous investor, decided on a move to the country in Sussex. She chose Slindon, where there was a small Catholic church, and took Slindon Cottage. Belloc, just eight years old, was delighted with his new home, as he recalled years later. 'In this place, when I was a boy,' he wrote, 'I pushed through a fringe of beeches … and I came to a glade called No Man's Land. I climbed beyond it, and I was surprised and glad, because from the ridge of that glade I saw the sea.'[36] Although schooling and life's adventures would take him away from Slindon, it remained his retreat, and in when asked in later life where was 'home', he would reply: 'Sussex, whither I had been brought by my family as a little child, and where I have lived all my life.'[37] His wife Elodie grew to love the county too. When Belloc was away lecturing or politicking, Elodie spent less time in their London house and more and more staying with her mother-in-law, Bessie. In the early summer of 1903,

Elodie found that Bleak House, in Slindon village, was up for rent, and with Belloc's agreement she took it, from June to October. For Belloc, it was a symbolic 'coming home', and a spur to find somewhere more permanent in Sussex. Three years later, in 1906, he found the place that they had been looking for – an ancient, rambling property called King's Land, in the hamlet of Shipley, near Horsham. It was to be his home for the rest of his life. He had five acres there, and when not away on his travels would help to farm the land – as near as he would ever get to his 'three acres and cow' – and felt himself close to the Sussex soil which he now claimed as his own. After the Second World War, as he grew yet older, the journeyings that had characterised his busy life came to an end, and he lived quietly in Sussex thereafter. On Thursday 16 July 1953 he died – not at King's Land, unfortunately, but in a nursing home in Guildford in neighbouring Surrey. Nonetheless, he remembered his adopted county at the last:

> When I get to my own country
> I shall lie down and sleep;
> I shall watch in the valleys
> The flocks of sheep.
> And then I shall dream, for ever and all,
> A good dream and deep.[38]

'Yea, Sussex by the sea!'

The only other writer really to match this passionate devotion to Sussex was, perhaps, Rudyard Kipling. Politically, as a conservative Imperialist, he was as far removed from Hilaire Belloc as it was possible to be; moreover, he was suspicious of Roman Catholicism. Yet Kipling was touched by the all-pervading Arts & Crafts influence in Sussex, and was to acquire his own version of the 'back to the land' imperative. And, like Belloc, Philip Webb and Virginia Woolf, he came to fret about the future of Sussex, as he saw it given over increasingly to development and creeping suburbanisation. Kipling was born in India; his wife Caroline 'Carrie' Balestier was an American. These two facts of life came to mould his world-view: of India as vital to Britain's global mission, and of America as a wayward child that might one day be persuaded to rejoin the British fold – the sister 'Five Free Nations' (as Kipling later called them) of Britain, Canada, Australia, New Zealand, and South Africa. Indeed, after their marriage in 1892, Kipling and Carrie lived in her native Vermont, until deteriorating Anglo-American relations over Venezuela and a very public family squabble with Carrie's brother Beatty drove them to England in 1896. Arriving in the UK, the Kiplings lived first at

Torquay, in Devon. But, finding this 'English Riviera' staid, damp and claustrophobic, they were enticed instead to Rottingdean in Sussex by Kipling's 'Aunt Georgie' (his mother's sister) and 'Uncle Ned', the Pre-Raphaelite artist Sir Edward Burne-Jones.

Among other things, Burne-Jones was responsible for seven painted glass windows in Rottingdean church, notably the east window above the altar. Depicting the archangels Gabriel, Michael and Raphael, the window was designed by Burne-Jones to commemorate the marriage of his daughter Margaret, and was executed by his close friend William Morris, himself a frequent visitor to Rottingdean. Not exactly another Ditchling, Rottingdean had nonetheless proved a popular destination for artistic and literary types – and would remain so: Margaret Burne-Jones's daughter, Angela Thirkell, became a popular novelist of note, and Enid Bagnold – of *The Chalk Garden* and *National Velvet* fame – lived in the village from 1923 until her death in 1981. Kipling found Rottingdean congenial, renting 'The Elms', opposite the church, from 1897 until 1902, and it was there that he composed some of his finest and best-known work, including *Stalky and Co*, *Kim*, and the *Just So Stories*, as well as poems such as 'A Smuggler's Song', 'The Absent-Minded Beggar', and his prophetic 'Recessional'. Among this prolific outpouring was his lengthy song of praise to his adopted county, simply entitled 'Sussex', with its memorable and uplifting refrain:

Rudyard Kipling was born in Bombay (today Mumbai) in India on 30 December 1865, and died in London on 18 January 1936. However, he lived in Sussex for much of his life, first at Rottingdean and then at Batemans, near Burwash, from 1897 until the eve of his death. It was in Sussex that he wrote much of his most important and memorable work, including poems and stories about his adopted county. This photograph, taken in 1907, shows Kipling at the height of his powers. In that year he was awarded the Nobel Prize for Literature, becoming the first English-language writer to receive the honour.
ELLIOTT & FRY, BONHAMS

> God gives all men all earth to love,
> But, since man's heart is small,
> Ordains for each one spot shall prove
> Beloved over all.
>
> Each to his choice, and I rejoice
> The lot has fallen to me
> In a fair ground – in a fair ground –
> Yea, Sussex by the sea!

Penned in 1902, 'Sussex' revealed not only Kipling's deep affection for the county but also an intimate knowledge of its history and topography. For example:

> No tender-hearted garden crowns,
> No bosomed woods adorn
> Our blunt, bow-headed, whale-backed Downs,
> But gnarled and writhen thorn –
> Bare slopes where chasing shadows skim,
> And through the gaps revealed,
> Belt upon belt, the wooded, dim,
> Blue goodness of the Weald.
> Here through the strong and shadeless days
>
> The tinkling silence thrills;
> Or little, lost, Down churches praise
> The Lord who made the hills:
> But where the Old Gods guard their round,
> And in her secret heart,
> The heathen kingdom Wilfrid found
> Dreams, as she dwells, apart.

And again:

> I will go out against the sun
> Where the rolled scarp retires,
> And the Long Man of Wilmington
> Looks naked towards the shires;
> And east till doubling Rother crawls
> To find the fickle tide,
> By dry and sea-forgotten walls,
> Our ports of stranded pride.
>
> I will go north about the shaws
> And the deep ghylls that breed
> Huge oaks and old, the which we hold
> No more than Sussex weed;
> Or south where windy Piddinghoe's
> Begilded dolphin veers,
> And red beside the wide-banked Ouse
> Lie down our Sussex steers.[39]

The years at Rottingdean were those when Kipling discovered the pleasures of motoring. Although he was soon to share Belloc's fears for the future of Sussex, Kipling was an enthusiastic motorist, and it was his forays into the Sussex countryside that accounted for his detailed appreciation of the county. Yet he and Carrie continued to travel overseas. In 1898 they spent four months in South Africa, the latest of Kipling's imperial obsessions, and they visited again every year between 1900 and 1908. In 1899, the Kipling family visited America for the last time. Unfortunately, all three children became ill during the voyage, and Kipling and Carrie went down with sickness on arrival in New York. Kipling himself became desperately ill with pneumonia, and only on his recovery did he learn the dreadful news that his daughter Josephine – aged only six – had already died. Those who knew Rudyard Kipling said that he was never the same again. Returning to Rottingdean, he busied himself with his work, but he also began to look elsewhere. As David Gilmour has remarked, Kipling 'wanted a place where Josephine had never played'.[40] He was also increasingly irritated by the trippers from Brighton and elsewhere who peered into the house in the hope of catching a glimpse of the famous writer, and he felt that Rottingdean was becoming too popular. People were moving in from outside, and the village was losing its sense of peace and tranquillity. Accordingly, the Kiplings began house-hunting, seeking privacy and seclusion.

Kipling at Bateman's

They first saw Bateman's, near Burwash, a Sussex ironmaster's house from the seventeenth century, in 1900. But before they could decide upon it, someone else had snapped it up. As Kipling described it in his autobiography, *Something of Myself*, he and Carrie had driven out to Bateman's in response to an advertisement in a newspaper:

> and we reached her down an enlarged rabbit hole of a lane. At very first sight the committee of ways and means said: 'That's her! The only she! Make an honest woman of her – quick!' We entered and felt her spirit – her *feng shui* – to be good. We went through every room and found no shadow of ancient regrets, stifled miseries, nor any menace, though the 'new' end of her was 300 years old. To our woe the owner said: 'I've just let it for twelve months.' We withdrew, each repeatedly telling the other that no sensible person would be found dead in the stuffy little valley where she stood. We lied thus while we pretended to look at other houses till, a year later, we saw her advertised again, and got her.[41]

Kipling paid £9,000 for the house together with its accompanying thirty-three acres of land. Over the years he added to the holding, acquiring land from neighbours as he settled into his role as countryman. His intrepid chauffeur could whizz him to the heart London more effectively than could the train from nearby Etchingham, so he was by no means isolated or cut off. Yet Bateman's offered the illusion of utter remoteness (Kipling even refused to have a telephone installed), providing the calm and quiet that he sought. It also offered the prospect of a 'Merrie England' that matched his imagination, in which the reality of deep agricultural depression in Sussex – prompted by the arrival of abundant meat and cereals from the New World – simply did not exist. Instead, at Bateman's Kipling could indulge his agricultural fantasies. He kept a dairy herd of Guernsey cows ('largely for aesthetic reasons', according to Adam Nicolson) which, as his secretary, Dorothy Ponton, observed wryly, cost more to feed than the value of the milk it produced.[42] Kipling gave each calf a name, delightfully light-hearted and fun – 'Bateman's Baby', 'Bateman's Bunting', and so on – and was inordinately proud when they won prizes at local agricultural shows. He also acquired a herd of deep-red Sussex beef cattle to add to the Wealden scene, and kept pigs, chickens, geese and bees.

Bateman's also appealed to Kipling's deep sense of history, and allowed him to imagine his own Sussex version of England's story. The Dudwell valley, in which Bateman's was situated, and the surrounding Weald, became the often-mystic setting for his later work. *Puck of Pook's Hill* (published in 1906) and *Rewards and Fairies* (1910), addressed to the fictional Dan and Una, were meant for his own children – Elsie and John – as entertaining history lessons, and were steeped in Sussex landscape and lore. 'Puck's Song' asks, enchantingly:

See you the dimpled track that runs
All hollow through the wheat?
O that was where they hauled the guns
That smote King Philip's fleet.

(Out of the Weald, the secret Weald,
Men sent in ancient years
The horse-shoes red at Flodden Field,
The arrows at Poitiers!)

See you our little mill that clacks,
So busy by the brook?
She has ground her corn and paid her tax
Ever since Domesday Book.

See you our stilly woods of oak,
And the dreadful ditch beside?
O that was where the Saxons broke
On the day that Harold died.[43]

But within this rural idyll, Kipling sometimes suffered. Bursts of creative energy were matched by bouts of depression, made worse by the pain of an undiagnosed duodenal ulcer, and the memory of Josephine's untimely death. Carrie – physically and mentally robust (as she is depicted in the portrait by Philip Burne-Jones) – managed to hold everything together, providing the strength for Kipling to keep going in difficult times. Kipling admired the ancient skills of the country folk around him at Bateman's – the hedgers and ditchers and woodmen – but came to loathe 'modern progress', concerned, like Eric Gill, that it was turning working people into 'meritorious menials'.[44]

Most especially, Kipling resented the 'development' of Sussex. In 1925 he complained that Rottingdean was now 'all one dirty mess of bungalows',[45] and in *Something of Myself* he wrote with deep regret that years before 'the motherly Downs' had 'moved me to write some verses called "Sussex". Today, from Rottingdean to Newhaven is almost fully developed suburb, of great horror.'[46] The First World War had provided another 'great horror', when the Kiplings' only son John was reported missing – and eventually presumed killed – at the Battle of Loos in 1915 (see p.202). Thereafter, Kipling's introspection increased, exacerbated by a gradual literary fall from grace in which he was seen increasingly as a relic, forlorn, from an earlier era. He died in 1936, aged seventy. Yet Kipling's lengthy Sussex sojourn had changed him, allowing him to discover for himself an England that bestowed upon him a different kind of Englishness to that of India and Empire:

> *The Weald is good, the Downs are best –*
> *I'll give you the run of 'em, East to West.*
> Beachy Head and Winddoor Hill,
> They were once and they are still.
> Firle, Mount Caburn and Mount Harry
> Go back as far as sums'll carry.
> Ditchling Beacon and Chanctonbury Ring,
> They have looked on many a thing,
> And what those two have missed between 'em,
> I reckon Truleigh Hill has seen 'em.
> Highdown, Bignor and Duncton Down
> Knew Old England before the Crown.
> Linch Down, Treyford and Sunwood
> Knew Old England before the Flood;
> And when you end on the Hampshire side –
> Butser's old as Time and Tide.
> *The Downs are sheep, the Weald is corn,*
> *You be glad you are Sussex born!*[47]

Sussex continued to attract writers and other artists. It was at Crowborough, for instance, that W.B. Yeats proposed to his future wife, Georgie Hyde-Lees, in September 1917 (they married the following month), and it was at Forest Row that the newly wed Mrs Yeats experimented with the spiritualist 'automatic writing' ('performed through the agency of subconscious intelligence') that so fascinated her husband.[48]

In 1925 A.A. Milne purchased Cotchford Farm at Hartfield, near East Grinstead, and surrounding Ashdown Forest became the setting for the 'Winnie-the-Pooh' stories which have delighted successive generations of small children (and not a few adults). *Winnie-the-Pooh*, the first book, came out in 1926, to be followed by *The House at Pooh Corner* in 1928, along with a volume of verse *Now We Are Six* in 1927, each illustrated by the incomparable E.H. Shephard. 'Nobody can be uncheered with a balloon', observed Pooh philosophically to his friend Piglet in one of these stories. Eeyore, with equal home-spun wisdom and an innocence characteristic of the Pooh volumes could likewise announce that 'weeds are flowers too, once you get to know them'. Such picturesque truths help to explain the enduring popularity of Milne's books.

The late poet laureate, Sir John Betjeman, wrote fondly of Brighton – 'Few places gave so much pleasure as Brighton,'[49] he insisted – and in 'Original Sin on the Sussex Coast' evoked a familiar Downland scene where: 'Now over Polegate vastly sets the sun; / Dark rise the Downs from darker looking elms, / And out of Southern railway trains to tea / Run happy boys down various Station Roads.'[50]

A less enthusiastic observer of Sussex was school-boy Evelyn Waugh, who in his autobiography *A Little Learning* (first published in 1963) recalled his unhappy time at Lancing, the public school near Shoreham, during and after the First World War. He arrived there by train on 9 May 1917 – 'a black day in my calendar' – and was instantly repelled by the school's seemingly bleak environment in that 'cold, damp spring'. 'The River Adur at low-water revealed empty mud flats', he remembered, 'on one side lay a hutted army camp, on the other a field occasionally used by aeroplanes; eastwards the sea-shore ran desolate to the suburbs of Brighton; westwards to Worthing, broken only by the hamlets of Lancing and Sompting, pasture and arable fields running down to the edge of the shingle'.

In the school itself, 'everything was grimly correct at Lancing in 1917 and 1918', and Waugh was slow to make friends. 'Boys from perfectly civilised homes seemed to glory in savagery', he wrote, and he sought solace in the library and the chapel. There was 'black misery', and one of his 'most bitter ... experiences' was the loneliness of Ascension Day, during his first term at Lancing, when, to his surprise, the whole school emptied for a day's holiday and parents took their sons to Brighton or Worthing or 'to Bramber, where there were river-side tea-gardens, a ruined castle and a repository of stuffed animals'. Waugh managed to scrounge a few slices of bread and some unpalatable sausage meat from a steward, and 'wandered out with my damp packet of food and after a time took shelter among the trees called Lancing Ring, ate a little, and, for the first and last time for many years, wept'. Things improved at Lancing as the war came to an end but Waugh was bored by school work, despite winning a prize for poetry. He also won a prize for an illuminated hymn, having taken up calligraphy, and as a reward for his interest was taken to see Eric Johnston, 'the scribe' as Waugh described him, at Eric Gill's Catholic community at Ditchling. 'He received me with exquisite charm', Waugh recalled, 'and demonstrated how to cut a turkey-quill into a chisel-pointed pen and there and then wrote a few words for me on the title page of his book in what is now called his "foundational" hand'. It was, perhaps, one step on Evelyn Waugh's eventual conversion to Roman Catholicism.[51]

Another literary convert to Roman Catholicism was Sheila Kaye-Smith, born at St Leonards-on-Sea in 1887. Reputedly a lesbian, she nonetheless married an Anglo-Catholic clergyman, one Thoedore Penrose Fry, and together they lived in a converted oast-house at Northiam (where eventually she died in 1956). Increasingly drawn to Catholicism, the couple took the plunge and both went over to Rome in 1929. Kaye-Smith's first novel, entitled *Sussex Gore*, was published in 1916 to general acclaim, and was followed by others such as *The End of the House of Alard* (1923) and *Joanna Godden* (1921), the latter set in Romney Marsh and later (in 1947) made into a film, entitled *The Love of Joanna Godden*. Sheila Kaye-Smith's 'realistic' depiction of Sussex rural life caught the attention of Stella Gibbons (1902–1989), remembered today for her satirical novel *Cold Comfort Farm* (1932), also set in Sussex, who is said to have used Kaye-Smith's work as an authentic 'secondary source' for her own writing.[52] Employed as a reviewer for the *Lady*, Stella Gibbons had read countless popular novels of varying quality in the 1920s, many in the so-called 'loam and lovechild' genre, which 'portrayed nature as rough and wild, men and women ruled by their passions, sexual and otherwise', with 'rural families [seen] as combative'.[53] Gibbons decided to write a humorous antidote, *Cold Comfort Farm*, an amusing parody which sees sophisticated Flora Poste visit (and ultimately reform) her country relatives, the dysfunctional Starkadders, on their gloomy run-down property in the fictional Sussex village of Howling. Gibbons even made satirical use of the 'purple prose' characteristic of those 1920s novels, helpfully marking them with asterisks to jokingly inform the reader that they had been inserted following the practice 'perfected by the late Herr Baedeker'.[54] According to the critic

Edward Lucie-Smith, Stella Gibbons in her *Cold Comfort Farm* 'offers a delicious, unforgettable comic fantasy about rural life in the remoter parts of the county', and is 'a rustic counterpart to E.F. Benson's comedies about Sussex small-town life, which belong to the same epoch, but is a good deal sharper in tone'.[55]

Indeed, perhaps the most unusual Sussex author in this period was E.F. Benson, son of the archbishop of Canterbury, who lived at Rye – where he was mayor, 1934–37 – and wrote the incomparable 'Lucia' series of novels. 'We will pay anything for Lucia books,' exclaimed Noël Coward, Gertrude Lawrence, Nancy Mitford and W.H. Auden in unison, expressing their delight at the absurdities of 1920s' leisured middle-class life captured so unerringly by Benson. Lucia, the protagonist, who decides to set up home in 'Tilling' (a thinly disguised Rye), is the arch-snob and engages in all the subtleties and rivalries of small-town English intrigue, always to deadly effect. The genteel hostility that exists between Lucia and her arch-enemy, Miss Mapp, is caught neatly in *Mapp and Lucia,* in an exchange with her devoted male friend, Georgie, where they recall how they first met the dreadful woman. Miss Mapp, Lucia remembered, 'talked about a place called Tilling, where she had a Queen Anne house. We rather despised her for that.' And:

> Oh, yes, and she came to a garden-party of mine. And I know when it was, too. It was that summer when you invented saying 'Au reservoir' instead of 'Au revoir'. We all said it for about a week and then got tired of it. Miss Mapp came here just about then,

Lamb House in Rye was built in 1722, and from 1897 until his death in 1916 was home of the American-born author Henry James, where he wrote novels such as *The Turn of the Screw* and *The Awkward Age.* Two years later Lamb House became the residence of E.F. Benson, shortly to become author of the amusing social commentaries, the *Mapp and Lucia* series, as well as mayor of Rye in 1934. When he died in 1940, he was buried in his beloved Rye. 'Tilling', the fictional home of the *Mapp and Lucia* characters, is a thinly disguised Rye, its name inspired by the nearby river Tillingham. Benson imagined Lamb House as the residence of Miss Mapp (and later of Lucia herself), renaming it 'Mallards' in his stories, and in 2014 it did indeed serve as 'Mallards' in the BBC TV adaption of *Mapp and Lucia.*
ALISON AVERY, WWW.BEAUTIFULENGLANDPHOTOS.UK

One of the most picturesque villages in England, and made famous by E.F. Benson's *Mapp and Lucia* stories, Rye is home of the celebrated Mermaid Inn (seen here on the right), whose cellars date back to the early thirteenth century, the rest of the building having been reconstructed in the 1420s and comprehensively renovated during the sixteenth century. In the early eighteenth century, the Mermaid Inn was the haunt of the notorious smugglers, the Hawkhurst Gang. During the First World War, the Inn was run as a club for servicemen by Mary Aldington, mother of Richard Aldington, author of the anti-war novel *Death of a Hero*. DAVID MOYES PHOTOGRAPHY

> because she picked it up at my garden-party. She stopped quite to the end, eating quantities of red-currant fool, and saying that she had inherited a recipe from her grandmother which she would send me. She did, too, and my cook said it was rubbish.[56]

Although Benson did not say so, behind the inconsequential but ardent socialising of refined Sussex society in the 1920s and 1930s which he recorded so penetratingly was the unspoken spectre of the Great War, where bright and cheerful garden-parties, village fetes, art exhibitions, musical soirees, bridge evenings, luncheons and dinners disguised the collective loss suffered by all. Even as Benson was merrily producing his Mapp and Lucia stories, so Richard Aldington was writing his novel *Death of a Hero*, published in 1929, based on his wartime experiences and inspired in part by his mother's purchase of the Mermaid Inn in Rye in 1913 – which became a servicemen's club during the First World War of 1914–18.

NINE

War and an uncertain peace, 1914–1939

'Sussex by the Sea'

IN 1907 WILLIAM WARD-HIGGS penned his patriotic song 'Sussex by the Sea'. With its rousing words and stirring tune, 'Sussex by the Sea' had, before long, been adopted as the regimental march of the Royal Sussex Regiment, and was soon regarded widely as the county's unofficial anthem. It is said that Ward-Higgs composed the song for the wedding ceremony of his sister-in-law, Gladys, to Captain Roland Waithman of the 2nd Battalion, Royal Sussex Regiment, on which occasion it was performed to great acclaim. The march also proved immensely popular far beyond the bounds of Sussex, capturing the attention of military units throughout the Empire – even as far as Victoria in Australia, where the Bendigo Regiment adopted 'Sussex by the Sea' as its official march.[1]

Sussex men had fought and suffered in the Boer War – out of 116 volunteers from the Royal Sussex Regiment, sixteen had perished in the conflict – and in its aftermath fears of German intentions had heightened. The vast German field army, with its fearsome reputation for ruthless efficiency, was not so far away in mainland Europe, and Sussex people contemplated nervously their own close proximity to the Continent. The naval race between Britain and Germany also reminded them that Sussex was a 'front line' maritime county. In such an atmosphere, 'Sussex by the Sea' struck a chord of defiance and resolution, tinged with a little eye-moistening sentimentality, which readily appealed to a people proud of their native county but increasingly apprehensive about the future:

> Now is the time for marching,
> Now let your hearts be gay,
> Hark to the merry bugles
> Sounding along our way.
> So let your voices ring, my boys,
> And take the time from me,

And I'll sing you a song as we march along,
Of Sussex by the Sea!

Chorus
For we're the men from Sussex, Sussex by the Sea.
We plough and sow and reap and mow,
And useful men are we;
And when you go to Sussex, whoever you may be,
You may tell them all we stand or fall,
For Sussex by the Sea!

Refrain
Oh Sussex, Sussex by the Sea!
Good old Sussex by the Sea!
You may tell them all we stand or fall,
For Sussex by the Sea.

Prescient in its anticipation of the mood of 1914, it was quintessentially a soldier's song, to be sung by the long-suffering infantry in the trenches of France and Flanders and further afield:

Up in the morning early,
Start at the break of day;
March till the evening shadows
Tell us its time to stay.
We're always moving on, my boys,
So take the time from me,
And sing this song as we march along,
Of Sussex by the Sea.

Sometimes your feet are weary,
Sometimes the way is long,
Sometimes the day is dreary,
Sometimes the world goes wrong;
But if you let your voices ring,
Your care will fly away,
So we'll sing a song as we march along
Of Sussex by the Sea.

And, inevitably, there were always the fond thoughts of home, and the girls left behind:

Light is the love of a soldier
That's what the ladies say –

Lightly he goes a wooing,
Lightly he rides away.
In love and war we always are
As fair as fair can be,
And a soldier boy is the ladies' joy
In Sussex by the Sea.

Far o'er the seas we wander,
Wide thro' the world we roam;
Far from the kind hearts yonder,
Far from our dear old home;
But ne'er shall we forget, my boys,
And true we'll ever be
To the girls so kind that we left behind
In Sussex by the Sea.[2]

'The most tremendous cataclysm that has ever happened'

There were those who had seen the war coming. Among their number was Edward Heron-Allen, a noted polymath with an array of scientific and literary interests, who in 1911 had retired to his country house 'Large Acres' at Selsey. Throughout the First World War, Heron-Allen kept a journal. At midnight on 3 August, he pondered the momentous events of recent days, including the ominous outbreak of hostilities between Germany and Russia. 'I believe,' he recorded, 'though I am laughed at, that the European war, which is to involve the whole world into the most tremendous cataclysm that has ever happened, has begun.'[3] He hoped that Germany would shrink from the enormity of the situation it had created, and undo the damage before other nations were drawn in. But he doubted whether that was possible now, and on the following day (4 August) he got his answer. 'We are in it,' he exclaimed, Britain having delivered an ultimatum to Germany insisting on respect for Belgium neutrality, a demand that was bound to be ignored.[4] Over the next few days, Nour, his wife, scoured Chichester to stock up with meats, and found to her dismay that shops would not take cheques but insisted instead upon payment in gold sovereigns. Stories of food hoarders were already emerging, and Heron-Allen observed that hostilities would very likely cut off or seriously diminish the import of foodstuffs from abroad. As District Commissioner for South-west Sussex, he also noted that the Boy Scouts had been 'mobilised' (as he termed it) to guard telegraph lines, run messages, and even look out for spies. The war, only a few days old, was already having its effect in Sussex.

When war was declared on 4 August, units of the Territorial Army

It is 1913 and a crowd of curious onlookers has gathered on Brighton beach to watch the attempted recovery of a Royal Navy seaplane, which has ditched in the Channel. A little over a year since the first successful flight from a warship at sea, HMS *Africa*, in January 1912, naval aviation – like British airpower generally – was still in its infancy. Yet by the end of the Great War, the aeroplane had become an indispensable part of military operations, over land and at sea, such had been the pace of technological innovation and advances in strategic thinking since hostilities had commenced in 1914.

had marched through Lewes, the county town of East Sussex, in an impressive display of military preparedness. At the railway station they embarked in special trains, bound for Dover and so to France as part of the British Expeditionary Force sent to halt the German advance through Belgium. But, as elsewhere in Britain, Sussex proved equivocal about the prospect of war. The patriotic outpourings of the press were tempered by the acute anxiety felt by many people – especially those who foresaw the widespread disruption to everyday lives that conflict would bring, together with the blissful ignorance of others who could not imagine what war might be like. There were those, for example, who complained that the rash of troop trains from Lewes and elsewhere was already playing havoc with the timetabling of specials organised for the Brighton races. More informed observers, such as Edward Heron-Allen, were annoyed by such selfish reactions to minor irritations, and knew that more profound inconveniences lay ahead. Heron-Allen likewise dismissed silly notions that 'our army will be in Berlin by Christmas', and considered that 'this is going to be a long war, and one in which the price of victory will be fully as great as the penalty of defeat'. He had seen 'a wild rush of enthusiastic young men' to join the colours, he said, yet on a visit to Eastbourne was astonished to find the beach crammed with deck-chairs, their youthful occupants joking and flirting as if they had not a care in the world, oblivious to the great war that was about to engulf them.[5]

By September recruiting had begun in earnest for Kitchener's Army, and the new civilian volunteers undertook their basic training in camps at Bexhill, Seaford and Shoreham. Herstmonceux Castle, acquired in 1911 by Claude Lowther MP, became the focus of an especially impressive recruiting campaign, in which Lowther's energetic efforts raised no fewer than three 'Southdown' battalions, as they were called. Local men clamoured to join the 'Southdown Brigade' (or Lowther's Lambs, as it was sometimes known), and marched to their own martial song:

Oh the Sussex boys are stirring
In the Wood-land and the Downs;
We are moving in the hamlet
We are rising in the town;
For the call is King and Country
Since the foe has asked for war,
And when danger calls, or duty
We are always to the fore.

We have come from shop and sheepfold
We have come from deck and store,
We have left our peaceful callings
To be taught the trade of war;
For our hearths, and homes and honour
As a bulwark we shall stand
Fighting hard for England's glory
And the pleasant Sussex land.[6]

An armed camp

The arrival of Belgian refugees brought the first real taste of war to Sussex. They were met with tea and sympathy, and found temporary accommodation in homes that had room to spare; their harrowing tales of the German advance through their country seemed to confirm what local people had read already in the press about the 'barbarism' of the Hun. Local organisations, such as Southwick Patriotic Committee (run by women anxious 'to do their bit'), raised money to send 'trench comforts' to soldiers at the front. Brighton and Hove Grammar School was hastily converted into a military hospital, to receive the inevitable casualties from the front, and by early 1915 parts of Sussex were already assuming the aspect of an armed camp. Plans for the defence of Sussex, should an invasion occur, were drawn up by the Lord Lieutenant, the duke of Norfolk, and before long the Weald resounded to the noise of the Women's Forestry Corps as they chopped down trees to make trench props and telegraph poles. At Polegate, a Royal Naval Airship Station was established to keep a watch on the coast. A mounted troop of the Hampshire Yeomanry was quartered at Selsey, their officers invited by the ever-generous Edward Heron-Allen to make free use of Large Acres and its grounds.

At Bateman's, at the other end of Sussex, Rudyard Kipling provided billets for a few of the many British soldiers now arriving in the county from all corners of the kingdom. He wrote to his son, John, on 27 February 1915, to explain that: 'The billetees (I don't know how you spell it) have just gone to pick up their men in Burwash and to march back to Eastbourne via Dallington and Pevensey. I think they have had a good time of it.' As Kipling added: 'They turned up yesterday evening about 6.30 … preceded by a young transport officer. … Also three or four soldier servants [who] carried their kit to Bateman's – and you can imagine the joy of the maids.' He went on: 'There were six chaps altogether – a Captain Dryden with a Northcountry accent you could cut with a brick; a Glasgow boy with a ditto Scotch accent; another Scotchman and the rest mixed and curious but all interesting.' Having posted their sentries and outposts, the officers 'set the rest of their company to digging trenches near the golf course. Apparently the 10th Battn Loyal North Lancs love trench-digging.'[7] For Kipling, who entertained the officers to dinner and breakfast, and provided packed lunches, here was an important opportunity to get the measure of Kitchener's New Army:

> They, naturally, talked shop all the time. Three of 'em had been in the Public School battalions and had got their commissions from the ranks. They said it was a great pull in the New Armies, if a man had passed through this mill. They said that the weakness of the new armies was in the NCOs, and they told me awful yarns of Sergeants (aged 21) larking with the men. Of the men themselves they could not speak too highly … there's no doubt that the new armies work like beavers and they are getting some sort of discipline.[8]

Kipling was duly impressed when the officers, after 'a decent dinner', went out into the cold night 'at ten to inspect trenches, outposts etc.

They were hung with revolver, binoculars, water bottle and all whole mass of muckings.' The next morning, the soldiers left 'with the highest expressions of esteem on both sides. It was a pretty wet day and I feel sorry for 'em.'[9]

Military hospitals and convalescence

Rudyard Kipling, with his intimate Indian connections and close personal friendship with George V, was no doubt also aware of recent moves to convert the Royal Pavilion in Brighton into a hospital for wounded soldiers from the Sub-continent. Diverted from the Middle East to bolster the Empire's presence in France, troops from the Indian army had begun to arrive on the western front as early as September 1914. By now military hospitals were being established across the United Kingdom to cope with the anticipated influx of casualties, and there was recognition that those from India – Hindus, Muslims and Sikhs – would require special facilities. The onion-domed Royal Pavilion, with its evocations of India and the Orient, was deemed eminently suitable – Indian troops would feel culturally at home in such an environment – and urgent negotiations led swiftly to its conversion to a hospital in November 1914. On 5 December, the *Brighton Gazette* announced the arrival of the first wounded Indian soldiers at the Pavilion Military Hospital (as it was now designated), a week later adding that another 345 had arrived by two special trains.[10] The 'walking wounded' had marched proudly from Brighton railway station to the Pavilion, it was reported, their route lined with cheering crowds who saluted these fine sons of Empire. The more seriously wounded were transported by ambulance. In the Pavilion itself, arrangements were made for the provision of separate drinking taps and foods (including the ritual slaughter of animals) to satisfy the needs of different religions. A marquee was erected in the grounds to act as a Sikh temple, and Muslims were allowed to worship on the lawns outside the Dome.

Between 1914 and 1916, when the last inmates left the hospital, more than 12,000 Indian troops were treated in Brighton. Alas, not all recovered from their wounds. Muslims who succumbed were buried at the mosque in Woking, Surrey. But the fifty-three Hindus and Sikhs who died at the Pavilion Military Hospital were cremated on funeral pyres – or 'ghats' – on the South Downs, near Patcham, their ashes scattered at sea. After the war, a Chattri (literally, 'umbrella') was constructed on the site of the ghats, as a permanent memorial to those Indians who had fought and died. 'To the memory of all Indian soldiers who gave their lives for their King-Emperor in the Great War,' explained an inscription on the Chattri, 'this monument, erected on the site of the funeral pyres where the Hindus and Sikhs who died in hospital at Brighton, passed through the fire, is in grateful admiration and brotherly affection dedicated.' The Chattri was formally unveiled in February 1921 by Edward, Prince of Wales, and among the honoured guests, as the *Brighton Herald* put it, was 'Rudyard Kipling, our story-teller of India and poet of the Empire'.[11]

The presence of recuperating Indian troops had brought a touch of the exotic to wartime Sussex. Far more commonplace were the wounded from other British and Empire units – notably the Australians, Canadians and New Zealanders – who filled the county's hospitals and convalescent homes to capacity during the war years. Each major offensive – Loos, the Somme, Passchendaele, Amiens, and all the rest – led to a new wave of maimed and injured young men from the front. Writing in 1928, Edmund Blunden – the war poet, as he had become – remembered his days in Sussex before deployment to France in March 1916. A pupil at Christ's Hospital school in Horsham, he had joined the 11th Battalion Royal Sussex Regiment (one of the 'Southdowns'), and trained at Shoreham Camp. As a young subaltern at Shoreham, Blunden had been put in charge, as he recalled, 'of a squad of men nominally recovered from wounds and awaiting their next transmigration'.[12] As he explained:

> It had been my happiness to march them out to a place at once as sequestered and sunny as I could find, overlooking the lazy Adur, and there let them bask on the grass, and tell their tales, and be peaceful. How contentedly they had rested in the lucky sun! Nor was much said among them – their thoughts were their conversation ... I began to love these convalescent soldiers, and their distinguishing demeanour sank into me.[13]

He went on:

> They hid what daily grew plain enough – the knowledge that the war had released them only for a few moments, that the war would reclaim them, that the war was a jealous war and long-lasting. 1914, 1915, 1916. ... Occasionally I would ask the silly questions of non-realization; they in their tolerance pardoned, smiled and hinted, knowing that I was learning, and should not escape the full lesson.[14]

In June 1915, Edward Heron-Allen's wife, Nour, was appointed commandant of the Red Cross Voluntary Aid Detachment (the 'VADs') at Selsey. Her VADs were put to work attending the wounded soldiers in Graylingwell Hospital, Chichester, where in April 1917 the Heron-Allen children and their friends gave a concert for the inmates. Heron-Allen found it a poignant and in some respects harrowing occasion. One of the soldiers, a 'poor creature', lay on his bed moaning and crying, he recorded, 'a living skeleton', according to the ward sister, who would surely die in a day or two.[15] Later, in August 1919, Heron-Allen chanced upon an ambulance train at Chichester railway station, consisting of ten large hospital carriages fitted out with cots, together with two additional coaches for the walking wounded. Again, he was moved by the terrible and pitiful sights, as the train's occupants were transferred to Graylingwell Hospital.

George Orwell, the writer, likewise observed the war wounded, this time in their wooden hospital huts in the camp near Eastbourne, the 'chicken-houses stuck right on top of those beastly icy downs', as he described them. The bracing fresh air was supposed to aid convalescence, but mostly the soldiers looked, usually in vain, for somewhere to shelter from the biting winds. Sometimes, Orwell noted, local schoolboys would be brought to hand out cigarettes and peppermint creams to the recuperating Tommies. 'A pink faced boy of about eight.' he wrote, 'would walk up to a knot of wounded men sitting on the grass, slit open a packet of Woodbines and solemnly hand one fag to each man, just like feeding a monkey at a zoo.' Meanwhile, soldiers recovering their strength and appetites would 'wander for miles over the downs in the hope of meeting girls'.[16] Orwell did not say so, but for many of the convalescing men the dread thought of returning to the front once pronounced fit, was made more awful by the distant sound of artillery on the Western Front. Arthur Conan Doyle, at Crowborough, wrote that he too heard 'the mutter of the guns'[17] far off in distant France (his son Kingsley was wounded on the Somme and died of pneumonia), while Marian Allen was likewise disturbed:

> The Downs be silent and untouched by war
> But I can hear beyond the distant hill
> The guns that boom and echo, throb and roll.[18]

For some wounded soldiers, succour was provided at the Chailey Heritage Craft School and Hospital for Crippled Boys on North Common, near Ditchling. Founded in 1902 by Grace Kimmins, Chailey Heritage was designed to give medical assistance to disabled children as well as to equip them with a useful craft or trade which might stand them in good stead for the future. Inspired in part by the Arts & Crafts movement, Kimmins believed that these children were 'wounded soldiers, fighting the battle for an independent life'.[19] The military allusion proved prescient, for during the First World War injured soldiers found themselves alongside the 'crippled' boys at Chailey Heritage, studying in open-air workshops where they learned skills such as carpentry and book-making which would ease their rehabilitation back into civilian life. Meanwhile, wounded officers who had been blinded in action found solace at St Dunstan's, near Brighton, an annexe of the recently opened charity at Regents Park, devoted to those who had lost their sight in service of their country.

The home front

As the war dragged on, so it became a yet more integral part of Sussex life, much of it recorded in the journal kept by Edward Heron-Allen. Little escaped his eagle eye or critical pen, as he ranged across subjects as varied 'the elaborate system of machine gun (Maxim) emplacements, dotted all along the shore from Bognor to Wittering', and venereal diseases (VD) which had 'almost become subjects of conversation among the most delicately nurtured women'.[20] The spread of VD, Heron-Allen opined, reflected the promiscuous nature of soldiers billeted in Sussex and the willing local girls of easy virtue. The latter were encouraged – he argued – by the multiplicity of Flag Days, where young women became unhealthily accustomed to stopping strange men in the street to ask for money for the wounded. He took a dim view of these 'flag hags', as he called them, insisting that their activities were but a short step from prostitution. He was also scathing about 'war marriages', as he termed them, especially those where soldiers on leave would marry any disreputable women 'on terms'. Such women, he insinuated, would offer their soldiers a home and 'a good time' when on leave, in return for 'housekeeping', and if the newly wed husbands were killed on their return to the front, then their recently acquired spouses would receive pensions for life. But Heron-Allen, with his myriad prejudices, also

The French passenger ferry *Sussex*, torpedoed off the Sussex coast by a German U-boat in March 1916. Among the eighty people who lost their lives were the noted Spanish pianist and classical composer Enrique Granados and his wife Amparo. Seeing his wife struggling in the water, Granados leapt to her aid from the safety of his lifeboat, only to be drowned in his attempt at rescue. The appalling casualties shocked Edward Heron-Allen, as he recorded in his journal.

conceded that many respectable middle-class women could scarcely tell a cad from a gentleman, and that all too often unsuspecting brides were simply deserted by their new husbands – especially those Australians and Canadians who no doubt, he said, already had wives in their own countries.

When in March 1916 the passenger steamship *Sussex* was torpedoed by a U-boat off Selsey Bill, 'with terrible loss of life', and on 25 September that year a Zeppelin passed over Selsey on its way to bomb Portsmouth, Heron-Allen reflected how close to home the war had come.[21] Later, in 1917, Norwegian soldiers who had survived a torpedo attack off Selsey Bill were washed up on a raft near Pagham, and when in the September a New Zealand ship was sunk off the Bill, blocks of butter came ashore, to be snapped up eagerly by local foragers. By now shortages were commonplace and rationing a fact of life. But the home-front spirit was nurtured by fund-raising events (including those Flag Days of which Heron-Allen so disapproved), and 30 July 1918 was designated 'France's Day'. Nour Heron-Allen and her female neighbours worked hard for several weeks to prepare Selsey's contribution to the celebrations. Jumble was collected, and garden produce – fruit, vegetables, flowers – was assembled for the various stalls. Sweets were sold for a penny each, and a small basket of raspberries was auctioned for the remarkable sum of 8*s.* 6*d.* In all, over £77 was raised for the French Red Cross. As Edward Heron-Allen observed in admiration: 'It is really amazing how good and generous people are on these occasions.'[22]

The arrival of German prisoners of war – such as the squad of thirty or so held at Chichester, who ploughed and sowed a plot of land on the nearby golf course – added another curious dimension to Sussex life. Edward Heron-Allen thought them a pathetic sight, and considered that their presence on Selsey soil brought home to local residents the reality of war. But nothing could be more affecting than the departure from local stations of reinforcements bound for the front. Heron-Allen found such occasions hard to bear, especially the fond farewells as the soldiers boarded their trains. The band would play 'Auld Lang Syne', and as the train pulled out slowly the regimental march would be struck up, the officers on the platform overseeing the departure standing rigidly to attention and saluting the young soldiers as they headed inexorably for the trenches. As they fell out, the officers could not look at each other. They were glad that it was dark, so that they could not see the tears in each other's eyes, or that their hands were shaking.

'My boy Jack'

Of course, a great number of the departing soldiers never did return, and many Sussex families suffered bereavements. Early in the war, in February 1915, Edward Heron-Allen had learned of the loss of his Canadian cousin, Roger Pepler, who only in January had been a guest at Large Acres. He had been killed at St Eloi on 21 January, just a handful of days after having arrived at the front. A few months later, at Bateman's, Rudyard and Carrie Kipling learned that their only son, John, had been posted as 'missing' at the Battle of Loos. At the beginning of September, the British and French had gone on the offensive in Artois, the British Expeditionary Force assaulting Loos while their French allies attacked to the south. Sir John French, the British commander, had looked askance at the task he had been set by his superior, the French general Joseph Joffre. Surveying the terrain, he saw that it was difficult country – full of factories, mine buildings, shafts, slag heaps, tightly packed rows of terraced houses – and thought it best fought over by artillery. But Joffre insisted on a full frontal attack by infantry, and when Sir John French expressed his misgivings, he was overruled by Kitchener himself, who opined that the resultant heavy casualties would be a fair price to pay for supporting the French army in their joint enterprise. The die was cast.

Loos was the biggest battle fought by the British army thus far – in this war, or in any other. Among the array of military units pitted against the Germans were two inexperienced Kitchener New Army divisions, which would be held in reserve to exploit early successes. Included in their number was 2nd Battalion The Irish Guards, only recently formed and fresh from its training in England, with Second Lieutenant John Kipling one of its officers. When war had broken out, John had been keen to volunteer but was under-age and poorly sighted, leading to his rejection. But his father pulled strings, using his friendship with Field-Marshal Lord Roberts to obtain a commission for his son in The Irish Guards. John had joined just in time to complete his training before the battalion sailed for France.

The Battle of Loos began early on the morning of 26 September 1915, with the infantry going forward at 6.30. First reports indicated success – Loos itself was captured, and German first positions overrun – but it was not possible to deploy the reserves quickly enough. The early momentum was lost, and as the New Army divisions – the 2nd Battalion Irish Guards among them – moved up, they were met with insuperable opposition from the enemy second line. In just under four hours, these two divisions, comprising some 10,000 officers and men, suffered 8,000 casualties. The official history of the German 26th Infantry Regiment described the slaughter:

> Never had machine guns had such straightforward work to do, nor done it so effectively; with barrels burning hot and swimming in oil, they traversed to and fro along the enemy's ranks unceasingly. … The effect was devastating. The enemy could be seen literally

> falling in hundreds, but they continued their march in good order and without interruption … they went doggedly on, some even reaching the wire entanglement in front of the reserve line, which their artillery had scarcely touched. Confronted by this impenetrable obstacle, the survivors turned and began to retire.[23]

Second Lieutenant Kipling fell early in the action. Witnesses said that he had been hit at a place called Chalk Pit Wood, leading his men in the open, and was still walking upright after being wounded. But the last man to see John Kipling alive, according to one report, had 'watched him weeping with pain as he tried to fasten a field dressing around his shattered mouth'.[24] Kipling crawled into a building, later re-occupied by the enemy, presumably to die. He was officially designated 'wounded and missing', and Rudyard and Carrie Kipling – like all parents in their position – clung to the hope that their son had somehow survived and had perhaps been taken prisoner. The Red Cross made enquiries on their behalf, and the Royal Flying Corps dropped leaflets over the German lines, requesting information about the fate of the 'son of the world-famous author'.[25] John's body was never found, and gradually the Kiplings accepted that their boy would not be coming home. Perhaps they always knew that he never would. Months before, Carrie had been asked how she could bear John's joining the colours. She replied firmly that 'one can't let one's friends' and neighbours' sons be killed in order to save us and our son'. As she explained, with great candour and not a little courage: 'There is no chance John will survive unless he is so maimed from a wound as to be unfit to fight. We know it and he does. We all know it, but we must all give and do what we can and live on the shadow of hope that our boy will be the one to escape.'[26]

'My Boy Jack': Second Lieutenant John Kipling, 2nd Battalion The Irish Guards, only son of Rudyard and Caroline ('Carrie') Kipling, was born at Rottingdean on 17 August 1897 and killed in action at the Battle of Loos on 27 September 1915. His body was never found during his parents' lifetimes, and was not discovered until 1992. After a period of uncertainty, it was finally confirmed as the remains of John Kipling in January 2016.
RUDYARD KIPLING PAPERS, UNIVERSITY OF SUSSEX LIBRARY

In 1917 Rudyard Kipling was asked to write the official history of The Irish Guards, a work which was published in two volumes in 1923. In perfunctory and matter-of-fact language that would infuriate Edmund Blunden, Kipling recorded the action at Loos:

> Of the officers, 2nd Lieutenant Pakenham-Law had died of wounds; 2nd Lieutenants Clifford and Kipling were missing. Captain and Adjutant the Hon. T.E. Vesey, Captain Wynter, Lieutenant Stevens, and 2nd Lieutenants Sassoon and Grayson were wounded, the last being blown up by a shell. It was a fair average for the day of a debut, and taught them somewhat for their future guidance.[27]

Indeed, many hard lessons were learned that day, and many more would be before the Allies finally asserted themselves over their formidable enemy, leading to the final victory of autumn 1918. But Kipling's stiff upper lip surely quivered when he penned his haunting poem, 'My Boy Jack':

> 'Have you news of my boy Jack?'
> *Not this tide.*
>
> 'When d'you think that he'll come back?'
> *Not with this wind blowing, and this tide.*
>
> 'Has any one else had word of him?'
> *Not this tide.*
> *For what is sunk will hardly swim,*
> *Not with this wind blowing, and this tide.*
>
> 'Oh, dear, what comfort can I find'
> *None this tide,*
> *Nor any tide,*
> *Except he did not shame his kind –*
> *Not even with that wind blowing, and that tide.*
>
> *Then hold your head up all the more,*
> *This tide,*
> *And every tide;*
> *Because he was the son you bore,*
> *And gave to that wind blowing and that tide!*[28]

Undertones of War

Reviewing Kipling's *The Irish Guards in the Great War,* Edmund Blunden objected to phrases, such as the reference to 'annoying fights and checks round the concreted machine-gun posts', which seemed to underestimate the infantryman's experience of warfare. Blunden had participated in such bloody encounters himself, and knew that 'annoying' was not the right word to describe them. Instead, he set out to offer his own account of the conflict, his *Undertones of War*, first published in 1928, giving a soldier's eye view of life and death on the western front. As well as his story, it was also that of the 11th Battalion Royal Sussex Regiment, and mapped the unit's progress from the early years when it was full of 'Southdown' men, 'singing some rhymes by Mr Belloc' as they marched along, to later days when gaps left by casualties were filled by strangers from any part of the country where they could be found.[29] The 11th Battalion went overseas in March 1916, and at first found itself in a relatively quiet sector on the Belgian border. But the Somme offensive involved it in diversionary attacks, a prelude to a move southwards to participate in the assault on Hamel in September 1916 – an action in which Blunden was awarded the Military Cross. In 1917 the 11th Battalion was at Ypres, where between 23 and 27 September it suffered 200 casualties. The following year it was back in the Somme sector, and played a significant role in stemming the German 'spring offensive' of 1918, losing twenty officers and 300 other ranks on 29–30 March. Thereafter, the remnants of the badly mauled 11th Battalion were split up, half being employed to help train recently arrived American troops, the rest deployed to northern Russia as part of the anti-Bolshevik intervention force.

In August 1915 Edmund Blunden was commissioned into the 11th Battalion (1st South Downs) as a Second Lieutenant, and saw action in many of the great battles of the Western Front in the Great War. Although gassed, he managed to survive the war unscathed physically (but not mentally), which he attributed to his short stature. He recorded his war experiences in his memoir *Undertones of War* and in his poetry. After the war he pursued a literary and academic career, and was elected to the prestigious Oxford Professorship of Poetry in 1966. He married three times. His first wife, pictured here, was Mary Daines. They married in 1918 and were divorced in 1931.

Edmund Blunden served with the battalion until sent home to take up a training post in February 1918. His wartime experiences, with all their conflicting and powerful emotions, were captured unerringly in *Undertones of War*, a cathartic process which – like his poetry – allowed vent to his deepest feelings. There were intimate descriptions of trench warfare, such as the unnerving occasion when he was asked to patrol, at night, the ground over which an assault was intended. On each of the two preceding nights, an officer and one or two men had been sent out on the mission, but none had returned. 'It was believed that these had been taken prisoner,' Blunden observed, 'but I was not inclined to that view when, the third night, I was sent up with one or two old hands to see what I could see.' Having crawled over the top and made their way carefully through the British wire, they were suddenly confronted by 'crash and flame on all sides' as an enemy barrage began. Blunden described how they

Beginning his association with Sussex, Edmund Blunden attended Christ's Hospital, known popularly as the Bluecoat School, situated south of Horsham, before joining the Royal Sussex Regiment during the First World War.
WWW.CHRISTS-HOSPITAL.ORG.UK

dodged the shells 'in wild disorder', plunging ever deeper into No Man's Land. 'The barrage followed our direction like a net,' he added, 'and when it stopped, as we lay panting and muttering in the smell of explosive mixed with that of dewy weeds and broken clods, I saw we were a few yards from a German sap.' Hearing the sounds of stealthy movement within the enemy trench, Blunden and his men beat a hasty retreat, making their 'shaky way' as 'shells flinging out bright terrible phosphorus howled' past. Soon after, they encountered 'in the sickening brightness a column of artillery wagons, noiseless, smashed, capsized, the remains of mules and drivers sprawling among the wreckage'.[30]

Yet there were also moments of intense tenderness that would remain with Blunden for ever. 'I sauntered by the canal,' he wrote, describing a peaceful interlude, 'and then settled myself with a book in an empty cattle-truck' on the nearby railway line. 'There came along a girl of fourteen or so, with a small brother, and looked in. We talked – and fell in love.' Years later, in *Undertones of War*, he mused: 'That "I" may be still in love with her, Marie-Louise of course, so black-eyed, and serious, and early-old with the inheritance of peasant experience – I have seen her alone since in many a moment of escape and fantasy.'[31] He sighed:

> Still she looks in on this life's sultry cattle-truck, halted awhile in some drab siding, and once again we kiss, innocent as petals in the breeze. With what sad resignation to the tyrannical moment, which she hardly credits to be true, lifting her slow hand doubtfully to wave farewell, does that child-love of only one day's courting

watch me pass into the voluminous, angry, darkening distance:
ah, Marie-Louise![32]

Blunden's poetry matched his prose, capturing moments as terrible as they are incidental, such as 'Pillbox', where the fortunate/unfortunate Sergeant Hoad cops a coveted blighty one – an injury serious enough to return him to England, but not life-threatening – only to succumb unaccountably to his wounds:

Just see what's happening, Worley. – Worley rose
And round the angled doorway thrust his nose,
And Sergeant Hoad went too, to snuff the air.
The war brought down his fist, and missed the pair!
Yet Hoad was scratched by a splinter, the blood came,
And out burst terrors that he'd striven to tame.
A good man, Hoad, for weeks. *I'm blown to bits.*
He groans, he screams. *Come, Bluffer, where's your wits?*
Says Worley. *Bluffer, you've a blighty, man!*
All in the pillbox urged him, here began
His freedom: *Think of Eastbourne and your dad.*
The poor man lay at length and brief and mad
Flung out his cry of doom; soon ebbed and dumb
He yielded. Worley with a tot of rum
And shouting in his face could not restore him.
The ship of Charon over channel bore him.
All marvelled even on that deathly day
To see his life so spirited away.[33]

During the First World War, the Royal Sussex Regiment had expanded to twenty-three battalions. The 2nd Battalion, the so-called 'Iron Regiment', had arrived in France as early as 23 August 1914 and saw action in the defence of the Marne, later participating in many of the great battles of the western front. The 4th (Territorial) Battalion, by contrast, was at the landing at Suvla Bay in August 1915, serving in the ill-fated Gallipoli campaign. The 1/6th (Cyclist Battalion), with its Headquarters at Hove cricket ground, was raised in Brighton in November 1914, and was employed in coastal defence duties in Norfolk, Sussex and Kent before being sent to Ireland to guard munition works. Other units served equally widely, from garrison duty in India, action on the Italian front, and ceremonials at the Tower of London, to deployment to northern Russia, fighting in the second Battle of Gaza, and participation in the capture of Jerusalem. When at last it was all over, the names of 6,800 officers and men of the Regiment who had fallen were recorded in Chichester Cathedral.

Edward Heron-Allen was in London when he heard news of the Armistice, and witnessed the metropolis go mad with joy, but he was back in Selsey by 16 November. He had been collecting tree prunings at Large Acres since August 1914, with the intention of lighting a huge victory bonfire when the moment came. Now was that moment, and he sprinkled the pile with two cans of 'hoarded' petrol, and set it ablaze – it smouldered for four days. Heron-Allen had also designed and planted a 'war maze' at Large Acres in the summer of 1915, and now, with hedges over five feet high, it had matured in time for victory, a memorial to all those from Sussex who had fought or otherwise been caught up in the conflict.

'A land fit for heroes'?

Memorialisation, indeed, became a major pre-occupation of the post-war years. Returning servicemen were greeted with often sumptuous 'Welcome Home' dinners, such as that organised by the vicar and Ladies Committee

The war memorial in the Market Square at Midhurst was erected, like many others across Sussex, in the aftermath of the Great War, as local people tried to come to terms with their losses and to remember in perpetuity those who had fallen. The memorial commemorates the names of fifty men from the district, many of whom had served in the Royal Sussex Regiment, who gave their lives in the First World War. There are an additional eleven names of those who died in the Second World War.
ALISON AVERY, WWW.BEAUTIFULENGLANDPHOTOS.UK

at Horsham in May 1919, but soon attention was turned to more tangible and lasting commemoration – especially of those who had fallen. At St Peter's church, Selsey, a Saxon cross, similar to that brought to Sussex by St Wilfrid when he converted the county to Christianity, was erected as a war memorial. At Bramber, Clayton, Lyminster, Sompting, and other places across Sussex, memorial lych gates were constructed using distinctive local materials. During 1917, Rudyard Kipling had joined the Imperial (now Commonwealth) War Graves Commission, and among his tasks was the composition of appropriate inscriptions for memorial stones, such as those for Merchant Navy seamen 'who have no grave but the sea', and for – unidentified remains – 'A Soldier of the Great War Known unto God'. In 1920 he and Carrie visited Chalk Pit Wood at Loos, to see for themselves where their son had fallen, and Kipling toured the commission's cemeteries, reporting on their conditions and making recommendations. By now he was often ill, yet he continued to travel frequently until shortly before his death in 1936. He was succeeded as literary advisor to the Imperial War Graves Commission by his arch critic, Edmund Blunden.

David Lloyd George (who in the summer and autumn of 1918 had spent time at Danny, near Hassocks, devising the Armistice terms), had promised 'a land fit for heroes', and Brighton Corporation did its best to respond to this new imperative. Between 1920 and 1938 it built no fewer than 3,588 new houses and flats, many in the new developments of Moulsecoomb and Whitehawk. The former, with its fine rural views across open Downland, incorporated some of the best of modern planning, with attractive 'cottages' set in curved streets, and proved popular with its new residents. Whitehawk, designed specifically to relocate families from the inner slums to land near the ancient hill-fort (much of which was destroyed by the new building work), was less successful. For slum-dwellers used to rent of 7*s*. 9*d*. per week and a short walk to work, their new council houses seemed extortionate at 12*s*. – to which was added the cost of bus journeys to and from central Brighton.

Other building work was of the type that so offended Philip Webb, Virginia Woolf, Hilaire Belloc, Rudyard Kipling and other champions of rural Sussex, with its piece-meal and speculative development – or despoliation – of vast tracts of countryside. The chief culprit was Charles Neville, who during the war years had acquired land east of Rottingdean, in 1916 announcing that the resultant development would be named 'New Anzac on Sea' in recognition of the contribution to the Empire's cause of the Australians and New Zealanders. Eventually, this rather grandiose title was replaced by the simpler 'Peacehaven', and sombre road names such as Mons, Marne and Ypres were discarded in favour of more jolly examples such as Sunview, Gladys and Dorothy. But the scale of the development itself did not become more modest. On the contrary,

An early aerial view of Peacehaven, as it developed in the inter-war period, showing the *ad hoc* sprawl that so offended many devotees of the Sussex countryside and coastline, and yet which appealed to many who, after the trials of the Great War, wished for a home of their own and the freedom to rebuild (quite literally) their lives anew.

Neville's plans became ever more ambitious. He tapped in to government funding which had been made available to house returning servicemen, acquiring large amounts of otherwise scarce building materials, and allowed purchasers of plots of land to build their bungalows where and how their fancies took them, creating a general sense of disorder – what one critic called 'a colony of shacks'.[34]

Neville's own newspaper, the *Peacehaven Post* (later the *Downland*), emphasised the supposedly idyllic nature of the new settlement, where dreams of independence and happiness might at last be realised by a new generation of homeowners. 'Leave all your troubles in those drab old towns,' exhorted the *Peacehaven Post* in a parody of the First World War song 'Pack Up Your Troubles in Your Old Kit Bag', as it urged its readers to 'fly, fly, fly / There's still a plot upon the Downs / Left for you to buy'.[35] And, whatever the deleterious aspects of Neville's activities (and they were many), his schemes did indeed prove popular with the house-buying public. Peacehaven itself became the prototype for any number of look-alike developments all along the Sussex coast from Pevensey in the east to Bognor in the west. The latter, despite George V's reputed famous last words, 'Bugger Bognor', had always considered itself a cut above other Sussex seaside resorts, and looked askance at this slide into vulgarity, especially when in 1933–34 Billy Butlin opened a zoo and funfair on the town's Eastern Esplanade. Worse still, in the eyes of conservationists, were the motley collections of grounded railway carriages, former trams, Nissan huts and other shacks that sprung up in coastal locations such as Camber Sands, Shoreham and Pagham.

Autumn sunset at Beachy Head. Situated close to Eastbourne, and just east of the Seven Sisters, Beachy Head offers stunning views of the Sussex coast in both directions, from Dungeness (in Kent) in the east to Selsey Bill in the west. Towering above the lighthouse, Beachy Head is a favourite spot for walkers, cyclists and site-seers. It is also a popular venue for the scattering of ashes – those of Friedrich Engels (author of *The Condition of the Working Class in England*, published in Germany in 1844) were scattered into the sea here in 1895. Alas, Beachy Head has also been the scene of more than a few suicides (about twenty each year), and the Beachy Head Chaplaincy Team conducts regular patrols of the cliff-top to persuade would-be suicides not to take their lives. Beachy Head has also featured in a number of films, including the 2010 remake of Graham Greene's *Brighton Rock*, and was the location for the music video of David Bowie's 1980 song 'Ashes to Ashes'.
DAVID MOYES PHOTOGRAPHY

The interior of the De La Warr Pavilion, built in 1935 on the seafront at Bexhill-on-Sea, exhibits the Art Deco and International Style features deployed by its architects, Erich Mendelsohn and Serge Chermayeff, leading proponents of the Modern movement. Herbert Sackville, 9th Earl De La Warr and mayor of Bexhill at the time, was an advanced socialist and persuaded the local council of the public amenity value of his proposed building. When completed, the pavilion had seating for 1,500 and a 200-seat restaurant, together with a spacious reading room and lounge.
CHRIS BROCKBANK

Charles Neville went on to develop Saltdean (where Billy Butlin later opened a 'holiday centre' in the Ocean Hotel built 1938), although there were now other builders in the business who drove up standards – notably Braybon's, who enjoyed an enviable reputation for style and quality, exemplified in their outstanding work at Bevendean, where they produced well-planned and -constructed housing in an attractive and healthy environment. But such improvement did not lessen the growing sense of discomfort among those concerned for the future of the countryside, and in 1931 the Sussex Rural Community Council was founded with the express purpose of monitoring housing developments and calling for more effective planning regulations. Here and there, there were important victories for the conservationists, especially when Eastbourne Corporation purchased the iconic and internationally renowned Beachy Head to prevent the eastward spread of bungaloid development. Other local authorities also took the planning initiative, such as Bexhill, which commissioned a new leisure centre for the town, selecting a modernist Bauhaus design by the German architects Mendelsohn and Chermayeff. The resultant De La Warr Pavilion, unveiled in 1935, was one of the most striking and architecturally important public buildings of the inter-war Britain. Also significant was the new 1934 Art Deco-style terminal building at Shoreham Airport, part of the joint development of the aerodrome by Brighton, Hove and Worthing Corporations, which sought to strengthen air links with France and the Channel Islands.

Such initiatives hinted at growing middle-class prosperity and middle-class tastes. More explicit was the conversion in 1934 of Glyndebourne, the historic seat of the Christie family near Ringmer, into an operatic centre of international excellence. Assisted by his wife, the soprano Audrey Milday, John Christie moved swiftly from a relatively modest repertoire – consisting mostly of Mozart – to the impressively broad range of performance that Glyndebourne had achieved by the eve of war in 1939. The appearance of well-attended picture houses (cinemas) in many towns across Sussex was also a measure of increased affluence, as those with a little more spare cash in their pockets looked for new forms of entertainment. Indeed, for those with funds, there was much fun to be had. The annual Veteran Car Run from London to Brighton, for example, attracted motorsport enthusiasts keen to put their much-prized vehicles through their paces. In November 1932, L.T.C. 'Tom' Rolt – later to become a leading canal and railway preservationist and author – entered his 1903 Humber into the Run, dreaming of a triumphant entrance into Brighton: 'This was the life, I thought; Brighton here we come!' Alas, the Humber expired long before Rolt had reached the Sussex border. Undeterred, he tried again in 1934, and this proved to be a 'most memorable experience'. The Humber 'ran like a watch and it was with immense satisfaction that I drove on to the Madeira Drive at Brighton

BRIGHTON
For Health & Pleasure
all the year round
T.F.
THE FAMOUS SHELTERED WALK, MADEIRA DRIVE.

Brighton for Health and Pleasure all the Year Round. Published *c.*1920, probably by the London Brighton & South Coast Railway, the poster indicates that the holiday industry is getting back into its stride after the dark days of the Great War (although among the figures depicted is an Army officer in uniform). The wrought-iron colonnade of the famous walk at Madeira Drive features centre-stage (finishing line from 1927 for the London–Brighton Veteran Car Run), while in the background is the Palace (now Brighton) Pier.

Young women on Brighton Beach in 1926. Although extremely popular in the eighteenth and nineteenth centuries, 'bathing machines' such as these had all but disappeared by the 1920s, surviving examples now serving as static 'bathing boxes' where individuals might change their clothes, shelter from the breeze or brew a cup of tea. The Collins brothers, Daniel and Thomas, were successful bathing machine operators at Broadstairs in Kent in the 1860s, so perhaps one of their venerable machines had by now migrated to the Sussex coast for its 'retirement'.

Beach huts at Littlehampton. The fictional Stevens family, whose simple holiday pleasures were described fondly in *The Fortnight in September*, rented a cosy, unpretentious beach hut, where they brewed tea and enjoyed looking out to sea. Their hut was at Bognor, but countless others could be found along the Sussex coast, at West Wittering, Lancing and other vantage points, including Littlehampton, where these two examples survive today.
ALISON AVERY, WWW.BEAUTIFULENGLANDPHOTOS.UK

well within the time limit'.[36] Tom Rolt entered again in 1935, and in the three succeeding years. Only on the last occasion did the Humber let him down, refusing to go any further than Bolney crossroads, just a dozen or so miles short of Brighton.

The introduction of paid holidays in the 1930s also made the Sussex coast more accessible to visitors of modest means. Some made the relatively short journey from inland towns in the county, but others came from farther afield, usually courtesy of the Southern Railway. In 1931 R.C. Sherriff's novel, *The Fortnight in September*, appeared, 'a perfect, relentlessly detailed evocation of a lower middle-class family's fortnight by the sea in the 1930s', as Juliet Gardiner has described it.[37] Every year the Stevens family, the novel's protagonists, go to the same boarding house in Bognor – 'Seaview' – at the cost of £3 10*s*. a week. Mr and Mrs Stevens had stayed there for their honeymoon, and it is now a place of annual pilgrimage, where the cosy, safe familiarity of the Sussex seaside amply rewards the Stevens family for their patient anticipation of each year's visit. There is 'the first walk along the front, the first ice cream of the holiday', together with entertainment on the pier, snoozing in deck-chairs, bathing on the beach (where they hire a hut and brew tea), and the buying of postcards to send to friends and relations at home. Eventually it is time to return to Dulwich (changing at Clapham Junction), secure in the happy knowledge that they will be back in Bognor next year. Others longed to share the Stevens' simple pleasures. The initial print run of *The Fortnight in September* sold out instantly, with sales reaching 20,000 copies within a month of its appearance, and publishers in America and Europe clamoured to produce their own editions.

The road to war ... again

However, for many in Sussex in the inter-war period – especially as the Depression stuck in the 1930s – such contentment could only be dreamed of. Although unemployment rates in Sussex were about half the national level (the worst year was 1932, when the jobless rose to 10 per cent), there were pockets of both rural and urban poverty. Brighton, especially, was hit hard by the recession. The building industry was in the doldrums by the late 1930s, impacting on Moulescoombe in particular, where many local men who had been employed in the trade were now thrown out of work. Earlier, in May 1928, Brighton had experienced conflict between workers and the authorities during the General Strike. The mood was set on 8 May when a body of strikers, said to be 200 strong, marched to the Town Hall, where they were turned back by the police. However, as they moved away, the strikers were suddenly confronted by a woman in a small car who drove straight at them. They jumped for their lives, and fortunately there were no injurious. But the incident had created a new atmosphere of discontent, especially when it was learned that the woman had been neither apprehended nor charged. Fearing further trouble, the authorities mobilised special mounted constables – known to their detractors as 'Black and Tans' in an unflattering comparison with the auxiliaries in Ireland – who were armed with stout staves and ready for action. The 'specials' got their chance on 11 May, when a group of high-spirited students decided to break the strike by driving trams from the Lewes Road depot. They were prevented from doing so by the strikers and their supporters, who blocked their way. This was the cue for which the 'Black and Tans' had been waiting. Lashing out with their staves, they charged the crowd in a paroxysm of unprovoked violence that has survived in popular memory as the 'Battle of Lewes Road'. Brighton Corporation later treated the 'specials' to a civic banquet in recognition of their prompt despatch of the 'Bolsheviks', while twenty-two workers received gaol sentences of, on average, three months each.

Although relatively few workers in Brighton – or elsewhere in Sussex – had participated in the General Strike, the Battle of Lewes Road had

Despite the growth of tourism and the holiday trade, Brighton remained an important fishing centre in the inter-war period, when daily fish sales were still held, the fish industry being a welcome source of employment locally in the depressed 1930s. Here a fish market is in full swing at dawn on the beach at Brighton on 7 December 1931, local fishermen intent on selling their overnight catches.

hardened attitudes on both sides. Brighton Corporation, anxious to protect the town's reputation as an attractive holiday destination, did not wish to see discontented workers on the streets, whose presence might deter the visitor. But they could not disguise the hunger and want that now existed in the town. By 1932 5,800 people in Brighton were on the dole, and in neighbouring Hove soup kitchens were providing nourishment for up to 750 people a week. The local Labour Party and trade unionists did what they could to address the conditions. But the initiative was taken by the Communist-inspired Brighton branch of the National Unemployed

Workers' Movement, whose antics ranged from lying down in front of double-decker buses and carrying coffins through the streets in mock funerals, to disrupting George V's jubilee celebrations. The Movement was also active in Horsham and Battle, and likewise in Eastbourne where in 1939 it staged a 'March of History'. Linking 'revolutionary' moments in Sussex history – Jack Cade's rebellion, the Captain Swing riots, and the more recent Battle of Lewes Road – by depicting these events on their flags and banners, some 400 Communists and their sympathisers marched through Eastbourne, singing an ironic version of Ward-Higg's 'Sussex by the Sea':

> Now is the time for marching, under our banners red,
> Rank upon rank advancing, surely we forge ahead.
> So let your voices ring, comrades, all you who would be free,
> And we'll sing a song as we march along,
> Of peace and liberty.[38]

The previous year, 1938, Brighton Corporation had been outraged by another attack on the town's good name, in the form of Graham Greene's novel, *Brighton Rock*. As John Lowerson has observed, it was a work 'replete with descriptions of vile slums, gang warfare and physically and psychologically malformed characters'.[39] The Brighton and Hove Hotels Association found the book 'loathsome', and the *Brighton and Hove Gazette* newspaper thought it a 'gross libel'.[40] But Greene had depicted faithfully a Brighton criminal underworld that could not be ignored, and had used it to develop a plot (with its underlying Catholic message of the unexpected strangeness of God's mercy) centred around 17-year-old 'Pinkie', the psychopathic would-be gang leader, and his new wife, the innocent Rose, aged just 16. Pinkie has murdered a journalist, Hale, to further his violent ambition, and marries the infatuated Rose only to prevent her giving evidence against him in court. Pinkie resorts to further crime, as Hale's friend – the ebullient Ida – does what she can to thwart Pinkie and save Rose. Pinkie meets his inevitable death, although not before he has recognised that Hell is not some distant place, but all around him and of his own making. In 1947 *Brighton Rock* was made into a memorable film starring Richard Attenborough as Pinkie, a 'movie' that entered the national consciousness and accounted for a sometimes ambivalent popular attitude to Brighton that is with us still (the film was remade in 2010) – much to the chagrin of Brighton Corporation.

To the unsettling activities of the National Unemployed Workers' Movement and the controversial impact of *Brighton Rock*, should be added the demonstrations of Oswald Mosley's Black Shirts, which greatly aggravated the sense of uncertainty and danger. Brighton had emerged as a regional focus for fascist sentiment, with local admirers of

Mussolini and Hitler among those determined to spike the strikers and Communists. When Mosley addressed a Black Shirt rally in the Dome in 1934, violence broke out between rival left- and right-wing groups, both armed with knives and other offensive weapons, which the police struggled to contain. Hastings, Newhaven and Worthing also became centres of fascist sympathy, especially as Appeasement – the desire to prevent another war at any price, even if it meant buying off Mussolini and Hitler – became a popular political creed. The outbreak of the Spanish Civil War heightened still further the atmosphere of popular disquiet, with local opinion split between supporters of the fascist Franco and those of his Republican opponents. Sussex gained its own taste of the war when, in 1937, the British government agreed to allow 4,000 Spanish children, aged five to fifteen, to come as refugees to the UK. Some of these *evacuados* found themselves in Sussex, a number boarded at Herstmonceux Castle, and others attending Knoll school in Hove – with merely the smattering of English picked up in the playground, these poor ragged Basques could only reply 'bang, bang' and point imaginary rifles when other pupils asked them where their fathers were.[41]

Richard Attenborough stars as the troubled youth Pinkie in this 1938 screen version of Graham Greene's classic novel *Brighton Rock*, as depicted in this cinema poster. The film also included an early appearance by the actor William Hartnell, later to earn fame in the 1960s as the very first of a long line of Dr Who characters in the eponymous BBC television series.

Meanwhile, the local branch of the Anglo-German Friendship Ring had joined forces with the Brighton police to invite a German police football team to visit in 1938. The resultant match was not without controversy. When the Germans arrived at Hove railway station, crowds singing the 'Red Flag' attempted to drown out the German national anthem played by the Brighton Police Force band. Before the kick-off at the Goldstone ground of Brighton & Hove Albion, the German team treated the assembled fans to the Nazi salute. Supporters of the visit insisted that it was a social occasion, and that sport and politics should not be mixed, and that anyway it was up to the Germans to decide what form of government they preferred. When it was time for the visitors to depart, the two sides agreed – without irony – that they looked forward to a replay in 1939. By now, of course, the real nature of the Nazi regime was plain for all to see. George Bell, Bishop of Chichester, had opposed rearmament, and at his behest prayers for peace were said fervently throughout the diocese. But when A.C. Headlam, Bishop of Gloucester, praised the Nazis for their discipline and self-sacrifice, Bell called for his

The Army on manoeuvres 'somewhere in Sussex' in October 1928. The neat rows of bell tents and marquees in the background suggest that this is a Territorial Army 'fortnight camp'. The ancient armoured car seems hardly equal to the demands of modern warfare, a measure perhaps of the extent to which the armed services were starved of funds in the inter-war period. Eleventh-hour rearmament only occurred when the threat from Hitler's Germany appeared acute.

resignation and demanded that the archbishop of Canterbury dissociate the Church of England from such views (which he did). Bell also led the work to help Jewish victims of Nazi persecution – although he loathed the prospect of another world war, he had no illusions about those in power in Berlin, and said so.[42] No doubt he spoke for the overwhelming majority in Sussex.

TEN

Sussex at war again

The trauma of war

When the redoubtable Esther Meynell penned her *Sussex*, first published in 1947, she could not bring herself to discuss the impact of the late war upon her beloved county. Sussex had found itself in the front line once more, yet this time the danger had seemed even more acute, the threat palpable and tangible. The Sussex landscape was transformed as, like everything else, it was put on a war footing, and the conflict intruded in myriad ways upon the lives of ordinary people. German bombs fell, bringing death and destruction to town and country, and after the fall of France invasion had seemed a real possibility. When it was all over, the return to normality that people sought so earnestly was not easily achieved, and indeed many things – and many people – remained changed for ever. Like others, Esther Meynell had experienced first-hand the trauma of war over Sussex, and at its end mourned all that had been destroyed or disfigured. But the memory was too raw and too immediate for her to write about it now. 'I have deliberately refrained,' she admitted, 'from any allusions to the recent war in Sussex – troops and searchlights on the Downs, aerodromes, damage done by enemy bombs. These things will pass,' she agreed, 'Sussex will absorb them into her long history,' But, she insisted, 'they cannot take their place in that history till they have receded into the past'.[1]

Her sentiments were shared by others in Sussex who had suffered in the Second World War, but few had the opportunity to muse in print or to make public their disclaimers. Instead, most had to carry on quietly, putting the dreadful experiences of the war behind them and not pondering upon them too closely until the passage of time had begun to heal the wounds. Such was the experience of the perhaps typical Williams family, who had moved to Brighton from Cornwall on the eve of war. 'Pop' (Cecil) Williams had taken up the position of resident engineer at Roedean, the girls' public school soon to be transformed into HMS *Vernon*, the Royal Navy's torpedo, mining and electrical training establishment for the duration of the conflict. Setting up home in a large terraced town house at 246 Eastern Road in Kemptown, Pop and his wife Dorothy ('Dottie May') and their several children were only a few minutes' walk from what would shortly be the heavily defended coastline at Black Rock, and soon felt themselves vulnerable and exposed.

In January 1939, as Dottie May recorded in her diary, her son Roy had 'passed for the army', and in the May he was joined by his elder brother Doug, the two of them leaving for Aldershot and Colchester. Dottie May's eldest son, Garfield, a granite quarryman and mason, had been left behind in Cornwall, and there was an uncomfortable sense that her tight-knit family was suddenly unravelling.[2] 'Home so different,' she noted in her diary, the days seeming quieter now that the boys had gone, and she passed the time making frocks and coats for her daughters or going to the cinema. During the spring and summer months of 1939 Roy and Doug came home periodically on weekend leave (though rarely together), and on Friday 18 August Doug arrived for a much anticipated seven-day leave period. But early on the following Thursday morning he received a telegram, telling him to report immediately to his unit, cutting short what was left of his time at home. Dottie May fretted over his hurried departure and the looming 'war crisis', as she described it.

A week later, as she wrote in her diary entry for 1 September, 'Germany invaded Poland very upset and worried'. Evacuation was already in progress (Dottie May had been asked to collect her youngest son, Cyril, recovering from an illness in the Royal Alexander Hospital for Sick Children, which was being emptied of its inmates), and even as evacuees left London for the Sussex countryside, so children were also being removed from urban, front-line Brighton to rural safety inland. 'Seeing the evacuated children made my heart sore … a sight I shall never forget,' wrote Dottie May: 'very upset seeing Ambulances with stretcher cases.' On Sunday morning, 3 September, she listened on the wireless – as did countless millions across the country – to the weary tones of Neville Chamberlain explaining how all his hopes for peace had been shattered. 'War declared 11 o'clock,' recorded Dottie May, 'first air raid warning sent Cyril's temperature up, he was very upset.' Over the next few days she professed herself 'overcome with worry of Doug and Roy'. But, for the moment, there was a strange air of normality.

From the 'phoney war' to Dunkirk

The 'phoney war', as it came to be known, was a temporary stand-off when little seemed to be happening, although behind the scenes Britain was busily preparing for total war. The 7th Battalion, Royal Sussex Regiment, had been mobilised in August (Doug Williams was not the only one to receive an urgent wire that fateful day) to help form the proposed British Expeditionary Force (BEF) that would be deployed to France if needs be. But, despite the digging of trenches, gas-mask

Mass gas attacks against the civilian population were feared during the Second World War, a threat that was taken extremely seriously by the authorities. Here schoolchildren in Brighton, escorted by an Air Raid Protection (ARP) Warden, participate in a gas exercise on 17 February 1941. Tear gas was released in one sector of Brighton, and those people foolish enough not to have their gas-masks to hand were required to remain outside the area until the exercise was over and the gas had dispersed. Meanwhile, everyone else was encouraged to carry on as usual, going about their daily tasks while wearing their respirators. All ARP personnel in Brighton were involved in the exercise, which lasted thirty minutes.

drills and air-raid warnings, few took seriously the threat of imminent invasion, the beaches for now remaining only lightly defended. Despite the dramatic rise of air power since 1918, and the doctrine that 'the bomber will always get through', popular opinion continued to imagine that the war would be fought on the Continent, as it had been in the Great War. Nonetheless, there were those who thought it best to be prepared, the Royal Victoria Hotel at St Leonards-on-Sea advertising in *The Times* to the effect that its 'ballroom and adjacent toilets have been made gas- and splinter-proof'.[3] At neighbouring Hastings, the White family decided that far-away Somerset would make an altogether safer home, and duly moved to Weston-super-Mare where, ironically, they would be bombed out in a heavy air raid in October 1942.[4]

Pop and Dottie May had the welcome diversion of a trip to Cornwall, for Garfield's wedding, and over the next few months Doug and Roy even managed to make it home occasionally on weekend leave. But Roy's posting to France that autumn as part of the BEF was an ominous sign, and did much to concentrate the mind. 'Had first letter from Roy in France,' wrote Dottie May on 14 October: 'Thinking a lot about the dear boy.' The Williams family celebrated an early Christmas together when both boys were home briefly in December, but their departure left Dottie May 'very much down in the dumps' and fearful of what the year ahead might hold. It had cost her an astronomical 3*s.* 6*d.* to send a parcel overseas to Roy, she recorded in her diary, but she felt it was worth it, forwarding home comforts to her son at the front and keeping in touch. Yet Christmas Day 1939, when it came, seemed flat and lonely: she 'missed the boys terribly'.

Tom Payton, dressed here in the uniform of a Boy Seaman, left Hove to attend the Prince of Wales Sea Training School at Ingham Old Hall, Norfolk, which trained boys between the ages of fifteen and seventeen as deck ratings for the Merchant Navy.
AUTHOR'S COLLECTION

By now some 114,000 children from London had been evacuated to the Sussex countryside. Black-out had become part of the wartime routine, as had rationing. At schools across the county, pupils practised their gas-mask and air-raid drills. Cinema footage still survives of children being put through their paces at the Knoll school in Hove.[5] The youngsters in the film are shown continuing with their lessons while wearing their gas-masks, and then – led by their teacher – trotting smartly out of the classroom to the safety of the air-raid shelters nearby. Owen Payton is prominent among those doubling across the playground, his younger brother Tom behind and just out of camera. The Payton brothers lived close by, in Godwin Road, and, bicycling around the streets of Hove in those early war days in their Boys Brigade or Boy Scout uniforms, delivering messages from the Royal Naval Volunteer Reserve (RNVR) centre at HMS *King Alfred* to local shops or boarding houses, they felt that they were making vital contributions to the war effort. Later, when he was 15, Tom was despatched to Merchant Navy training school in Norfolk, and went to sea in time to experience the last days of the Atlantic convoys and to participate in the Pacific war, the latter taking him to Hawaii, New Zealand and best of all (in his estimation), Australia.

In the spring of 1940, as Dottie May Williams had feared, the Germans struck. In a lightning attack – the classic 'blitzkrieg' assault – across the Low Countries and then into France, Hitler's armoured columns by-passed the heavily defended Maginot Line, throwing the French army into disarray and with it denting the BEF's hitherto firm belief in its ally's military capacity. The BEF was now fighting for its collective life, and among those units facing the full force of the German onslaught was the 7th Battalion, the Royal Sussex Regiment. Moving forward to engage the enemy on 18 May, the train carrying the battalion from Rouen to Amiens was bombed by the Luftwaffe, resulting in more than sixty dead or wounded. The locomotive had been derailed by a direct hit, and the train left the rails, the violence of its destruction accounting for some of the more gruesome injuries sustained – a soldier with the top of his head sliced clean off, another man wandering among the wreckage with half his face missing.[6]

That night the battalion took cover in a nearby wood, fearful that the German bombers would return to complete their task, and on 20 May it found itself holding a stretch of the Amiens–Poix road. Unaware that neighbouring units, the Tyneside Scottish and the 36th Brigade, had already been swept aside, the men of the Royal Sussex Regiment had no idea that the Germans were at that moment approaching in overwhelming force. Suffering the awful paralysis of denial, the battalion's commander clung optimistically but hopelessly to French intelligence assessments that the enemy was at least forty miles away, angrily dismissing reports to the contrary from his own officers. But when tanks from 1st Panzer Division appeared that afternoon, it was clear that the unequal contest was about to commence. Years later, on those rare occasions when he could be persuaded to talk about the war, Roy Williams remembered the horrifying sight of British soldiers – and French civilians, too, including women and children – being run down by the panzers as the enemy thrust forward. Doug Swift, another private in the Royal Sussex Regiment, recalled likewise, marvelling at the courage of his colleagues. 'Some had been run over by tank tracks,' he said, 'They advanced with bayonets fixed, bloody heroes the lot of them, against tanks. Bayonets!'[7]

It was a rout, the beginning of an inexorable retreat to the beaches of Dunkirk, from which large sections of the BEF (some 198,229 men), together with 139,997 French soldiers, were evacuated to England in Operation Dynamo between 26 May and the early hours of 4 June 1940. Most were landed at Kentish ports, being closest to the French coast, but others arrived along the Sussex shore – notably at Newhaven, where the Southern Railway laid on troop trains to ferry them inland. The escape from Dunkirk was dependent upon the might of the Royal Navy, together with the air cover provided by the Royal Air Force and gallant rearguard actions on the ground which delayed the enemy's advance. The Southern Railway's cross-channel fleet also performed sterling service, and among its losses at Dunkirk was the steamship *Brighton*.[8]

In popular memory, however, pride of place in the evacuation is given

For most soldiers, such as Roy Williams, the retreat from Dunkirk in 1940 was an appalling nightmare, a lengthy and patient but nerve-wracking wait for rescue among rising and falling tides, enemy aircraft bombing and machine-gun raids, filthy water, and drownings as men succumbed to fatigue or their wounds or were simply overwhelmed by the waves.

to the 'little ships'. Responding to Admiralty pleas for assistance, owners of small vessels of all kinds participated in the rescue of the British army. From all along the Sussex coast, pleasure craft, yachts, fishing boats, lifeboats and other 'little ships' joined this remarkable flotilla. Pleasure steamers from Brighton, Newhaven, Hastings and elsewhere played especially distinguished roles. The *Brighton Belle* and the *Brighton Queen II* were both sunk by enemy action, as were the *Waverley II* and at least two vessels named *Starling*, with the stricken *Devonia* abandoned for ever on the beach at Dunkirk. Of all the household names among the pleasure fleet remembered so fondly by day-trippers to Sussex coastal resorts before the war, only the *Glendower* had survived unscathed – or so it was said.

Among those evacuated from Dunkirk was Roy Williams. Having waited his turn among the dunes, he joined the lines of soldiers wading out into the sea to be picked up. It seemed liked hours, he recalled later (it probably was), made worse by the continual dunking he experienced as waves washed over his head, or when he and others ducked down beneath the surface to avoid the strafing runs by German aircraft. In later years, Roy suffered severe mastoiditis, which he (and his doctors) attributed to the filthy, oily salt water that had invaded his ears, nose and throat during that agonising wait for rescue. Otherwise uninjured, he was soon home. But what Dottie May, his mother, had to say is unrecorded, no diary entries having survived from the spring of 1940, the trauma of those terrible days perhaps inhibiting her from putting pen to paper. Roy later saw active service in north Africa and Italy, where the Royal Sussex Regiment played its part in combating Rommel's Afrika Korps and in the struggle for Monte Casino, as did his brother Doug. All three Williams boys in uniform (including Garfield) survived the war, returning home safely to Sussex and to Cornwall.

Among those assisting in the evacuation of the BEF from Dunkirk, were volunteers drawn from the trainees of HMS *King Alfred*, the RNVR shore establishment at Hove where the Payton boys had thought themselves key players. Built as the Hove Marina complex, with an impressive swimming pool and excellent supporting facilities, HMS *King Alfred* had been requisitioned by the Admiralty in 1939, even before it had been opened for its civilian use. Situated next door to the existing headquarters of the RNVR Sussex Division, *King Alfred* was conveniently placed as well as superbly equipped. The pool was covered over and became the main instructional hall, while the restaurant and dance hall were converted into the wardroom, or officers' mess. Formally commissioned on 11 September 1939, the new establishment was getting into its stride when the Dunkirk crisis loomed. Initially, yachtsmen and other 'gentlemen' with maritime interests or connections had been invited to apply for commissions in the Royal Naval Volunteer Special Reserve (RNV[S]R), with successful applicants being sent to *King Alfred* for officer training. By May 1940, however, RNVR and Royal Navy 'Hostilities Only' ratings recommended for commissions had also begun to arrive at the establishment, swelling its ranks and considerably expanding its role.

On the evening of Thursday 29 May, a 'guest night' mess dinner at *King Alfred* was interrupted with the urgent news that volunteers were required for an important mission. Thirty-two were chosen from the eager trainees, and by 10 p.m. that evening they found themselves *en route* to Dunkirk to assist in the evacuation effort. Arriving by bus at Dover, several were earmarked for the Dutch freighter *Hilda*, and others assigned to the pleasure boat *Skylark* (one of no fewer than nine vessels with that name at Dunkirk). At Sheerness, two trainees were given command of the riverboats *Empress* and *Tigris One*. The *Hilda* arrived off Dunkirk on the evening of 30 May, towing several motorboats that were subsequently despatched to pick up soldiers waiting in the shallows.

The following morning *Hilda* rescued fifty survivors from the stricken destroyer, HMS *Keith*, and shortly after took on another sixty or so when the minesweeper HMS *Skipjack* was also bombed. Now with some 530 men embarked, the *Hilda* returned to Dover, her task accomplished. The *Skylark*, meanwhile, assisted in the rescue of seventy British soldiers and an equivalent number of Frenchmen. The *Tigris One* was similarly active, ferrying troops from the shore to larger ships farther out until, having completed half-a-dozen runs, she was badly damaged and abandoned. In all, it had been an impressive contribution, and HMS *King Alfred* was justly proud of its courageous trainees.[9]

HMS *King Alfred*

Indeed, *King Alfred* was to make a continuing contribution of great significance throughout the war. It was commanded for the duration by Captain John Pelly, who had entered the Royal Navy as long ago as 1903, at the age of fourteen, and had acquired wide-ranging experience of operations at sea before, during and after the First World War, retiring some thirty years later in 1934. On the outbreak of the Second World War, he was recalled to active service. A reserved yet determined man, Pelly proved the ideal appointment for the task of developing HMS *King Alfred* as a major training establishment, and for turning civilians and ratings swiftly but effectively into naval officers capable of command at sea. He enjoyed the support of an equally dedicated staff of regular and RNVR officers who taught a range of academic subjects as well as practical training in areas such as seamanship, communications, gunnery, and torpedoes. They, in turn, managed an extensive staff of senior ratings, whose job it was to instruct the trainees in all manner of naval knowledge (as it was known), and to inculcate the values, ethos and traditions of the Royal Navy. As Ewen Montagu, famous much later as one of the architects of Operation Mincemeat – the deception plan that, employing a disguised dead body carefully dumped at sea, caused the Germans *not* to expect the Allied invasion of Sicily in 1943 – was to recall:

> From the very first day of operations in the *King Alfred* the staff of that 'ship' began, not only to train us in the skills which we would need, navigation, seamanship, gunnery and so on, but also instill into us what was more important – the spirit of the Navy and its discipline … my admiration for, and devotion to, the Navy became fixed and has persisted to the present day.[10]

As the numbers of trainees continued to grow, so *King Alfred* extended its tentacles across Hove and neighbouring districts. Boat-handling and seamanship drills were practised in Shoreham Harbour, for example, and a local football field was commandeered periodically for bayonet training. The canal at Portslade, where half-a-dozen Admiralty launches were kept, was another seamanship venue. Lancing College, a public school some six miles away, became *King Alfred (L)* in January 1941, its pupils evacuated to distant Shropshire, their place taken by officer candidates – ratings recommended for commissions. When, after six weeks' initial training, they were transferred to Hove, they found that they were required to live in an austere underground car-park hastily converted to serve as a naval barracks. Directly recruited officers-under-training, by contrast, were allowed to live 'ashore' in boarding houses or small hotels but with strict instructions that on no account should they be 'adrift' when required 'on board' each day for training. Ludovic Kennedy, later a distinguished television journalist, broadcaster and author, found himself in one of 'Hove's numerous genteel hotels where the residents were mostly retired service people and old ladies'.[11] But at least there was the prospect of escaping this staid atmosphere from time to time, seeking out the altogether more racy venues of neighbouring Brighton, with its bars, restaurants and theatres. On the whole, trainees would look back on their *King Alfred* days with affection.

Those who graduated successfully from HMS *King Alfred* saw active service in major conflicts throughout the war, and served in numerous roles – from key positions ashore in naval intelligence to convoy work or underwater operations in submarines. Alongside Ewen Montagu and Ludovic Kennedy, HMS *King Alfred* welcomed through its doors a string of talented young men who in years ahead would go on to play prominent parts in British life. Alec Guinness, the distinguished actor, Nicholas Monsarrat, the novelist whose book *The Cruel Sea* was so powerful in describing the realities of the Battle of the Atlantic, and Peter Scott, the naturalist, all passed through *King Alfred* during the war years. So, too, did William Golding, of *Lord of the Flies* fame, who joined the establishment in November 1941 and later went on to command a rocket-firing landing craft at the D-Day landings in Normandy and at Walcheren on the Scheldt estuary, near Antwerp.[12] Edward Young, peacetime publisher who had designed the Pelican Books logo, became the first RNV[S]R officer to command an operational submarine, later recording his experiences in the classic wartime autobiography *One of Our Submarines*.[13] Leon 'Goldy' Goldsworthy, one of several exceptional Australian mine disposal trainees to pass through *King Alfred*, was shortly to become the most decorated officer in the Royal Australian Navy: George Cross, George Medal, Distinguished Service Cross, Mentioned in Despatches. Much of his early work was accomplished along the Sussex coast, where he quite literally learned on the job. He successfully defused a 'horned' mine on Brighton beach, and went on to deal with a number of other mines washed up on the long coastline between Selsey

Bill and St Leonards. At Bexhill, having disarmed a mine, he and his Wren driver (Pamela Darlington) clambered down a sandhill for a closer look at his handiwork. As they did so, they were machine-gunned by a flight of German aircraft that had suddenly appeared over the horizon, and were lucky to escape with their lives. Later, Goldsworthy was again called to Brighton beach, only to find that the suspected parachute mine lurking beyond the shallows was actually the body of an unfortunate German pilot who had bailed out and drowned in the Channel.[14]

The Home Guard

After Dunkirk, the public mood had grown more serious. On 14 May 1940 Anthony Eden, Secretary of State for War, announced the formation of the Local Defence Volunteers (LDV). LDV companies were formed across the county, ostensibly for men aged 17 to 65 but in practice recruiting youths as young as fifteen and elderly ex-soldiers in their late sixties or seventies. In those early days, when uniforms and weapons were in short supply, the more self-conscious Volunteers felt awkward or inadequate in their makeshift guises, not helped by their being lampooned in the press as the 'Look, Duck and Vanish' brigade. But, like the Payton boys who cycled around the streets of Hove on their errands, they were anxious to do their bit. Soon they would be re-invented as the Home Guard, becoming progressively better trained and better equipped, although never quite losing that air of well-meaning amateurism so fondly remembered in British folk culture.

Yet for those who enlisted in the Home Guard, there was a sense of deadly earnest. Gerry Wells, who joined the Eastbourne detachment of the Royal Sussex Home Guard, recalled that: 'I often did night guard duty together with my Father … it was a surreal experience to be patrolling with a loaded rifle slung from my shoulder, along a darkened promenade that I'd so often seen full of people doing their holiday thing in deck chairs, licking ice-cream cornets and cooking in the sun.' It was a remarkable contrast, he explained:

> How different was that part of the front at 2 a.m. in 1943 – how cold and deserted then – the beach shadowed by endless coils of barbed wire and skeletal traceries of linked steel poles set into the shingle that we knew harboured countless mines. A spill of moonlight on the sea would sometimes illuminate the pier with a 50 yd gap cut out of its length – it was no holiday spot any more and not much of a landing place either.[15]

On Sunday mornings, Wells added, the Home Guard practised street fighting in the Bourne Street area of Eastbourne, where enemy air raids had reduced buildings to rubble. Here Wells and colleagues 'cleared houses of fanatical SS with much shouting, and discharging of blanks from our antiquated rifles'. They were also taught to use explosives, learning how to pack drainpipes and propel them as makeshift missiles. Then, after 'a satisfying morning session we packed up and went home to Sunday lunch and a quiet afternoon'.[16] As Gerry Wells understood, the deployment of the Home Guard across Sussex was designed to complement the elaborate defensive arrangements put in place to hamper the German invasion, if and when it came. Even small villages sported a Home Guard platoon, and large commercial organisations such as the Southdown bus company established their own units. There was also the shadowy 'Auxiliary' arm of the Home Guard, intended to form the kernel of a resistance movement had the Germans landed, and which trained in sabotage, booby-traps and the like. Its regional headquarters was Tottington Manor, at Small Dole near Henfield in West Sussex, which controlled the twenty or so patrols – comprising some 135 men all told – that ranged silently across the county in strict secrecy, intent on wreaking havoc on the enemy should the opportunity present itself.

As part of this increasingly determined defensive posture, Sussex beaches were closed and mined, and became a tangle of barbed wire and anti-tank and anti-personnel obstacles. As Gerry Wells noted, spans were removed from piers to prevent their use by enemy shipping, and anti-aircraft batteries were set up to defend strategic points, especially along the coast. The most vulnerable coastal areas, such as the flat grounds around Pevensey, were bolstered by heavy naval guns, hastily brought out of storage and erected along the shoreline. Meanwhile, so-called 'Stop Lines' had been established across Sussex, designed to hinder the Germans as they attempted to move inland. Among the most significant was the GHQ Stop Line, which began at Newhaven, following the courses of the rivers Ouse and Uck, making eventually for the Medway and the Thames. Similarly important was the Corps Stop Line, which ran from Guildford in Surrey to Uckfield in East Sussex. These Stop Lines were provided with many hundreds of pillboxes of various shapes and sizes, with gun emplacements designed to accommodate light artillery or machine-guns.[17]

There were also 'Nodal Points', as they were designated, towns and villages of particular strategic importance that warranted enhanced defensive measures – concentrations of pillboxes, road-blocks, anti-tank cubes, minefields, and so on. Barcombe Mills, for example, with its several crossings of the river Ouse and its vital railway junction, was protected by nine pillboxes, roadblocks and anti-tank obstacles. Crowborough, with its railway station, road junction and location on the GHQ Stop Line was another Nodal Point, guarded by a plethora of pillboxes and anti-tank ditches. So, too, was Arundel, where the castle helped form part of the defensive arrangements for the locality, alongside the ubiquitous pillboxes – one of these, indeed, was constructed against the south-east gate of the castle, cleverly camouflaged by the use of flint to make it appear part of the ancient walls. Such devices were replicated across Sussex, in sometimes unlikely and improbable places, turning the county quite literally and very visibly into a front line in waiting – for an invasion that never came.

The Battle of Britain

Hitler's decision to postpone Operation Sealion, the proposed invasion of Britain, rested upon his knowledge that, having failed to achieve mastery of the air in the Battle of Britain, his flotilla of barges and other craft earmarked for the operation would have been easy pickings for the might of the Royal Navy's Home Fleet. The epic struggle for air superiority had been fought in large measure over Sussex and adjoining counties. Tangmere, near Chichester, was the most important of the five Royal Air Force airfields in Sussex in 1940, and provided air cover along the south coast from Bournemouth to Brighton. Farther east, protection was provided by fighters from RAF Kenley in Surrey. From the beginning, Tangmere pilots, flying Hurricanes, were in the thick of it. Through August and into September they flew almost without respite. On 13 August all available aircraft were scrambled over Arundel and Petworth to turn back a huge enemy formation intent on attacking Farnborough. Later that afternoon, the Tangmere squadrons scattered another formation over the Isle of Wight. The Luftwaffe had expected 13 August – 'Eagle Day' – to be the decisive phase of the contest, but poor weather contributed to its disappointing performance. Three days later, however, the Germans attacked Tangmere itself, recognising its strategic importance and determined to knock the airfield out of the battle. Two hangars and fourteen aircraft on the ground were destroyed, with buildings damaged and water and electricity supplies disrupted. Next day, German aircraft attacked the radar station at Poling, putting it out of action for the rest of August, and bombed the airfields at Thorney Island and Ford. The latter was only lightly defended, and thirteen aircraft were lost in the raid. Yet somehow Tangmere managed to hold on, continuing to drive off Luftwaffe assaults until the last of the daylight raids on 30 September 1940. By then, the Royal Air Force had begun to hit back, its bombers destroying some 200 invasion barges marshalled in the Channel ports of France and the Low Countries. The Battle of Britain had been won; Operation Sealion was postponed.

One individual who observed the contest in the skies over Sussex in the summer of 1940 was Laurie Lee, then an up-and-coming young poet working for the GPO Film Unit. One sunny August day – very likely the 13th, or perhaps the 15th – he found himself near Arundel, visiting his lover Lorna Wishart and their daughter Yasmin. As he wrote later, the 'drone of planes was continuous. About one o'clock it grew louder, more threatening, like a swarm drawing near. Suddenly the ground shook beneath our bodies and the dull thump of bombs sounded in the distance.' It was over as quickly as it had started, however, 'and presently we saw English fighters flying back to their aerodromes in threes and singly'. But the lull was illusory, for 'there was a sudden burst of machine-gun fire, loud, in the sky. It rattled across the hills like an oath … the machine-gun cracked again … all around the ground shook, the dry leaves crackled with repeated bombs.' Once more the 'sky heaved and boiled. I saw planes whirling around each other like little wooden crosses tossed up by a juggler.' Now the battle seemed to be directly overhead: 'everything seemed aimed at us, we heard the vicious tearing whines of crashing planes coming straight down to us.' Yet once again the fighting dissipated as swiftly as it had flared up. 'We walked down the road again,' wrote Lee, 'and looked once more down into the sky. … The aerodrome was blazing.' Finding themselves near a cottage hospital, they sat on the gate 'and very soon the ambulances began to arrive'.[18]

Later, in the October, Laurie Lee rented a caravan near Storrington, right under Chanctonbury Ring. One night a German plane jettisoned its bomb load close by, destroying several houses and bursting a water main – one piece of stray shrapnel landed six feet from the caravan. Other nights were 'loud with bombs & planes & tenseness'.[19] It was not until the spring of the following year that a plain-clothes policeman arrived to explain that this was a restricted area, and that Lee was breaking the law by living in the caravan. He was moved on, but not before he had experienced first-hand the Battle of Britain and its aftermath.

Such brushes with the law could have a lighter side, as the youthful Ian Allan (born in Horsham), then a very junior Southern Railway employee but shortly to embark upon the creation of his railway publishing empire, discovered. As he put it, reflecting on the events years later, his 'railway enthusiasm nearly landed me in deep trouble'. His elderly grandmother, he explained, had lived at Burgess Hill, then within the ten-mile exclusion zone from the coast where a wide variety of activities was restricted. Ian Allan's parents periodically visited Granny at Burgess Hill, and on one occasion Ian went with them. Soon he wandered off to train-spot on the nearby London–Brighton mainline, taking his camera with him. 'After an hour', he recalled, 'a real Sussex Mr Plod arrived on his bicycle and averred that I was acting in a suspicious manner and what was I doing in Burgess Hill?'. Ian Allan's seemingly lame excuse that he was only visiting his grandmother failed to convince the police constable, 'and he arrested me and marched me to the Police Station where I was interviewed by a very stern and serious inspector' who likewise disbelieved the grandmother story and 'was convinced I was a German parachutist or at least a fifth columnist'. Eventually, of course, Ian Allan's identity was established, and he was grudgingly sent on his way but not before the film from his camera had been confiscated for processing and examination. As Ian Allan recalled: 'I heard no more. I was a rotten photographer anyway'.[20]

The literary couple, Virginia and Leonard Woolf, were among those who had faced the air battle over Sussex. Bombed out of their London residence in September 1940, they retreated permanently to their Sussex home, Monk's House at Rodmell, near Lewes. Leonard, who was Jewish, had no illusions about what might happen if the Germans did invade. He joined the Local Defence Volunteers, and prepared to meet the enemy. Later, in his autobiography, he recalled the horror that he and Virginia had felt in that summer of 1940. 'Jews were hunted down, beaten up, and humiliated everywhere' under Nazi domination, he wrote. 'I saw a photograph of a Jew being dragged by storm-troopers out of a shop in one of the main streets in Berlin; the fly-buttons of the man's trousers had been torn open to show that he was circumcised and therefore a Jew.' On the man's face, he added, was the 'look of blank suffering and despair'. But equally shocking 'was the look on the faces of respectable men and women, standing on the pavement, laughing at the victim'.[21] On 13 May 1940, the Woolfs had made a suicide pact. If the Germans overran England, they would poison themselves with fumes from their car. Later, they were able to get hold of sufficient morphia to administer a fatal dose each, and that became their preferred method of terminating their lives. Virginia, with her history of mental instability, already considered that the war was lost and began to look forward to ending it all.

Yet the events as they unfolded provided a strange fascination for her, as she watched the dogfights in the Sussex skies. On one occasion, she wrote, the 'aircraft came very close. We lay down under the tree. The sound was like someone sawing in the air just above us. We lay flat on our faces, hands behind head. Don't close your teeth, said L[eonard].'[22] Bombs fell and 'shook the windows of my lodge', and they heard the boom of the anti-aircraft guns at Ringmer as they joined the battle. Virginia found such experiences oddly therapeutic. On 29 September a bomb fell close to Monk's House. Virginia thought the noise the result of Leonard slamming a window, and shouted a rebuke, only then going into the garden to see a German raider chased back over the Channel at Newhaven. From Monk's House, Virginia could look out across the countryside to Mount Caburn. In the November, a bomb burst the banks of the Ouse, and the river spilled over the surrounding meadows, right up to her garden. She was enchanted, and for the moment quite placid, although thoughts of suicide never really disappeared – eventually, on 28 March 1941, she drowned herself in her beloved river Ouse. The Battle of

Anti-aircraft guns and their crews became a familiar sight in Sussex from the earliest days of the Second World War. Here anti-aircraft gunners grab a bite to eat alongside their gun at Rye in November 1944, ready to leap into action should enemy raiders appear. By now the Allies had gained air superiority over the Sussex coast, with raiding usually occurring in the other direction, but there remained the tantalising prospect of maybe shooting down a 'doodlebug' flying bomb.

Britain might have been won, but this had not prevented Virginia Woolf's long struggle with her personal demons from ending finally in sad defeat.

Victory in the skies over Sussex was only the beginning, however, and in the autumn of 1940 Britain continued to stand alone against the Nazi menace. Sussex lost none of its front-line atmosphere, and indeed much of the county assumed the nature of an armed camp, as it would remain until the end of the war. In March 1941 the air ace Douglas Bader, recently promoted wing commander, became 'Wing Leader' of several Spitfire squadrons based at Tangmere. Between 24 March and 9 August he flew no fewer than sixty-two sweeps or 'circus operations' (where fighters supported bomber raids) over the Channel and France, adding numerous 'kills' to his already impressive tally, before his aircraft was lost in action. Bader believed that he had collided with an enemy plane, but there is some evidence to suggest that he was shot down by 'friendly fire'. He spent the rest of the war in German prisoner of war camps, including the notorious Colditz.[23] Meanwhile, at East Grinstead, Archibald McIndoe had established his celebrated burns unit, where his 'guinea pigs' – RAF aircrew who had suffered appalling burns in combat – were treated with the latest plastic surgery techniques. Pilots were apt to be fatalistic. 'People who stayed in a burning cockpit for ten seconds were overcome by the flames and heat,' recalled one RAF flyer: 'Nine seconds and you ended up in Queen Victoria Hospital in East Grinstead in Dr Archie McIndoe's burns surgery for the rest of the war. If you got out in eight seconds you never flew again, but you went back about twelve times for plastic surgery.'[24]

The renewed sense of urgency after Dunkirk was also heightened by the arrival of the Canadians. At Roedean, where Cecil 'Pop' Williams worked, some of the schoolgirls had been evacuated to Nova Scotia, and among the servicemen who replaced them was a number of Canadians. One of these, a young army captain named Basil, began courting Pop and Dottie May's eldest daughter, Doris. Like the Americans later in the war, the Canadians were thought glamorous and affluent, and their success with local women caused resentment among British servicemen and civilians, as well as considerable alarm among local mothers who feared for their daughters' virtue. It is said that officers accommodated in the girls' dormitories at Roedean were much encouraged by the signs reputedly located above each bed: 'If you want a mistress during the night, please press the bell.'[25] The Canadians and their Sussex hosts did not always see eye to eye, and there were various clashes – some physical, some verbal – in towns across the county such as Hastings, Seaford and Worthing. Basil, however, was approved of in the Williams family, not least on account of the fact that his nineteenth-century forebears had hailed from Cornwall, and he became a frequent visitor at their house in Eastern Road in Brighton. In due course, Basil and Doris became engaged to be married.

Canadians and the Dieppe Raid

By the autumn of 1941 the 1st Canadian army was firmly ensconced in Sussex, and gradually integrated into the local community, its heavy anti-aircraft artillery providing much of the coastal defence until 1944. The 2nd Canadian Division, part of this vast army, was stationed in West Sussex. Here it prepared for the ill-fated Dieppe Raid in August 1942. Early on the morning of 2 August, the Canadians left their camps in convoys, travelling to Newhaven, Shoreham and the Solent ports to participate in a major amphibious assault designed to probe the enemy's defensive capabilities. Dieppe, on the Channel coast of occupied France, had been selected for the operation, its situation close to Newhaven and the Sussex shore ensuring a relatively short journey for the attacking forces. Nonetheless, any element of surprise was soon lost, and the Canadians found themselves pinned down on the beach by withering enemy fire. Finally, when the order was given to withdraw, two-thirds

The enigmatic glance of wartime lovers. Major-General J. Hamilton 'Ham' Roberts, born in Manitoba, was appointed General Officer Commanding the 2nd Canadian Infantry Division, and directed the ill-fated raid on Dieppe from the warship HMS *Calpe*, for which role he was awarded the Distinguished Service Order. Like many Canadian servicemen in Sussex, he met and fell in love with a local woman, in this case Mrs Anne C. Fullerton, widow of the late John Fullerton of Thribergh Park, Yorkshire. General Roberts was himself a widower (his first wife had died in 1931), and Ham and Anne were married 'at a little church in Sussex' (according to a contemporary newspaper report) on 13 February 1943.
© PLANET NEWS/SCIENCE & SOCIETY PICTURE LIBRARY

of the 6,000 raiders had been killed, wounded or captured, the beach at Dieppe strewn with dead bodies, debris and the remains of twenty-eight knocked-out Allied tanks. The Germans, by contrast, had suffered only 591 casualties. Although a disaster by any reckoning, the Dieppe Raid taught the Allies many invaluable lessons about the conduct of amphibious warfare, and confirmed British military opinion that a full-blown Allied invasion of occupied Europe was not an option in 1942–43.

The return from Dieppe, though vastly smaller in scale than the escape from Dunkirk and 'hushed up' by the authorities, further sharpened the sense of Sussex as front-line. Continuing Luftwaffe activity likewise brought the war to the local home front, and although Sussex was not targeted to the extent of the large industrial conurbations elsewhere, it nonetheless had its own taste of the 'Blitz' – the nightly bombing raids over the United Kingdom which followed the end of the Battle of Britain. The eastern part of the county was 'bomb alley', where German aircraft often jettisoned their unused ordnance to alarming effect, and many Sussex towns and villages were also subject to the unpredictable 'tip-and-run' day-light raids by fighter-bombers – sudden attacks where civilians were machined-gunned in the streets, and local infrastructure, such as railway lines and gasometers, was targeted. In the early afternoon of 16 December 1942, for example, a north-bound train travelling between Lewes and East Grinstead was shot up by one such raider. There was damage to the locomotive and the train's three coaches, and several passengers were injured. The most serious casualty was Daisy Wilkins, from Newick, who lost an eye and suffered gunshot wounds to the face when she threw herself on top of a schoolgirl travelling in her compartment to shield her from the bullets. The girl survived unscathed, as did the other pupils from the Girls' Secondary High School in Lewes, returning home for the Christmas holidays, who had taken shelter on the floor and under the seats, despite worries about getting their school uniforms dirty. The engine driver, meanwhile, with great presence of mind, had accelerated his train into the 63-yard Cinder Hill Tunnel, situated between Barcombe and Newick & Chailey stations, which was just long enough to provide a refuge. He remained there until he decided it was safe to proceed.[26]

The Blitz

Towns such as Bexhill, Selsey, Eastbourne (which claimed to have had more air-raid warnings than any other place in Sussex), Littlehampton, Hastings, Worthing, and Lewes were all hit periodically. Gerry Wells recalled the strangeness of the mundane everyday existing side by side with the extraordinary. In Eastbourne, he slept with the rest of his family under a steel Morrison table in the dining room. Here at night

The remains of a Heinkel bomber, one of a group of nine German planes shot down on the Sussex-Surrey border on the night of 12 March 1941, at the height of the Blitz. Four aircrew from the Heinkel were killed, one corpse – as a local newspaper reported with grim relish – 'being found four miles from the blazing aeroplane'.

they listened to the drone of German bombers as they passed overhead on their way to and from London. Sometimes a German plane might 'dump a load of incendiaries on the Downs between us and the sea as a parting bonus – and then around 6 a.m. we would hear the milkman and the clink of bottles on the doorstep'.[27] Often such jettisoning did little material damage and, as Wells remembered, local people tried to take it all in their stride. But occasionally there were devastating consequences. In 1942 a single bomber ditched its load over Petworth, hitting the boys' school and inflicting thirty-one fatalities. In the following year, 108 people were killed when the Whitehall Cinema in East Grinstead was bombed. It was Brighton, however, that received the most sustained attention from the enemy. Between Monday 15 July 1940 and Wednesday 22 March 1944, according to local historian David Rowland, there were no fewer than fifty-six aerial attacks on the town, accounting for 198 deaths together with 790 injuries, almost half of them serious. Over 200 houses were destroyed, with a further 894 badly damaged and another 14,232 slightly damaged. As Rowland explains, it was east Brighton that bore the brunt of the bombing, around Kemptown and Black Rock, with the prominent block of flats at Marine Gate a favourite target for German raiders.[28]

In local memory, one of the most horrific episodes was 'the day they hit the Odeon' in Kemptown, on the afternoon of Saturday 14 September 1940. Trying desperately (but unsuccessfully, it gratifyingly transpired) to shake off a pursuing Spitfire, a German raider shed its half-a-dozen or so bombs, attempting to lighten its load and make good its escape. One bomb hit the Odeon cinema, where the audience, many of them children, had just finished viewing the presciently titled *It Could Happen to You* and were now watching a comedy *The Ghost Comes Home*, starring the popular Ann Rutherford. Two children and two adults were killed instantly or died in the ruins; a further ten died later in the nearby Royal Sussex County Hospital in Eastern Road. Included in the latter was eleven-year-old Monica Diplock, with a shrapnel wound to her neck, whose younger brother Neil had somehow found the superhuman strength to carry her to the hospital, although to no avail. Luckier was Cyril Williams, youngest son of Dottie May. News that the Odeon had been struck travelled quickly and among those who hurried to Royal Sussex County was Cyril's sister Hazel, younger sister of Doris. Looking anxiously from one broken body to the next, she could not identify Cyril in the row of dead and dying laid out on the hospital floor; fortunately he was by then already safe on one of the wards, being treated for a nasty gash to his arm. In all some fifty-two people across Kemptown died that day, with another eighty-five seriously injured. Some died in their homes when the bombs struck, others were caught in the street by shrapnel and debris. Seventeen-year-old Joyce Thomas was killed in the newsagent's shop in Bedford Street; Frederick Ball, aged fifty-seven, an Air Raid Warden, was injured at Chesham Place and died later that day in Royal Sussex County.[29]

There were further raids, and mounting casualties, during the autumn and winter of 1940 and the spring of 1941. Thereafter there was something of a lull, until the Luftwaffe was back with a vengeance in the summer of 1942. On 26 June, for example, a gasometer at Black Rock was destroyed by cannon fire in a lightning tip-and-run attack. Such raids continued into 1943, the most devastating being that of Tuesday 25 May when twenty-five enemy aircraft appeared suddenly in the early afternoon. In the resultant carnage, 600 people were made homeless and twenty-four lost their lives. The Black Rock gasometers were hit again, resulting in a huge conflagration, and a bomb detonated at nearby St Mark's school killed two local policemen – one of whom had just seen pupils safely across the road. The other had been placing a notice on the wall of Wilson's Laundry, at the corner of Eastern Road and Arundel Road. This area remained a favourite target in subsequent raids. On the chilly night of Wednesday 23 February 1944, a lone German aircraft was caught in a searchlight beam above the streets of Kemptown. Shortly after it released its high-explosive bomb load, perhaps in an effort to

Doris Caroline Lucy Williams' coffin, draped in the Union Flag, rests in the chapel at Roedean School, before interment at Rottingdean on 29 February 1944 at 11.00 a.m.
AUTHOR'S COLLECTION

escape or – as local witnesses thought – to hit the Black Rock gasworks once more. Alas, among those caught in the raid was twenty-three-year-old Doris Williams, daughter of Pop and Dottie May, and only recently betrothed to Basil, the Canadian. Out for the evening, Doris had had the misfortune to be walking past Wilson's Laundry when it was hit by one of the bombs, and was struck in the head by shrapnel. Carried the short distance home by passers-by, she was already dead by the time they arrived. Subsequently, Doris was laid to rest in Rottingdean churchyard, her granite headstone brought especially from Cornwall.

For nearly five years Dottie May had fretted for her children – Roy at Dunkirk, Cyril in the Odeon – and now the worst of her fears had been realised. Yet the Williams family carried on, as was expected in wartime Britain. Roy, Doug and Garfield continued their service in the army abroad, and on the home front Diana and latterly Pamela – two of Dottie May's three surviving daughters – worked as civilians at Bletchley Park, playing their part in the vital unravelling of the enemy 'enigma' codes. Hazel, the third daughter, had joined the Women's Land Army, and saw a different kind of front-line war in the fields of East Sussex and the Kentish border.

The Women's Land Army

Many areas of the Sussex Downs not given over to military training were ploughed up, for the first time in centuries if not millennia, as agricultural production was expanded vigorously in the 'Dig for Victory' campaign. The agricultural college at Plumpton became a training centre for the 'Land Girls' – recruits to the Women's Land Army (WLA) – who soon became familiar and welcome additions to the country scene. They learned new skills (Hazel Williams, for example, was taught how to thatch), from tractor driving and maintenance to lambing and milking and poultry raising. Replacing rural male workers who had been called up for the forces, the Land Girls were generally well received by local farmers who appreciated their hard work and commitment to the war effort. As early as September 1939, Diana Countess De La Warr, the appropriately named chair of the East Sussex Committee of the WLA, had explained 'to farmers in East Sussex' through the pages of the *Sussex Express* that: 'the Women's Land Army is now in a position to

Members of the Women's Land Army lift a crop in 1940. Despite some initial misgivings from those who suspected they would be unequal to their task, the 'Land Girls' performed magnificently in Sussex, as they did elsewhere, 'digging for victory' and learning a wide range of new skills. They were also on the 'front line' in Sussex, often drawing the unwelcome attention of German raiders.

supply trained and partially trained women ready to go out to farms as milkers, tractor drivers, and general farm workers.'[30] These Land Girls were mainly of two types, she added, those 'fully trained' in all branches of agriculture, and those who had completed the four-week course at Plumpton. Both were eligible for employment by local farmers, there being no charge for their allocation to farms, and with a government allowance of fifteen shillings a week payable to farmers to cover the costs of board and lodging for each girl they took on.

Hazel May Williams, dressed in the full uniform of the Women's Land Army. AUTHOR'S COLLECTION

Yet despite these favourable circumstances, there was some hostility to the WLA – from those who imagined that women generally unaccustomed to farm life could not possibly assume such demanding duties, and from others who feared the malign influence of 'fast' Girls from towns and cities who might seduce their simple country menfolk. Experience dealt swiftly with the first prejudice, and the second proved vastly exaggerated. Instead, demand for Land Girls developed apace in the Sussex countryside, for the reasons explained by one William Brown, a farm manager, in the *Sussex Express* in December 1942. 'These girls work all the year round in all weather (despite inadequate clothing),' he wrote in admiration. 'They work capably, cheerfully, even enthusiastically, and I am prepared to back them against any man of equal experience.'[31] As they integrated into country life, so the Girls became involved in all manner of community activities – sometimes even staging their own reviews or variety shows in local towns and villages, as they did at Burwash and at Battle, performing songs, reciting poetry, acting in sketches. They tackled all kinds of farm work – threshing during the harvest at Uckfield, for example, or helping to plough up Romney Marsh (where the Girls were billeted at nearby Rye) – and after the war the contribution of the Sussex Women's Land Army to the Allied victory was celebrated at a WLA Exhibition at the Corn Exchange, Brighton, in February 1947.

Hard work and inclement weather led to calloused and chapped hands, sunburn, cuts and bruises, and occasional nasty accidents, as well as the unpleasantness of toiling in mud and slurry. There was also the *frisson* of excitement, even sense of responsibility, as Hazel Williams recalled, of being put to work alongside Italian prisoners of war. Although generally glad to be out of the war, and most hoping for an Allied victory, the Italians initially caused some anxiety – until the Land Girls discovered that the POWs were friendly and helpful and made good working companions. Far more sinister were the German raiders that flew at low level across the fields, looking for targets. On one occasion, Hazel remembered, the plane came in so low that, as they had donned their tin helmets and flung themselves into the nearest ditch, the Girls could see the pilot looking left and right for victims as he machine-gunned the ground ahead. By 1944 'doodlebugs', V1 flying bombs, had added to the dangerous uncertainty of working in the fields of Sussex, a danger also experienced by the seasonal East End hop-pickers in the summer months, the rockets' random appearance and tendency to fall short (they were intended for London) causing real terror. One Land Girl working on Romney Marsh recorded several 'near misses', including the unpleasant experience of being blown over by the blast when a doodlebug exploded in a nearby meadow. Hazel Williams had a similar escape when a V2, one of the next generation of flying bombs, crashed near where she was working on the Sussex/Kent border. In all, some 886 doodlebugs and four V2 rockets fell on the Sussex countryside, although they caused remarkably little damage in the county.

D-Day and Victory in Europe

By now victory was in sight, the D-Day landings on 6 June 1944 having successfully landed British, Canadian and American forces ashore in Normandy. Again, Sussex had played its role to the full in preparation for the assault on occupied Europe. RAF Tangmere and its satellite airfields flew 730 sorties over northern France on a single day in May 1944, such was the intensity of operations in advance of D-Day. Five new airfields were built in Sussex to give improved air cover – four around Chichester and one at Coolham, near Billingshurst – from which flew British, Canadian, Czech, Free French and Polish squadrons. Additionally, auxiliary landing grounds (ALGs) were laid out across the county, little more than rudimentary airstrips where aircrew could practise landing without supporting facilities – experience that would stand them in good stead when operating in Europe. The tight formations of German aircraft which had once flown over 'bomb alley' were now a thing of the past, replaced by similar formations of Allied planes flying in the opposite direction in search of enemy targets on the Continent. The Americans flew by day, and Gerry Wells observed a formation of perhaps 100 Flying Fortress bombers over Eastbourne, its flanks guarded by Mustang fighters. As he watched, a Mustang came too close or maybe was disturbed by turbulence, crashing into one of the Fortresses. Of seven aircrew, only three survived the ensuing explosion and plunge into the sea – picked up by the Eastbourne lifeboat.

At the end of February 1944, the 30th United States Division arrived in the Chichester/Bognor area. The 15th Scottish Infantry Division was now based at Knepp Castle, near West Grinstead, and Petworth Park

The silent expanse of Pagham Harbour, where before D-Day and the Allied invasion of France in June 1944, massive floating Mulberry Harbours were marshalled in advance of being transported across the Channel.
BARRY TURNER

became a vast camp for thousands of troops and vehicles assembled for the assault. Practice amphibious landings were enacted at Bracklesham and Littlehampton. Large areas of the Downs became military training areas, and the downland village of Stanmer was commandeered for practising hand-to-hand street fighting – again, vital experience for what would soon be encountered in France. Streets adjacent to the seafront in Brighton became jammed with vehicles of the Guards Armoured Division, and the Williams family was alarmed when a tank slithered out of control in Eastern Road, one set of tracked wheels hanging precariously over the basement of 246 and momentarily threatening to smash into the downstairs living room.

Sussex also participated in the manufacture and deployment of the top-secret Mulberry Harbours, prefabricated monsters that would be towed to France to assist the invasion force in getting its men, vehicles and supplies ashore. Selsey was selected for the assembly of one of these Mulberrys, which was hauled from Pagham harbour in the wake of the first D-Day landings. Elsewhere along the south coast of Britain, thousands of men and their equipment had already embarked for the invasion, the

These remains of Second World War invasion defences on the beach at Bognor Regis are but one example of the many structures still to be found scattered across Sussex, reminders of the dark days early in the war when it was fully expected that German troops would have to be confronted on the coast and halted at the county's strategic Stop Lines and Nodal Points.
ALISON AVERY, WWW.BEAUTIFULENGLANDPHOTOS.UK

first struggling ashore on the beaches of Normandy on the morning of 6 June. Bosham, Shoreham and Newhaven were the embarkation ports in Sussex, the roads in their hinterlands jammed with military vehicles. Once the invaders had departed, however, an unfamiliar quiet descended over Sussex, a sense of release that anticipated final victory.

Although the V1 and V2 menace continued, Sussex began to look forward to the return of peacetime normality. The Home Guard was stood down at the end of 1944, although the Women's Land Army continued until 1950, with some rationing still in place as late as 1954. But as early as July 1944 place-names and road signs had re-appeared in towns and villages across Sussex, having been carefully stored after their hasty removal during the invasion scare, and the task of dismantling the county's extensive defences began. Of course, some of those defences never were removed, and across Sussex today is ample evidence of the pillboxes and other emplacements that guarded Stop Lines and Nodal Points. New names were added to war memorials, a perpetual reminder that Sussex men and women had fallen in war service, and civilian casualties lay in their freshly dug graves. For families such as Pop and Dottie May Williams and their sons and daughters, the war had visited great sorrow but had also instilled a stoicism that had somehow kept them going. Now, with the war coming to an end, they could at last draw breath. But, as Esther Meynell observed, it was still far too early to make sense of all that had occurred, of all that had happened to them.

ELEVEN

Into the new millennium

Rations and bonfires

In July 1954 meat rationing in Britain at last came to a close, with ration books remaining now only in the hands of mothers with children entitled to free milk. Across the country, people tore up their redundant ration books more in relief than joy, nine years having passed since the end of the war, but here and there individuals and communities allowed themselves a moment's celebration. At Heathfield in East Sussex, for example, the end of rationing was an excuse for a procession and bonfire. As the *Sussex Express & County Herald* reported, the parade was led by the undertaker, suitably attired for the occasion, and 'behind him, two by two, came local representatives of those who had been most involved in rationing'.[1] There were housewives, grocers, confectioners, bakers, millers, dairy and poultry farmers, and, appropriately bringing up the rear, the last of those occupational groups to have been constrained by the rationing system, the butchers. The bonfire itself was lit by a young lad, 14-year-old Colin Saunders, the choice a symbolic look to the future, with its hopes of better times ahead for the next generation.

As the flames flared up, the townsfolk threw their ration books into the blaze. Stage-managed to the last, the ritual reached its climax when an official from the Eastbourne Food Office (hitherto responsible for administering rationing) was seized from the crowd (having been duly warned beforehand), and – complete with his bureaucrat's briefcase and brolly – was raised shoulder high and thrust menacingly towards the fire. Three times he was passed in front of the flames before his freedom was restored, the people's desire for vengeance against 'the system' now symbolically assuaged. At last, they felt, wartime austerity had come to an end.

This highly ritualised procession and bonfire, marking the final vestiges of food rationing and reaffirming the community's faith in the future, looked optimistically to the years to come. Yet it also reached into its Sussex past, reawakening memories of the rural unrest and discontent that had characterised the county a century before. Then ritualised protest and resistance had fuelled semi-secret 'bonfire societies' and often violent demonstrations, such as the desperate battle fought in 1847 between the Lewes Bonfire Boys and opposing police and troops. East Sussex, in particular, with its puritan and dissenting background, readily adopted the religious language of 'No Popery', and local bonfire societies focused their volatile enthusiasms on 5 November, Guy Fawkes night. Despite intimations of loyalty to crown, parliament and state inherent in the 'Fifth', there were frequent outbursts of anti-establishment anger during bonfire celebrations. As Brigid Chapman has observed, the 'Fifth' remained 'one of the few opportunities an oppressed and half starved agricultural community had to let its collective hair down',[2] and in 1906 the authorities in Sussex took concerted action to stamp out the practice of bonfires in the streets and fireworks on the public highway. As Chapman noted, at 'a stroke it put a stop to most of the village celebrations and was the beginning of the end for many of the bonfire societies', especially 'in the coastal towns and resorts'.[3]

Despite some attempts at revival, such as the reformation of the Newick Bonfire Society in 1936, when hundreds of spectators were drawn from Haywards Heath, Brighton and surrounding areas, the tradition had all but died out before the Second World War, except principally in Lewes itself, which continued to celebrate the 'Fifth' in fine style. After the war, however, in a change of mood and purpose, there was a determined attempt to revive the old customs. As in Heathfield, perhaps, this reflected a new desire to embrace change by reasserting local identity, to recognise that the Sussex of post-war 'reconstruction' could be both dynamic and traditional in outlook. As change gathered pace – some aspects of which were welcome, some not – so the preservation of old Sussex ways became increasingly important in maintaining a reassuring sense of community. At Crowborough, for example, a Bonfire and Carnival Society was formed as early as 1948, eschewing the 'Fifth' and deciding instead upon the second Saturday in September as the preferred date for its procession and bonfire. At Eastbourne, meanwhile, the similarly innovative Old Town Bonfire Society was reformed during the 1950s: a torchlight procession would wind its way through the town for up to three hours but ended up (in 1959, at least), not with a bonfire, but rather a formal dinner and dance at the Drive Hotel!

Other towns and villages, mainly in central and eastern Sussex, quickly followed suit. The Rye Bonfire Boys led a spectacular revival in the 1950s and 1960s, which in 1958 attracted the attention of British Movietone News, the proceedings filmed for the benefit of the UK cinema-going public. At Battle, the Battel [*sic*] Bonfire Boys were likewise active, and so too were societies at Littlehampton and Newhaven. At Mayfield, where bonfires had continued to be lit during the inter-war period, the Bonfire Boys and Belles led another major revival in the 1950s. Increasingly, the accent was on family fun and fund-raising for charity, the political–religious connotations of previous generations now largely forgotten. In 1958, for example, the Mayfield society collected some £32 for the local Darby & Joan Club and the Home Physiotherapy Service.[4] A relative late-comer to this upsurge, the Rotherfield and Mark Cross society, revived in 1970, managed to raise £8,000 for good causes in the first twenty years of its existence, its celebrations on August bank holiday marking the start of what had by now become the 'bonfire season'. Burgess Hill, Barcombe, Uckfield, Lindfield and a host of other towns and villages joined the bonfire throng, some affiliating to the Sussex Association of Bonfire Societies (founded in 1955) to co-ordinate their efforts and to plan a calendar of events stretching from late summer until after the 'Fifth'. Processions became ever more spectacular – flaming torchlights; banners; marching bands; carnival queens; Guy Fawkes effigies; floats and tableaux; fancy dress ranging from Aztecs, Zulus and Red Indians to Vikings, Normans and Crusaders; guize-dancing; battle re-enactment groups – and the bonfires themselves were equally impressive, often with accompanying firework displays. By 2013 there were no fewer than twenty-eight bonfire societies active in Sussex, eleven of them affiliated to the association.

Cliffe Bonfire Society's 'No Popery' skull-and-crossbones is tongue-in-cheek and done for effect. But it is redolent of Lewes' turbulent past, and a reminder of the days when religious bigotry mattered in England. There are still those who are disturbed by such iconography, as Anne Widdecombe has demonstrated. The *Daily Telegraph*, however, commenting on 1 November 2008, considered the Lewes bonfire celebrations an eclectic and somewhat bewildering mix drawn from a wide variety of contrasting influences, a sort of 'head-on collision of Halloween and Mardi Gras'. In recent years, David Cameron, Jeremy Clarkson and Donald Trump have all been among those burned in effigy at Lewes, alongside the more traditional Guy Fawkes and the Pope.
DAVID MOYES PHOTOGRAPHY

Yet despite all this post-war activity, Lewes remained the undisputed heart of the bonfire tradition. Here too something of the old religious feeling survived, lurking in the collective subconscious. As Brigid Chapman wrote in 1994, 'anti-Catholic reaction has long ago died down, yet a No Popery banner still appears across Cliffe High Street on the morning of November 5, and papal effigies are paraded through the streets before being consigned to the flames'.[5] The Protestant martyrs, burned for heresy in Lewes in 1555 during 'Bloody' Mary's reign, were duly honoured, she explained, and the old 'prayer' remembered:

> A penny loaf to feed old Pope, a farthing cheese to choke him,
> A pint of beer to rinse it down, a faggot of sticks to burn him
> Burn him in a tub of tar, burn him like a blazing star
> Burn his body from his head, then we'll say old Pope is dead.[6]

The Firestarter initiates the blaze at the Cliffe Bonfire Society's bonfire at Lewes in 2011, the lurid glow from the flames illuminating the town's streets as participants from all over Sussex and beyond parade to 'Remember, Remember, the Fifth of November'. The Cliffe Bonfire Society traces its origins back to 1853.
DAVID MOYES PHOTOGRAPHY

In 1989 the several bonfire societies in Lewes rejected an invitation from the BBC to participate in a 'Songs of Praise' programme filmed in Lewes Castle, fearing a negative portrayal of their activities. Two decades later, Anne Widdecombe MP, a recent convert to Rome from Anglicanism, visited Lewes during the 'Fifth' and on television admitted to being intimidated and discomforted by what she had witnessed. Nonetheless, with its six separate bonfire societies, blazing tar barrels, coach-loads of visiting societies, and general party atmosphere, Lewes today manages to conduct itself on the 'Fifth' 'with the greatest good humour',[7] any lingering hint of religious antagonism dwarfed and made irrelevant by an overwhelmingly inclusive sense of carnival and fun.

'And we're going up to win the cup/ For Sussex by the sea'

This resurgence in local identity was also manifest in the ever-growing popularity of stoolball in the post-war era. Allegedly more than 500 years old, the sport was comprehensively revived in Sussex during the Great War when Major William Grantham, of Barcombe, introduced the game at auxiliary hospitals in the county in 1917–18. Teams such as the East Preston Ladies entertained recuperating soldiers, and those troops well enough to play took part themselves in keenly fought matches, stoolball proving so popular that its distinctive wickets and bats – together with copies of the rules – were soon finding their way across the globe to places as far distant as India and Australia.[8] Yet Sussex remained the focus of the game, as it had been before and as it was to remain, and grew in popularity across the county. By the 1950s there were few towns, villages or schools that could not boast their own stoolball teams. Claimed by its adherents to be a forerunner of cricket, stoolball was considered by many to be primarily a women's sport. Indeed, in the days before ladies' cricket, it was almost a female alternative to the game, especially as taught in Sussex schools, yet it has always had its male devotees, with mixed teams being much in evidence at both adult and junior level. The Chanctonbury Ladies League, formed in 1972, with its vigorous programme of local contests, attests to the continuing association of the sport with women's teams. But recent events – such as the 'Hastings Games' in June 2013, where mixed teams from ten schools took part, or the 'Let's Play Stoolball' day for schoolchildren at the Weald & Downland Living Museum at Singleton in the July – evidenced youthful enthusiasm for stoolball across the gender divide.

Stoolball had been considered an appropriate pastime for young ladies in mid-Victorian Sussex, although the dress code – as this illustration of 1866 shows – was not entirely practical.

Unlike stoolball, cricket can hardly be claimed as a quintessentially Sussex sport. But Sussex was an integral part of the Home Counties heartland where the game grew up and reached maturity, and after the Second World War white-clad cricketers remained an essential and picturesque element of village-green life across the county – as indeed they do today. Moreover, the Sussex County Cricket Club, with its headquarters and county ground in Hove, is claimed as the 'oldest club in the UK', the very first first-class county cricket club to have been established in England. Formed in 1839, the club has always been at the forefront of English county cricket, although it did not win its first county championship until as recently as 2003. This victory was the prelude to the club's 'Golden Decade', ten years of glittering success foretold in Joe Haddon's 1957 famous cricketing version of 'Sussex by the Sea':

The Weald and Downland Living Museum at Singleton, near Chichester, was founded in 1967, the brain-child of the Sussex historian and author Dr J.R. Armstrong MBE and his small band of devotees, and was opened to the public on 5 September 1970. As well as rescuing for permanent preservation and display representative vernacular buildings from across Sussex and south-east England, the Museum has a variety of collections and exhibits reflecting country crafts and agricultural practices – including a blacksmith's forge, depicted here. The Museum also hosts a variety of activities, from rare breed shows to outdoor theatre and stoolball games.
BARRY TURNER

Now is the time for playing
Now let your hearts be gay
List what your captain is saying
While off the field of play
So put your best foot forward, my lads
And time each ball you see
If you sing the old song
Well you can't go wrong
Of Sussex By the Sea

Good Old Sussex by the sea
Their cricket is a pleasure to see
They will give you a show
For they don't play slow
And useful men are they
So when you go to Sussex
Six Martlets men to see
They will delight you all
With the bat and ball
In the County Ground by the Sea.[9]

By the eve of the remarkable 'Golden Decade', Sussex cricket supporters – and players – had enthusiastically adopted a shortened version of the chorus, already made popular by the fans of Brighton & Hove Albion Football Club:

Good Old Sussex by the Sea
Good Old Sussex by the Sea
And we're going up to win the cup
For Sussex By the Sea.

Indeed, Brighton & Hove Albion, like the County Cricket Club, had also acted as an important vehicle for Sussex identity and local patriotism in the years since 1945. But in 1997 the club's much-loved Goldstone ground was given up as no longer fit for purpose, and the team and its followers were reduced to several peripatetic years until the sparkling new American Express ('Amex') Community Stadium was opened in July 2011 at Falmer, on the outskirts of Brighton. Here the players – the 'Seagulls' – could again run out to the rousing strains of 'Good Old Sussex by the Sea', specially recorded for the occasion by The Grenadier Guards, a fitting blend, perhaps, of the old and new, of the accommodation of 'traditional' and 'reconstruction' Sussex.

From Crawley to the 'Haywards Heath-Burgess Hill axis'

The epitome of post-war 'reconstruction' Sussex was Crawley New Town. Here, for defenders of ancient Sussex, was the greatest challenge to the old order, the most subversive and threatening aspect of the wide-ranging socio-economic change now being visited upon the county. Designated a New Town in 1947, under the auspices of the 1944 Greater London Plan, Crawley was to become a centre for 'overspill' (as it was termed) from the over-crowded metropolis, with new housing, facilities and jobs created to cater for this rapidly expanding population. The original market town, with some 10,000 people, was shortly to be overwhelmed by this new development, and the arrival of streams of newcomers from the capital, Crawley's population rising to 80,000 in just three decades. The duke of Norfolk headed a vociferous campaign against the plan, leading via a public inquiry to the House of Lords and the Court of Appeal, before being finally dismissed by the Master of the Rolls.[10]

Crawley New Town was designed on the 'neighbourhood' principle, each neighbourhood equipped with differing proportions of different types of houses, the idea being to encourage integration by mixing social classes. Writing in 1980, John Lowerson looked back on the previous three decades and decided that the 'social engineering' underpinning the neighbourhood scheme had 'proved an almost complete disaster'. As he explained, 'London newcomers tended to gravitate towards people with similar backgrounds and interests, and the upper-middle-class groups who worked in the town found their homes in the more traditional commuter areas of East Grinstead or Forest Row'. Although Lowerson conceded that Crawley (the 'New Town' suffix was soon abandoned) had 'achieved a fairly well-balanced structure', the class divisions within it had merely replicated what the newcomers had known in London, defeating the idealistic aspirations of the post-war planners.[11] He might have added that many of the resettled Londoners pined for their old homes, despite the obvious superiority of the new housing at Crawley, while local conservationists were alarmed at the scant attention paid by the Crawley Development Corporation to the intrinsic value of historic buildings within the town, fearing their imminent destruction. Some facilities were a long time coming – the town did not get its arts centre, 'The Hawth', until the 1980s – yet by the turn of the millennium observers were able to reflect that, during the previous half century, Crawley had 'come good'. Denys Skinner, writing in 2002, decided that, after 'early teething problems', Crawley had become 'a major player in the Sussex team'.[12] Four years later, Peter Brandon could add that Crawley was now 'a pleasant place to live, with many trees and open spaces, and local people feel it still is "a town in the country"'.[13]

Associated with Crawley's identification as a hub for economic development in northern Sussex, was the expansion of nearby Gatwick as London's second airport. Situated immediately adjacent to the London–Brighton railway line, and with the main A23 north–south trunk road diverted towards the airport, Gatwick developed apace after the war, its status as London's second airport assured when in 1980 its North Terminal for international flights was opened. In the Local Government Re-organisation of 1974, the northern border of Sussex was redrawn slightly to accommodate Gatwick, removing it from Surrey, one of very few alterations to be welcomed in a county that generally resented boundary changes – such as that which located Haywards Heath in West Sussex, severing its links with nearby Lewes, county town of East Sussex, and placing it instead under the sway of distant Chichester.

Indeed, what John Lowerson darkly called 'the Haywards Heath-Burgess Hill axis',[14] had also emerged as a centre for population and economic growth in the post-war era – and, inevitably, as a focus for those conservationists criticising and lamenting the rapid suburbanisation of mid-Sussex and other parts of the county. No fewer than three local stations on the main line sped commuters northwards to London, or down to Brighton, the two towns and their village hinterlands becoming dormitories for large numbers of business people and white-collar workers. Dubbed 'Bugs Hole' by a generation of irreverent school-children, Burgess Hill was also the butt of John Betjeman's satire. In his scathing poem 'Executive', Betjeman pokes withering fun at the 'young executive', with his shallow lifestyle and jumped-up aspirations. 'No cuffs than mine are cleaner,' exclaims the young executive: 'I have a Slimline brief-case and I use the firm's Cortina. / In every roadside hostelry from here to Burgess Hill / The *maitres d'hotel* all know me well and let me sign the bill.'[15]

Yet there was no evidence of hurt civic pride in *Burgess Hill, Sussex: The Official Guide*, published in the early 1960s by the local urban district council – quite the reverse, in fact. 'Burgess Hill's reputation as a progressive, modern, residential town and business centre is a comparatively recent one,' the *Guide* explained. 'Only ten years ago it was little more than a large village of about 9,000 people – today that population has nearly doubled, and the town has one of the newest and best shopping centres in mid-Sussex and a thriving light industrial estate which makes a variety of goods which are sent all over the world.' Not only that: although 'the potentialities of the town remained undiscovered for so long, this has proved a blessing in disguise because it has enabled the growth of the district to be carefully planned to secure the proper integration of the industrial development and,' the *Guide* continued, 'to ensure that the residential development was matched with proper public services and adequate educational, cultural, recreational and sports facilities.' It was an undisguised hymn to progress, a declaration of passionate and uncritical faith in post-war 'reconstruction' Sussex: 'the Burgess Hill of today is already a well-planned, increasingly self-contained community which is looking ahead to consolidate and continue the remarkable progress made in the last decade.'[16]

The modern band stand at Burgess Hill sits centre stage in the recently pedestrianised town centre on Church Road. The town remains a key focus for development on the London–Brighton corridor in mid-Sussex.

In similar mood, Haywards Heath considered itself *The Metropolis of Mid-Sussex*, the title of a celebratory book published in 1981, not least as an important centre for secondary education. After the 1939–45 war, great excitement attended the planning and construction of a new grammar school at Harlands Farm, half a mile or so to the west of the railway station. Opened at last in September 1958, with 270 pupils selected by '11 Plus' examination from Haywards Heath, Lindfield, Burgess Hill and surrounding towns and villages, the school developed swiftly under the leadership of its first headmaster, Donald Jarvis. Consciousness of its newness among the august company of the great British grammar schools, Haywards Heath swiftly invented its own traditions, adopting a Latin motto *Usque Conabor* ('I will try my utmost') and resurrecting the colours and house names – Borde, Flower, Molyneux, Spicer – connected with the old Cuckfield Grammar School, which had flourished from its foundation in the sixteenth century until closure in 1820. Jarvis retired in 1962, to be succeeded by the legendary E.C.C. Wynter ('Ted', to those irreverent schoolchildren), who took Haywards Heath Grammar School to new heights. By 1967 there were 876 pupils, along with 49 full-time and 10 part-time members of staff, and an array of extra-curricular activities that ranged from fencing, model railways, radio and electronics, Scouts, the Christian Union, drama and debating, to educational day-trips to France, or visits to Brighton, London and elsewhere to see the latest plays or films. For Wynter, it was a matter of pride that, despite being the youngest grammar school in East Sussex, it was already a leading place of learning. 'We now have pupils in almost every university in Great Britain,' he said, 'and in many other institutions of higher education.'[17]

HAYWARDS HEATH
AND DISTRICT
BUILDING SOCIETY
Established 1890

Assets £5,450,000
Reserves £247,000

ADVANCES ON
ALL CLASSES OF
LANDED PROPERTY
ENTERTAINED

INVESTMENTS ACCEPTED
AT CURRENT RATES
OF INTEREST
and are
TRUSTEE SECURITIES

For full Particulars, apply to the Secretary,
PATRICK D. HANNA
Haywards Heath Building Society Offices,
The Broadway, Haywards Heath. Phone No. 51844/5
or
117 London Road, East Grinstead. Phone No. 21936

The 1960s, when this advertisement for the Haywards Heath & District Building Society appeared in *East Grinstead: The Official Guide*, published by the local council, was the heyday of the mutually owned building society throughout the United Kingdom, with a plethora of locally based and relatively modest societies catering for local financial needs. In Sussex, such building societies played a major role in post-war reconstruction and expansion, not least in encouraging families to save to purchase their own homes and to take out mortgages.
AUTHOR'S COLLECTION

The foundation and drive of Haywards Heath Grammar School was emblematic of the expansive mood of post-war Sussex. Across the county, housing estates went up, industrial parks were developed, and new institutions were inaugurated. The plethora of 'official guides' produced by local councils during the 1960s attest to this atmosphere, partly through their breathless rhetoric but also in the multiplicity of advertisements for estate agents, builders, light-engineering firms, and the like. Especially revealing are the many local building societies, positively extolling people to buy houses or to save for the future – or, preferably, to do both. The

Haywards Heath & District Building Society, for example, advertising in *East Grinstead: The Official Guide*, boasted that its assets were an impressive £5,450,000, its reserves a reassuring £247,000, while the Eastbourne Mutual could intimate that its assets 'exceed £12,750,000', its reserves 'over £580,000'. The Horsham Building Society was more coy about precise amounts but informed readers that it had 'doubled its assets in three years'. The Steyning & Sussex County Building Society gave no-nonsense advice, urging potential clients to get in touch at once: 'Whether you are thinking of buying a house ... or Whether you wish to save or invest.'[18]

All things Brighton beautiful

Perhaps the most ambitious of all these post-war schemes was the foundation of the University of Sussex at Falmer in 1961, under its first vice-chancellor John (later Lord) Fulton. Although financial constraints would soon curb some of its architectural ambition, the university was innovative from the first, both in its physical design and its imaginative provision of interdisciplinary study. Fulton was replaced six years later by Asa (later Lord) Briggs, the distinguished historian (author of the highly regarded *A Social History of England*, published in 1983) who had been the very first academic appointed to the university. Sussex soon acquired an enviable reputation for scholarly excellence, but relations between 'town' (in this case, Brighton) and 'gown' were not always easy, partly as a result of the campus being 'marooned' out at Falmer, and partly because the sit-ins and upheavals of 1968 confirmed all the locals' worst fears about the moral character of the student body. Suspicions were not eased when a polytechnic was opened in the heart of Brighton, although this too developed as a prestigious institution, specialising in vocational education from nursing to design, and which by the early 1990s had been re-designated the University of Brighton.

Despite the initial misgivings of the local populace, Sussex and Brighton universities added immeasurably to the cultural, social and economic life of Brighton, Hove and district, and together were a powerhouse for the county as a whole. After the dislocation and destruction of the war, Brighton and environs appeared to be bouncing back in every direction. 'Where, in the whole of Britain, is there an equal to Brighton?' wrote Cecile Woodford with great excitement in her 1972 book *Portrait of Sussex*. 'Surely in no other place in this country is it possible to step, literally, straight out of the past into the future,' she conjectured, thinking of the close juxtaposition of the ancient Lanes and the new Churchill Square shopping centre, but also admiring the reconciliation of the 'traditional' with 'reconstruction' that she imagined epitomised post-war Brighton. Those who lived in Brighton but commuted to London, less than an hour away by train, could 'enjoy the best of both worlds in every sense', she added. 'Soon the dream of the motorist and shopper alike will be realized,' she enthused, 'for the massive planning scheme ahead [in Brighton] will relieve the closely knit and condensed streets where early planners defied present-day attempts to find an easy or quick solution to increasing traffic and pedestrians.'[19] Woodford could not have foreseen the extraordinary expansion of car-borne travel that would typify the next four decades and defeat even the most brilliant of planners. But her unbounded optimism, touchingly naïve as it appears today, captured the mood of the moment. Amid great fanfares in May 1979, for example, the Queen opened the new Brighton Marina at Black Rock, the first stage of an ambitious regeneration project that was also to include new luxury flats and a jetfoil service to Dieppe.

Mods and Rockers rampage along the beach at Hastings in the early 1960s, one of several south coast locations that saw pitched battles between the two rival groups of teenagers in this period. Extra police were drafted in at Hastings, Brighton and elsewhere to restore order and deal with the hooligans. The clashes, often occurring over long weekends, were thought to be 'bad for business', and it was feared that respectable holidaymakers, especially families, would decide to go elsewhere in future. In this scene, however, the trippers relaxing in their deck-chairs seem unperturbed by the mayhem unfolding around them.

Part of Brighton's enduring fascination and attraction, argued Cecile Woodford, was its 'cosmopolitan atmosphere, where the lowliest rub shoulders with the highest'. As she explained, 'It is famous for its appeal to every taste from the sophisticated to the primitive … a town that stands apart from the rest of Britain.'[20] In its intimations of the 'lowliest' classes, with their 'primitive' desires, Woodford's portrait admitted that the seamier side of Brighton life remained much as it had been before the war. In the early 1960s the Brighton seafront became the scene of violent confrontations between teenage Mods and Rockers, the former devotees of the motor-scooters that then seemed so cool, the latter aggressive proponents of motorbike culture. Underworld Brighton lurked somewhere just below the surface, a lingering sense of malevolence that was caught in the 2010 remake of *Brighton Rock*, the gangster film now set in 1964 against the background of Mod and Rocker warfare. Later, as the optimism of the early post-war decades gave way to the harsher socio-economic environment of the Thatcher period, existing problems of social deprivation in parts of Brighton became more pronounced, with Whitehawk in particular notorious as a centre for drug dealing and taking. By 2013 Brighton suffered the unenviable reputation of having one of the UK's highest drug-death rates, with 104 fatalities between 2009 and 2011, while more than 2,000 local people were said to have a serious abuse problem.[21]

In a British Railways (Southern Region) poster of 1961, the description 'Brilliant and Beautiful' is subtly applied by the artist to both Brighton & Hove *and* the young woman cheerfully drying herself with a towel, presumably after a dip in the sea. Although people of all descriptions were encouraged to 'Go By Train', such advertisements were invariably tailored for the male gaze, probably because men were seen (rightly or wrongly) as the breadwinners and thus the final arbiters of where couples and families might take their holidays, in this case Brighton and Hove. Single men might also choose accordingly, expecting to find jolly good-natured company on the beach.

Yet it would be unfair, as well as profoundly wrong, to suggest that all of Brighton's 'lowliest' inhabitants or visitors lived on the fringes of criminality or degradation. For many the simple pleasures of the seaside were – and are – more than enough, as Cecile Woodford conceded. 'The rather garish vulgarity of the mixture of shops that adorn the sea-front in no way detract from its [Brighton's] character,' she wrote in her 1972 volume, 'rather the reverse.' Indeed, 'the kaleidoscope that is Brighton seems to stem from this point'. Within such emporiums, she said, one could find '"rare antiques", inexpensive perms, pink-rock and "keys cut while you wait"', along with 'peaches and crabs; knife-grinders, curtains and lollipops, arms and ammunition,

A bikini-clad young lady lavishes attention (and sun-cream) on her beau, as he tries to relax on the shingle beach at Brighton. In the background, other trippers snooze in deck chairs or gaze out to sea. The scene was captured *c.*1964 by photographer Tony Ray-Jones (1941–72), who created many memorable images of work and leisure in the mid- and late 1960s, before his untimely death from leukemia in 1972. Typically, his photographs convey a mixture of sadness and humour, windows to a quiet and often stoic English eccentricity. As he explained in the magazine *Creative Camera* in October 1968, his aim 'was to communicate something of the spirit and mentality of the English, their habits and way of life, the ironies that exist in the way they do things, partly through their tradition and partly through the nature of their environment and mentality'.

Another of Tony Ray-Jones' classic studies of ordinary English life, taken at Brighton *c.*1966. Sitting under the shadow of the Palace (Brighton) Pier, a formally dressed couple in late middle age relax with their backs to the sea. Unobserved by them, a gaggle of young men, probably up to no good (this was the era of Mods and Rockers and beach warfare), stalk along the shore line.

marbles, second-hand books, fishing-rods, and fashionable "gear".' One even might discover, she added, a '"biscuits to tempt the palate" range beside herbal laxatives and "cure-all" tablets in the several health shops'.[22] In this way, as Woodford brightly concluded, 'the face Brighton presents to the world at large is impregnated with vividly startling colour'.[23]

The promise of sexual adventure was often part of this allure; in the 1950s as young people benefited from the more broad-minded attitudes encouraged in the war, and then in the 'permissive society' of the

Brighton's West Pier at sunset presents a surreal and eerie sight, a sad remnant of the once famous seaside attraction yet also elegant and imposing, in a post-modern way.
DAVID MOYES PHOTOGRAPHY

Brighton's West Pier in happier times, before it fell victim to decay, storm and fire in the years between 1975 and 2002. Prominent too are the Sussex Heights flats and the Bedford Hotel, with the South Downs beyond.
© DAILY HERALD ARCHIVE/NATIONAL MUSEUM OF SCIENCE & MEDIA/SCIENCE & SOCIETY PICTURE LIBRARY

Brighton Pier (originally known as simply the Palace Pier) was built between 1891 and 1899, and is one of the most outstanding examples of its type in Britain. Housing a theatre (until its closure in 1986) and numerous 'fun fair' attractions, the pier has been consistently popular as a mecca on Brighton beach for visitors and locals alike. In view of its iconic status, many Sussex residents, led by the *Argus* newspaper, resisted the pier's change of name in 2000, and in 2016 there was an uneasy compromise when its owners rebranded it the 'Brighton Palace Pier'.
ALISON AVERY, WWW.BEAUTIFULENGLANDPHOTOS.UK

'swinging sixties' and beyond. One woman, interviewed in 2000 for the book and television series *Some Liked it Hot*, an examination of British holiday habits, recalled that as a south London teenager in 1952 she went to Brighton for a week with her parents. 'Mum and Dad had gone to the pub and left me and my sister by the pier,' she explained, and when 'they'd gone we secretly put all our make-up on and I got chatting to this well-dressed bloke with a gold medallion.' As she reflected, ruefully, 'I can't even remember his name. It was getting dark and he invited me for a walk. We found a quiet spot and did it.' Alas, 'it was all over so quickly, and there was no pleasure at all for me, I just thought, "is that it, is that what I've been looking forward to? Am I really not a virgin any more?' No doubt many others were disappointed by such rough and ready first-time encounters, with little time for romance or affection, but it remained a private rite of passage: 'Of course, I didn't tell my mum; I didn't even tell my sister when I got back; they never knew.'[24]

The two Brighton piers, Palace and West, had long been the focus of sea-front entertainment. But the latter was gradually overshadowed by its larger and more centrally situated sister, and was closed in 1975 as structurally unsafe. There it survived in semi-derelict state until it partially collapsed in a storm in December 2002. A few months later, the remains were swept by fire, producing the eerie tangle of blackened metal framework that rises from the sea today like some dark, monstrous crustacean. The Palace, meanwhile, had been re-christened the Brighton Pier and continued to thrive. The varying fortunes of the twin piers were somehow a metaphor for the two sides of the Brighton experience since the Second World War – a robust and energetic faith in the future alongside a slide, in some areas at least, into urban decay and inner-city under-privilege.

Although this is the 1960s, this nostalgic portrait of a Brighton Music Hall by photographer Tony Ray-Jones exudes a certain timelessness but perhaps also a sense of impending loss, an intimation that the old days and ways may be numbered.

Perhaps the lowest moment was the 'Brighton bombing' of 20 October 1984, when the IRA planted a massive bomb in the Grand Hotel on the seafront, designed to kill Margaret Thatcher and other attendees at the Conservative Party annual conference. Thatcher survived the ensuing explosion unscathed, but five others were killed and 34 injured, some seriously. Yet in many ways, despite its reverses, Brighton remained the exciting, cosmopolitan, progressive place that Cecile Woodford had identified in 1972. A leading centre of gay culture, Brighton also elected Britain's first Green Party MP – Caroline Lucas – in 2010. The crowning achievement of all, perhaps, was the granting of city status in 2000, as part of the celebrations to mark the new millennium, creating the new Brighton & Hove City Council which brought together the two erstwhile towns, burying, perhaps, their long-standing rivalry.

Holidays and 'Hoppers'

As Brighton had demonstrated, reality on the ground did not always match the post-war rhetoric of 'reconstruction' that had swept Sussex in the 1950s and 1960s. Coastal towns, in particular, suffered as a result of the changing habits of the British holidaymaker. All around the UK, resorts found themselves losing out to the new 'package tours' which tempted sun-seekers to the surer climes of the Mediterranean, and Sussex was no exception. Victorian and Edwardian infrastructure began to look tired and shabby (the West Pier at Brighton being the most extreme example of such decrepitude), and local economies suffered. In an effort to promote diversification, some civil service departments were relocated to seaside towns. Hastings was one beneficiary of this dispersal policy, yet by the mid-1970s it still suffered the highest youth unemployment in Sussex. As Akhtar and Humphries observed, by the

1970s such resorts 'were now resigned to being the poor relation of the holiday abroad'.[25] Luckily, there were some individuals and families who retained a sentimental attachment to the bucket-and-spade holidays of their childhoods, and if their main annual holiday was now spent overseas, they might still find time for a few days or a long weekend in Bognor, or Worthing, or Bexhill.

Bexhill-on Sea on the Sunny Sussex Coast, published in 1964 as the Corporation's Official Guide, was typical of such publications produced during this period by local authorities anxious to advertise their 'patch'. Bexhill employed its own Publicity and Entertainments Manager to promote the town and its environs, and, as the Mayor explained in his introduction to the volume, the Council was endeavouring 'to attract both those people seeking a pleasant town in which to live and those who wish to spend an enjoyable holiday'. As the Mayor emphasised, Bexhill projected itself as a town 'with a difference and one which has much to offer both residents and holiday-makers alike'.
AUTHOR'S COLLECTION

In the 1960s Bexhill, like other resorts, had tried vigorously to protect its position in the face of change, its official guide *Bexhill-on-Sea: On the Sunny Sussex Coast*, published in 1964, reminding readers that the it 'enjoys an all-the-year round sunshine record comparable with any other part of England'. As the guide explained, 'Bexhill-on-Sea is one of the most attractive and beautiful holiday resorts in southern England', with no fewer than five miles of coastline within the borough boundaries. Attractions ranged from 'land and water sport in abundance' to the 'peace, rest and relaxation' offered by a fine array of hotels and superior guest houses, while the famous De La Warr Pavilion remained an unrivalled venue for a wide variety of activities, including beauty queen competitions and morning and afternoon concerts. There was an Annual Festival of Music, featuring Sir John Barbirolli and the Hallé Orchestra, together with frequent visits by 'well-known Dance Bands' from London. In addition to adult entertainment, there was plenty to keep the youngsters occupied: 'Popular Uncle Tom Kemp will present Punch and Judy and Children's Magic each Monday and Friday and Children's Sports on Wednesdays during August.'[26] It was a mix that had not changed much since the pre-war era, and while it appealed to those who had returned loyally year on year, there was nonetheless an inexorable decline as potential visitors were seduced by more exotic destinations abroad. However, Bexhill was fortunate in that it possessed a certain up-market charm, which made it increasingly attractive as a residential town for both retirees and commuters, an advantage enhanced by fast rail communication with London. A national survey in 2007 discovered that it was now considered the third-best seaside town in Britain in which to live, while in 2009 the Halifax bank was able to explain that Bexhill residents enjoyed on

Although the towering cliffs at Beachy Head are not for the faint-hearted or light-headed, British Railways in the 1950s and 1960s actively promoted 'Downland Rambles' along the adjoining coast road, this tranquil scene depicting pedestrians entirely at ease with their breathtaking environment, along with cyclists intent on enjoying the bracing air and stupendous views. The poster emphasised 'cheap tickets' and 'frequent electric trains' (to Eastbourne from London, Brighton and elsewhere, safe from the Beeching axe). Cyclists, of course, could also take the train, placing their bicycles in the roomy guard's compartment.
© NRM/PICTORIAL COLLECTION/SCIENCE & SOCIETY PICTURE LIBRARY

average four extra hours of sunshine per week compared to people in other British seaside towns.

Those destinations which had retained their rail connections were lucky, for the 1950s and 1960s – in one of the great paradoxes of post-war expansion in Sussex – saw the county's railway network shrink by half.[27] By and large, coastal destinations were spared, but their hinterlands suffered, especially links into the Weald, which vanished completely in some areas. Ironically, one important coastal closure in 1964 was the branch from Bexhill West to Crowhurst on the Hastings main line. Elsewhere, the line northwards from Shoreham-by-Sea through

Bramber, Steyning, Partridge Green and West Grinstead to Christ's Hospital was shut in March 1966, although the short section from Shoreham to Breeding Cement Works remained open for freight until 1988. Farther west, the line from Chichester to Midhurst had been abandoned as early as 1935, with the exception of the Chichester–Lavant stretch which survived until 1991 for freight workings. The route from Petersfield in Hampshire to Midhurst and Pulborough was closed to passengers in 1955, with freight lingering on a few sections until the mid-1960s, and in the north of the county services from Ashurst Junction, near Groombridge, to Three Bridges, via Forest Row and East Grinstead, were withdrawn in January 1967. Farther east, the death of the old 'Cuckoo Line' between Polegate, near Eastbourne, and Eridge was a particular blow for communities such as Hailsham and Heathfield. There were other closures, notably the section between Uckfield and Lewes, and also the Kent & East Sussex which – having been acquired by British Railways from the Colonel Stephens empire (see p.153) – was partially abandoned in January 1954 when the Headcorn–Tenterden stretch was closed and lifted. As the railway historian Terry Gough observed angrily in 1984, 'the railway in East Sussex has virtually been destroyed'.[28] And, as he also noted, those lines throughout the

Eastbourne in 1968, one of Tony Ray-Jones' penetrating and slightly wistful, even melancholy, depictions of ordinary English life, often at the seaside. Here young and not-so-young enjoy the pleasures of the sea, from paddlers in the shallows to the more adventurous canoeists venturing far from the shore line. Although the railway had already disappeared from much of rural Sussex, coastal resorts such as Eastbourne continued to welcome their traditional rail-borne holidaymakers.

Hop-pickers at London Victoria station in 1919, waiting for special trains for the 'hop gardens' of East Sussex and Kent. This party seems surprisingly well dressed and well equipped – most of the habitual hop-pickers were from the poorer families of the East End, for whom a week or two toiling in the country was a surrogate holiday as well as a means of earning some extra cash.
© NATIONAL RAILWAY MUSEUM/SCIENCE & SOCIETY PICTURE LIBRARY

Joy, exuberance, freedom! The excitement of being back in the 'hop gardens' for their annual 'holiday' is written across the faces of young and old as the East Enders leap from the back of the lorry that has brought them from the local railway station on the last leg of their much-anticipated journey in August 1950.
© DAILY HERALD ARCHIVE/NATIONAL MUSEUM OF SCIENCE & MEDIA/SCIENCE & SOCIETY PICTURE LIBRARY

county which had survived the cull were largely the ones that had been electrified before the Second World War.

Following partial closure in 1954 until the eve of its final abandonment in 1961, the Kent & Sussex was used occasionally – in the high summer months of August and September – for hop-pickers' specials. There were usually three Saturday afternoon trips from Robertsbridge (with its mainline connection) to Junction Road Halt, Bodiam and Northiam. Hop-pickers travelling from London could change for the Kent & East Sussex at Robertsbridge, and then alight at whichever of these stations was most convenient for the particular hop-gardens at which they were to work. On Sundays, when many pickers returned to London on the expiry of their contracts, there was a special through-train from Bodiam to London Bridge, departing at 6.40 p.m. This train – 'the Bumper' in pickers' parlance – was worked to Robertsbridge with a diminutive 'Terrier' tank engine at each end, where it was then taken forward by a mainline locomotive. For many, especially the young children, the train journey was an integral part of the 'paid holiday' fun of the annual hop-picking season. It was a way of life that stretched back to before the First World War and which lasted until the 1960s, when manual labour was at last replaced by machinery. Sadly, no hop-pickers' trains were run on the Kent & East Sussex in the summer of 1959, and thereafter the practice stopped. Some blamed this demise on the newly introduced machines, but others thought that the railway was surreptitiously being prepared for closure. Both opinions were correct. Following flood damage in November 1960, a 5 m.p.h. speed limit was imposed on the railway, with an impossible three-hour journey time between Tenterden and Robertsbridge. In June 1961 the line was abandoned altogether.[29]

Not all hop-pickers came from London – some lived locally on farms and in villages, while others were recruited from nearby towns such as Hastings – but the East End was overwhelmingly the main source of seasonal labour. Here families who could not afford to go on holiday were offered a chance to get away to the country for several weeks at a time, with accommodation (albeit rudimentary) provided and an opportunity to earn much needed cash. Many went to the so-called 'Guinness gardens' around Bodiam and Northiam, but countless more would head for other destinations in East Sussex and across the border into Kent, with attendant special trains from London to speed them on their way. Some of these would leave the metropolis as early as 4 a.m. – the proverbial 'milk train' – and for hours before extended families of sometimes three generations pushed their make-shift 'hopping barrows' down the Old Kent Road to get to the station on time. On the Kent & East Sussex, the hop-pickers' trains were met at the various wayside stations by lorries owned by Huxfields, the local coal merchants, pleased to have the business in the otherwise slack summer months. Although the lorries were thoroughly hosed down beforehand, coal dust had a habit of sticking, just one of the hardships that faced the 'hoppers' as they arrived at and settled into their temporary homes. Families were allotted their own 'hoppers' huts' (often made of corrugated iron, with no windows), and had to make up their own beds using whatever blankets they had brought with them, placed on faggot bundles covered with straw. Work started early in the morning, by 7.30 at the latest, and continued into early evening until at last the overseer shouted 'pull no more bines'. Lunch was usually a sandwich eaten in the fields, with tea brewed over a small campfire. Those who worked swiftly and 'cleanly' could earn a reasonable wage, but slower or 'dirty' pickers (those who threw leaves and twigs into their bins along with hops) would be penalised. Bins were emptied into bushel baskets twice a day, and an efficient family team could produce twenty to thirty bushels from one bin, rewarded at about a shilling per bushel.[30]

In the evening, the hoppers made dinner and sang songs around the campfires or went to the pub. For many, the social dimension was an important component of the hop-picking holiday, an opportunity to work and play in what they found an exhilarating and liberating environment, and where they would meet up again with old friends not seen since the previous season. Sometimes romance blossomed in the hop-gardens. Staid marriages were refreshed, young people fell in love, and occasionally there were illicit liaisons that led to complications later on. Hilary Hefferman, in her oral history of hopping, tells one of the happier tales. 'I was born as a result of hop picking,' explained one of her informants. Exasperated that his wife was working late in the hop-garden, when she should have been be back preparing dinner, the informant's father complained bitterly that 'you think more of those damned hops than you do of me'. To show that this was not true, the wife led her husband back to their hut, and, as Hefferman's informant put it: 'I was born nine months later.'[31] Not all encounters were so felicitous, and Jennifer Worth in her memoir *Call the Midwife* recounts the altogether more distressing story of an East End hop-picking couple in which the wife, entranced by the West Indians who were now joining the hopping throng, formed a fleeting relationship with one of these exotic (as they appeared to her) newcomers. When the resultant child was born, the outraged husband threatened his wife with physical violence and insisted that the babe be deposited in a children's home.[32]

Although the hop-pickers brought money into the community, spending it in the pubs and shops, and provided useful business for firms such as Huxfields the coal merchants, they were not always made welcome by the locals. They were thought to be 'common' or 'rough', dismissed pejoratively as 'Gypsies' and 'Romanys', or at least 'Cockneys', and considered to be light-fingered as well as bad company. In some public houses, there were hostile signs: 'saloon bar – no hoppers'.[33] But when mechanisation brought manual hop-picking swiftly to an end, there was general regret at the passing of a colourful era in Sussex history. There was also widespread sorrow at the apparent demise of the Kent & East Sussex Railway, so much so that at a meeting in the Rother Valley Hotel in Northiam in April 1961, a preservation society was launched. Progress was slow, and it was not until 1974 that the first section west of Tenterden was opened. The restored line did not reach into Sussex until 1990, when the extension to Northiam was opened. A further extension to Bodiam became operational in 2000, and by 2011 track had been laid farther westwards to the site of Junction Road Halt, restoring much of the line familiar to the hop-pickers of the 1950s and confirming the Kent & East Sussex as one of Britain's leading heritage railways.

'Does Sussex still exist?'

Equally miraculous as a preservation project was the fall and rise of the Bluebell Railway. Although the dismantling of much of the rural railway system in Sussex is routinely blamed on Richard Beeching (ironically, a long-term resident of East Grinstead) and his infamous report, there had been significant closures before those of his notorious regime. Chief among these was the so-called 'Bluebell' line between Lewes and East Grinstead, which British Railways (Southern Region) publicly earmarked for closure in May 1954. Energetic work by accountants had begun in 1951 to demonstrate that the route was unremunerative, and that there was no possibility of reversing the downward financial trend. When the closure proposal was announced, there was an outcry locally but after the usual 'consultation' the final date was fixed as 13 June 1955. In fact, the line shut a few weeks earlier, without ceremony, on 28 May, as a result of a railwaymen's national strike. An enthusiasts' special, the 'Wealden Rambler', had to be postponed but eventually ran over the route on 14 August 1955, in what all assumed was the final act.

However, British Railways had not reckoned with the determined opposition of Miss Rose Ellen Margaret Bessemer, a local 'worthy' at nearby Chailey and determined advocate of good causes. Feisty 'Madge' Bessemer formed a 'fighting committee', and discovered that the original Act of Parliament of 1878, authorising the railway's construction, had insisted upon the provision of four trains each way each day, including Sundays, in perpetuity. A reluctant British Railways acknowledged that this was the case, and trains ran again on 7 August 1957, inaugurating what the local press dubbed the 'Sulky Service'. Needless to say, measures were soon taken to rescind the Act, but not before a further round of protests had provoked increased public interest in what was then 'a remote, mysterious part of the Sussex Weald', as Klaus Marx so aptly

Bluebell, a diminutive P class locomotive, was one of the first steam engines acquired by the preserved Bluebell Railway in 1960, and is still performing sterling service today, as this scene at Horsted Keynes indicates. The P class, consisting of eight locomotives, was built by the South Eastern & Chatham Railway in 1909–10.
DEE CLEARY

described it.[34] This time, when the line was shut again on 16 March 1958, there was intense national media scrutiny. Alan Whicker had turned up a few weeks before the end to report on the impending closure for the BBC news programme *Tonight*, provoking a great upsurge of curiosity, and when the final moment came the *Sussex Express and County Herald* announced proudly that the 'Bluebell line closes in a blaze of glory'.[35]

Among those emboldened by this surge in public enthusiasm, were four students – Chris Campbell, David Dallimore, Martin Eastland, and Alan Sturt – who called a meeting in Haywards Heath on 16 March 1959, a year after the line's closure, to form what became the Bluebell Railway Preservation Society. The meeting was chaired by Bernard Holden, a railwayman and former soldier, who proved inspirational in taking the 'Bluebell' forward and remained its passionate supporter until his death, aged 104, in 2012. Initially, progress was difficult. The wise decision was taken to concentrate on preserving the section between Sheffield Park and Horsted Keynes, for which British Railways was asking £34,000. With only £89 in the society's bank account, the task seemed formidable. But by the end of 1959 an agreement had been reached to rent the line for £1,850 per annum, and in May 1960 the Bluebell's very first locomotive, 'Stepney', a 'Terrier' tank, arrived along with two coaches, all for £850. In July 1960 a Light Railway Order was granted, allowing the Bluebell

Another South Eastern & Chatham Railway locomotive preserved on the Bluebell Railway is H class No.263 (later British Railways No. 31263). Some sixty-six of these successful locomotives were built in 1904–9 and 1915, and several saw service in and around East Grinstead. The South Eastern & Chatham became part of the Southern Railway at the 'Grouping' in 1923, which in turn became the Southern Region of British Railways on Nationalisation in 1948.
DEE CLEARY

to run passenger trains, and soon other locomotives and rolling stock arrived. Unfortunately, British Railways closed its electrified branch from Haywards Heath to Horsted Keynes in 1963, foolishly severing the Bluebell's link to the national network. Ironically, Bluebell engines were soon hired to assist in the lifting of the abandoned line between Horsted Keynes and East Grinstead, providing much needed income for the embryonic railway. In 1968 an agreement was reached for the outright purchase of the Sheffield Park to Horsted Keynes stretch, and with this under its belt the Bluebell could look to the future with increased confidence, launching a long-term development plan in 1972 which, among other things, dared to contemplate an extension northwards over the recently lifted track-bed to East Grinstead. As Terry Cole, a leading Bluebell activist, wrote in 1974: 'It's been a hard fight … but "Bluebell" is rightly proud of its unique achievement. No "big business" has subsidised and shielded us. Everything we have and own has been achieved by a devoted band of amateurs.'[36]

This 'devoted band of amateurs' was to scale new heights in the years ahead, the most remarkable being the extension northwards to East Grinstead and, with it, a renewed connection to the national network. There had been those who wondered whether the project was viable, especially as the track-bed cutting south of East Grinstead had been filled as a municipal rubbish dump. As the seasoned railway observer, Michael S. Welch, opined in 1995: 'The Bluebell will need a lot of luck – not to mention money – if their ambitious scheme is to succeed.'[37] In fact, the extension had already reached Kingscote station by April 1993 but, as Welch rightly forecast, the final lap was an altogether tougher prospect. However, with the Bluebell's customary determination, local authority encouragement, community goodwill, and a great deal of luck and money (including vital environmental grants to clear the rubbish), the final section into East Grinstead was completed at last in March 2013, some forty years since it was first mooted. It was one of the greatest achievements, perhaps *the* greatest, in British railway preservation history. The first passenger train arrived at East Grinstead to triumphant scenes on 23 March, a supremely confident Bluebell Railway now turning to contemplate the possible restoration of the old railway southwards from Sheffield Park towards Lewes, or westwards from Horsted Keynes to Ardingly on the former Hayward's Heath branch![38]

Horsted Keynes, one of four stations on the Bluebell Railway, has been preserved to reflect a typical Southern Railway junction station of the 1930s and 1940s.
DEE CLEARY

Attention to period detail is part of the secret of the Bluebell Railway's great success in creating an authentic atmosphere. Here two genuine examples of Southern Railway signage provide warnings still applicable today, notwithstanding the warm welcome awaiting visitors to the line.
DEE CLEARY

In its way, the experience of the Bluebell Railway also reflected those twin imperatives of post-war Sussex – protection of the 'traditional' on the one hand, and support for 'reconstruction' on the other. The Bluebell had succeeded handsomely in its aim of running classic steam trains through the Wealden countryside, preserving a rural scene and way of life that many in the Beeching era had feared would be obliterated. But it had also created a powerful heritage tourism attraction in the heart of Sussex, a significant generator of regional economic activity which the local authorities were not slow to acknowledge. The Bluebell experience had also shown that the 'traditional' and 'reconstruction' need not be in conflict, although many recognised that there was a sometimes difficult line to tread, the prospect of unrestrained development in the tourist industry posing a threat to the very 'traditional' things that visitors came to see. The National Trust, for example, was supremely aware of this conundrum, carefully husbanding its properties such as the splendid gardens at Sheffield Park, and new preserved railways – such as the Spa Valley, between Eridge and Tunbridge Wells, and the Lavender Line at Isfield – emerged to follow the Bluebell's inspirational example of 'getting it right'.

Yet there remained those, like Philip Webb, Virginia Woolf and Hilaire Belloc before them (see chapter 8), who considered that Sussex was now more or less permanently under threat. Mass in-migration from London, elsewhere in the South East, and beyond, had swollen the combined population of West and East Sussex, including Brighton & Hove, to beyond 1.6 million by 2011, and the attendant expansion of housing provision – embraced so enthusiastically by local authorities in the 1960s and thereafter – had turned quiet villages into bustling towns as well as devouring large swathes of countryside. Wholesale closure of the rural railway network combined with often indifferent public transport alternatives to promote reliance on the motor-car, which in turn encouraged the construction of out-of-town shopping facilities. As early as 1995, Desmond Seward had dared to ask 'Does Sussex Still Exist?', wondering whether the fair county of Belloc's and Kipling's day had already disappeared for good under 'roads choked by traffic (with blaring radios) and gentrified hamlets whose barns have been turned into expensive weekend "cottages"'.[39]

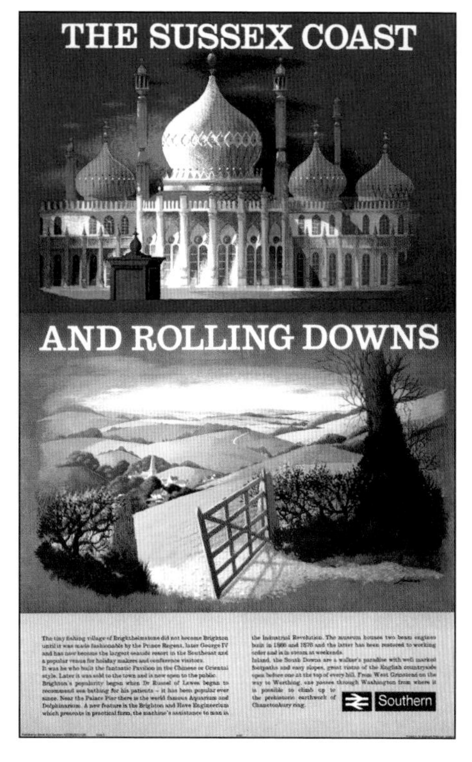

The Sussex Coast and Rolling Downs. Published in 1980 by the Southern Region of British Rail, this poster encourages rail travel to two contrasting but nonetheless equally iconic Sussex destinations – the Royal Pavilion at Brighton on the south coast, and the rolling Downland landscape. The former indicates the hold that the Prince Regent's exotic early nineteenth-century creation still had on the popular imagination in the new 'heritage' era of the 1980s, while the latter shows the enduring influence of Belloc and Kipling on the way rural Sussex continued to be portrayed and understood by those concerned for its future.

Others worried that Sussex would be overwhelmed by cultural as well as demographic change. Patience Strong, the much-loved but reactionary composer of sentimental light verse, who died at Sedlescombe in East Sussex in 1990, had opposed the building of the Channel Tunnel. 'I'm against that,' she had explained. 'It would fill Kent full of foreigners on motor-cycles.'[40] Presumably, she also feared that, given the opportunity, some of these cheeky foreigners would bike across the Sussex border. Indeed, following the expansion of the European Union, there was a noticeable influx of foreigners into Sussex, many of them young people looking for employment and better opportunities. Bulgarians toiled in the hop-fields of niche-market micro-breweries, Czechs worked as hotel receptionists, and Poles as waiters in

Rottingdean Windmill (also known as Beacon Mill) was built in 1802 on the site of an earlier mill, grinding corn for the village and supplying flour to local bakeries. It fell into disrepair after 1881. Restored in 1905, the mill was again derelict by the early 1920s. Following basic repairs in 1929, it was fully renovated in 1935. Today in the care of Rottingdean Preservation Society, the windmill is a Grade II listed building, a fine example of an English smock mill situated in superb Downland countryside, emblematic of the desire to conserve the best of Sussex architecture and landscape.
DAVID MOYES PHOTOGRAPHY

restaurants, enhancing further the cosmopolitanism that Cecile Woodford had detected approvingly in Brighton forty years earlier, and adding to an ethnic diversity already created by Asian and Afro-Caribbean immigration. There were those who resented the Europeans, especially in those towns with pockets of high unemployment, where it was feared that the newcomers – with their determined work ethic – might take jobs away from locals. But, like the Huguenots and Flemings of the early modern era, whose skills and energy had helped build the distinctive Sussex iron, glass, brick and brewing industries, the newcomers added to the spice of Sussex life. Change was by no means the harbinger of cultural extinction, indeed quite the reverse. At Sedlescombe, for example, Roy Cook and his German-born wife, Irma, produced the very first English organic red wine to win an international award, at a prestigious event in Germany in June 2013.[41] The Cooks had established a vineyard at Robertsbridge back in 1979, part of an upsurge in local wine production that was soon recognised as inextricably part of a modern Sussex identity, in many ways Continental in character.

In Sussex, as elsewhere, identities are dynamic, subject to constant contestation and renegotiation. As we have seen, Sussex since the Second World War had struggled to cope with wide-ranging socio-economic change, sometimes promoting the new and sometimes resisting, and often finding positive compromises and accommodations. Yet the influx of European workers, filling work vacancies that locals often felt unable or unwilling to fill themselves, combined with a general hostility to the European Union 'project' to ensure that Sussex (like much of England) voted for 'Brexit' in the referendum in 2016. Only in cosmopolitan, progressive Brighton and Hove was the 'Remain' vote dominant.

The Sussex of the early twenty-first century is indisputably a different place from that which existed in 1945. Yet, for admirers of the county, not only is there much to celebrate among the new, but there is also a perhaps surprising degree of continuity from the past. Desmond Seward, having posed his awkward question, went on to answer it himself. Looking beyond contemporary depredations, as he saw them, he recognised that Sussex was still 'a wild and lonely land with an ancient and even sinister history'. Indeed, he said, behind 'the suburbia and the motorways the old, secret Sussex can still be found by those who try hard enough to find her, still beautiful and mysterious'.[42] Obstinate Sussex men and women continued to insist that they 'won't be druv', and Seward detected in their voices survivals of Sussex dialect and pronunciation, evidence of the county's durability in the face of change. Ardingly remained firmly Arding*lye,* he wrote, despite the competing accents of Dagenham or Croatia or Slovenia. Reassuringly, he recalled the old rhyme:

> If true Sussex you would be,
> Say sure*lye*, not surely.
> In names of places stress should dwell
> Upon the final syllable.
> Thus, Arding*lye* doth well accord
> With South*wick*, Ber*wick* and Sea*ford*.[43]

Like Desmond Seward, other writers were aware of the enduring qualities of Sussex life and the county's powerful sense of historical continuity. 'At times,' wrote Olivia Laing in her book *To The River*, a lyrical description of her journey along the river Ouse, 'it feels as if the past is very near.'[44] Candida Lycett Green agreed. 'Sussex is a kingdom in its own right,' she declared, musing on its long history and seeking to define its essential nature: it is 'Saxon through and through.'[45] Yet it was a European 'outsider' who put his finger on the ultimate meaning of the county's identity. In 2000 Pieter Boogaart, a retired Dutch teacher of English language and literature, published his *A272: An Ode to a Road*, a nostalgic – if somewhat eccentric – evocation of the ninety-mile long A272 that runs, east to west, through the heart of Sussex, from the Kentish border to eastern Hampshire.

Exploring the A272 and its hinterlands, Pieter Boogaart explained 'why I have come to love this road'. 'It represents England,' he said. 'It epitomises England.' To travel the A272 was to journey through Englishness. 'Past Uckfield and Cuckfield, Wineham and Twineham' and onwards, glancing sideways at 'places like Lewes, Brighton and Chichester, at Barcombe and Balcombe', Boogaart unravelled for his readers what was for him the fundamental 'Englishness of English life'. Driving along the A272 was nothing less, he insisted, than 'doing England'. 'The A272 *is* England.'[46]

Here, then, was the secret of Sussex. It was, for Pieter Boogaart and countless others, locals and visitors alike, quintessentially and uncompromisingly English, the 'real England' of popular imagination. However much Sussex had changed in the years since 1945, it had remained – undiluted and indisputably – an exemplar of all that was England and Englishness.

Notes and references

Notes to chapter 1: Ancient landscapes, ancient peoples

1 Janet and Colin Bord, *A Guide to Ancient Sites in Britain*, (London, 1979), p. 28.
2 http://www.sussexpast.co.uk/property/ accessed 11 April 2011.
3 Hilaire Belloc, *The County of Sussex* (London, 1906); cited in Esther Meynell, *Sussex* (London, 1947), p. 259.
4 Cited in Desmond Seward, *Sussex* (London, 1995), p. 229.
5 Ibid., p. 3.
6 Denys Skinner, *Sussex: People and History* (Marlborough, 2002), p. 38.
7 Cited in Meynell, *Sussex*, p. 33.
8 Alan Charig, *A New Look at the Dinosaurs* (London, 1979), pp. 45–50; Tim Haines, *Walking with Dinosaurs: A Natural History* (London, 1999), p. 174.
9 Meynell, *Sussex*, p. 26
10 Ibid., p27.
11 Ibid., p. 27.
12 Skinner, *Sussex: People and History*, pp. 37–40.
13 J.R. Armstrong, *A History of Sussex*, new edn by Richard Pailthorpe and Diana Zeuner (Chichester, 1995), p. 17; Skinner, *Sussex: People and History*, p. 41; Peter Brandon, *Sussex* (London, 2006), pp. 47–8.
14 Derek Simpson, 'Prehistoric and Roman Archaeology', in Ian Nairn and Nikolaus Pevsner (eds), *Sussex* (New Haven, CT, 2003), p. 18.
15 John Lowerson, *A Short History of Sussex* (Folkestone, 1980), p. 17.
16 Candida Lycett Green, *Unwrecked England* (London, 2009), p. 77.
17 Simpson, 'Prehistoric and Roman Archaeology', p. 21.
18 Cited in Armstrong, *A History of Sussex*, p. 26.
19 Barry Cunliffe, *Fishbourne* (Chichester, 1977); S.S. Frere, *Bignor Roman Villa*, n.p, n.d.
20 Charles Knightly, *Strongholds of the Realm: Defences in Britain from Prehistory to the Twentieth Century* (London, 1979), pp. 33–6.
21 Cited in Armstrong, *A History of Sussex*, p. 35. Dates in the *Anglo-Saxon Chronicle* are thought to be twenty years out.
22 Ibid., p. 35.

Notes to chapter 2: The South Saxons

1 Cited in Lloyd Laing and Jennifer Laing, *Anglo-Saxon England* (London, 1979), p. 36.
2 Norman Davies, *The Isles: A History* (London, 1999), p. 165.
3 Laing and Laing, *Anglo-Saxon England*, pp. 52–3.
4 For an epic account for the conflict between the Romano-British and the invading German peoples, see Peter Berresford Ellis, *Celt and Saxon: The Struggle for Britain, AD 410–937* (London, 1993).
5 Denys Skinner, *Sussex: People and History* (Marlborough, 2002), p. 67; Peter Brandon, *Sussex* (London, 2006), p. 69.
6 Esther Meynell, *Sussex* (London, 1947), p. 52.
7 Ibid., p. 51.
8 Ibid., p. 240.
9 Ibid., p. 52.
10 See Christopher Brooke, *The Saxon and Norman Kings* (London, 1978), pp. 89–93.
11 J.R. Armstrong, *A History of Sussex*, new edn by Richard Pailthorpe and Diana Zeuner (Chichester, 1995), p. 37.
12 Meynell, *Sussex*, p. 75.
13 David Arscott (ed.), *A Kipling Sussex: An Anthology of Poetry and Prose* (Lewes, 2007), pp. 134–5.
14 The ten stories later published as *Puck of*

Pook's Hill were first published in the *Strand* magazine from January to October 1906; see *Puck of Pook's Hill* (London, 1951).
15 Meynell, *Sussex*, pp. 76–8.
16 Ibid., pp. 78–9.
17 Cecile Woodford, *Portrait of Sussex* (London, 1972), p. 173.
18 Meynell, *Sussex*, p. 74.
19 W.S. Mitchell, 'Sussex: Introduction', in John Betjeman (ed.), *English Parish Churches* (London, 1958), p. 365.
20 Ian Nairn and Nikolaus Pevsner (eds), *Sussex* (New Haven, CT, 2003), p. 111.
21 Simon Jenkins, *England's Thousand Best Churches* (London, 1999), p. 698.
22 Ibid., p. 704.
23 Nairn and Pevsner, *Sussex*, p. 641.
24 Brandon, *Sussex*, p. 74.
25 Ian Nairn, 'West Sussex', in Nairn and Pevsner, *Sussex*, p. 23.
26 John Lowerson, *A Short History of Sussex* (Folkestone, 1980), pp. 37–41.
27 Armstrong, *A History of Sussex*, pp. 40–1.
28 Ibid, p. 38.
29 Skinner, *Sussex: People and History*, p. 78.
30 Ibid., p. 78.
31 Cited in Meynell, *Sussex*, p. 75.
32 Lowerson, *A Short History of Sussex*, p. 44.

Notes to chapter 3: The Normans

1 David C. Douglas, 'William the Conqueror: Duke and King', in Dorothy Whitelock, David C. Douglas, Charles H. Lemmon and Frank Barlow, *The Norman Conquest: Its Setting and Impact* (London, 1966), pp. 50–1.
2 See chapter X, 'The Conqueror and the Conquest' in Christopher Brooke, *The Saxon and Norman Kings* (2nd edn, London, 1978).
3 Terence Wise, *1066: Year of Destiny* (London, 1979), p. 144.
4 Brooke, *Saxon and Norman Kings*, p. 148.
5 Wise, *1066: Year of Destiny*, p. 172.
6 Ibid.
7 Charles H. Lemmon, 'The Campaign of 1066', in Whitelock *et al.*, *The Norman Conquest: Its Setting and Impact*, p. 97.
8 Peter Brandon, *Sussex* (London, 2006), p. 82.
9 Denys Skinner, *Sussex: People and History* (Marlborough, 2002), p. 85.
10 Michael Wood, *In Search of the Dark Ages* (London, 1981), p. 228.
11 Lemmon, 'The Campaign of 1066', p. 111.
12 Ibid.
13 Ibid.
14 John Lowerson, *A Short History of Sussex* (Folkestone, 1980), p. 47.
15 Ibid., p. 54.
16 J.R. Armstrong, *A History of Sussex* (4th edn, Chichester, 1995), pp. 47–9.
17 Plantagenet Somerset Fry, *Castles of Britain and Ireland* (London, 1980; repub. 2006 as *Castles: England – Scotland – Wales – Ireland*, Newton Abbot, 2005), pp. 40, 45.
18 Ian Nairn and Nikolaus Pevsner, *Sussex* (New Haven, CT, 2003), p. 91.
19 Fry, *Castles of Britain and Ireland*, pp. 38–9.
20 Armstrong, *A History of Sussex*, pp. 50–1.
21 Lowerson, *A Short History of Sussex*, p. 49.
22 Nairn and Pevsner, *Sussex*, p. 131.
23 Simon Jenkins, *England's Thousand Best Churches* (London, 1999), p. 699.
24 Ibid., pp. 694–6.
25 Armstrong, *A History of Sussex*, pp. 59–61.
26 Jenkins, *Thousand Best Churches*, pp. 693–4.
27 Brooke, *Saxon and Norman Kings*, pp. 150–3.
28 Lowerson, *A Short History of Sussex*, p. 48.
29 Brooke, *Saxon and Norman Kings*, p. 164.
30 Philip Payton, *Cornwall: A History* (Fowey, 2004), p. 90.

Notes to chapter 4: Medieval Sussex

1 Charles Kightly, *Strongholds of the Realm: Defences in Britain from Prehistory to the Twentieth Century* (London, 1979), p. 133.
2 Catherine Morton, *Bodiam Castle: Sussex* (Beckenham, 1981), p. 20.
3 David Thackray, *Bodiam Castle: East Sussex* (Swindon, 2003), p. 9.
4 Morton, *Bodiam Castle*, p. 5.
5 Ian Nairn and Nikolaus Pevsner (eds), *Sussex* (New Haven, CT, 2003), p. 419.
6 M.W. Thompson, *The Decline of the Castle* (Cambridge, 1987), p. 17.
7 Kightly, *Strongholds of the Realm*, p. 134.
8 Tom McNeill, *English Heritage Book of Castles* (London, 1992), p. 64.
9 O.H. Creighton, *Castles and Landscape: Power, Community and Fortification in Medieval England* (London, 2002), p. 75.

10 Morton, *Bodiam Castle*, p. 6.
11 Matthew Johnson, 'Reconstructing Castles and Refashioning Identities in Renaissance England', in Sarah Tarlow and Susie West (eds), *The Familiar Past? Archaeologies of Later Historical Britain* (London, 1999), pp. 73, 74.
12 Robert Liddiard, *Castles in Context: Power, Symbolism and the Landscape, 1066–1500* (Macclesfield, 2005), p. 9.
13 Creighton, *Castles and Landscape*, p. 76.
14 Liddiard, *Castles in Context*, p. 150.
15 Cited in J.R. Armstrong, *A History of Sussex*, new edn by Richard Pailthorpe and Diana Zeuner (Chichester, 1995), p. 75.
16 Ibid., p. 73.
17 Cited in Peter Brandon (ed.), *Sussex* (London, 2006), p. 188.
18 E.V. Lucas, *Highways and Byways in Sussex* (London, 1904), p. 310.
19 Brandon, *Sussex*, p. 164.
20 Asa Briggs, *A Social History of England* (London, 1994), p. 85.
21 Ibid., p. 83.
22 Thackray, *Bodiam Castle*, p. 23; Morton, *Bodiam Castle*, p. 21.
23 Liddiard, *Castles in Context*, p. 64.
24 Armstrong, *A History of Sussex*, p. 74.
25 Ibid., p. 78.
26 Garry Hogg and John Tomes, *The Shell Guide to Exploring Britain* (Waltham Abbey, 1995), pp. 278–9.
27 Simon Jenkins, *England's Thousand Best Churches* (London, 1999), p. 691.
28 Nairn and Pevsner, *Sussex*, p. 370.

Notes to chapter 5: Early modern Sussex

1 Esther Meynell, *Sussex* (London, 1947), p. 202.
2 Ibid; p. 203.
3 Ibid.
4 Ibid.
5 Alan M. Kent, *The Literature of Cornwall: Continuity, Identity, Difference, 1000–2000* (Bristol, 2000), p. 49.
6 Ibid.
7 Meynell, *Sussex*, p. 202.
8 E.V. Lucas, *Highways and Byways of Sussex* (London, 1904), p. 332.
9 Ibid., p. 215.
10 Meynell, *Sussex*, p. 130.
11 Nigel Nicolson, *The National Trust Book of Great Houses of Britain* (London, 1978), p. 155.
12 Ibid., pp. 155–6.
13 Simon Jenkins, *England's Thousand Best Houses* (London, 2003), p. 777.
14 Ibid., p. 779; Ian Nairn and Nikolaus Pevsner, *Sussex* (New Haven, CT, 2003), p. 290.
15 Naine and Pevsner, *Sussex*, p. 195.
16 Ibid.
17 Nicolson, *Great Houses of Britain*, p. 165.
18 John Lowerson, *A Short History of Sussex* (Folkestone, 1980), p. 95.
19 W.G. Hoskins, *The Making of the English Landscape* (London, 1955; repub. 1970), p. 211.
20 J.R. Armstrong, *A History of Sussex*, new edn by Richard Pailthorpe and Diana Zeuner (Chichester, 1995), pp. 92–3.
21 Barrie Trinder, *The Making of the Industrial Landscape* (London, 1982), p. 23.
22 Ibid.
23 Lowerson, *A Short History of Sussex*, pp. 91–3, 97–100.
24 Julian Cornwall, *Revolt of the Peasantry, 1549* (London, 1977), pp. 8–9.
25 Ibid., p. 88.
26 Lowerson, *A Short History of Sussex*, p. 84.
27 Ibid., p. 81.
28 Ibid., pp. 82–5.
29 David Underdown, *Revel, Riot and Rebellion* (Oxford, 1995); Mark Stoyle, *Loyalty and Locality: Popular Allegiance in Devon during the English Civil War* (Exeter, 1994).
30 Armstrong, *A History of Sussex*, p. 95.
31 Lowerson, *A Short History of Sussex*, p. 103.
32 Taylor Downing and Maggie Millman, *Civil War* (London, 1992), p. 88.
33 Armstrong, *A History of Sussex*, p. 97.
34 Downing and Millman, *Civil War*, p. 89.
35 Ibid.
36 Lowerson, *A Short History of Sussex*, p. 104.
37 Downing and Millman, *Civil War*, p. 68.
38 Armstrong, *A History of Sussex*, p. 100.

Notes to chapter 6: Hanoverians and Early Victorians: High Society and Social Crime

1 Douglas Hay, Peter Linebaugh, John G. Rule, E.P. Thompson, Cal Winslow, *Albion's Fatal Tree: Crime and Society in Eighteenth-century England* (London, 1975; repub. 1988), cover notes.
2 John Lowerson, *A Short History of Sussex*

(Folkestone, 1980), p. 115.

3 Jessica M.E. Rutherford, *The Royal Pavilion: The Palace of George IV*, Brighton, 1995.

4 Simon Schama, *A History of Britain: Volume 3, 1776–2000 – The Fate of Empire* (London, 2002), pp. 90, 92.

5 Nigel Nicolson, *The National Trust Book of Great Houses of Britain* (London, 1978), p. 156.

6 Ibid., p. 158.

7 Jane Austen, *Sanditon* (1817; new edn London, 1974), p. 172.

8 Roger Wells, 'The Militia Mutinies of 1795', in John Rule (ed.), *Outside the Law: Studies in Crime and Order, 1650–1850* (Exeter, 1982), p. 38.

9 Ibid., p. 44.

10 Ibid., p. 45.

11 Ibid., p. 46.

12 Ibid., p. 47.

13 Ibid., p. 49.

14 Ibid., p. 63.

15 Ibid.

16 Cal Winslow, 'Sussex Smugglers', in Hay et al., *Albion's Fatal Tree*, p. 120.

17 David Arscott (ed.), *A Sussex Kipling: An Anthology of Poetry and Prose* (Lewes, 2007), pp. 117–18

18 For an excellent overview, see Mary Waugh, *Smuggling in Kent and Sussex, 1700–1840* (Newbury, 1985).

19 Ibid., pp. 139–40.

20 Winslow, 'Sussex Smugglers', p. 119.

21 Ibid., pp. 119–20.

22 Ibid., p. 128.

23 Ibid., p. 129.

24 Ibid.

25 Ibid., p. 133.

26 Ibid., p. 136.

27 Ibid., p. 137.

28 Ibid., p. 165.

29 Waugh, *Smuggling in Kent and Sussex*, pp. 96–101.

30 Ibid., p. 101.

31 *Parliamentary Papers* (1834), 44, Vol. 28, p. 197A; cited in Lowerson, *A Short History of Sussex*, p. 131.

32 Lowerson, *A Short History of Sussex*, p. 128.

33 Samuel Edwards, *Rebel! A Biography of Thomas Paine* (London, 1974), pp. 24–7.

34 William Cobbett, *Rural Rides* (London, 1830; repub., ed. E.W. Martin, London, 1975), p. 109.

35 E.J. Hobsbawm and George Rudé, *Captain Swing* (London, 1970), p. 104.

36 Ibid., pp. 104–6.

37 Ibid., p. 108–13.

38 Roger Wells, 'Resistance to the New Poor Law in the Rural South', in John Rule and Roger Wells, *Crime, Protest and Popular Politics in Southern England, 1740–1850* (London, 1997), pp. 91–126.

39 Ibid., p. 113.

40 Roger Wells, 'Southern Chartism', in Rule and Wells, *Crime, Protest and Popular Politics*, pp. 127–54.

41 Roger Wells, 'Crime and Protest in a Country Parish: Burwash, 1790–1850', in Rule and Wells, *Crime, Protest and Popular Politics*, p. 184.

42 Ibid., p. 186

43 Ibid., p. 175.

44 Desmond Seward, *Sussex* (London, 1995), p. 129.

45 Esther Meynell, *Sussex* (London, 1947), pp. 246–7.

Notes to chapter 7: Sussex in the Railway Age

1 Cited in J.R. Armstrong, *A History of Sussex*, new edn by Richard Pailthorpe and Diana Zeuner (Chichester, 1995), p. 113.

2 See H.P. White, *A Regional History of the Railways of Great Britain: Volume 2 – Southern England* (4th edn, Newton Abbot, 1982), pp. 72–107.

3 John Stuart Mill, *Collected Works: Volume Six* (London, 1836), pp. 327–8; see also Jack Simmons, *Railways: A Anthology* (London, 1991), p. 63.

4 Cited in White, *Railways of Great Britain: Volume 2*, p. 81.

5 Jack Simmons, *The Railway in Town and Country, 1830–1914* (Newton Abbot, 1986), p. 236.

6 Ibid.

7 E.L. Blanshard, *Adam's Illustrated Descriptive Guide to the Watering Places of England* (London, 1848), p. 95.

8 *Illustrated London News*, 6 June 1946.

9 Kenneth Hopkins, *The Poetry of Railways: An Anthology* (London, 1966), p. 212.

10 Ibid., p. 214.

11 White, *Railways of Great Britain: Volume 2*, p. 76.

12 L.T.C. Rolt, *Red for Danger: A History of Railway Accidents and Railway Safety* (4th edn,

Newton Abbot, 1982), pp. 51–7; O.S. Nock, *Historic Railway Disasters* (Shepperton, 1966), pp. 24–8.
13 Rolt, *Red for Danger*, p. 57.
14 Ibid.
15 Simon Bradley, *The Railways: Nation, Network and People* (London, 2016) pp. 159–60
16 Glyn Kraemer-Johnson and John Bishop, *Trolley-bus Memories: Brighton* (London, 2007), p. 8.
17 Brian Haresnape, *Stroudly Locomotives* (Shepperton, 1985), p. 14.
18 Cecil J. Allen (ed.), *The ABC of British Locomotives, Part 2 Steam Locomotives: Southern Region* (London, 1948), p. 43; Thomas Middlemass, *Steam Locomotive Nicknames* (Kettering, 1991), p. 131.
19 O.S. Nock, *British Locomotives from the Footplate* (London, 1950), p. 141.
20 Edgar Larkin, *An Illustrated History of British Railway Workshops* (Yeovil, 1992), pp. 33–5; Derek Huntriss, *Steam Works: BR Locomotives and Workshops in the Age of Steam* (London, 1994), pp. 45–8.
21 White, *Railways of Great Britain: Volume 2*, p. 101.
22 Jennifer Worth, *Call The Midwife: A True Story of the East End of London in the 1950s* (London, 2002), p. 316.
23 John Betjeman, *Lovely Bits of Old England*, ed. Gavin Fuller (London, 2012), p. 14; *Daily Telegraph*, 6 November 1964.
24 John Betjeman and J.S. Gray, *Victorian and Edwardian Brighton from Old Photographs* (London, 1972), p. xi.
25 Ian Nairn and Nickolaus Pevsner, *Sussex* (New Haven, CT, 2003), p. 430.
26 Simon Jenkins, *England's Thousand Best Churches* (London, 1999), p. 687.
27 Cited in Simmons, *The Railway in Town and Country*, p. 239.
28 Frederick McDermott, *Life and Work of Joseph Firbank* (London, 1887), p. 116; John Hoare, *Sussex Railway Architecture* (Hassocks, 1979), p. 77.
29 Philip Shaw and Viv Mitchell (eds), *Colonel Stephens: Insights into the Man and his Empire* (Midhurst, 2005), p. 90; see also John Scott-Morgan, *The Light Railway Era, 1896–1996* (Penryn, 1997), and John Scott-Morgan, *The Colonel Stephens' Railways* (Shepperton, 1999).
30 Scott-Morgan, *The Light Railway Era*, p. 34.
31 Shaw and Mitchell (eds), *Colonel Stephens*, p. 90.
32 Scott-Morgan, *The Colonel Stephens' Railways*, p. 36.
33 D.W. Winkworth, *Southern Titled Trains* (Newton Abbot, 1998), p. 93.
34 Ibid.
35 Julian Morel, *Pullman: The Pullman Car Company – Its Services, Cars, and Traditions* (Newton Abbot, 1983), p. 54.
36 Tony Hillman and Beverley Cole, *South For Sunshine: Southern Railway Publicity and Posters, 1923–1947* (Harrow Weald, 1999), p. 39.
37 Ibid., p. 13.
38 David Wragg, *Southern Railway Handbook: The Southern Railway, 1923–1947* (Yeovil, 2011), p. 142.
39 Hillman and Cole, *South For Sunshine*, p. 11.

Notes to chapter 8: Literary Sussex

1 Dorothy Eagle and Hilary Carnell, *The Oxford Illustrated Literary Guide to Great Britain and Ireland* (Oxford, 1981), p. 28.
2 Claire Tomalin, *Charles Dickens: A Life* (London, 2011), p. 84.
3 Cecile Woodward, *Portrait of Sussex* (London, 1972), p. 155.
4 Cited in ibid., pp. 155–6.
5 Cited in Tomalin, *Dickens: A Life*, p. 193.
6 Cited in Woodward, *Portrait of Sussex*, p. 156.
7 Cited in Jack Simmons (ed.), *Railways: An Anthology* (London, 1991), pp. 231–2.
8 Quentin Bell, *Virginia Woolf: A Biography – Volume Two, Mrs Woolf, 1912–1941* (London, 1972), p. 65.
9 Nigel Nicolson, *Portrait of a Marriage* (London, 1973; repub. 1990), p. 184.
10 Ibid., p. 185.
11 Bell, *Virginia Woolf: A Biography – Volume Two*, p. 119.
12 Ibid., p. 183.
13 Nicolson, *Portrait of a Marriage*, p. 186.
14 Bell, *Virginia Woolf: A Biography – Volume Two*, p. 129.
15 Lyndall Gordon, *Virginia Woolf: A Writer's Life*, London, 2006, p. 322.
16 Bell, *Virginia Woolf: A Biography – Volume Two*, p. 219.
17 Gordon, *Virginia Woolf: A Writer's Life*, p. 361.
18 Jane Drake, *William Morris: An Illustrated Life*

(Norwich, 2004), p. 1.
19 Fiona MacCarthy, *Eric Gill* (London, 1989).
20 Ibid., p. 90.
21 Ibid., p. 131.
22 Cited in A.N. Wilson, *Hilaire Belloc: A Biography* (London, 1984; repub. 2003), p. 300.
23 Ibid., p. 299.
24 MacCarthy, *Eric Gill*, p. 115.
25 Wilson, *Belloc: A Biography*, p. 192.
26 MacCarthy, *Eric Gill*, p. 147.
27 Ibid., p. 163.
28 Cited in Peter Brandon, *Sussex* (London, 2006), p. 320.
29 Wilson, *Belloc: A Biography*, p. 116.
30 A.L. Rowse, *Portraits and Views: Literary and Historical* (London, 1979), p. 86.
31 Hilaire Belloc, *The Four Men* (London, 1912), p. viii.
32 Ibid., pp. viii–ix.
33 Hilaire Belloc, *The County of Sussex* (London, 1936), pp. 200–2.
34 Wilson, *Belloc: A Biography*, p. 17.
35 E.V. Lucas, *Highways and Byways in Sussex* (London, 1904), pp. 72–4.
36 Cited in Wilson, *Belloc: A Biography*, p. 17.
37 Belloc, *The County of Sussex*, p. ix.
38 Cited in Wilson, *Belloc: A Biography*, p. 390.
39 David Arscott (ed.), *A Sussex Kipling: An Anthology of Poetry and Prose* (Lewes, 2007), pp. 12–15.
40 David Gilmour, *The Long Recessional: The Imperial Life of Rudyard Kipling* (London, 2002), p. 167.
41 Rudyard Kipling, *Something of Myself: An Autobiography* (London, 1937; repub. 2007), p. 120.
42 Adam Nicolson, *Bateman's, East Sussex* (Swindon, 1996), p. 39.
43 Arscott, *A Sussex Kipling*, pp. 97–8.
44 Gilmour, *The Long Recessional*, p. 283.
45 Ibid.
46 Kipling, *Something of Myself*, p. 94.
47 Arscott, *A Sussex Kipling*, p. 136.
48 Ann Saddlemyer, *Becoming George: The Life of Mrs W.B. Yeats* (Oxford, 2002), p. 46.
49 John Betjeman and J.S. Gray, *Victorian and Edwardian Brighton from Old Photographs* (London, 1972), p. vii.
50 John Betjeman, *Collected Poems* (London, 1984), p. 219.
51 Evelyn Waugh, *A Little Learning: The First Volume of an Autobiography* (London, 1964; repub. 1983), pp. 97, 108, 110, 114, 146–7; for a more detailed insight into Waugh's time at Lancing, see Philip Eade, *Evelyn Waugh: A Life Revisited* (London, 2016), pp. 39–65, 66–68, 106.
52 Edward Lucie-Smith, *Sussex Writers and Artists* (Alfriston, 2007), p. 41.
53 Bill Peschel's webpage: plantpeschel.com/2009/09/stella-gibbons-kills-a-genre-1932/ accessed 1 April 2017.
54 Margaret Drabble, *The Oxford Companion to English Literature* (Oxford, 1985), p. 210.
55 Lucie-Smith, *Sussex Writers and Artists*, p. 40.
56 E.F. Benson, *Mapp and Lucia* (London, 1935; repub. 1984), p. 26.

Notes to chapter 9: War and an uncertain peace, 1914–1939

1 I am indebted to Tom Luke of Bendigo, Australia, for this information.
2 Keith Greaves (ed.), *Sussex in the First World War* (Lewes, 2004), p. 302.
3 Brian W. Harvey and Carol Fitzgerald, *Edward Heron-Allen's Journal of the Great War: From Sussex Shore to Flanders Fields* (Chichester, 2002), p. 3.
4 Ibid., p. 4.
5 Ibid., pp. 9–11.
6 Greaves (ed.), *Sussex in the First World War*, p. 13.
7 David Arscott (ed.), *A Sussex Kipling: An Anthology of Poetry and Prose* (Lewes, 2007), pp. 92–3.
8 Ibid., p. 93
9 Ibid.
10 Alexandra Ayton, *Sussex Remembered: Personalities and Events of the 19th and 20th Centuries* (Lewes, 2010), p. 40.
11 Ibid., p. 44.
12 Edmund Blunden, *Undertones of War* (London, 1928; repub. 2010), p. 3.
13 Ibid.
14 Ibid.
15 Harvey and Fitzgerald (eds.), *Edward Heron-Allen's Journal*, p. 85.
16 Peter Brandon, *Sussex* (London, 2006), p. 298.
17 Greaves (ed.), *Sussex in the First World War*, p. xxv.
18 Ibid., p. xxvi.
19 Ayton, *Sussex Remembered*, p. 81.
20 Harvey and Fitzgerald (ed.), *Edward Heron-Allen's Journal*, pp. 100, 207.

21 Ibid., p. 65.
22 Ibid., p. 204.
23 Richard Holmes, *Tommy: The British Soldier on the Western Front, 1914–1918* (London, 2004), p. 37.
24 Jeremy Paxman, *The English: Portrait of a People* (London, 1999), p. 182.
25 Foreword by George Webb in Rudyard Kipling, *The Irish Guards in the Great War: The First Battalion*, new edn (Staplehurst, 1997), p. 10.
26 David Gilmour, *The Long Recessional: The Imperial Life of Rudyard Kipling* (London, 2002), p. 257.
27 Adam Nicolson, *Bateman's: East Sussex* (Swindon, 1996), p. 44.
28 Arscott, *A Sussex Kipling*, p. 94.
29 Blunden, *Undertones of War*, p. 138.
30 Ibid., p. 152.
31 Ibid., p. 147.
32 Ibid.
33 Ibid., pp. 212–13.
34 Juliet Gardiner, *The Thirties: An Intimate History* (London, 2010), p. 236.
35 Ibid., p. 235.
36 L.T.C. Rolt, *The Landscape Trilogy: Part 1 – Landscape with Machines* (Stroud, 2010), pp. 159, 166.
37 Gardiner, *The Thirties*, p. 584.
38 John Lowerson, *A Short History of Sussex* (Folkestone, 1980), p. 181.
39 Ibid., p. 182.
40 Ibid.
41 I am indebted to my late father, Tom Payton, for this insight.
42 Gardiner, *The Thirties*, p. 494.

Notes to chapter 10: Sussex at war again

1 Esther Meynell, *Sussex* (London, 1947).
2 All entries are from Dorothy May Williams' diary, held by Philip Payton.
3 Cited in Max Hastings, *All Hell Let Loose: The World at War, 1939–1945* (London, 2011), p. 29.
4 Bournville Past & Present Group, *Yer tiz: Bournville Memories* (Weston-super-Mare), p. 28. I am indebted to Liz and Paul Coole of Moonta, South Australia, for this information.
5 *The Second World War in Colour*, Carlton Television video, 1999.
6 Hugh Sebag-Montefiore, *Dunkirk: Fight to the Last Man* (London, 2006, pp. 138–9).
7 Cited in ibid., p. 140.
8 Michael R. Bonavia, *The History of the Southern Railway* (London, 1987), p. 167.
9 Brian Lavery, *In Which They Served: The Royal Navy Officer Experience in the Second World War* (London, 2008), pp. 35–42.
10 Cited in ibid., p. 33; for a discussion of 'mincemeat' see Ben Macintyre, *Operation Mincemeat* (London, 2010).
11 Cited in Lavery, *In Which They Served*, p. 31.
12 John Carey, *William Golding: The Man who Wrote Lord of the Flies* (London, 2009), pp. 82–110.
13 Edward Young, *One of Our Submarines* (London, 1952).
14 Robert Macklin, *One False Move: The Australian Mine Defusers in World War II* (Sydney, 2012), pp. 218–20, 228, 300. I am indebted to Jan Lokan (née Goldsworthy) of McLaren Vale, South Australia, for drawing my attention to this important book.
15 Gerry Wells, *Growing Up in Sussex: From Schoolboy to Soldier* (Stroud, 2009), pp. 67–8.
16 Ibid., p. 68.
17 Chris Butler, *East Sussex Under Attack: Anti-Invasion Sites, 1500–1990* (Stroud, 2007); Chris Butler, *West Sussex Under Attack, 1500–1990* (Stroud, 2008).
18 Cited in Valerie Gove, *Laurie Lee: The Well-loved Stranger – The Biography* (London, 1999), pp. 126–8.
19 Cited in ibid., p. 135.
20 Ian Allan, *Driven by Steam* (Shepperton, 1992), p. 12
21 Cited in Quentin Bell, *Virginia Woolf: A Biography – Volume Two: Mrs Woolf, 1912–1941* (St Albans, 1976), p. 216.
22 Ibid., p. 217.
23 Paul Brickhill, *Reach for the Sky* (London, 1954; repub. London, 2001).
24 Cited in Hastings, *All Hell Let Loose*, p. 85.
25 Macklin, *One False Move*, p. 134.
26 Klaus Marx, *An Illustrated History of the Lewes and East Grinstead Railway* (Shepperton, 2000), pp. 146–7.
27 Wells, *Growing Up in Sussex*, p. 69.
28 David Rowland, *The Brighton Blitz* (Seaford, 1997), p. 9.
29 Ibid., pp. 15–21.
30 Cited in Ann Kramer, *Land Girls and their Impact* (Barnsley, 2009), p. 29.
31 Cited in ibid., p. 128.

Notes to chapter 11: Into the new millennium

1 David Kynaston, *Family Britain: 1951–1957* (London, 2009), p. 394.
2 Brigid Chapman, *Night of the Fires: Bonfire in Sussex from the Plot to the Present Day* (Seaford, 1994), p. 10.
3 Ibid., pp. 5–6.
4 Ibid., p. 74.
5 Ibid., p. 22.
6 Ibid., p. 27.
7 Ibid., p. 24.
8 Keith Grieves, *Sussex in the First World War* (Sussex, 2004), p. xxix.
9 'Martlets' is a reference to the mythical birds represented on the county arms of both West and East Sussex.
10 Peter Brandon, *Sussex* (London, 2006), p. 398.
11 John Lowerson, *A Short History of Sussex* (Folkestone, 1980), p. 192.
12 Denys Skinner, *Sussex: People and History*, Marlborough, 2002.
13 Brandon, *Sussex*, p. 399.
14 Lowerson, *A Short History of Sussex*, p. 193.
15 John Betjeman, *Collected Poems* (4th edn, London, 1980), p. 385.
16 *Burgess Hill, Sussex: The Official Guide* (Burgess Hill, *c.*1963), p. 7.
17 Wyn K. Ford and A. Conway Gabe, *The Metropolis of Mid-Sussex: A History of Haywards Heath* (Haywards Heath, 1981), p. 86. Haywards Heath Grammar School later became a Sixth-Form College, a prelude to today's Mid-Sussex College of Further and Higher Education.
18 *East Grinstead: The Official Guide* (East Grinstead, *c.*1963), pp. 14, 86; *Horsham Official Guide* (Horsham, *c.*1967), p. 94; *Chanctonbury Rural District, Sussex* (Storrington, *c.*1963), p. 42
19 Cecile Woodford, *Portrait of Sussex* (London, 1972), p. 162.
20 Ibid.
21 *Observer*, 14 April 2013.
22 Woodford, *Portrait of Sussex*, p. 165.
23 Ibid., p. 174.
24 Miriam Akhtar and Steve Humphries, *Some Liked it Hot: The British on Holiday and Abroad* (London, 2000), p. 31.
25 Ibid., p. 36.
26 *Bexhill-on-Sea: On the Sunny Sussex Coast* (Bexhill, 1964), pp. 1–14.
27 See Nigel Welbourn, *Lost Lines: Southern* (Shepperton, 1996).
28 Terry Gough, *The Southern in Kent and Sussex* (Poole, 1984), p. iv.
29 D. Cole, *The Kent and East Sussex Railway* (London, 1963), p. 32.
30 Hilary Hefferman, *Voices of Kent and East Sussex Hop Pickers* (Stroud, 2004).
31 Ibid, p. 50.
32 Jennifer Worth, *Call the Midwife: The True Story of the East End in the 1950s* (London, 2002; repub. 2012), pp. 256–61.
33 Akhtar and Humphries, *Some Liked it Hot*, p. 68.
34 Klaus Marx, *An Illustrated History of the Lewes and East Grinstead Railway* (Shepperton, 2000), p. 229.
35 Ibid., p. 239.
36 Terry Cole, *Guide to the Bluebell Railway* (Sheffield Park, 1974), p. 1.
37 Michael S. Welch, *Branch Lines to Horsted Keynes: Then and Now* (n.p., 1995), p. 189.
38 *Objectives, Aims & Plans of the Bluebell Railway Preservation Society* (Sheffield Park, 2013).
39 Desmond Seward, *Sussex* (London, 1995), pp. 1–3.
40 Alexandra Ayton, *Sussex Remembered: Personalities and Events of the 19th & 20th Centuries* (Lewes, 2010), p. 97.
41 *The Times*, 26 June 2013.
42 Seward, *Sussex*, p. 4.
43 Ibid., p. 278.
44 Olivia Laing, *To the River: A Journey Beneath the Surface* (Edinburgh, 2011), p. 8.
45 Candida Lycett Green, *Unwrecked England* (London, 2009), p. 77.
46 Pieter Boogaart, *A272: An Ode to a Road* (London, 2000), pp. 9–10.

Index

Adur, River 54, 186, 197
Aldington, Richard 189
Alfred the Great 30, 37–40, 43
Alfriston 25, 123
Allan, Ian 142, 233–234
Allen, Marian 198
Anderida (Pevensey) 17–20
Angles 1, 22
Anglo-German Friendship Ring 219
Anglo Saxon Chronicle 19–20, 22, 37–38, 44
Angmering 12, 82, 92, 121, 148
Anjou 43
Anne of Cleves 92
Anti-Corn Law League 120, 125
Ardingly 82, 122, 274, 277
Arlington 122
Arts & Crafts movement 152, 168–172, 174–175, 180, 198
Arun, River 56, 63
Arundel 37, 51, 53, 56, 61, 64, 66, 71, 74, 89, 92–93, 98–99, 109, 115, 121, 123, 177, 231–233, 240
Ashdown Forest 86–87, 121, 186
Asheham 163–164
Ashford 153
Ashurst 267
Atlantic, Battle of 224, 229
Attenborough, Richard 218
Auden, W.H. 188
Australia 122, 180, 190, 224, 251

Bader, Douglas 236
Bagnold, Enid 181
Balcombe 131, 133–134, 278
Ball, Frederick 240
Ball, John 70
Barbirolli, Sir John 265
Barcombe 238, 249–250, 278
Barcombe Mills 231
Barpham 68
Bateman's 2, 74, 183–185, 195, 201
Battle 17, 58, 71, 74, 89–91, 95, 108, 114, 119–123, 128, 151, 218, 243, 248
Battle Abbey 47, 51–53, 62, 68, 83
Bayeux Tapestry 49, 51–53
Beachy Head 3, 117, 159, 185, 212
Beauport Park 17
Beech 89
Beeching, Richard 271, 274
Bede, the Venerable 24, 26–27, 32
Belgium 192–194, 204
Bell, Quentin 165
Bell, Vanessa 163, 166–167
Belloc, Elodie 177, 179–180
Belloc, Hilaire 2, 4, 170–172, 174–180, 182, 204, 208, 275
Benedictine Abbey at Cluny 59–60
Benson, E.F. 188–189
Berkshire 47
Bersted 121
Berwick 35, 277
Bessemer, Rose Ellen Margaret 271
Betjeman, Sir John 34, 145, 186, 255
Bevendean 212
Bevin, Ernest 167
Bexhill 3, 115, 119, 151, 158, 194, 212, 230, 238, 265–266
Bignor 17, 76, 185
Bignor villa 17
Billingshurst 74, 244
Billinton L.B. 142
Billinton, R.J. 142
Bishop Odo 52
Black Death 68–69, 74–76
Black Rock (Brighton) 13, 148, 222, 239–241, 258
Black Shirts (British Union of Fascists) 218
Blackheath 70–71
Blackpatch 12
Blatchington 109–110
Blenheim Palace 85
Bloomsbury Group 163, 166
'Bluebell' line 151, 271–272
Bluebell Railway 152, 271–272, 274
Blunden, Edmund 197, 202–206, 208
Blunt, Wilfrid Scawen 174–175
Bognor 11, 13, 106, 121, 158, 199, 210, 215–216, 244, 265
Bognor Regis 5
Boleyn, Anne 90, 94
Bolney 215
Bonfire Societies 94, 127, 247–250
Boogaart, Pieter 278
Boorde, Andrew 77–81, 92
Borde Hill 77
Bosham 26, 33–34, 39–40, 44, 52, 57, 122, 246
Bournemouth 232
Bowen, Elizabeth 167
Boxgrove 10, 92
Boxgrove Man 10
Bramber 54, 120, 187, 208, 267
Brede 70
Bretwalda 24–26
Briggs, Asa 257
Brightling 121
Brighton (Brighthelmstone) 3, 11, 13, 17, 31, 57, 92, 94, 103, 106, 110–111, 117–118, 120, 123, 125, 129–139, 141–142, 144–145, 148–151, 154–156, 158–163, 166–167, 169, 171–173, 183, 186–187, 193, 195–197, 199, 206, 208, 212, 215–219, 221–222, 225–226, 229–230, 232–233, 236, 239, 243, 245, 248, 253–259, 261, 263–264, 266, 275–278
Brighton Belle 155–157, 226
Brighton & Hove Albion Football

Club 219, 253
Brighton Chain Pier 129
Brighton locomotive works 141
Brighton Pier, Palace 23–264
Brighton Pier, West 263–264
Britain, Battle of 232–234, 238
Britons *see Celts, Celtic* 20, 22–23, 27, 37
Brittany, Bretons 26, 42–43, 46, 48, 64
Broyle Heath 95, 116
Bulleid, O.V.S. 144
Bulverhythe 115, 117
Burgess Hill 233, 249, 253, 255–256
Burne-Jones, Sir Edward 149, 181, 185
Burpham 37
Burwash 2, 29, 74, 121, 124–126, 183, 195, 243
Bury Hill 100
Butlin, Billy 210, 212
Buxted 68, 86, 121, 123

Cade, Jack 70–71, 92, 218
Caedwalla, King of Wessex 24, 26, 38
Caen 58–60
Caesar, Julius 16
Calais 67
Caldbec Hill 46–47, 51
Camber Sands 154, 210
Camden, William 33, 86–87
Campion, Sir William 96, 98
Camps and hill forts
  Barkhale 11
  Chanctonbury 68
  Cissbury 14, 18, 20
  Coombe Hill 11
  Devil's Dyke 14
  Goodwood 14
  Mount Caburn 14, 16, 18, 185, 234
  Trundle 11, 14, 100
  Whitehawk 11–12
Canada 180
Captain Swing riots 120–124, 218
Casserley, H.C. 152–154
Castles
  Amberley 63
  Arundel 55, 93, 98–99
  Bodiam 63–64, 66–68, 70, 72–73
  Bramber 53–55
  Hastings 56
  Herstmonceux 73–74, 82, 194, 219
  Knepp 55, 244
  Lewes 9, 56, 70
  Pevensey 45, 56, 61
Catherine of Aragon 90, 94
Celts, Celtic *see also Britons* 14–15, 20, 23, 25–26, 174
Central School of Arts and Crafts 169
Chailey 4, 238, 271
Chailey Heritage 198
Chailey Union 122
Chamberlain, Neville 222
Chanctonbury 68, 82, 251
Chanctonbury Ring 4, 185, 233
Channel Islands 99, 212
Charles I 88, 95, 100
Charles II 100–101, 162
Charles, 6th Duke of Somerset 84–85
Charles the Simple 42
Charleston 164, 166
Chartism, Chartist 120, 122–125
Chattri (at Patcham) 196–197
Chichester 5, 10–11, 17–20, 23, 25, 36–37, 51, 53, 58, 63, 71, 74, 77, 83, 89–90, 94–95, 98, 102, 108–109, 114, 116, 120–123, 148, 151, 154, 159, 169–170, 192, 197–198, 200, 206, 219, 232, 244, 254, 267, 278
Chithurst 89, 122
Cholmondeley-Pennell, Henry 136–137, 140
Christ's Hospital 151, 197, 267
Christie, John 212
Cinque Ports 62
Cissbury 12, 20
Claudius, Emperor 16
Clayton 35, 38, 131, 134, 137–139, 141, 170, 208
Clayton Tunnel disaster 137–139, 141
Clubmen 99–100
Cnut, King of England 38–40, 42
Cobbett, William 120, 129, 135
Cobden, Richard 120
Cogidubnus, King of the Regni 16–17
Cole, Terry 273
Commius (Belgic leader) 15–16
Cook, Irma 276–277
Cook, Roy 276–277
Coolham 244
Coppard, A.E. 162
Cornish language 77, 80
Cornwall 14, 22, 24, 26, 32, 62, 77–78, 92, 163–164, 174, 221–222, 224, 227, 236, 241
Covent Garden 128
Coward, Noel 188
Cowdray 83–84, 95, 98–99
Cowfold 123
Cox, Ka 163
Crabbet Park 175
Craven, John 141
Crawley 13, 74, 177, 253–254
Cretaceous period 5
Cromwell, Oliver 55, 73, 88, 100–101
Cromwell, Thomas 77, 90
Crowborough 89, 121, 151, 186, 198, 231, 248
Cuckfield 6–7, 74, 76–77, 82, 89, 256, 278
Cuckmere Haven 112
'Cuckoo' line 151, 267

Daddy Long-Legs electric tramroad 148
Dalling Ridge 64
Dallington 195
Dalyngrigge, Sir Edward 64, 66–67, 70, 72
Danelaw 37–38
Danny Park 82, 96
Darwin, Charles 8
Dawson, Charles 8–10
de Chardin, Pierre 9
de Montfort, Simon 71–72
de Warenne, William 53, 60–61
De La Warr, Countess Diana 242
De La Warr Pavilion, Bexhill-on-Sea 212, 265
Defoe, Daniel 88–89, 114
Denmark 38–39
Devil's Dyke 31–32, 148, 170
Devon 181
Dickens, Catherine (Kate) 159–160
Dickens, Charles 159–162
Didling 35
Dieppe 237–238, 258
Dieppe Raid 237–238
Diplock, Monica 240
Dissolution of the Monasteries 80, 83, 90, 92, 95

Ditchling 4, 8, 77, 89, 134, 168, 170–171, 173–174, 181, 187, 198
Ditchling Beacon 4, 185
Ditchling Common 171–174
Domesday Book 36, 51, 57–58, 184
Dorset 1, 16, 24, 47, 116
Dover 37, 51, 153, 193, 227–228
Doyle, Arthur Conan 198
Duke of Norfolk 195, 254
Duncton Down 100, 185
Dunkirk 222, 225–227, 230, 236, 238, 241

East Anglia 24, 26, 118
East Grinstead 57, 64, 89, 94, 116, 151, 168, 186, 236, 238–239, 254, 257, 267, 271, 273–274
Eastbourne 1, 3, 11, 108, 112, 117, 122–123, 151, 155, 158, 194–195, 198, 206, 212, 218, 230, 238, 244, 247–248, 257, 267
Eden, Anthony 230
Edward I 66–67, 72
Edward III 64
Edward VI 79, 92–94, 145
Edward the Confessor 30, 37, 40–41, 43, 52
Elgifu of Northampton 38–39
Elizabeth I 84, 94
Ella (or Aella), King of the South Saxons 19–21, 23–25
Ellman, John 118
Emma of Normandy 38–40
Emsworth 122
Eridge 86, 89, 151, 267, 275
Essex 25, 69–70
Etchingham 184
Ethelred 'the Unready' 38–40
Ethelwalh, King of the South Saxons 27–28
European Union 275, 277
Eustace of Boulogne 49, 51
Evesham, Battle of 72
Ewhurst 122

Fabian Society 168–170
Fairlight 121
Falmer 253, 257
Farnfold 88
Fécamp 30, 40, 58
Fetherstonhaugh, Sir Harry 105
Fiennes, Celia 83
Fiennes, Sir Roger 73
Findon 12
Finglesham 1
Fishbourne 16, 19, 122
Fishbourne Palace 17, 19
Flanders 43, 67, 92, 177, 191
Ford 232
Forest Row 186, 254, 267
Forster, E.M. 164
Fowey 62
Fox, George 100–101
France 11, 15, 42–43, 59, 61–62, 64, 66–67, 71, 85, 88–90, 92, 100, 106, 114, 142, 162, 176–179, 191, 193, 196–198, 200–201, 206, 212, 221–222, 224, 232, 236–237, 245, 256
Frant 121
Funtington 122

Gatwick 254
Gaul 15–16, 19
Gaza, Battle of 206
George I 101–102
George IV (Prince of Wales, Prince Regent) 103, 105–106, 111, 129, 159, 161
George V 196, 210, 218
Germany 22, 190, 192, 222, 277
Gibbons, Stella 187–188
Gill, Eric 168–176, 185, 187
Gill, Ethel (Mary) 168–171, 174
Glastonbury 31
Gloucestershire 47, 71, 219
Glynde 96, 102, 108
Glyndebourne 212
Godwin, house of 39–40, 43–44, 57–58
Golding, William 229
Goldsworthy, Leon 'Goldy' 229–230
Goodwood 10, 121
Goodwood House 102, 106
Greene, Graham 162, 218
Groombridge 112, 114, 151, 267
Guildford 180, 231
Guinness, Alec 229
Guy of Ponthieu 40, 49, 52

Haddon, Joe 251
Hailsham 74, 94, 267
Hampshire 16, 24, 38, 47, 76, 98–99, 116, 122, 185, 195, 267, 278
Hamsey 35
Hangleton 69
Hanover 101–102
Hardham 60
Hardrada, Harald 39, 41, 44–46
Hartfield 82, 89, 121, 186
Harthancnut 39
Hassocks 19, 82, 133–134, 151, 208
Hastings 3, 24, 37, 40, 42, 44–46, 51–53, 56, 62, 69, 71, 74, 97, 106–107, 114–115, 117, 151–152, 158, 219, 223, 226, 236, 238, 251, 264, 266, 269
Hastings, Battle of 42, 46, 49, 52
Hawaii 224
Hawkhurst 113, 115, 189
Hawkins, Daisy 173–174
Haywards Heath 98, 134, 172, 248, 253–257, 272–273
Haywards Heath Grammar School 256
Headcorn 153, 267
Heathfield 71, 121, 128, 247–248, 267
Henfield 123, 231
Hengist and Horsa 22–23
Henry I 43, 61
Henry III 71–72
Henry IV 67
Henry VIII 77–78, 83, 90, 92–94
Heron-Allen, Edward 192–195, 197–201, 207
Heron-Allen, Nour 192, 197, 200
Herstmonceux 117, 172
Highdown 25, 185
Hinton, Martin A.C. 10
Hitler, Adolph 219, 224, 232
HMS *King Alfred* 224, 227–229
HMS *Vernon* 221–222
Holden, Bernard 272
Holland 99
Holland, Henry 104
Home Guard 230–231, 246
Hooe 58, 113, 117
Hopton, General Sir Ralph 98–99
Horsham 13, 100–101, 111, 120–123, 130, 151, 158, 180, 197, 205, 208, 218, 233, 257
Horsted Keynes 151–152, 272–274
Hove 13–14, 69, 145, 148, 151, 158, 195, 206, 212, 217–219, 224, 227–230, 251, 253, 257, 264, 275, 277
Huguenots 88, 93, 276
Hundred Years War 61, 63–64, 67
Hurst Green 115

Hurstfield 121
Hurstpierpoint 51, 134

Iguanodon 6–7
India 73, 104–105, 175, 180, 185, 196–197, 206, 251
Ireland 26, 152, 175, 206, 216
Isfield 68, 275
Isle of Man 26
Isle of Wight 24, 38, 44, 62, 232
Isles of Scilly 32
Italy 227

James I 95
James II 101
James VI 95
James, Henry 150, 162
Jevington 13, 35, 38
John of Gaunt, Duke of Lancaster 66
Johnson, Samuel 159, 162
Jurassic period 5
Jutes 22

Kaye-Smith, Sheila 187
Kemptown 141, 148, 221, 239–240
Kennedy, Ludovic 229
Kent 1, 16, 22–26, 37, 44, 47, 51, 63, 69–72, 88–89, 103, 106, 113–114, 116, 121, 152–154, 158, 164, 166, 206, 225, 241, 244, 267, 269, 271, 275, 278
Kent & East Sussex (Rother Valley) Railway 152–154, 267, 269, 271
Keymer 51, 133, 151
Keynes, John, Maynard 164, 166
Kimmins, Grace 198
King John 61
Kingscote 152, 274
Kipling, Caroline 'Carrie' (Balestier) 180, 183, 185, 201–202, 208
Kipling, Elsie 184
Kipling, John 184–185, 195, 201–202
Kipling, Josephine 183
Kipling, Rudyard 2–4, 28–29, 74, 112, 124, 180–185, 195–197, 201–203, 208, 275
Kirdford 74
Knollys, Sir Robert 64, 70

Labour Party 167, 217
Lancing 142, 186–187, 229
Lansbury, George 167
Lawrence, D.H. 163
Lawrence, Gertrude 188
Lee, Laurie 232–233
Lewes 6, 8–9, 17, 37, 51, 53, 60, 62, 71, 74, 89–92, 94–96, 98, 103, 110, 115–116, 119–123, 126, 130, 133, 150, 155, 163–164, 166, 193, 234, 238, 248–250, 254, 267, 271, 274, 278
Lewes, Battle of 71, 216, 218
Lewknor, Sir Thomas 72
Liberal Party 175
Lincolnshire 47
Lindfield 249, 256
Lindisfarne 26, 32
Littlehampton 5, 148, 151, 155, 238, 245, 248
London 7, 17, 31, 38, 44, 46, 51, 61, 63, 67, 69–71, 74–75, 84, 87, 93–94, 106, 112, 114, 124, 127, 129–131, 134–137, 139, 145, 149, 151–152, 156, 158, 161, 163–164, 166–167, 169–171, 174, 179, 184, 206–207, 212, 222, 224, 233–234, 239, 244, 254–257, 263, 265, 269, 275
London and South Western Railway 152
London, Brighton and South Coast Railway (LBSCR) 139–140, 142, 144–145, 150–152, 155, 169
Loos, Battle of 185, 197, 201–202
Lopokova, Lydia 166
Lord Curzon, Viceroy of India 73
Lord Grey of Werke, earl of Tankerville 83
Lucas, Caroline MP 264
Lyminster 208

Macauley, Rose 164
Manhood 27–28, 69
Manhood & Selsey Tramway 152, 154
Mantell, Dr Gideon 6–8
Mantell, Mary 6–7
Maresfield 17, 89, 122
Mark Cross 249
Marsh, D. Earle 142
Martello Towers 106
Maugham, Somerset 162
Maunsell, R.L. 144
Mayfield 31, 94, 112, 114, 121, 248–249
McIndoe, Archibald 236
McNabb, Father Vincent 171–172, 174–175
Mediterranean 25, 264
Mercia 24, 39
Mesolithic period 11–12
Meynell, Esther 8–10, 23, 128, 221, 246
Midhurst 11, 74, 76, 83, 89, 119–120, 151, 267
Milday, Audrey 212
Mill, John Stuart 131, 151
Milne, A.A. 186
Mitford, Nancy 188
Mocatta, David 134, 151
Monsarrat, Nicholas 229
Montagu Ewen 228–229
Morley, Colonel Herbert 96, 98–100
Morris, William 168, 170, 175, 181
Mortimer, Raymond 164
Moulsecoomb 208, 259
Mount Caburn 6, 14, 16, 18, 185, 234
Mountfield 122
Mussolini, Benito 219

National Unemployed Workers Movement 217–218
Neolithic period 10–13
Neville, Charles 208, 212
New Shoreham 59, 74
New South Wales 110
New Zealand 180, 200, 224
Newbridge 86
Newbuilding Place 175
Newenden 121
Newhaven 110–111, 114, 133, 151, 166, 185, 219, 225–226, 231, 234, 237, 246, 248
Newick 238, 248
Nicolson, Harold 83
Nicolson, Nigel 83, 164–166
Ninfield 46, 121
Norden, John 88
Norfolk 195, 206, 224, 254
Normandy 30, 39–45, 47, 52, 58–61, 64, 229, 244, 246
North Africa 227
North Marden 13
Northamptonshire 38–39, 47
Northiam 51

Northumbria 24, 26–27, 43
Norway 38–39, 41, 44
Norwich 71
Nottinghamshire 47, 80
Nova Scotia 236

Offham Hill 71
Old Shoreham 59
Olivier, Laurence 156
Orwell, George 198
Ouse, River 16, 37, 56, 62, 90, 131, 134, 151, 168, 182, 231, 234, 277
Ovingdean 162
Oxted 130, 151

Pacific War 224
Pagham 121, 154, 200, 245
Paine, Thomas 'Tom' 119–120
Palace Pier (Brighton Pier) 148, 264
Palmer, Sir Thomas 82–83
Parham 83
Paris 60, 129, 135, 176
Partridge Green 267
Patcham 134, 138, 196
Patching 12
Pavilion Military Hospital 196
Payton, Owen 224, 227, 230
Payton, Tom 224
Peacehaven 166, 208–210
Peasants' Revolt 68–70
Pelly, Captain John 228
Pepler, Hilary [Douglas] 172, 174
Petworth 83–85, 89, 100, 103, 121, 174, 232, 239, 244
Pevensey 7–20, 23, 37, 40–45, 52–53, 56, 61, 69, 71, 74, 78–80, 112–113, 117, 195, 210, 231
Pevensey Levels 3, 73, 106
Picardy 64, 67
Piddinghoe 35, 166
Piltdown 8
Piltdown Man 8 9
Pleistocene period 8
Plomer, William 164
Plumpton 51, 89, 242–243
Poland 222
Polegate 151, 186, 195, 267
Poling 232
Pook's Hill 29, 184
Poor Law Amendment Act (1834) 108, 118, 120–125
Porchester 37
Portslade 145, 148, 229
Portsmouth 137–139, 148, 151, 154, 158, 200
Pre-Raphaelite Brotherhood 149, 168, 174, 181
Preston 134, 251
Priory of St Pancras 60, 62
Pulborough 17, 63, 100, 121, 151, 267

Quakers 100–101
Queen Anne 101, 151, 188
Queen Mary 94
Queen Victoria 135, 236

Rake 116
Rastrick, John 133
Rennie, John 130–132
Richard II 63, 67, 70, 72
Richmond, dukes of 102, 106, 108–111, 115–117, 122
Ringmer 121–122, 212, 234
Ripon 26
Robert, duke of Normandy 61
Robert of Eu 53, 56, 58
Robert of Mortain 53, 56, 61
Robertsbridge 90–91, 121, 152, 269, 277
Rochester 116
Rodmell 163–168, 234
Roedean School 221, 236
Rogate 122
Rollo the Viking 42–43
Rolt, L.T.C. 'Tom' 212, 215
Rome 16, 19, 26, 28, 38, 78, 90, 92–94, 171, 176, 187, 250
Romney 45
Romney Marsh 3, 69, 187, 243–244
Rother, River 63–64, 66, 182
Rotherfield 57, 89, 121, 249
Rottingdean 2, 62, 114, 148, 166, 181–183, 185, 208, 241
Rouen 43, 60, 225
Rowfant 81
Rowse, A.L. 176–177
Royal Military Canal 106
Royal Pavilion 104–105, 111, 159, 196
Rural Constabulary Act, 1839 125
Russell, Dr Richard 103
Russia 192, 204, 206
Rye 3, 40, 62–34, 66, 74, 91, 96, 100, 106, 108, 115, 120, 123, 188–189, 243, 248
Rye & Camber Railway 152, 154
Sackville-West, Vita 83, 164–166
Salehurst 121
Salisbury 71
Saltdean 212
Sandwich 44
Saunders, Colin 247
Saxon Shore, the 19, 21
Scotland 24, 26, 90, 95, 100–101
Scott, Peter 229
Seaford 36, 69, 109–112, 114, 120, 122, 158, 194, 236, 277
Sedlescombe 122, 275–276
Selham 35
Selsey 15, 17, 20, 23, 27, 32, 36–37, 51, 58, 69, 152, 154, 192, 195, 197, 200, 207–208, 229, 238, 245
Selsey Bill 114, 116, 200
Senlac 46
Sheffield Park 102, 274
Sheffield Park (station) 152, 272–274
Shephard, E.H. 186
Shipley 60, 180
Shoreham 36, 69, 74, 100, 114, 130, 132–133, 148, 151, 186, 194, 197, 210, 212, 228, 237, 246, 266–267
Shropshire 229
Singleton 11, 35, 100, 251
Sissinghurst 165
Slaugham Place 82
Slindon 10, 179–180
Small Dole 231
Smith, Charlotte 159
Smith, Horace 162
Smith-Woodward, Sir Arthur 8–10
Somerset 47, 84, 223
Somme, Battle of 197–198, 204
Sompting 34, 38, 60, 186, 208
South Africa 180, 183
South Eastern and Chatham Railway 152
South Eastern Railway 130
South Harting 168
South Malling 101
Southampton 17, 83
Southease 35
Southern Railway 144, 155, 158, 215, 225, 233
Southwick 194, 277
Spain 94–95
Spanish Armada 95
Spanish Civil War 219
Stamford Bridge, Battle of 45–47
Standen 168, 175

Stanmer 102, 245
Stansted 98
St Augustine 25, 66
St Cuthman 29–30, 40
St Dunstan 30–31
St Ives 163
St Leonards-on-Sea 80, 106, 117, 187, 223, 230
St Michael's Mount 32
St Paul's Cathedral 85, 149
St Roche 100
St Wilfrid 26–29, 37, 208
Stephanus, Eddius (Eddi) 27–28
Stephens, Lieutenant-Colonel Holman Fred 150, 152–155, 158, 267
Stephenson, Robert 130–132
Steyning 30, 40, 51, 54, 58, 89, 94–95, 123, 151, 257, 267
Storrington 83, 168, 177, 233
Strachey, Lytton 163
Strong, Patience 275
Stroudley, William 141–142, 145
Sullington 35, 38
Surrey 24, 31, 47, 69–70, 72, 74, 84, 88–89, 92, 99, 108, 158, 180, 196, 231–232, 254
Sussex Association of Bonfire Societies 249
Sweden 38
Synod of Whitby 26

Tacitus 17
Tangmere 232, 244, 236
Tarring 76
Tarring Neville 35
Tenterden 152–153, 267, 269, 271
Thackeray, William Makepeace 159, 161–162
Thatcher, Margaret 259, 264
Thirkell, Angela 181
Thomas, Joyce 240
Thorney Island 232
Thrale, Hester 159
Three Bridges 155, 267
Ticehurst 89, 121
Tilgate Forest 7, 74
Tilton 166
Tonbridge 71, 152
Torquay 181
Tostig 43–45
Tottington Manor 231
Tunbridge Wells 31, 103, 112, 114, 275
Twineham 278
Tyler, Wat 70

Uck, River 231
Uckfield 89, 231, 243, 249, 267, 278
Up Marden 35
Uppark 83, 101, 105

Verica, King of the Atrebates 16
Viscount Montague 84, 93, 95
Vikings 37–38, 42–43, 249
Volk's Electric Railway 148
Vortigern, overlord of southern Britain 21–22

Wadhurst 89
Wagner, Revd Arthur (Father Wagner) 149
Wakehurst 121
Wakehurst Place 82
Wales 22, 24, 26, 66, 152, 159, 174
Waller, General Sir William 98–99
Warbleton 121
Ward-Higgs, William 190
Waltham Abbey 51
Warminghurst 101
Waugh, Evelyn 186–187
Weald & Downland Living Museum 251
Webb, Philip 168, 175, 180, 208, 275
Wells, Gerry 230–231, 238–239, 244
Wessex 24, 28, 37–40, 47
West Grinstead 55, 76, 151, 244, 267
West Pier 136, 148, 264
Westbourne 122
Westhampnett 11
Westminster Abbey 51, 61
Weston-super-Mare 223
Whicker, Alan 272
White family 223
Whitehawk 208, 259
Whiteman Green 6
Widdecombe, Anne MP 250
Wilkins, Daisy 238
William III 101
William, duke of Normandy, King of England 40–53, 56–57, 59–60
William of Montgomery 53, 57
William Rufus (William II) 60–61
Williams, Cecil 'Pop' 221, 236
Williams, Cyril 222, 240–241
Williams, Diana 241
Williams, Doris Caroline Lucy 236, 240–241
Williams, Dorothy 'Dottie May' 222, 224, 227, 236, 240–241, 246
Williams Douglas 222, 224, 227, 241
Williams, Garfield 222, 227, 241
Williams, Hazel May 240- 244
Williams, Pamela 241
Williams, Roy 222, 224–227, 241
Willingdon 122
Wilmington 1–2, 13
Wilmington, Long Man of 1–2, 182
Wilson's Laundry 240–241
Wiltshire 11, 16, 24
Winchelsea 40, 62–64, 66, 69, 74, 108
Winchester 30, 61, 74, 77, 99
Winddoor Hill 185
Windover Hill 1
Wineham 278
'Winnie-the-Pooh' 186
Wisborough Green 88
Wishart, Lorna 233
Wiston 68, 82
Withdean 134
Withyam 121
Wittering 199
Wolsey, Cardinal 90
Wolsonbury Hill 82
Women's Forestry Corps 195
Women's Land Army 241–243, 246
Woolf, Leonard 163–168, 171, 234
Woolf, Virginia 163–168, 171, 180, 208, 234, 236, 275
Worcester 31, 100
Worcester, Battle of 100
Wordsworth, William 159
Worth 34, 38, 74, 86
Worthing 5, 55, 68, 158, 186–187, 212, 219, 236, 238, 265
Wycliffe, John 70
Wynter, E.C.C. 'Ted' 256

Yapton 121
Yeats, W.B. 175, 186
Yorkshire 26, 47
Young, Edward 229

Zennor 163